AIRPLANE ADVENTURE

A

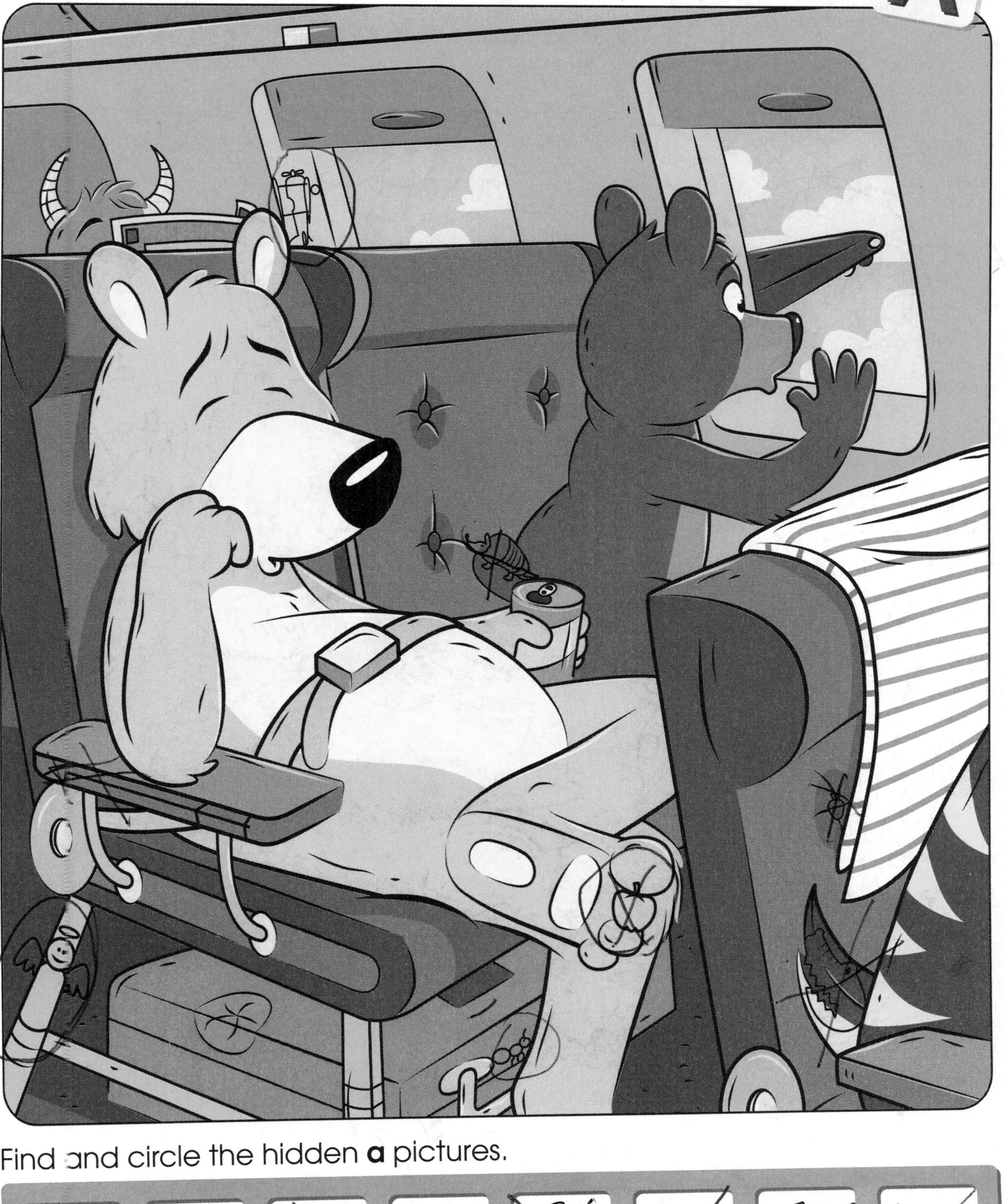

Find and circle the hidden **a** pictures.

apple | airplane | alligator | arrow | angel | armadillo | acorn | ant

©School Zone Publishing Company

W9-BPJ-545

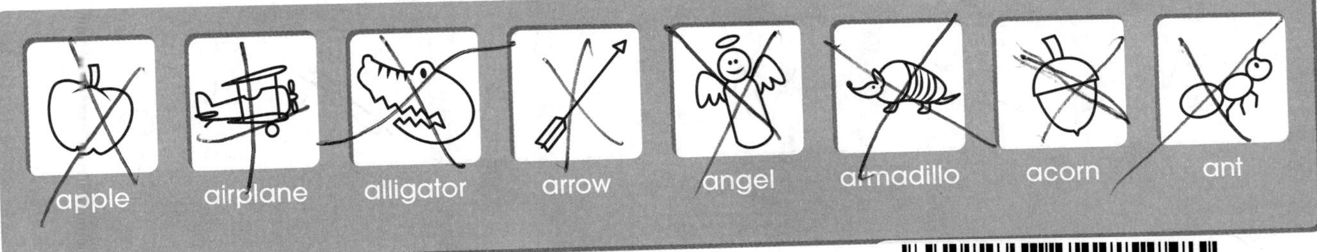

ANNA ALLIGATOR

Find and circle the hidden **a** pictures.

©School Zone Publishing Company

BEAUTIFUL BRIDGE

B

Find and circle the hidden **b** pictures.

©School Zone Publishing Company

B BASEBALL GAME

Find and circle the hidden **b** pictures.

butterfly | bird | baseball | banana | balloon | bat

 ©School Zone Publishing Company

B
B
B
brush
bee
boat
book
button
bell

C COWABUNGA!

Find and circle the hidden **c** pictures.

 ©School Zone Publishing Company

CHUNK OF CHANGE

C

CHEAP TODAY

Find and circle the hidden **c** pictures.

cookie

cat

cow

cake

carrot

cabbage

©School Zone Publishing Company

DIG THIS

Find and circle the hidden **d** pictures.

dress

dinosaur

drum

duck

door

doll

dragon

dog

 ©School Zone Publishing Company

DENTIST DAN

D

Find and circle the hidden **d** pictures.

duck

daisy

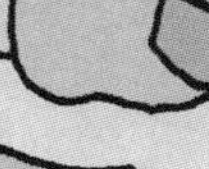

drum

doll

dog

diamond

©School Zone Publishing Company

E

EASY SHOT

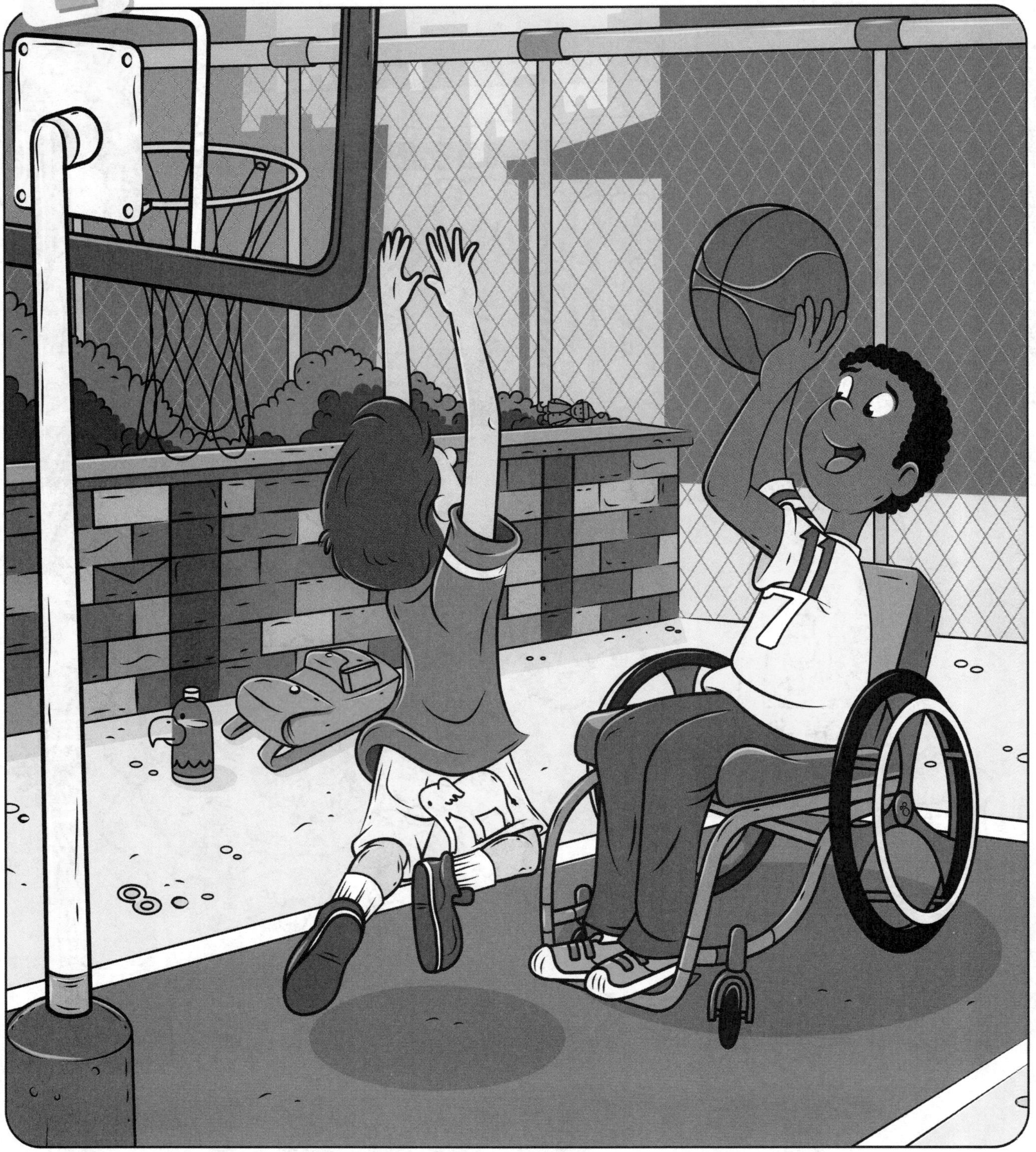

Find and circle the hidden **e** pictures.

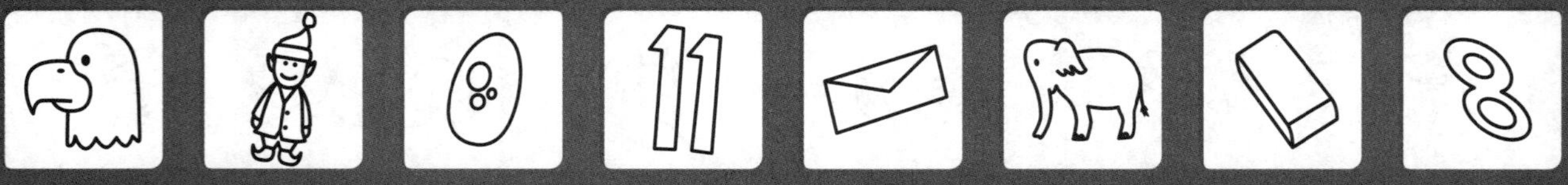

EATING OUT

E

Find and circle the hidden **e** pictures.

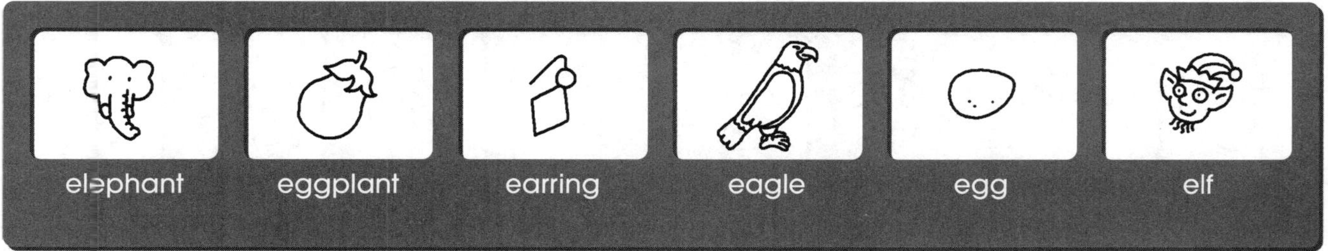

F FLOWER POWER

Find and circle the hidden **f** pictures.

FRIDAY NIGHT FOOTBALL

F

Find and circle the hidden **f** pictures.

footprint

flag

fish

flowers

football

firecrackers

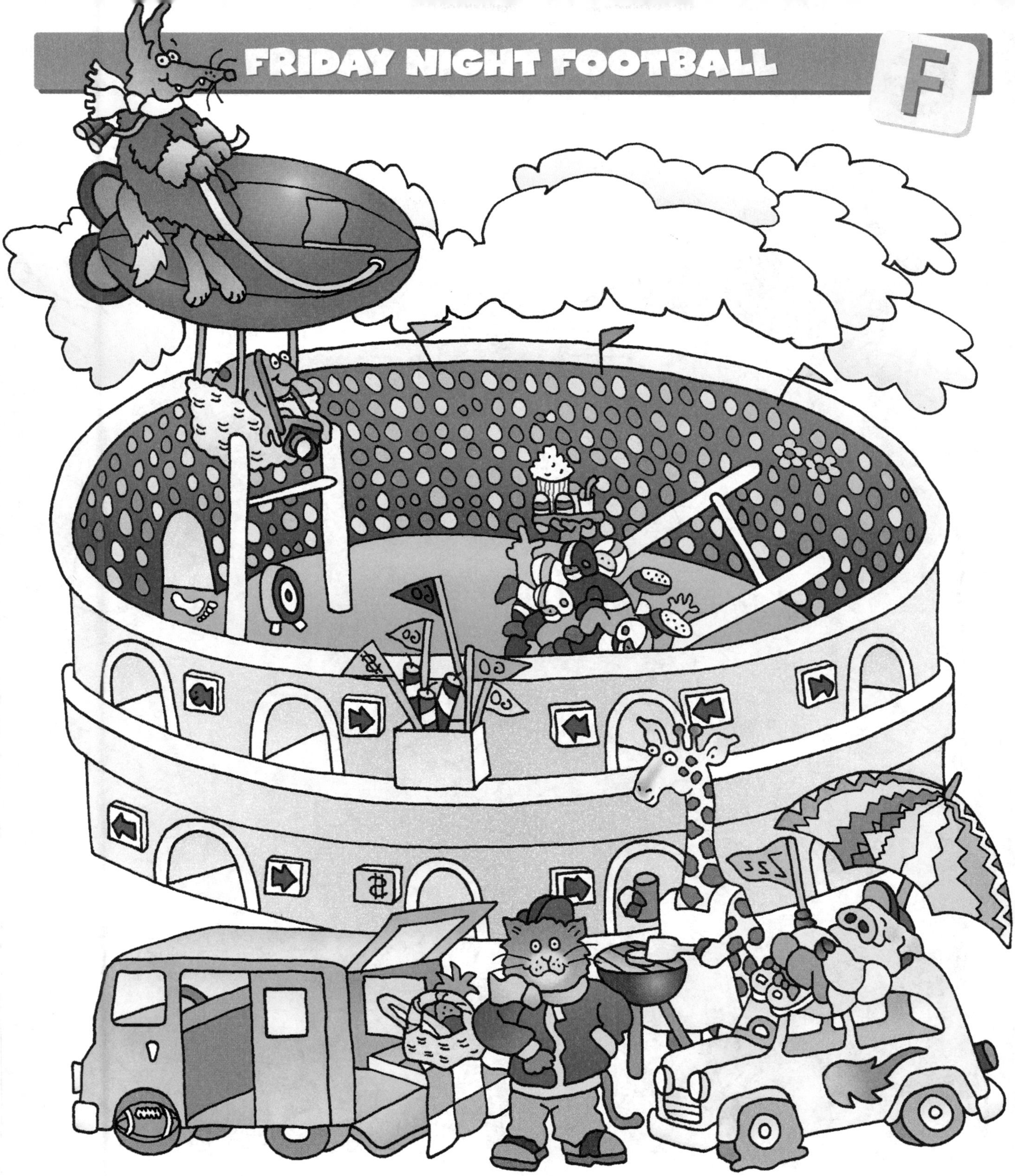

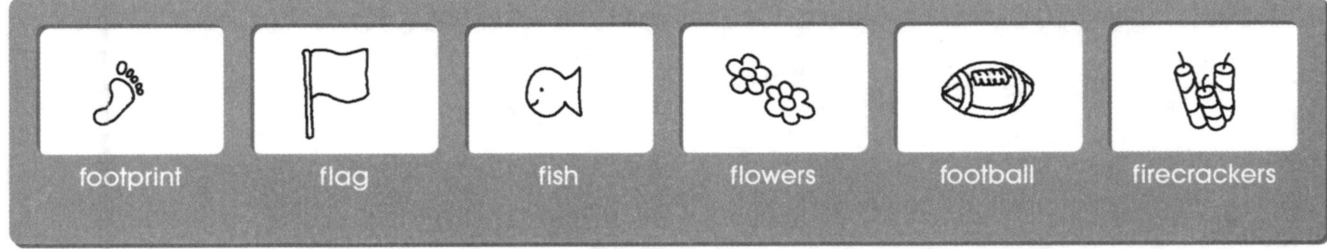

G

GARY'S GARDEN

Find and circle the hidden **g** pictures.

gift

goldfish

gold

gopher

goose

gate

©School Zone Publishing Company

G

ghost

gorilla

grapes

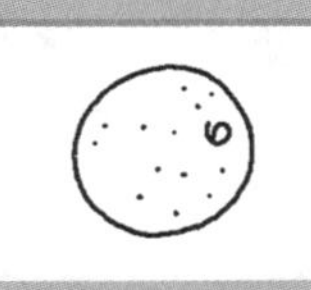
grapefruit

goat

GLIDING IN THE POND

Find and circle the hidden **g** pictures.

©School Zone Publishing Company

HOT HIGHWAY

H

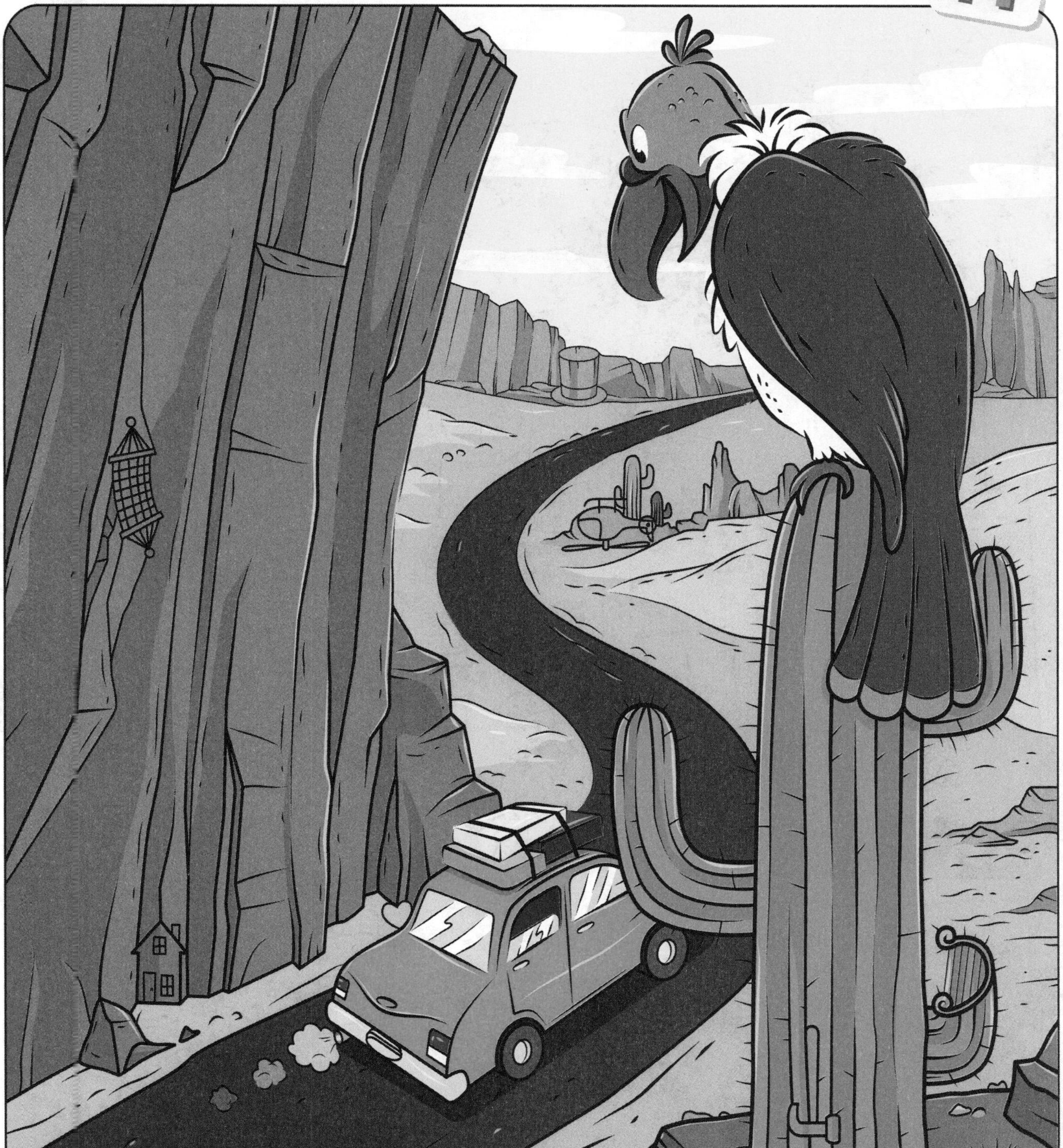

Find and circle the hidden **h** pictures.

hat | hammer | helicopter | harp | hammock | hot dog | house | heart

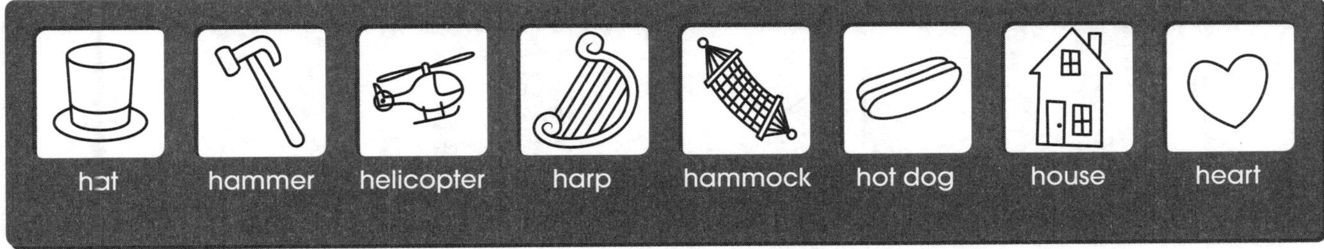

H HAPPY ANIMALS

Find and circle the hidden **h** pictures.

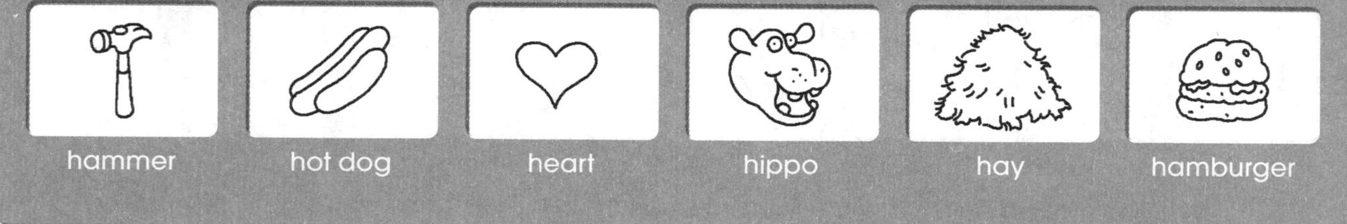

 ©School Zone Publishing Company

INCOMING STRIKE

I

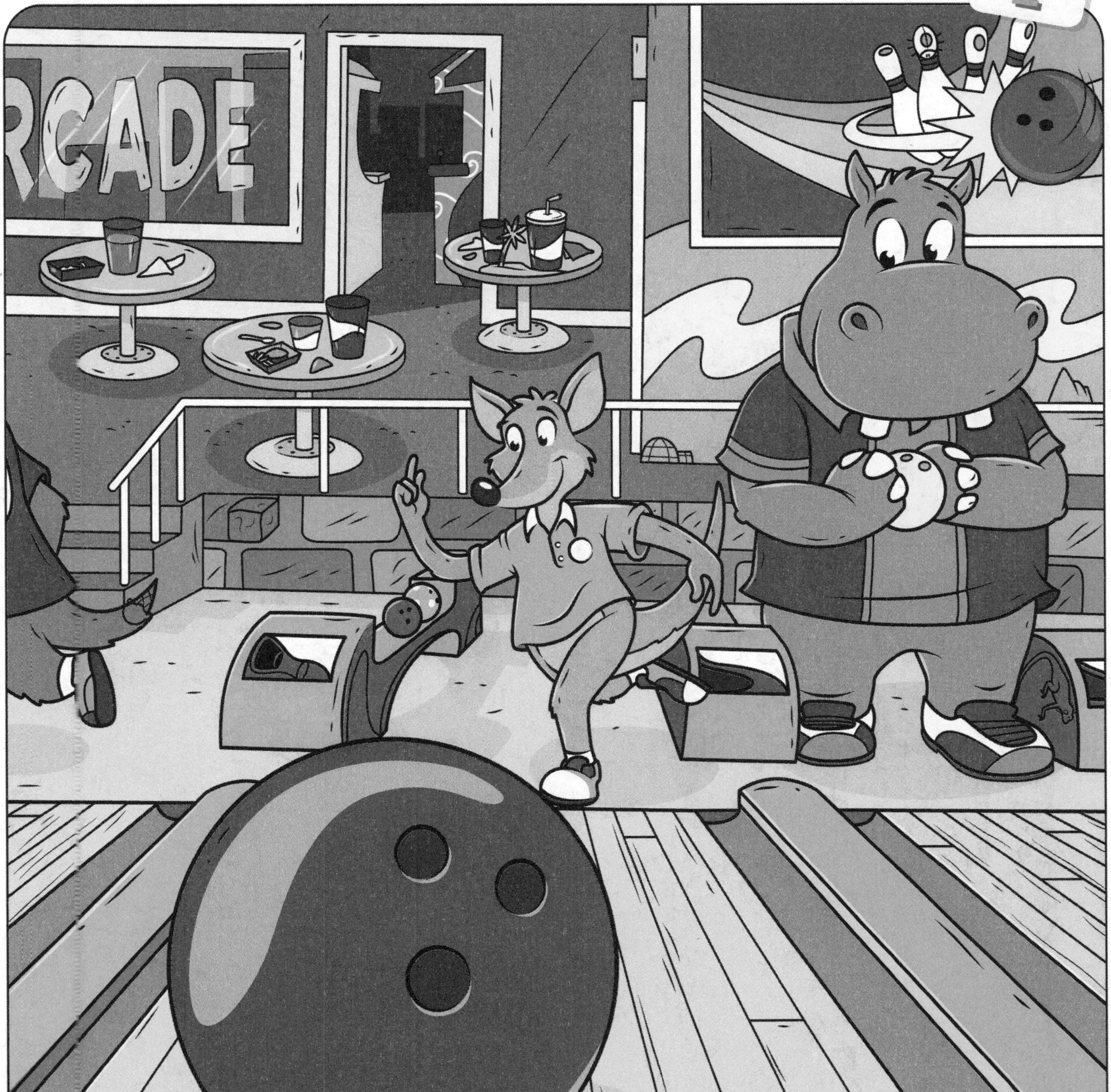

Find and circle the hidden **i** pictures.

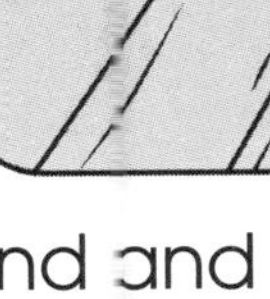
ice cube

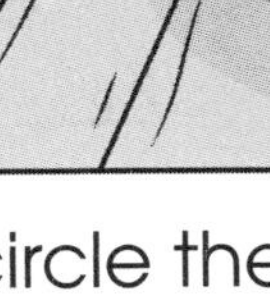
island

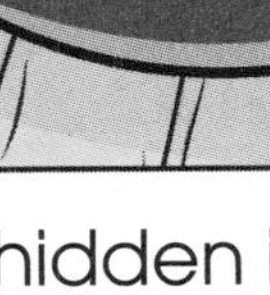
iceberg

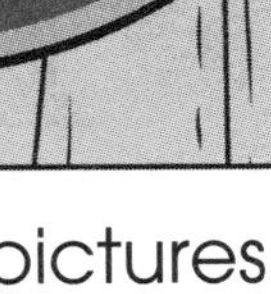
igloo

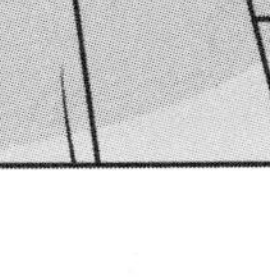
ink

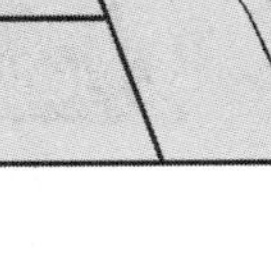
ice cream cone

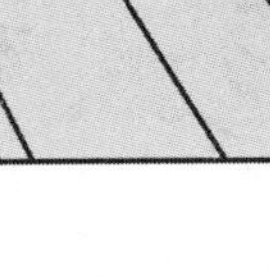
insect

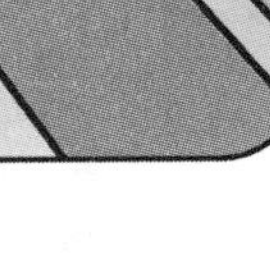
iguana

©School Zone Publishing Company

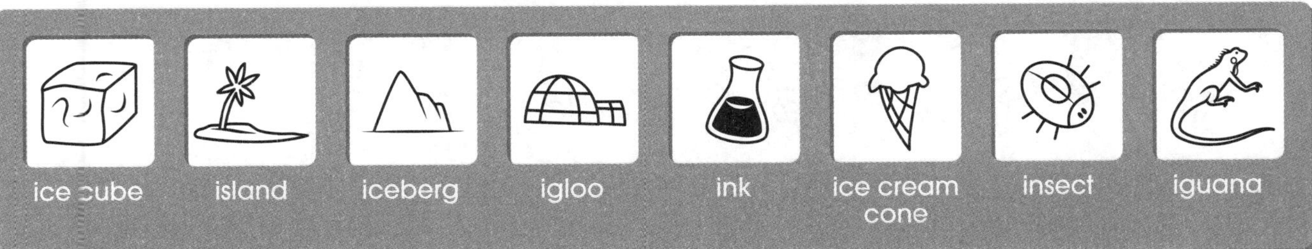

I

ICE CREAM TREAT

Find and circle the hidden **i** pictures.

insects

igloo

invitation

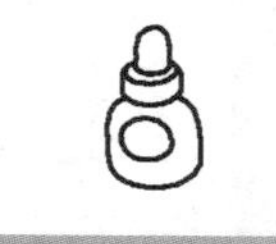
ink

ivy

ice cream cone

©School Zone Publishing Company

JACK'S ROUNDUP!

J

Find and circle the hidden **j** pictures.

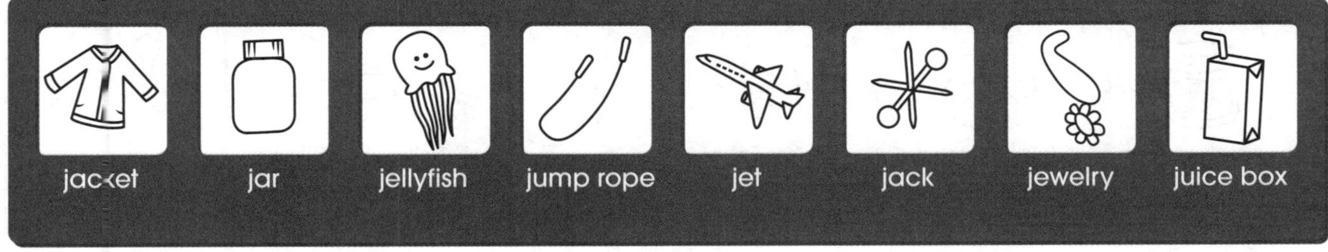

J JUMPING FOR JOY

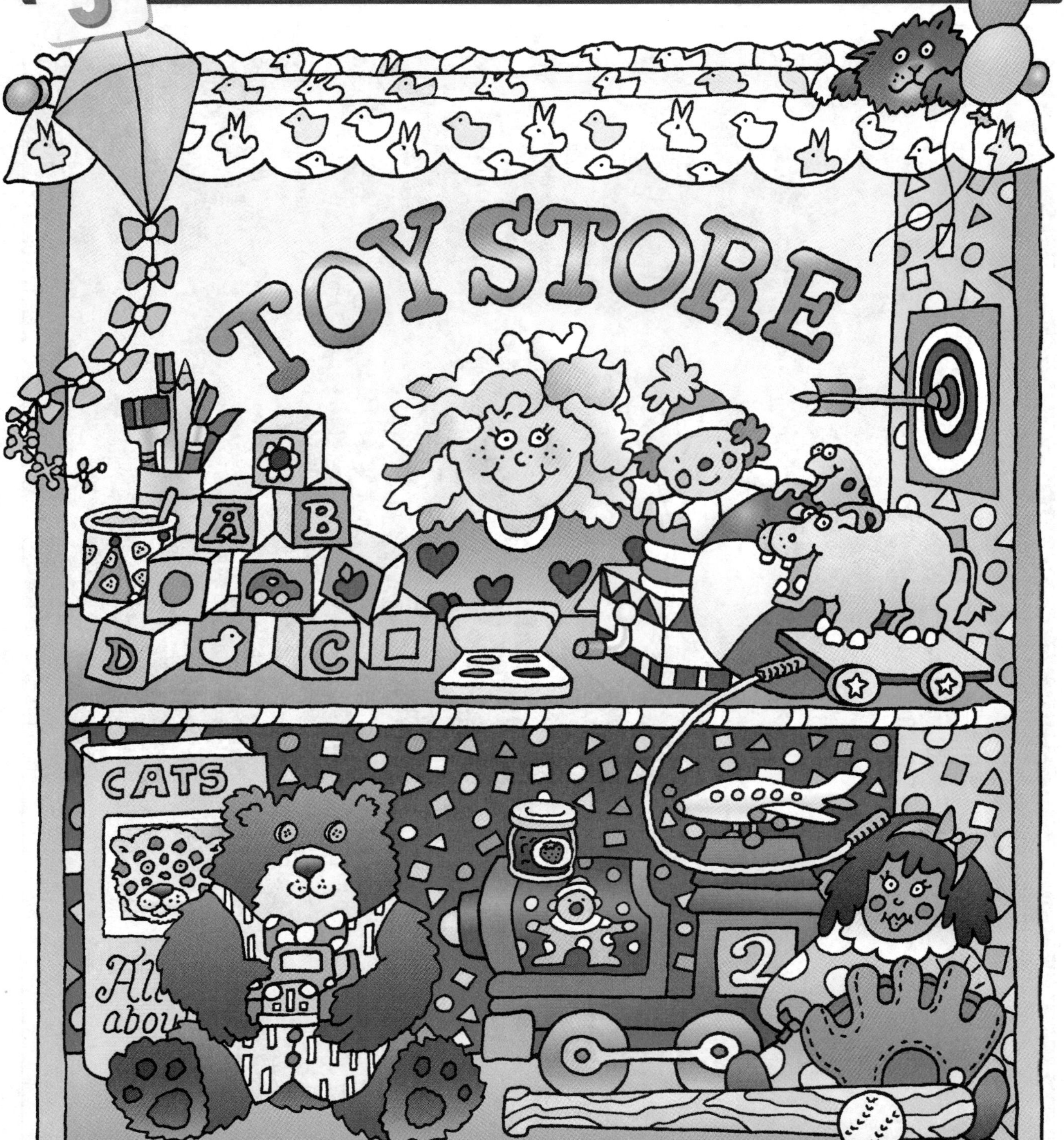

Find and circle the hidden **j** pictures.

jam

jaguar

jacks

jump rope

jet

jack-in-the-box

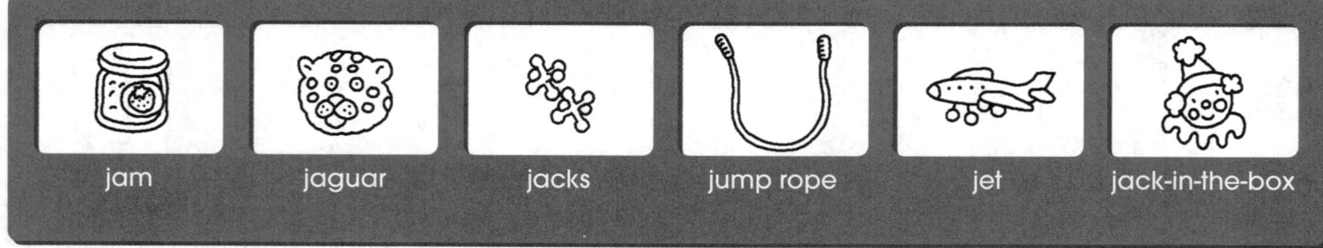

©School Zone Publishing Company

CAPTAIN KURT

K

Find and circle the hidden **k** pictures.

kiwi | kettle | king | kangaroo | kayak | kite | koala | key

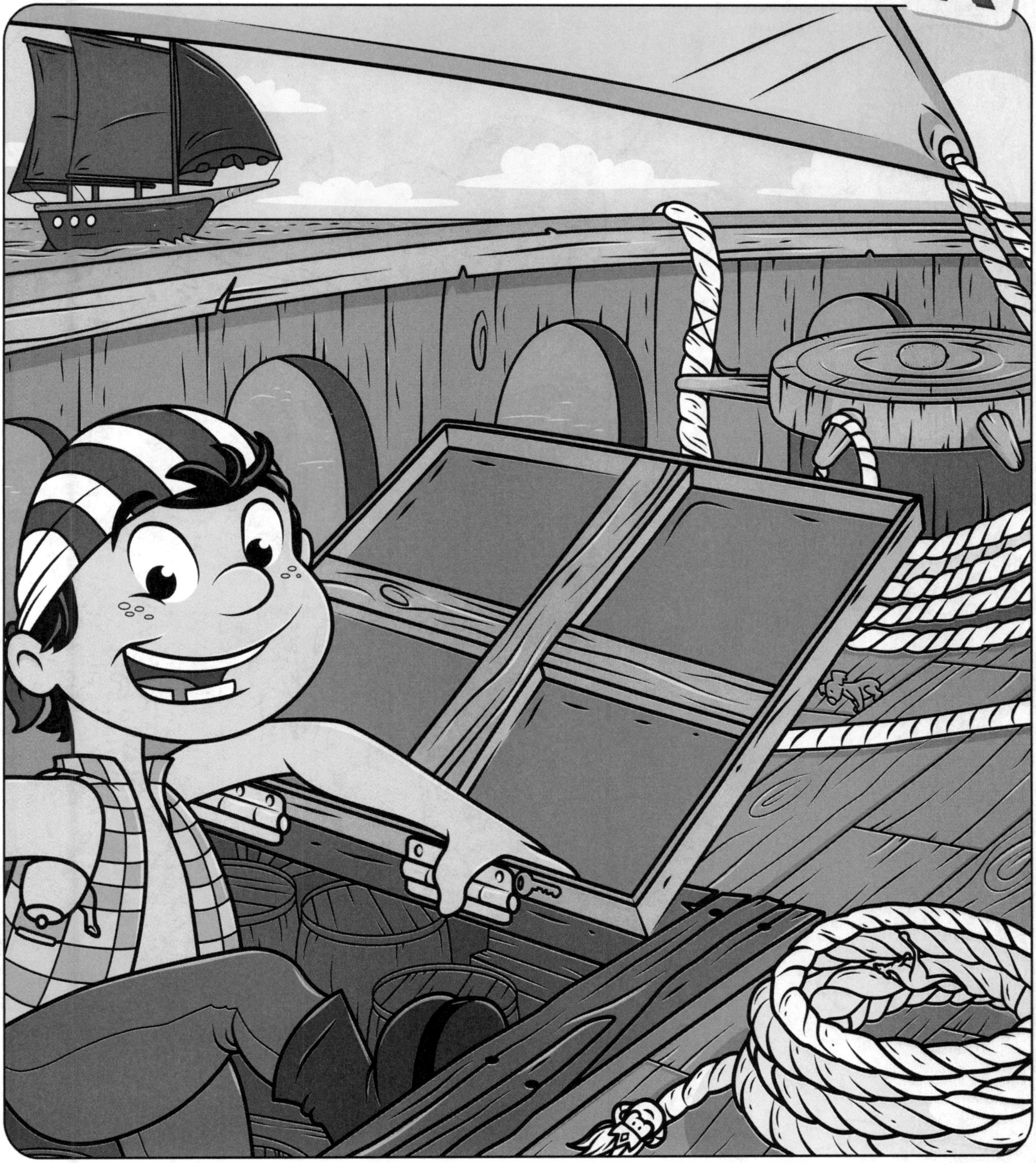

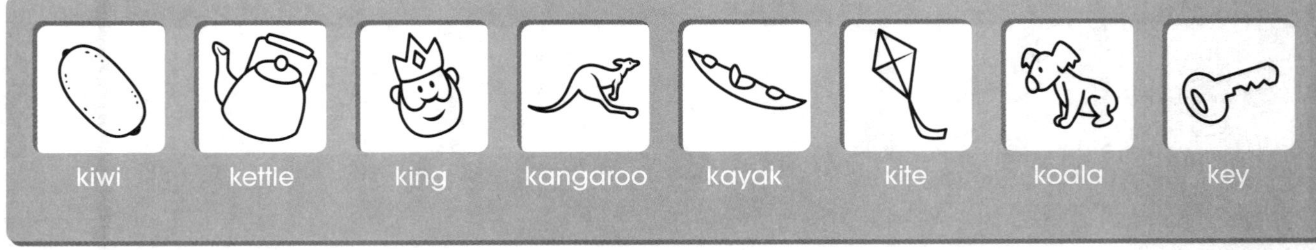

L

LIVELY PARTY

Find and circle the hidden l pictures.

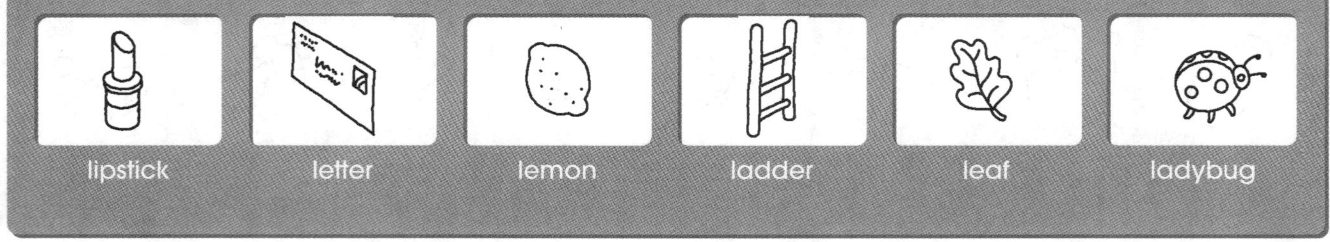

 ©School Zone Publishing Company

L

lobster
lamp
lion
lollipop
lizard
lamb

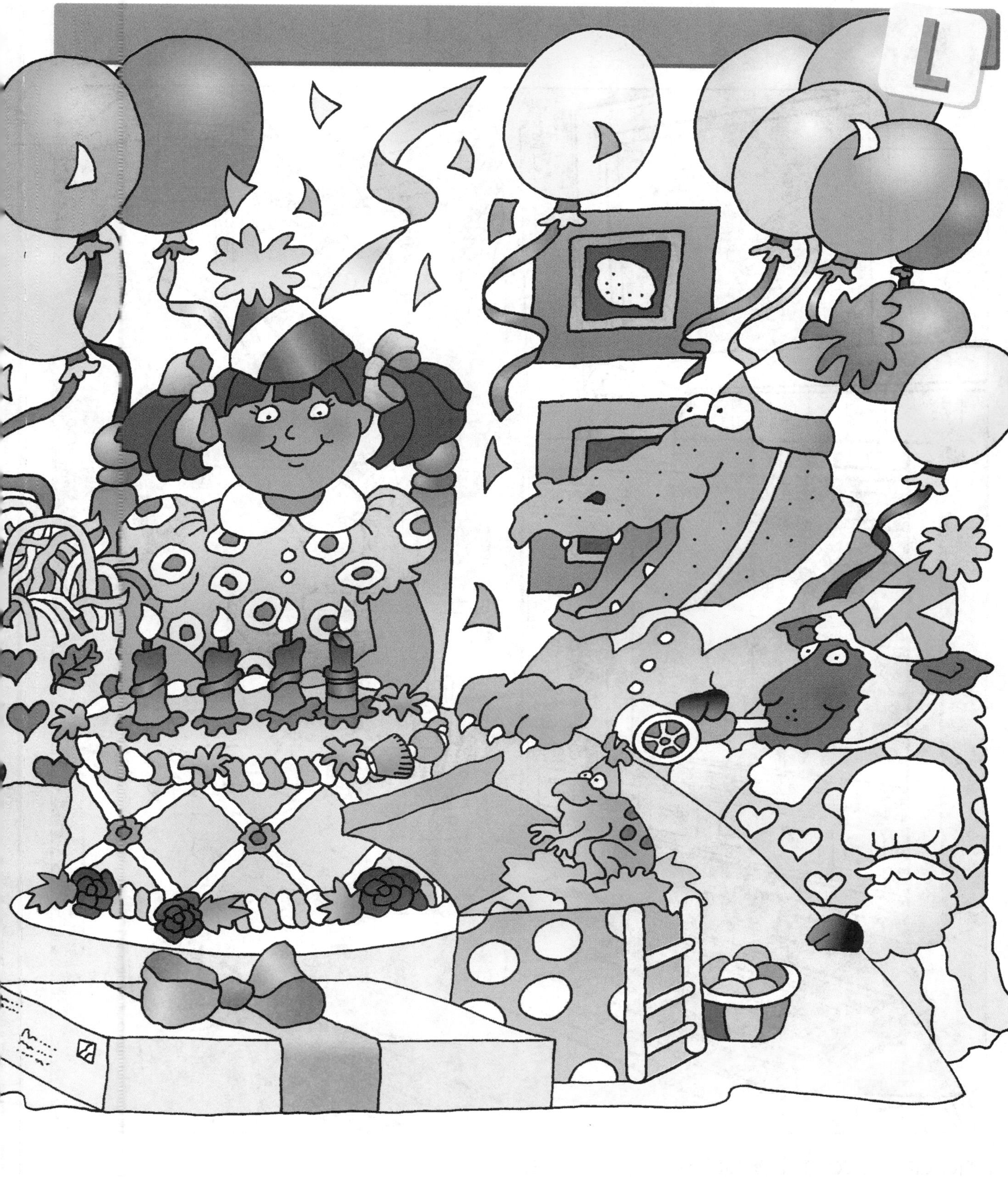

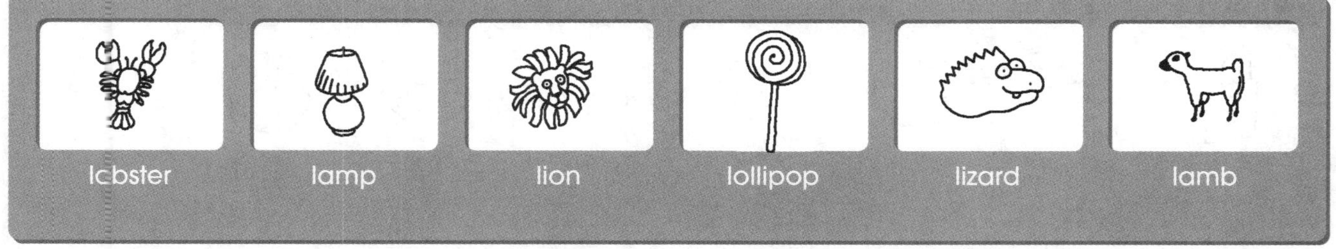

L

LAUGH OUT LOUD

Find and circle the hidden **l** pictures.

lock

ladder

lemon

ladybug

leaf

lime wedge

lettuce

lamp

©School Zone Publishing Company

MYSTERY BOAT

M

Find and circle the hidden **m** pictures.

M MOOSE'S CARNIVAL

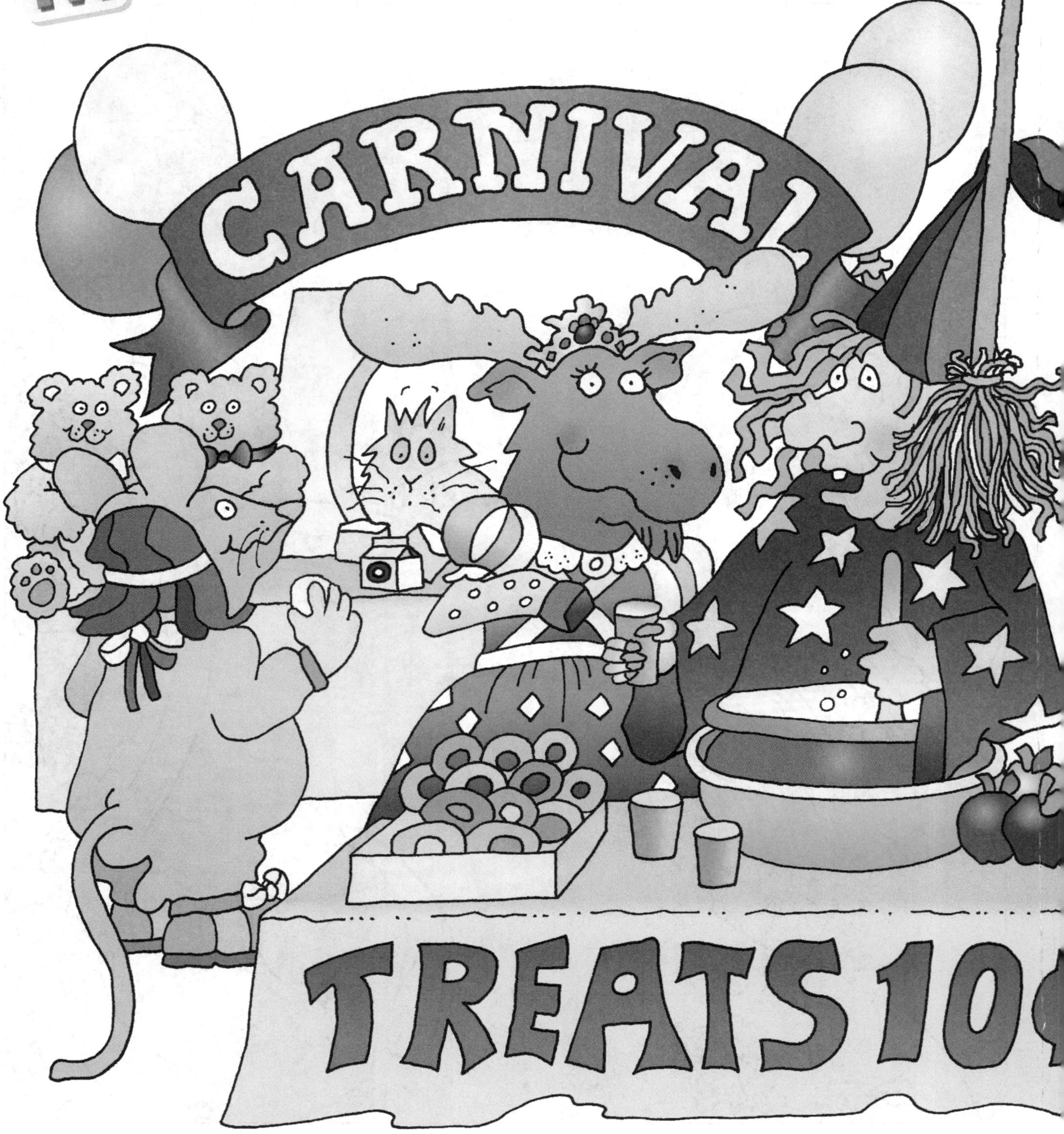

Find and circle the hidden **m** pictures.

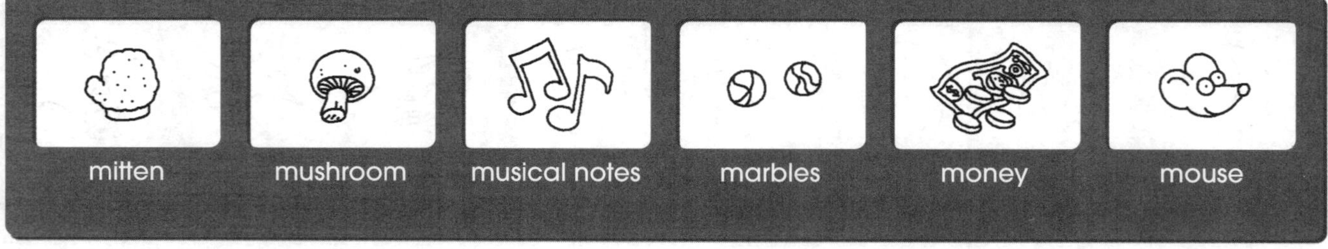

 ©School Zone Publishing Company

M
FACE 5¢
PAINTING
milk carton
monkey
moon
mop
mailbox
mask

N NATE'S CORNER

Find and circle the hidden **n** pictures.

nest

nail

newspaper

nut

needle

necktie

noodle

nine

©School Zone Publishing Company

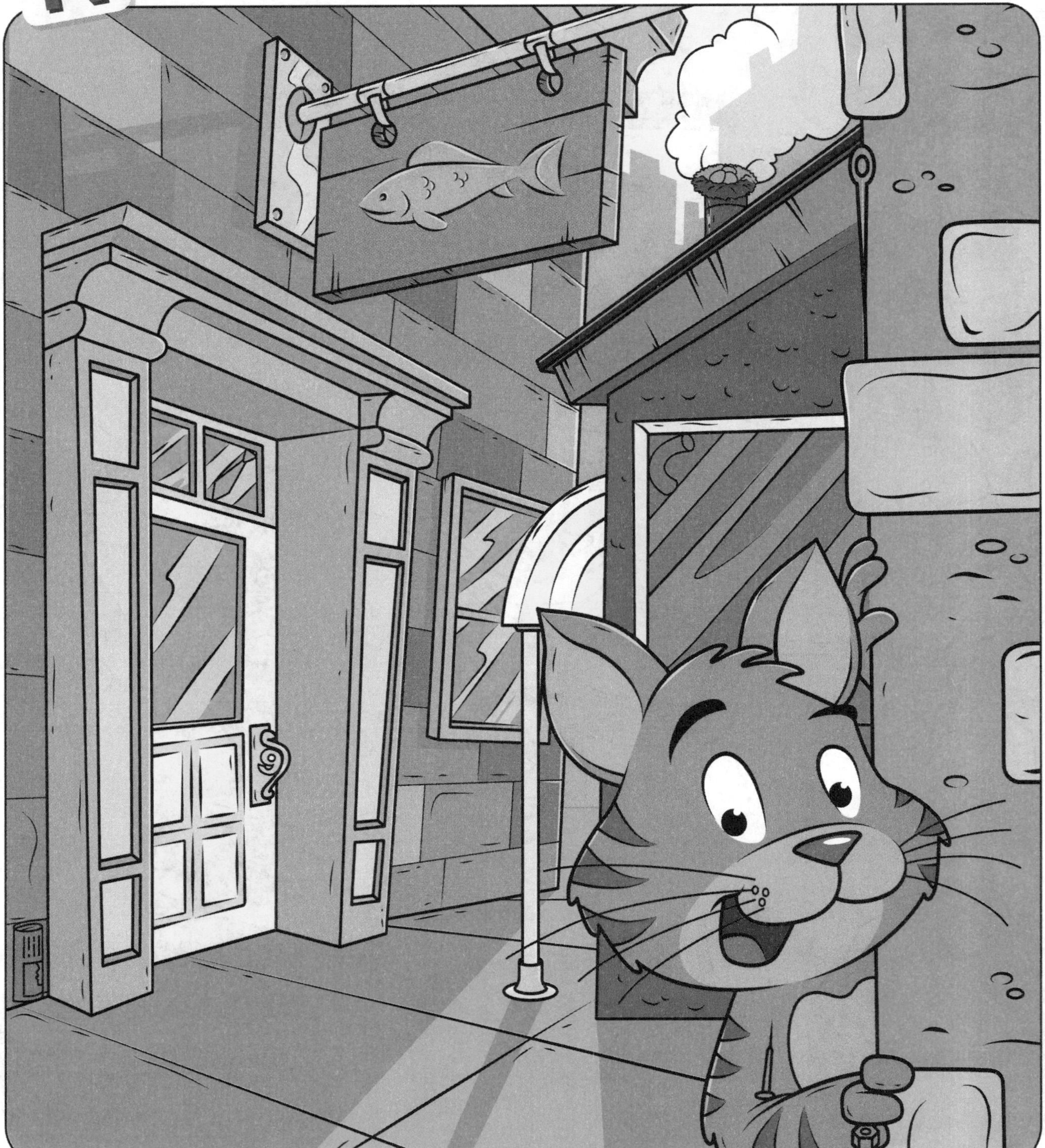

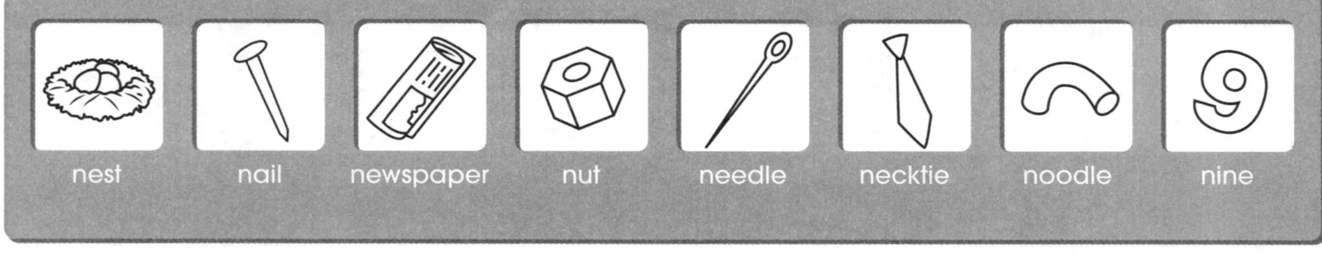

NICE NURSE

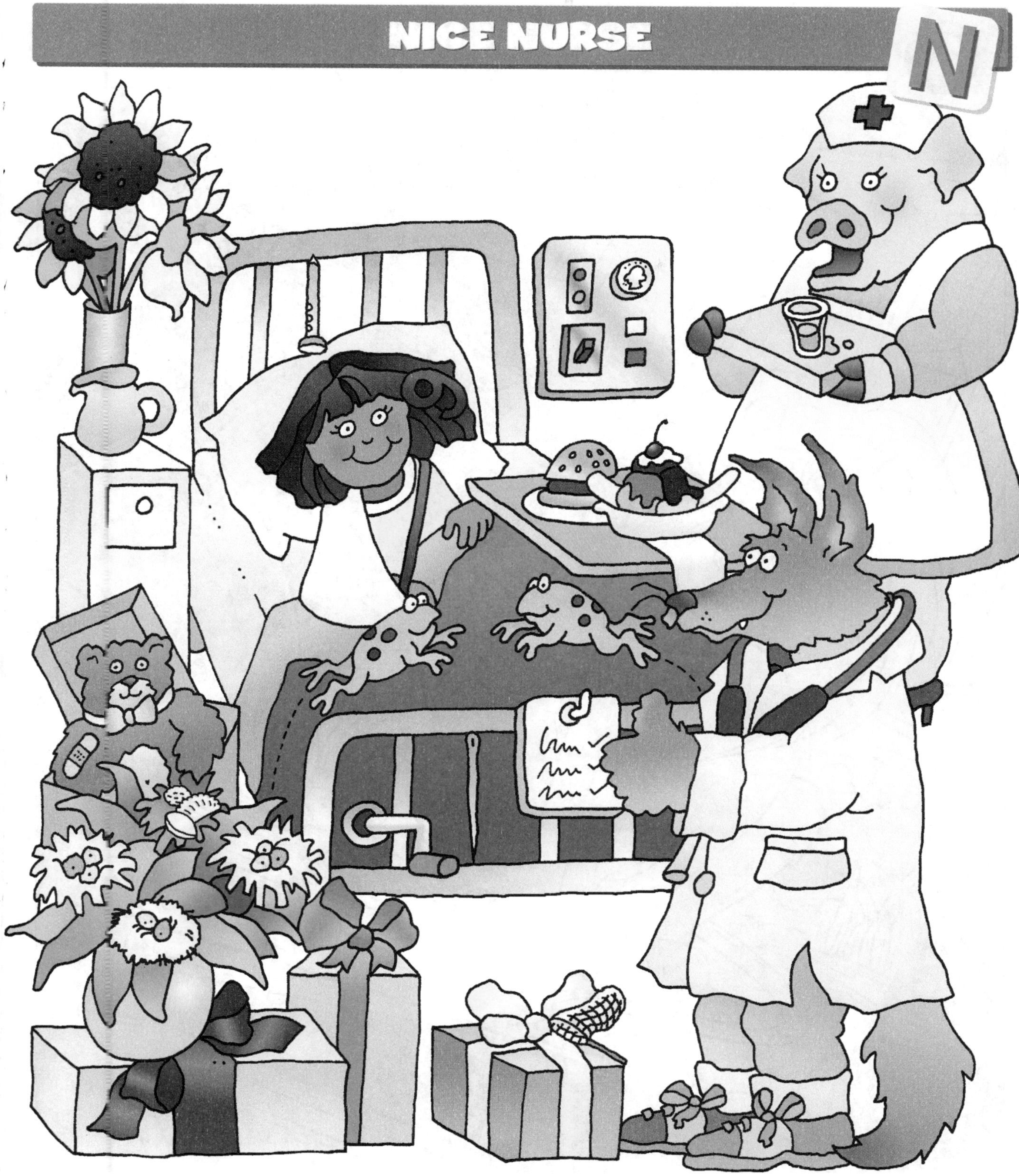

N

Find and circle the hidden **n** pictures.

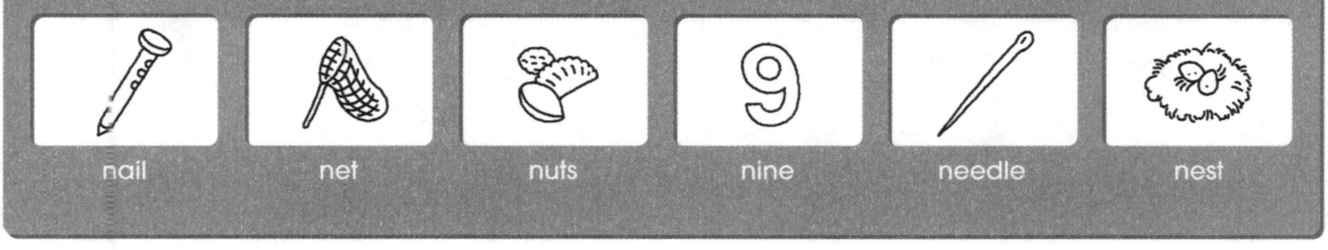

O OLIVER LION

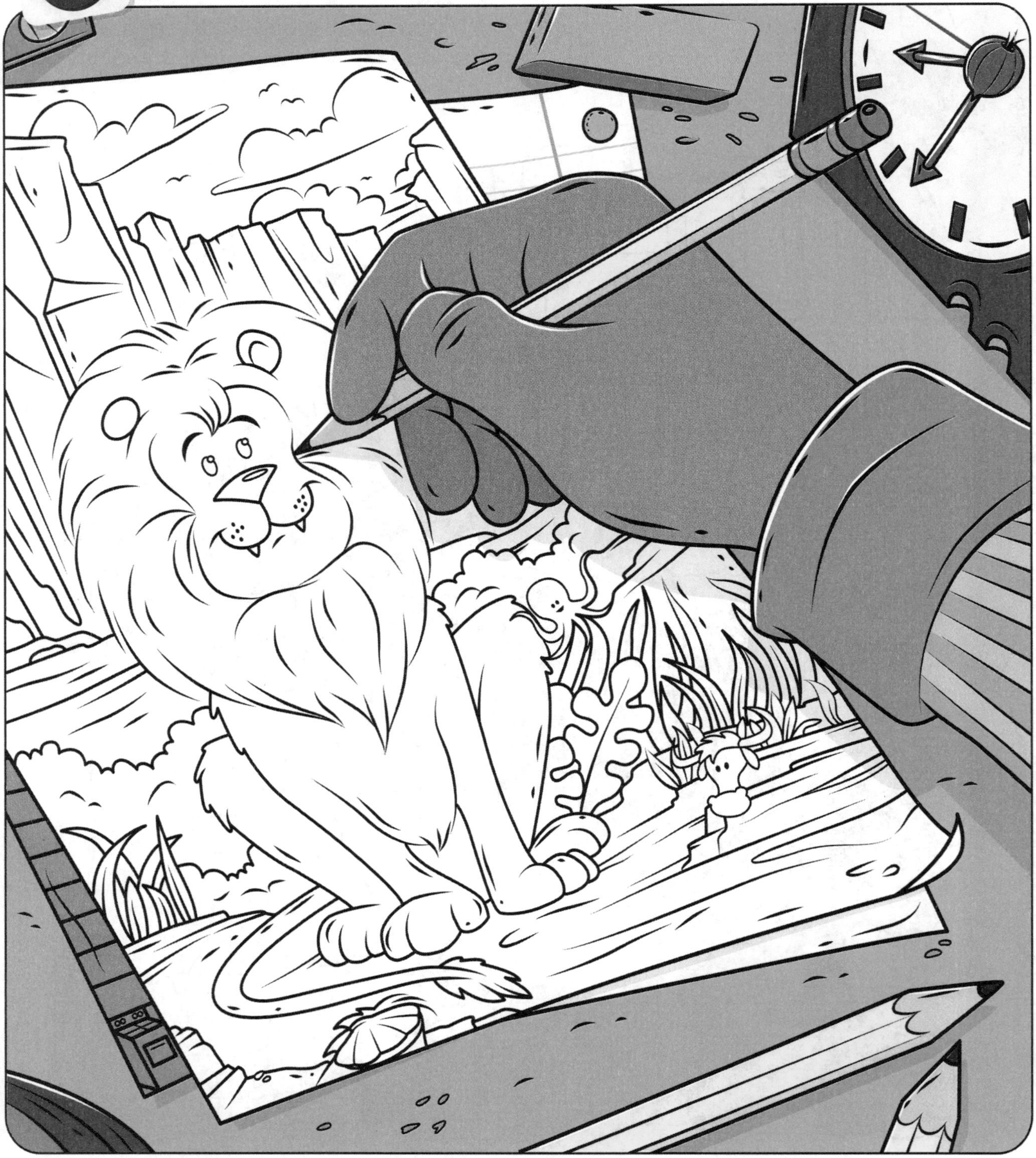

Find and circle the hidden **o** pictures.

oval onion ox oven orange oyster olive octopus

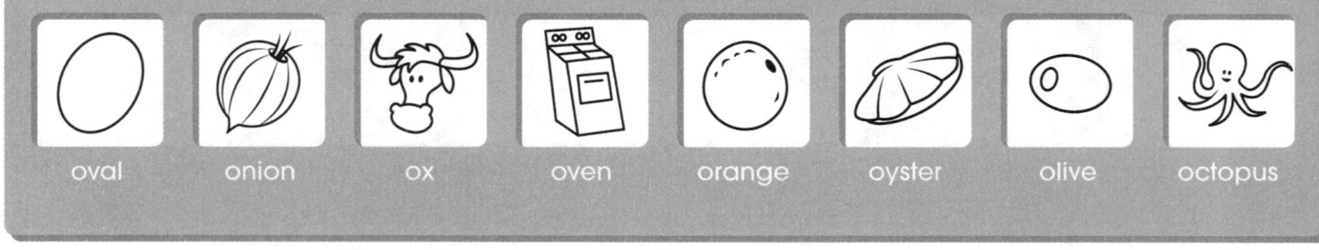

 ©School Zone Publishing Company

OLIVIA'S BREAKFAST

Find and circle the hidden **o** pictures.

P PARTY ANIMALS

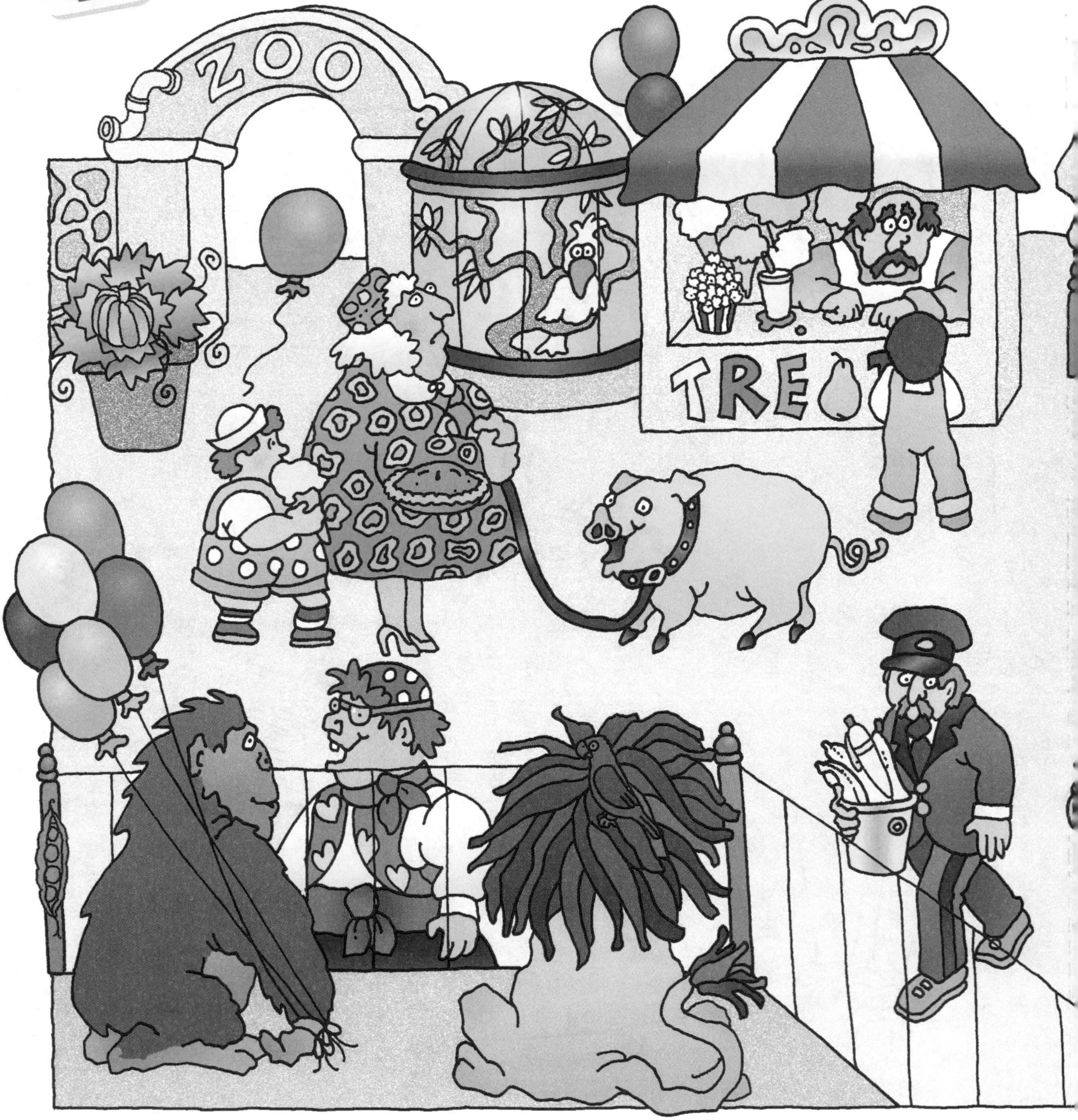

Find and circle the hidden **p** pictures.

pipe

paint

parrot

peanut

pen

pencil

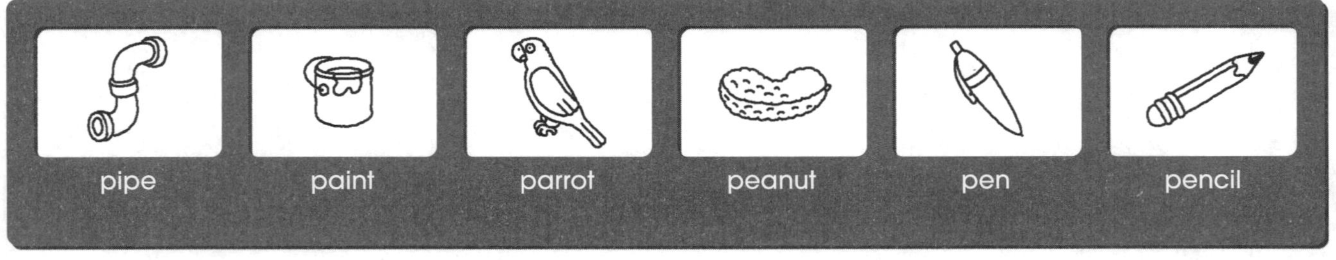

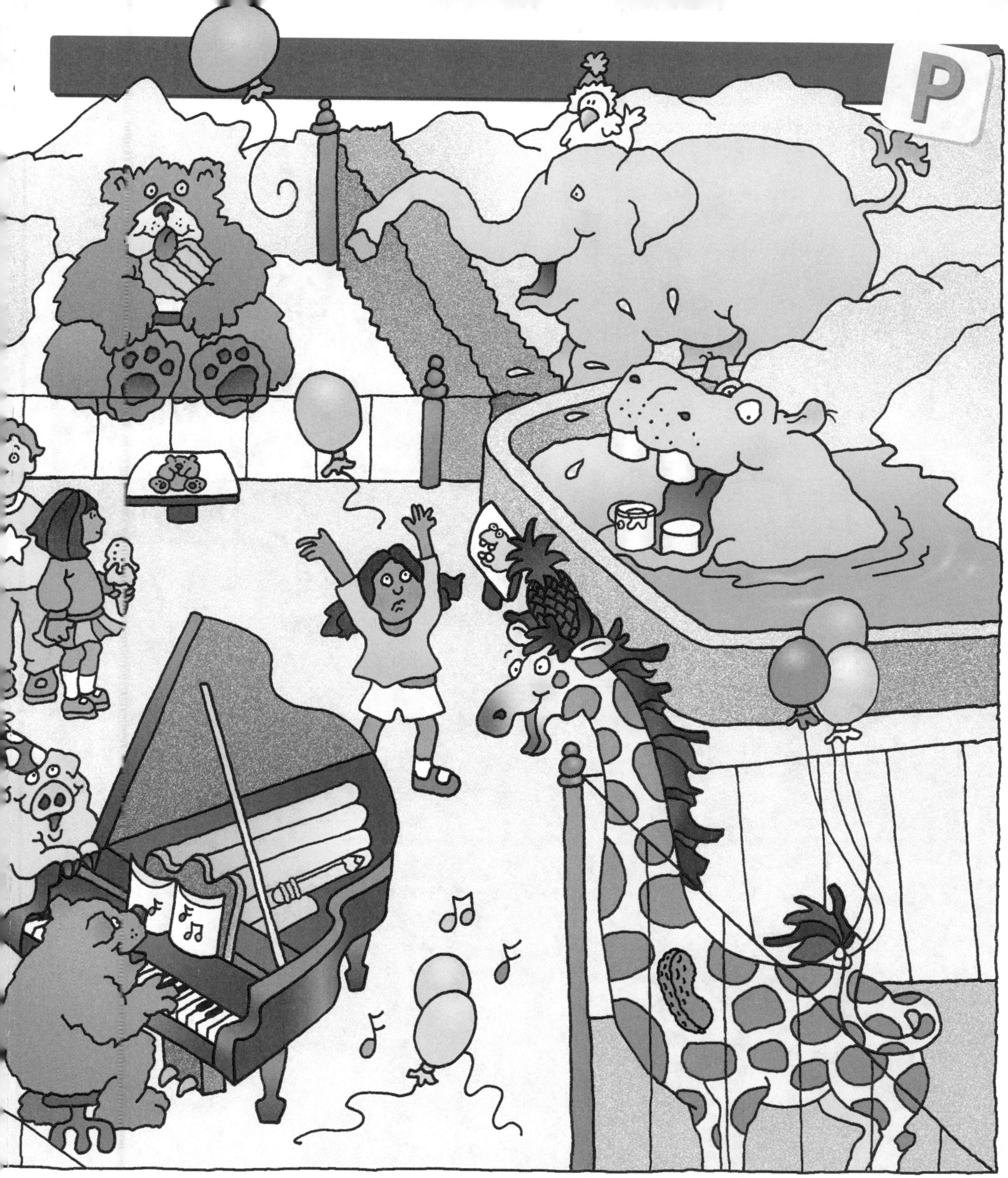

peas | pie | popcorn | pineapple | pumpkin | pear

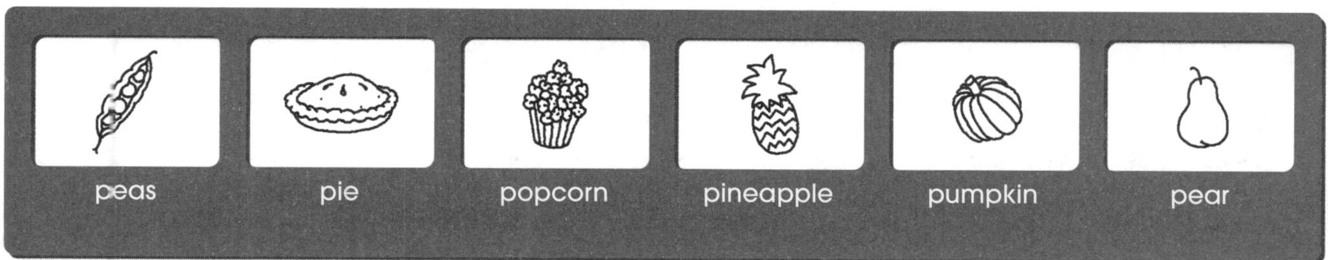

P PELICAN PLEASURE

Find and circle the hidden **p** pictures.

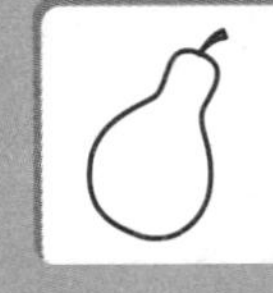
pear

penguin

pillow

pencil

parrot

peach

paint

peanut

©School Zone Publishing Company

QUIRKY CLOSET

Q

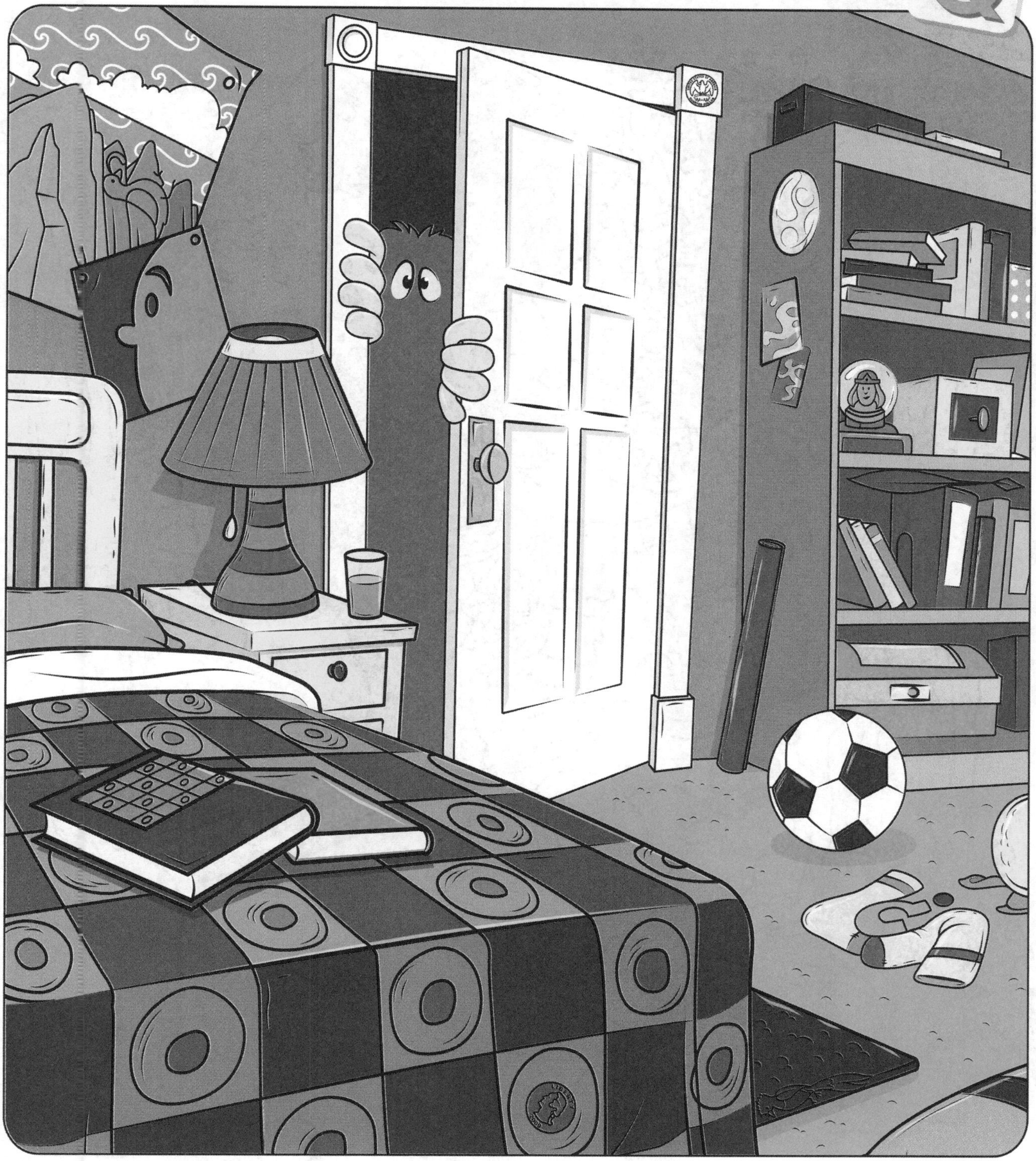

Find and circle the hidden **q** pictures.

queen

quarter

quill

question mark

quail

quarter

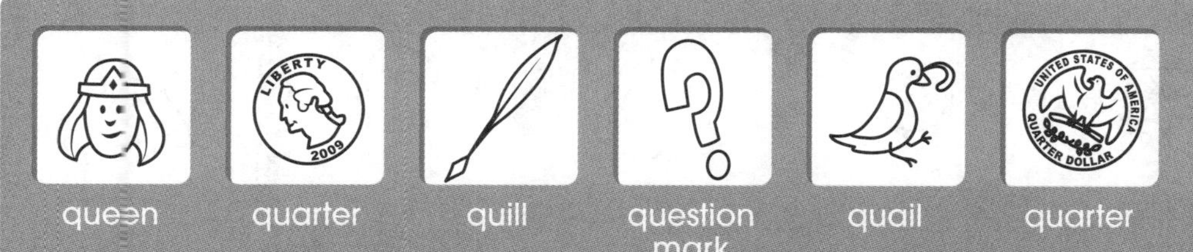

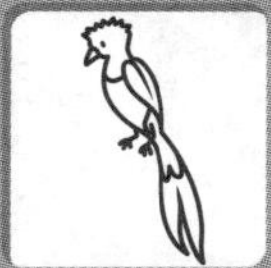

quetzal

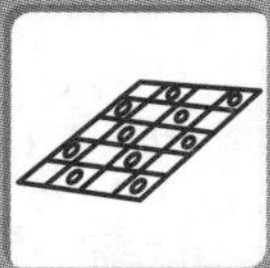

quilt

Q

THE QUEEN'S QUEST

Find and circle the hidden **q** pictures.

	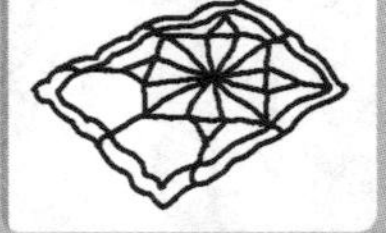				
quince	quilt	quarter	queen	question mark	quail

©School Zone Publishing Company

ROLLING SNOWBALLS

R

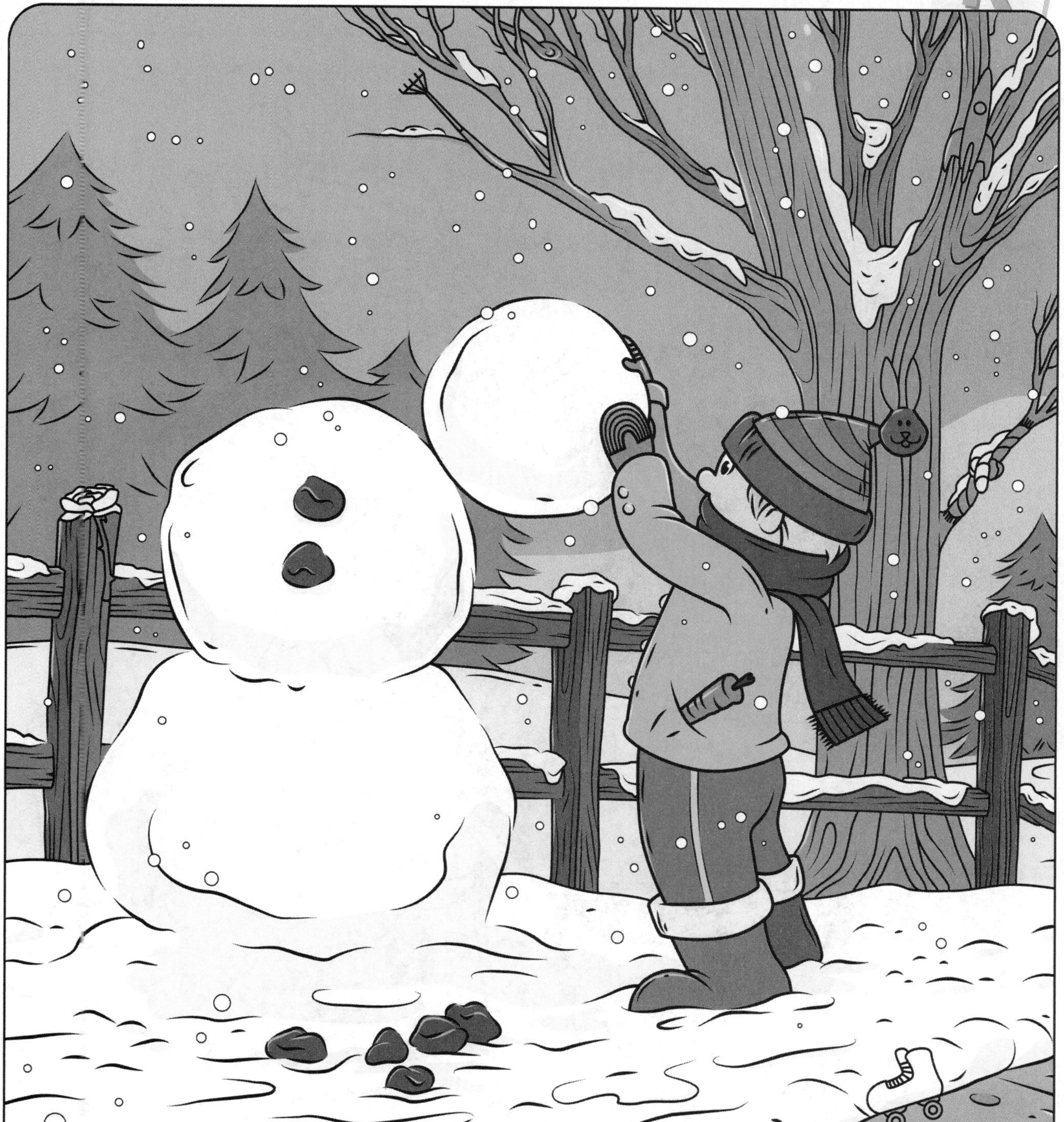

Find and circle the hidden **r** pictures.

rabbit | rug | rocket | rope | roller skate | rainbow | rose | rake

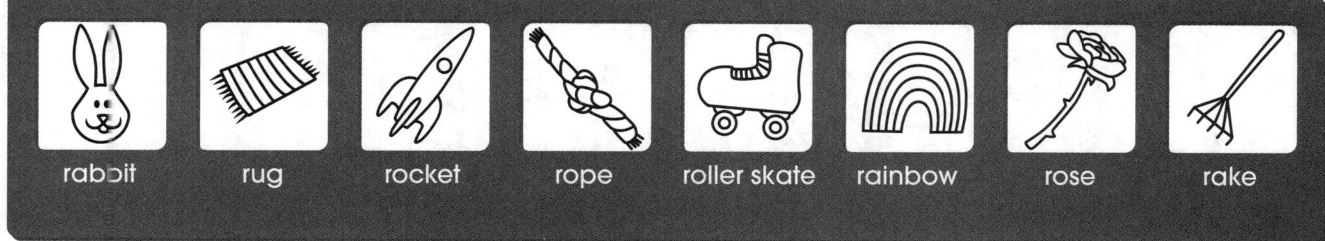

R RACHEL RHINO ROLLER-SKATING

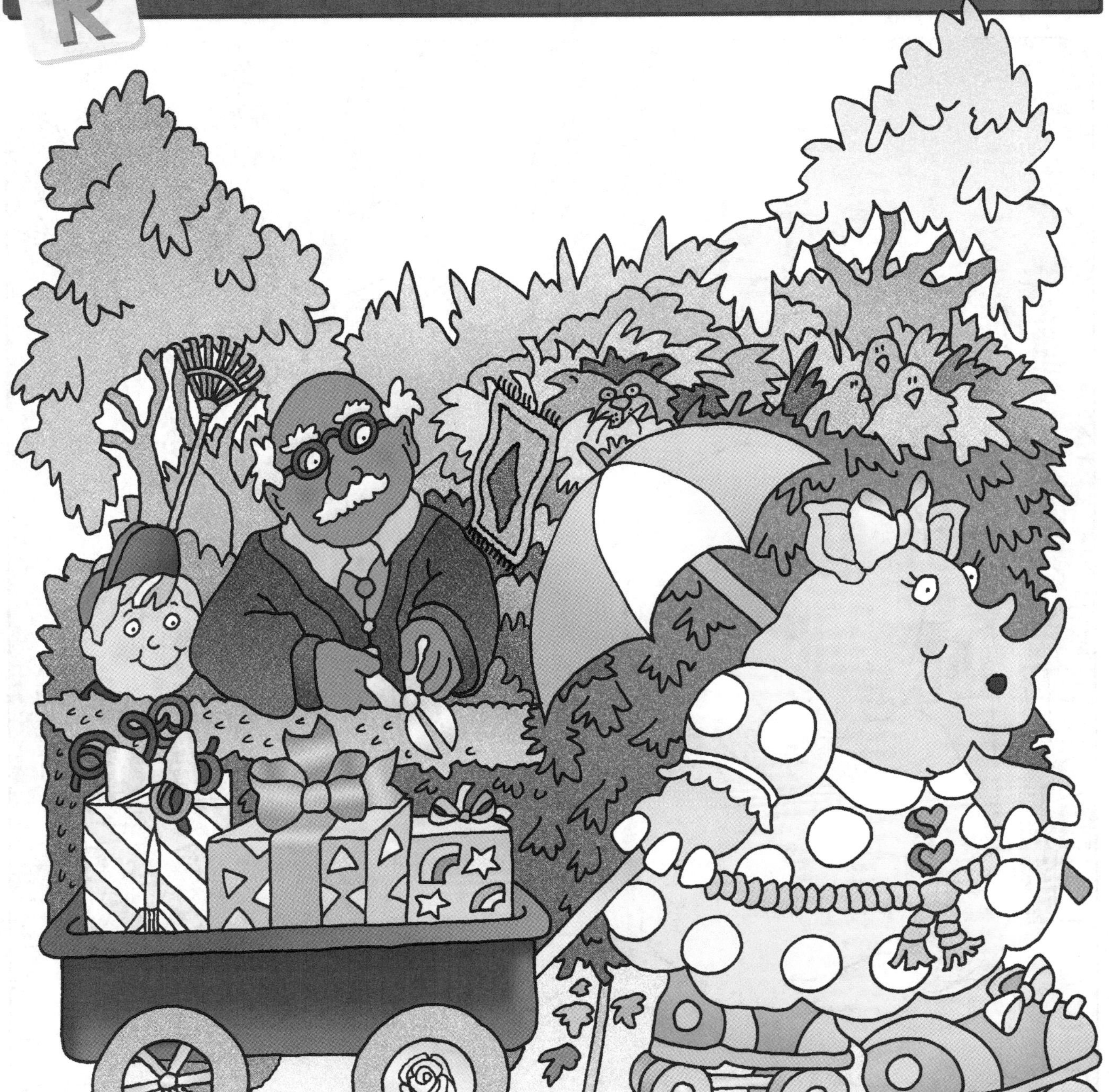

Find and circle the hidden **r** pictures.

rake

roller skate

rocket

rope

rose

rug

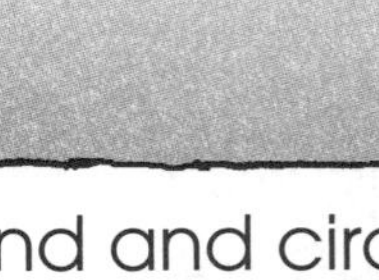

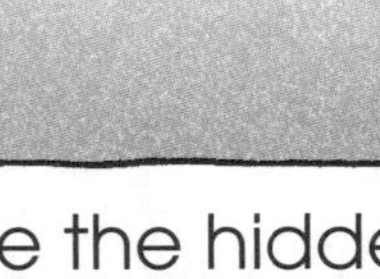

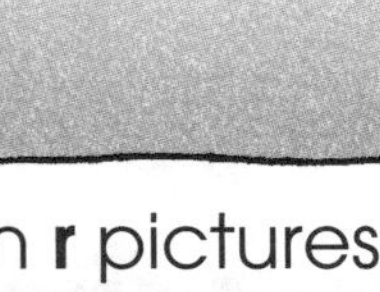

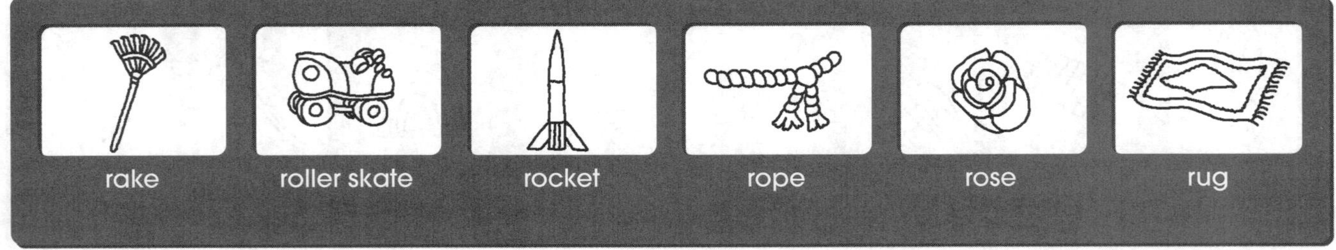

 ©School Zone Publishing Company

STUDY HALL DAYDREAM

S

Find and circle the hidden **s** pictures.

strawberry

spoon

snail

snowman

star

stamp

spider

sun

S SUMMER FUN IN THE SUN

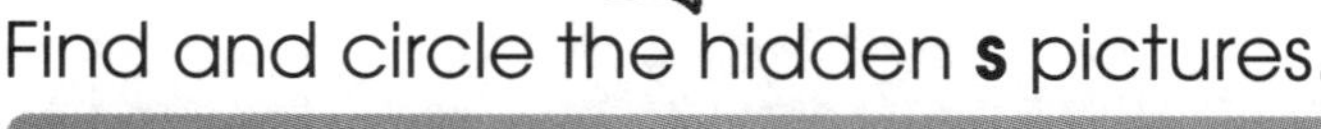

Find and circle the hidden **s** pictures.

©School Zone Publishing Company

S

©School Zone Publishing Company

T TROLLEY TIME

Find and circle the hidden **t** pictures.

train

television

ticket

truck

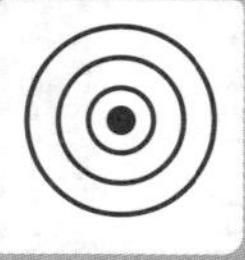
trumpet

target

turtle

tomato

©School Zone Publishing Company

TWO BEAR SCOUTS

T

Find and circle the hidden **t** pictures.

telephone | tulip | tomato | top | tent | turtle

©School Zone Publishing Company

U UP, UP, AND AWAY!

Find and circle the hidden **u** pictures.

 ©School Zone Publishing Company

UPTOWN CIRCUS

U

Find and circle the hidden **u** pictures.

umbrella

umpire

unicorn

unicycle

ukulele

V

VERTICAL VIEW

Find and circle the hidden **v** pictures.

valentine

vacuum

violet

violin

vest

volcano

van

vase

©School Zone Publishing Company

VIOLET & VICTOR DRESS UP

V

Find and circle the hidden **v** pictures.

violin

vase

vest

violets

vegetables

valentine

W WATCH OUT!

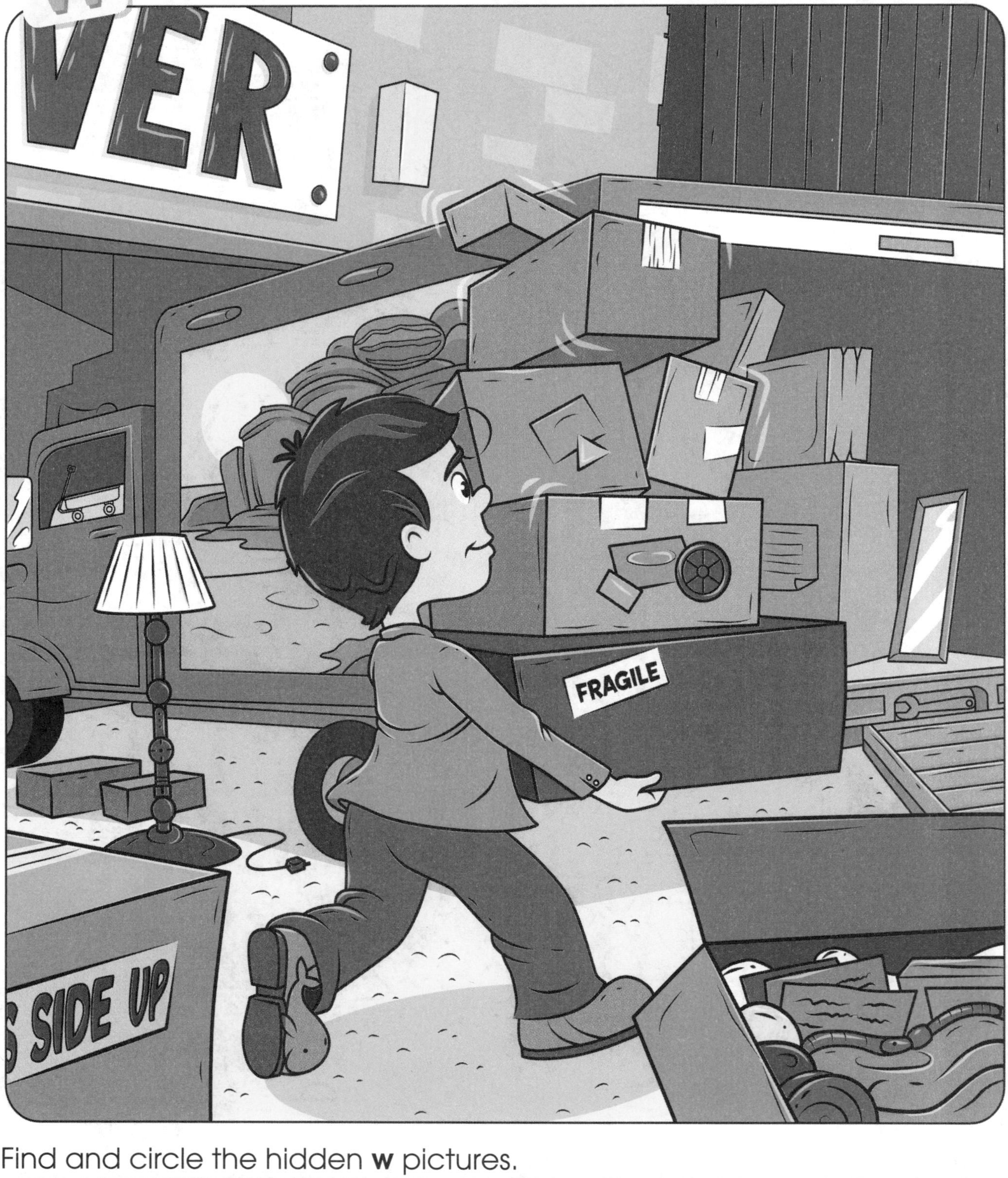

Find and circle the hidden **w** pictures.

wheel

worm

wood

wrench

watermelon

wagon

whale

watch

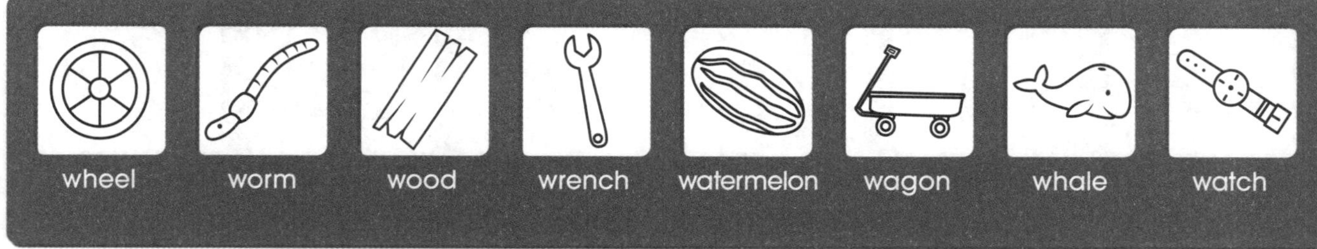

©School Zone Publishing Company

WALLY AND WANDA'S WEDDING

W

Find and circle the hidden **w** pictures.

watermelon slice	woodpecker	whale	watch	worm	wood

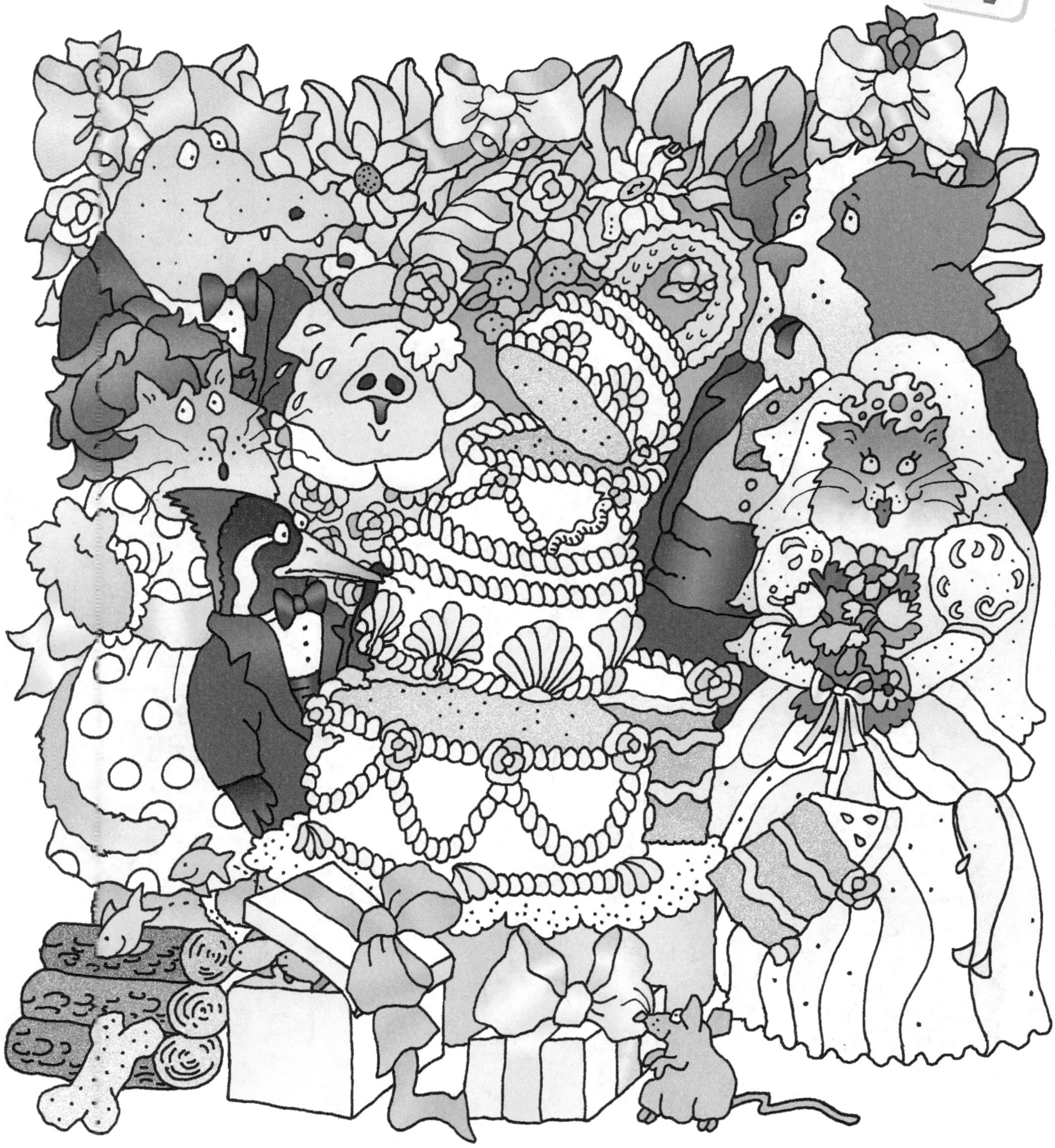

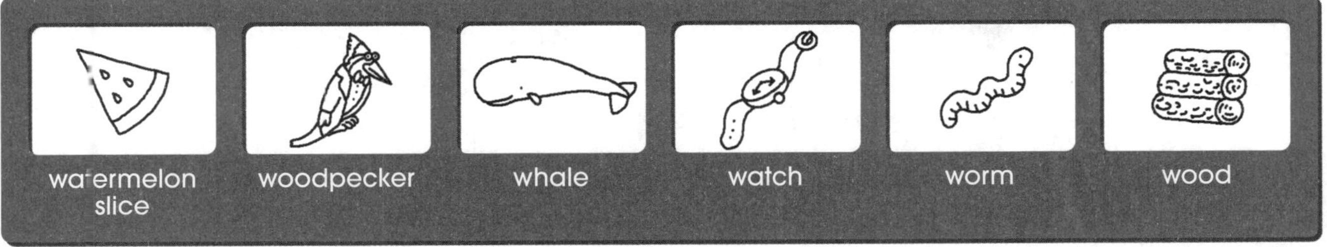

XY

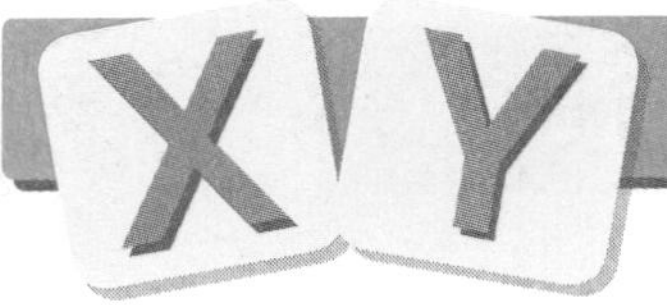

YEARLY CHECKUP

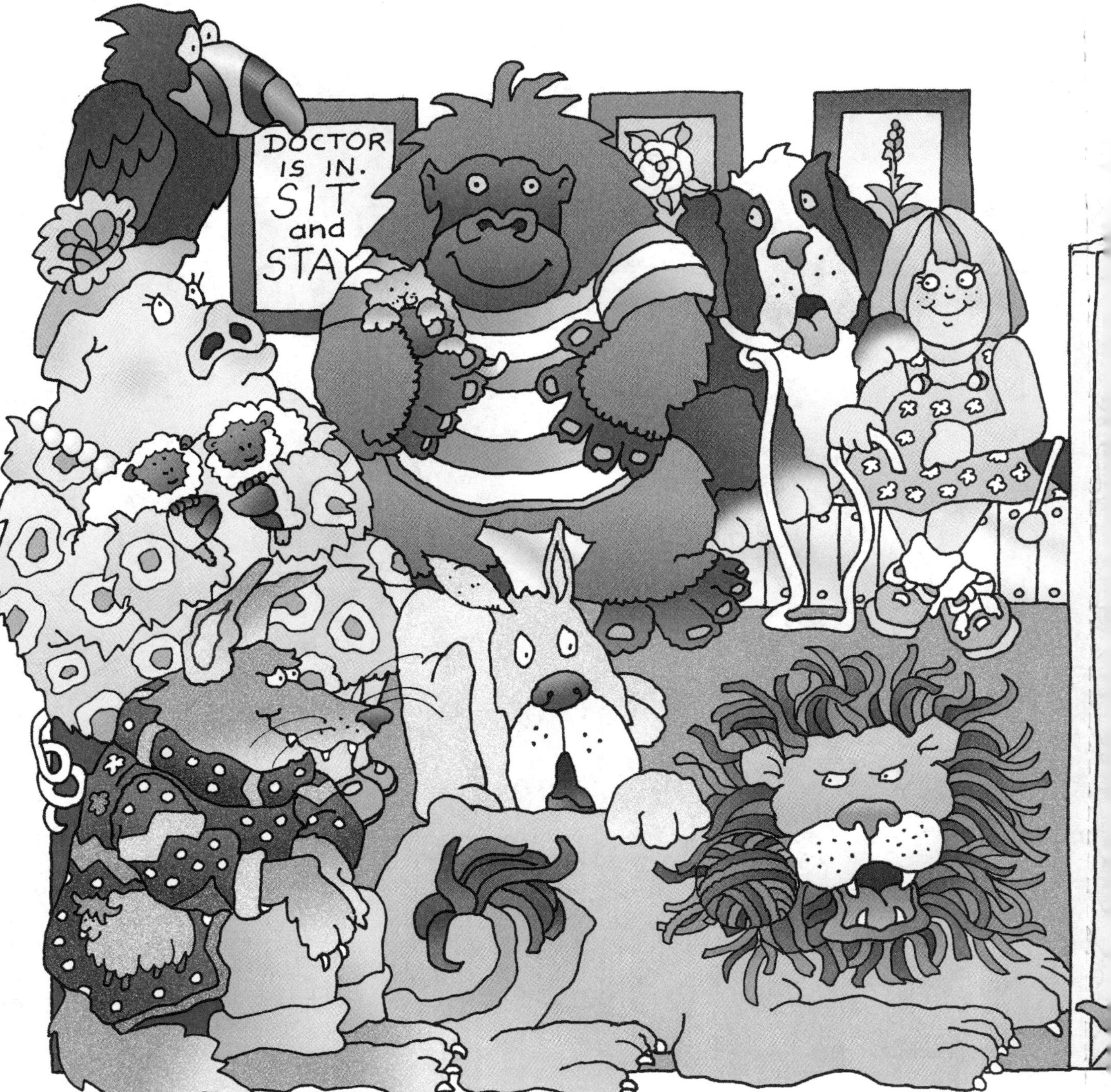

Find and circle the hidden **x** and **y** pictures.

xylophone

x-ray

yacht

yolk

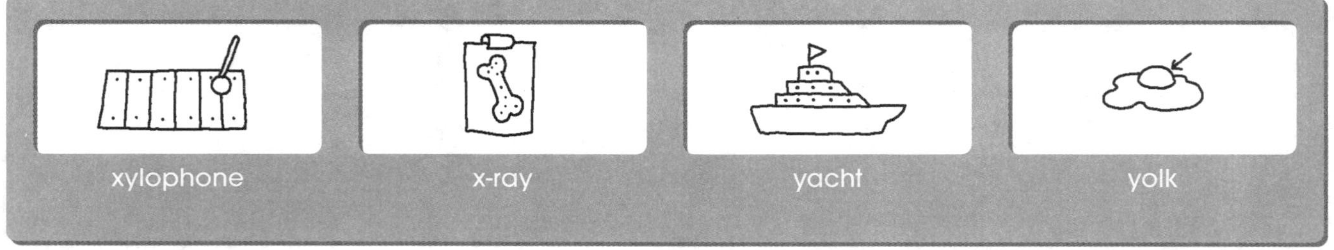

©School Zone Publishing Company

yo-yo

yak

yarn

yam

X Y Z ZESTY BATH

Find and circle the hidden **x**, **y**, and **z** pictures.

yarn

zero

zucchini

yo-yo

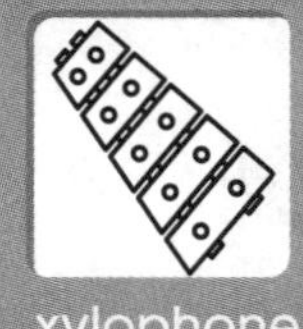
xylophone

x-ray

zipper

yacht

 ©School Zone Publishing Company

ZANY BEDTIME STORIES

Z

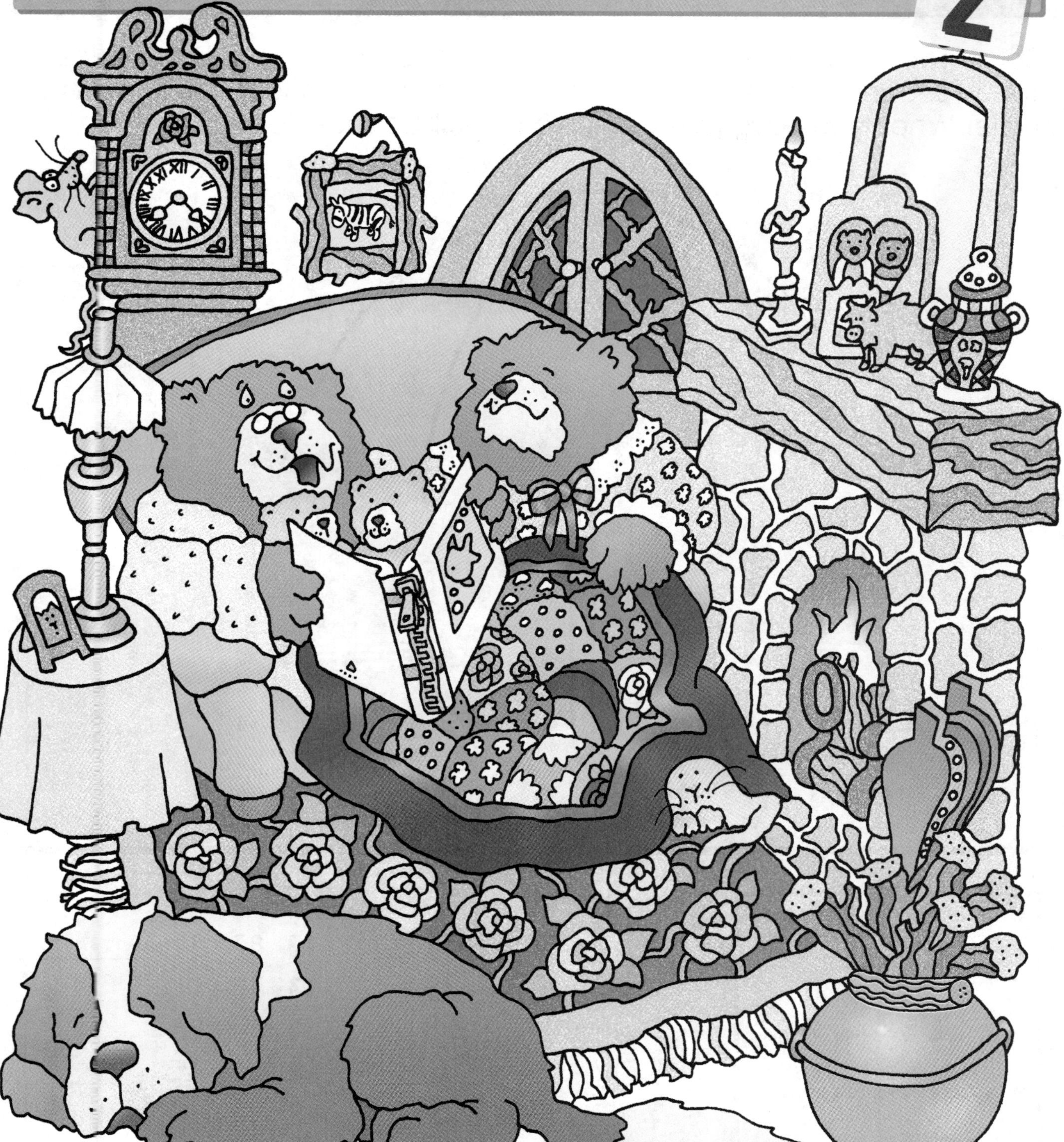

Find and circle the hidden **z** pictures.

zucchini

zero

zipper

zebra

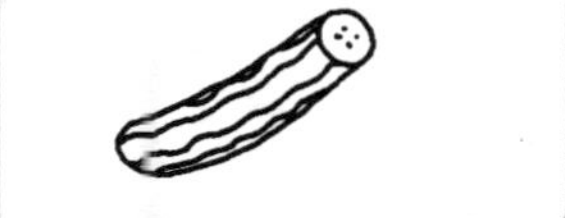

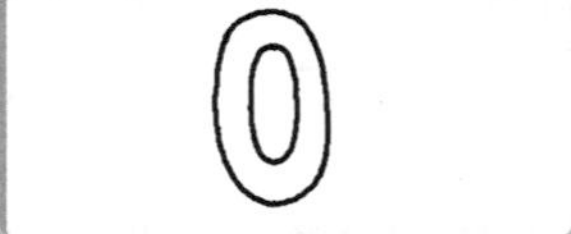

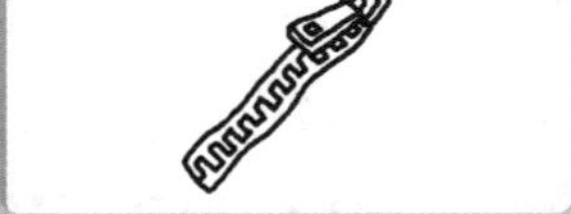

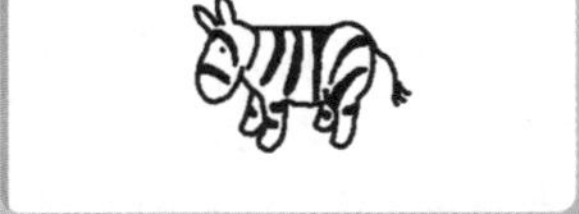

BRING ON THE RAIN!

Solve each math problem. Find the first answer on the grid. Draw a line to the second answer. Continue drawing lines to connect the answers in order. When you have finished, a picture will be revealed.

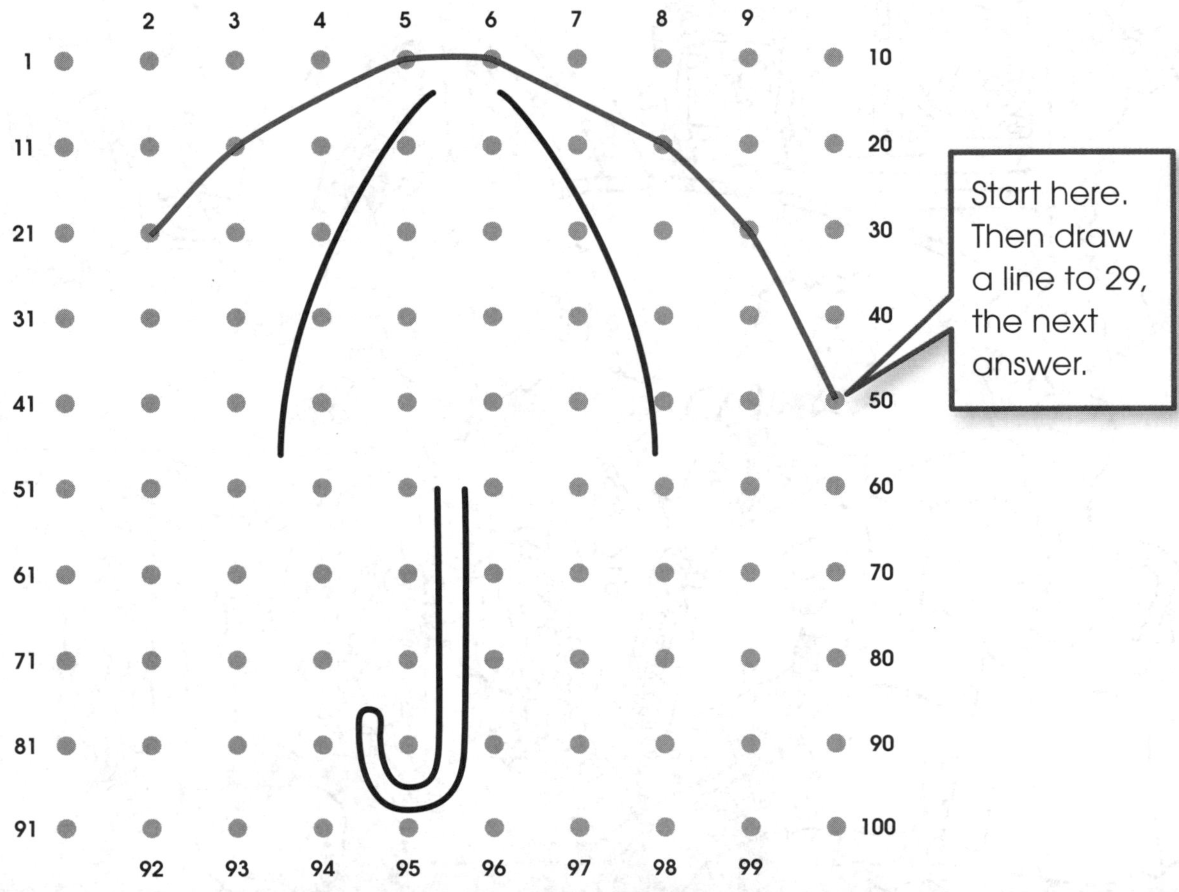

Grid Numbering Example:

1	2	3	4	5
11	12	13	14	15
21	22	23	24	25
31	32	33	34	35

Line 1

1. 20 + 30 = 50
2. 49 − 20 = 29
3. 14 + 4 = 18
4. 12 − 6 = 6
5. 4 + 1 = 5
6. 28 − 15 = 13
7. 11 + 11 = 22
8. 64 − 23 = ______
9. 31 + 22 = ______
10. 78 − 24 = ______
11. 40 + 15 = ______
12. 87 − 31 = ______
13. 43 + 14 = ______
14. 84 − 26 = ______
15. 25 + 25 = ______

©School Zone Publishing Company

MAZE CRAZE

Follow the maze from start to finish.

I'LL TAKE A BIG PIECE, PLEASE!

Solve each math problem. Find the first answer on the grid. Draw a line to the second answer. Continue drawing lines to connect the answers in order. When you have finished, a picture will be revealed.

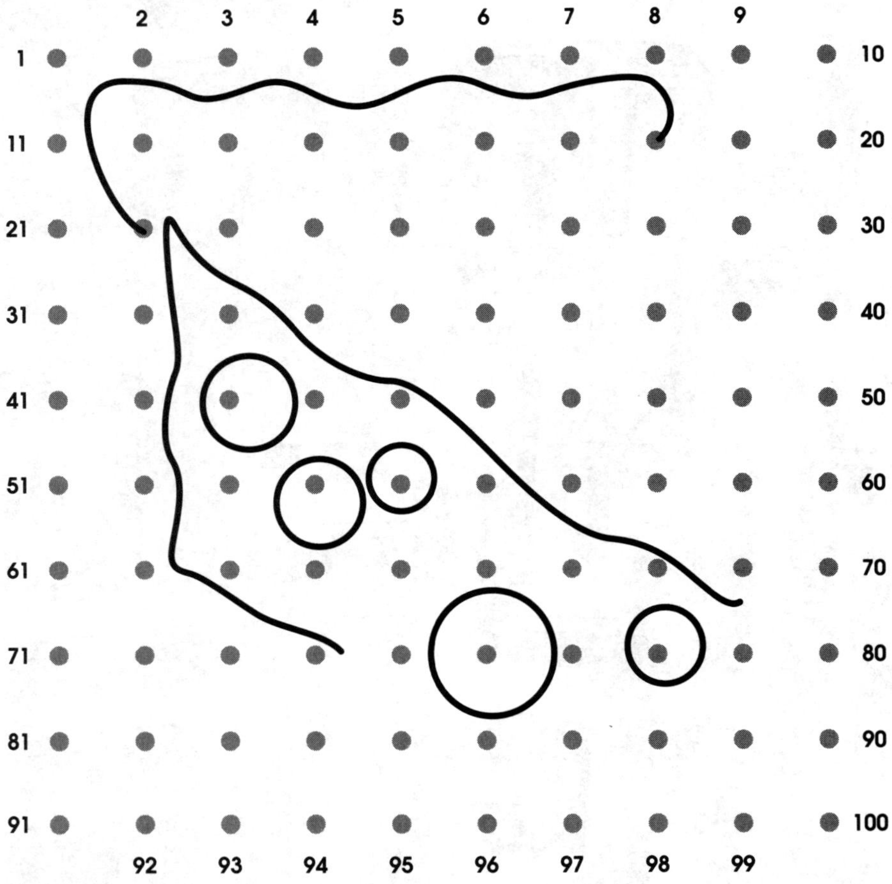

Line 1

1. 9 + 9 = ________

2. 25 – 8 = ________

3. 10 + 6 = ________

4. 25 – 10 = ________

5. 7 + 7 = ________

6. 49 – 36 = ________

7. 10 + 2 = ________

8. 11 + 11= ________

9. 47 – 15 = ________

10. 21+ 21= ________

11. 76 – 24 = ________

12. 31 + 31 = ________

13. 80 – 6 = ________

14. 100 – 14 = ________

15. 73 + 25 = ________

16. 100 – 1 = ________

17. 43 + 46 = ________

18. 90 – 11 = ________

19. 49 + 20 = ________

20. 70 – 11 = ________

21. 14 + 14 = ________

22. 12 + 6 = ________

Line 2

1. 6 + 6 = ________

2. 72 – 49 = ________

3. 30 + 4 = ________

4. 23 + 23 = ________

5. 69 – 12 = ________

6. 14 + 55 = ________

©School Zone Publishing Company

MR. T. REX

Color the picture below.

1 = **blue** 2 = **yellow green** 3 = **green** 4 = **yellow**
5 = **orange** 6 = **brown** 7 = **black**

FLOATING AWAY

Solve each math problem. Find the first answer on the grid. Draw a line to the second answer. Continue drawing lines to connect the answers in order. When you have finished, a picture will be revealed.

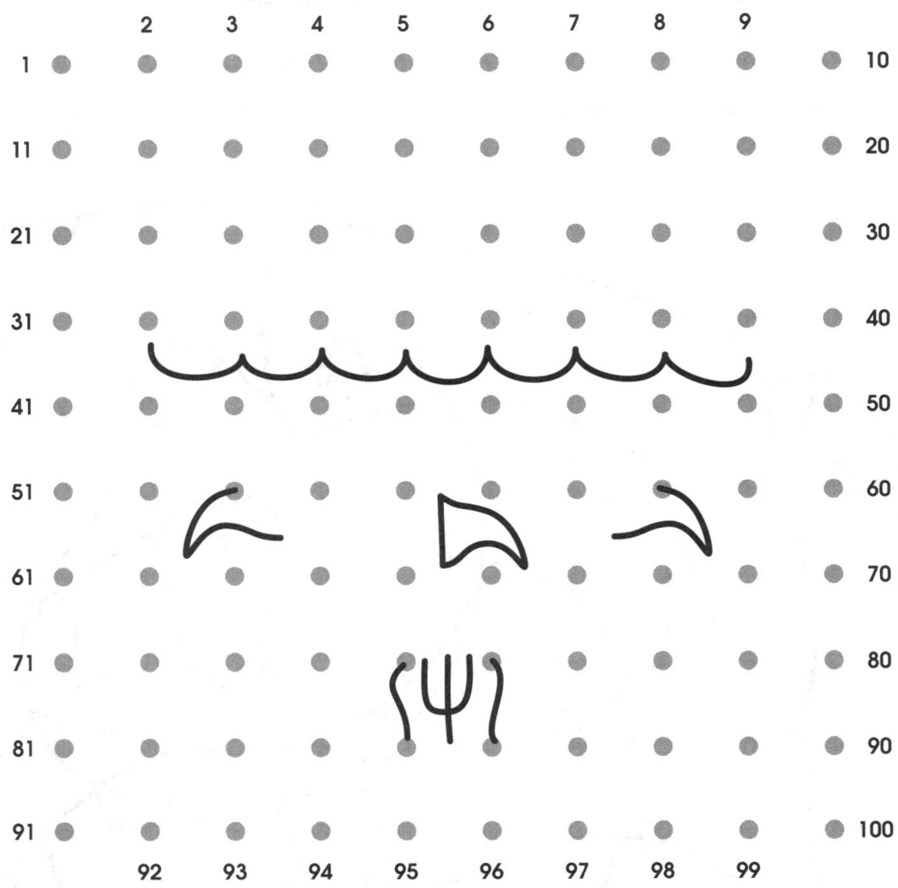

Line 1

1. 3 + 4 = ________
2. 17 – 11 = ________
3. 1 + 4 = ________
4. 14 – 10 = ________
5. 10 + 3 = ________
6. 11 + 11 = ________
7. 18 + 14 = ________
8. 66 – 24 = ________
9. 32 + 21 = ________
10. 99 – 35 = ________
11. 42 + 33 = ________
12. 88 – 12 = ________
13. 60 + 7 = ________
14. 79 – 21 = ________
15. 25 + 24 = ________
16. 46 – 7 = ________
17. 12 + 17 = ________
18. 39 – 21 = ________
19. 6 + 1 = ________

Line 2

1. 96 – 10 = ________
2. 63 + 22 = ________
3. 99 – 4 = ________
4. 69 + 27 = ________
5. 75 + 11 = ________

©School Zone Publishing Company

IN THE OUTBACK

Color the picture below.

1 = blue green　2 = green　3 = yellow　4 = brown
5 = orange　6 = black　7 = purple

<table>
<tr><td>1 / 1</td><td>1 / 1</td><td>1 / 1</td><td>1 / 1</td><td>1 / 1</td><td>1 / 1</td><td>1 / 1</td><td>1 / 1</td><td>1 / 1</td><td>2 / 1</td><td>2 / 2</td><td>2 / 2</td><td>2 / 2</td><td>2 / 2</td><td>2 / 2</td></tr>
<tr><td>1 / 1</td><td>1 / 1</td><td>7 / 7</td><td>7 / 7</td><td>7 / 7</td><td>7 / 7</td><td>1 / 1</td><td>1 / 1</td><td>1 / 1</td><td>1 / 1</td><td>1 / 2</td><td>2 / 7</td><td>7 / 7</td><td>7 / 7</td><td>7 / 7</td></tr>
<tr><td>1 / 1</td><td>1 / 1</td><td>3 / 1</td><td>3 / 3</td><td>3 / 3</td><td>3 / 3</td><td>7 / 7</td><td>1 / 7</td><td>1 / 7</td><td>1 / 7</td><td>1 / 7</td><td>7 / 3</td><td>3 / 3</td><td>3 / 3</td><td>2 / 2</td></tr>
<tr><td>1 / 1</td><td>1 / 1</td><td>1 / 1</td><td>1 / 3</td><td>3 / 3</td><td>3 / 7</td><td>7 / 7</td><td>7 / 7</td><td>7 / 7</td><td>7 / 7</td><td>7 / 7</td><td>3 / 3</td><td>3 / 3</td><td>2 / 2</td><td>4 / 4</td></tr>
<tr><td>1 / 1</td><td>1 / 1</td><td>1 / 1</td><td>1 / 1</td><td>3 / 7</td><td>7 / 7</td><td>7 / 6</td><td>7 / 7</td><td>7 / 7</td><td>7 / 6</td><td>7 / 7</td><td>3 / 7</td><td>1 / 1</td><td>1 / 4</td><td>4 / 4</td></tr>
<tr><td>1 / 1</td><td>1 / 1</td><td>1 / 1</td><td>1 / 7</td><td>7 / 7</td><td>7 / 7</td><td>7 / 7</td><td>7 / 6</td><td>6 / 6</td><td>7 / 7</td><td>7 / 7</td><td>7 / 7</td><td>7 / 4</td><td>4 / 4</td><td>4 / 4</td></tr>
<tr><td>1 / 1</td><td>1 / 1</td><td>1 / 1</td><td>1 / 1</td><td>7 / 7</td><td>7 / 7</td><td>7 /</td><td>6 / 6</td><td>6 / 6</td><td>7 /</td><td>7 / 7</td><td>1 / 1</td><td>4 / 4</td><td>4 / 4</td><td>4 / 2</td></tr>
<tr><td>1 / 1</td><td>1 / 1</td><td>1 / 1</td><td>1 / 1</td><td>1 / 1</td><td>7 / 7</td><td>7 / 7</td><td></td><td></td><td>7 / 7</td><td>7 / 7</td><td>1 / 4</td><td>4 / 4</td><td>4 / 4</td><td>2 / 2</td></tr>
<tr><td>2 / 1</td><td>1 / 2</td><td>2 / 1</td><td>1 / 1</td><td>1 / 7</td><td>7 / 7</td><td>7 / 7</td><td>3 / 3</td><td>3 / 3</td><td>3 / 3</td><td>7 / 7</td><td>4 / 4</td><td>4 / 6</td><td>7 / 7</td><td>7 / 7</td></tr>
<tr><td>2 / 1</td><td>2 / 1</td><td>1 / 2</td><td>1 / 1</td><td>1 / 7</td><td>7 / 7</td><td>7 / 7</td><td>7 / 7</td><td>7 / 7</td><td>7 / 7</td><td>6 / 4</td><td>4 / 4</td><td>4 / 6</td><td>7 / 7</td><td>7 / 1</td></tr>
<tr><td>4 / 4</td><td>1 / 2</td><td>2 / 1</td><td>1 / 1</td><td>1 / 7</td><td>7 / 7</td><td>7 / 7</td><td>7 / 7</td><td>7 / 7</td><td>7 / 7</td><td>6 / 4</td><td>4 / 4</td><td>4 / 4</td><td>1 / 1</td><td>1 / 1</td></tr>
<tr><td>2 / 4</td><td>4 / 4</td><td>1 / 2</td><td>1 / 1</td><td>7 / 7</td><td>7 / 7</td><td>3 / 3</td><td>3 / 3</td><td>3 / 3</td><td>3 / 4</td><td>4 / 4</td><td>4 / 4</td><td>4 / 7</td><td>7 / 7</td><td>1 / 1</td></tr>
<tr><td>1 / 1</td><td>4 / 4</td><td>1 / 1</td><td>1 / 1</td><td>7 / 7</td><td>7 / 7</td><td>7 / 7</td><td>7 / 7</td><td>7 / 7</td><td>4 / 4</td><td>4 / 4</td><td>4 / 4</td><td>7 / 6</td><td>7 / 7</td><td>1 / 1</td></tr>
<tr><td>1 / 1</td><td>4 / 4</td><td>4 / 4</td><td>1 / 1</td><td>1 / 1</td><td>7 / 7</td><td>7 / 7</td><td>7 / 7</td><td>7 / 7</td><td>7 / 7</td><td>6 / 4</td><td>4 / 4</td><td>7 / 6</td><td>7 / 1</td><td>1 / 1</td></tr>
<tr><td>5 / 5</td><td>4 / 4</td><td>4 / 4</td><td>4 / 4</td><td>5 / 5</td><td>5 / 5</td><td>7 / 7</td><td>7 / 7</td><td>7 / 7</td><td>7 / 7</td><td>6 / 4</td><td>4 / 5</td><td>5 / 5</td><td>5 / 5</td><td>4 / 4</td></tr>
<tr><td>5 / 5</td><td>5 / 5</td><td>4 / 4</td><td>4 / 4</td><td>4 / 4</td><td>5 / 5</td><td>5 / 4</td><td>4 / 4</td><td>4 / 4</td><td>4 / 4</td><td>4 / 4</td><td>5 / 5</td><td>5 / 5</td><td>4 / 4</td><td>4 / 5</td></tr>
<tr><td>5 / 5</td><td>5 / 5</td><td>5 / 5</td><td>4 / 4</td><td>4 / 4</td><td>4 / 4</td><td>4 / 4</td><td>4 / 4</td><td>4 / 4</td><td>4 / 4</td><td>4 / 5</td><td>5 / 4</td><td>4 / 4</td><td>4 / 5</td><td>5 / 5</td></tr>
</table>

A SPECIAL TREAT

Solve each math problem. Find the first answer on the grid. Draw a line to the second answer. Continue drawing lines to connect the answers in order. When you have finished, a picture will be revealed.

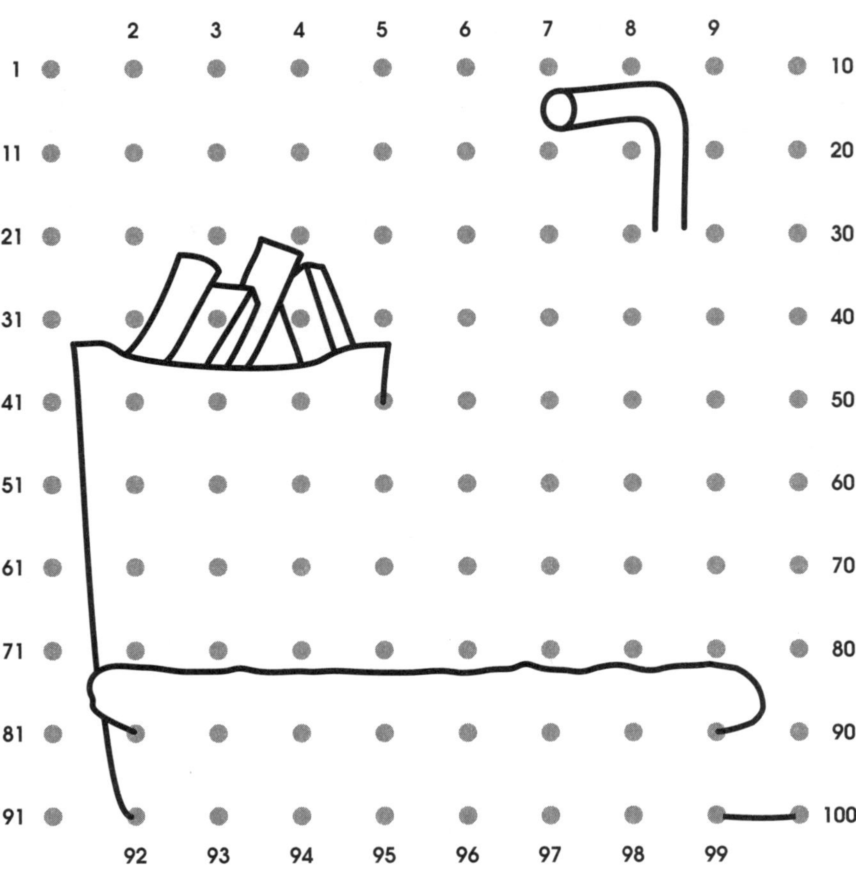

Line 1

1. 100 – 0 = ________
2. 45 + 45 = ________
3. 95 – 15 = ________
4. 40 + 30 = ________
5. 99 – 39 = ________
6. 36 + 14 = ________
7. 65 – 25 = ________
8. 15 + 15 = ________
9. 88 – 59 = ________
10. 15 + 13 = ________
11. 48 – 21 = ________
12. 26 + 11 = ________
13. 69 – 22 = ________
14. 33 + 13 = ________
15. 69 – 24 = ________
16. 36 + 8 = ________
17. 86 – 33 = ________
18. 32 + 30 = ________
19. 88 – 16 = ________
20. 40 + 33 = ________
21. 92 – 18 = ________
22. 39 + 36 = ________
23. 99 – 23 = ________
24. 60 + 17 = ________
25. 86 – 8 = ________
26. 63 + 16 = ________
27. 88 – 19 = ________
28. 44 + 14 = ________
29. 69 – 22 = ________

Line 2

1. 80 + 19 = ________
2. 95 – 6 = ________
3. 97 – 9 = ________
4. 80 + 7 = ________
5. 95 – 9 = ________
6. 43 + 42 = ________
7. 94 – 10 = ________
8. 62 + 21 = ________
9. 89 – 7 = ________
10. 56 + 36 = ________
11. 100 – 7 = ________
12. 82 + 12 = ________
13. 100 – 5 = ________
14. 73 + 23 = ________
15. 99 – 2 = ________
16. 61 + 37 = ________
17. 100 – 1 = ________

©School Zone Publishing Company

CAMP FOOD

Find and circle the hidden pictures.

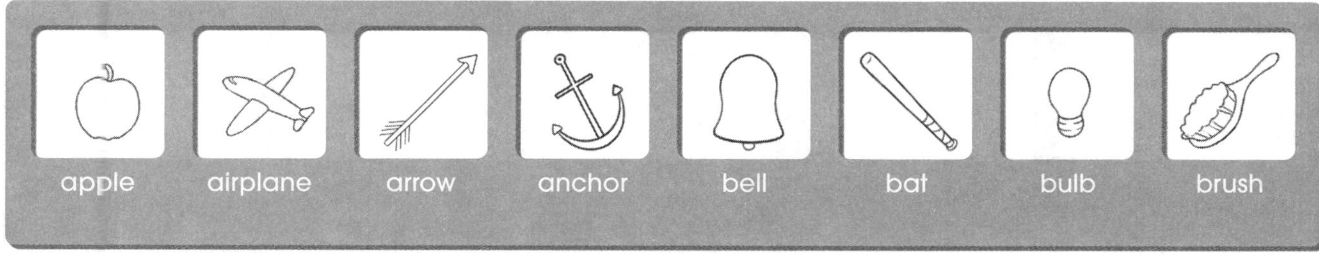

AN AFTERNOON IN THE ORCHARD

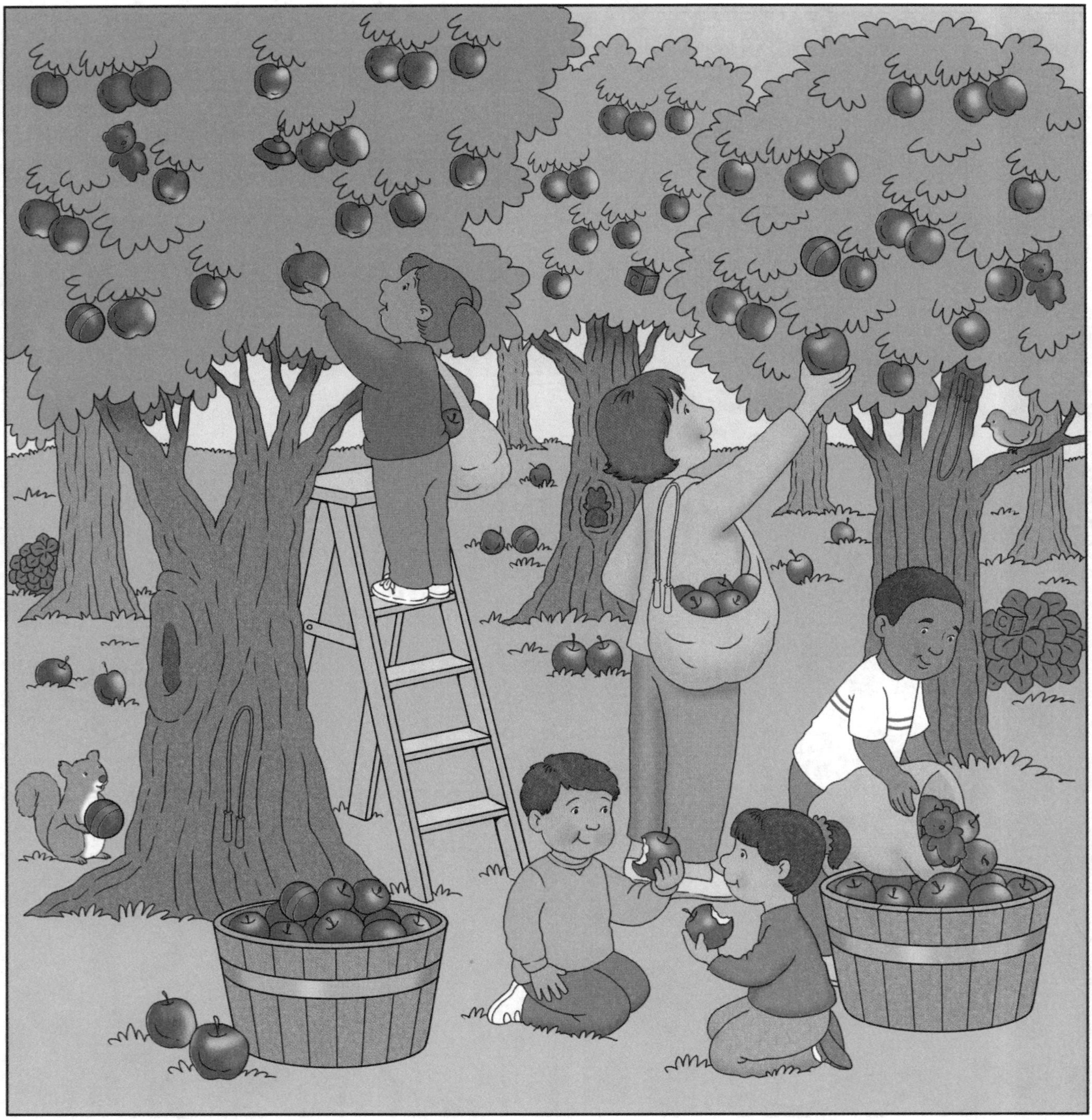

Find and circle the hidden pictures.

Find 1
top

Find 2
blocks

Find 3
jump ropes

Find 4
teddy bears

Find 5
balls

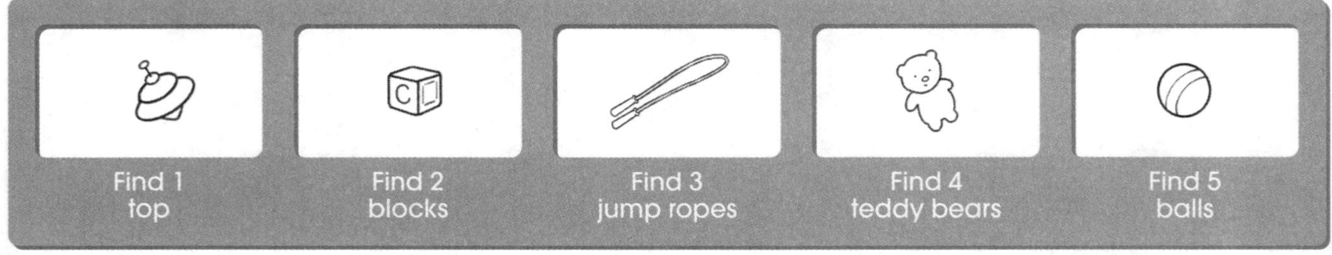

©School Zone Publishing Company

LOST IN SPACE

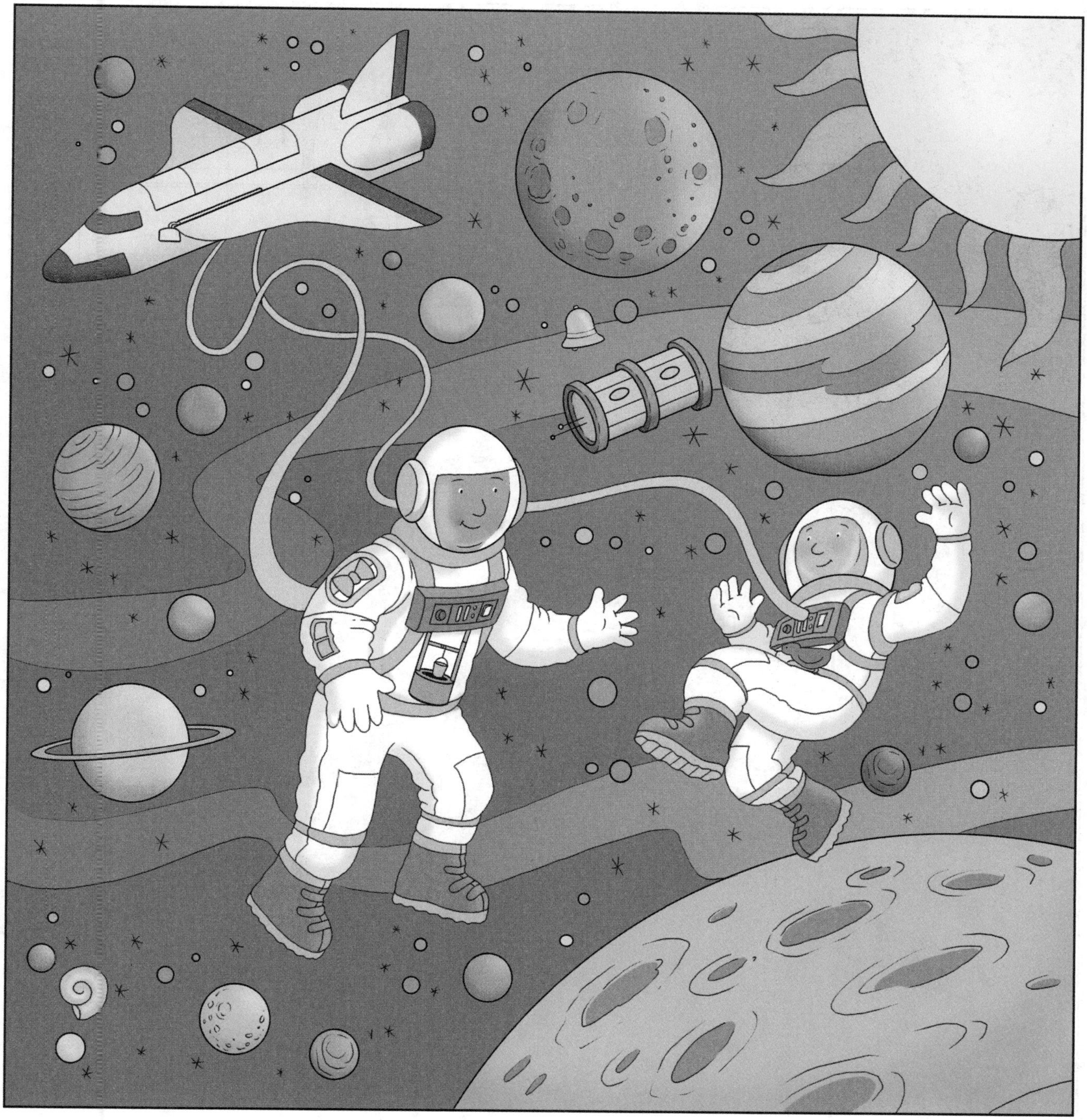

Find and circle the hidden pictures.

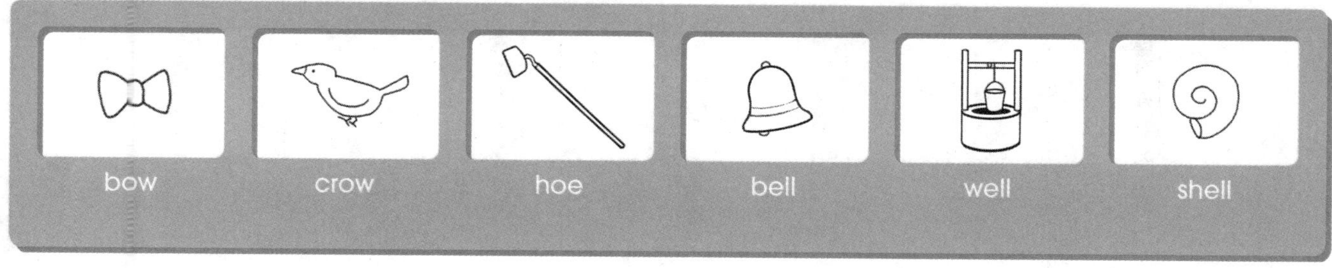

FUN IN THE SUN

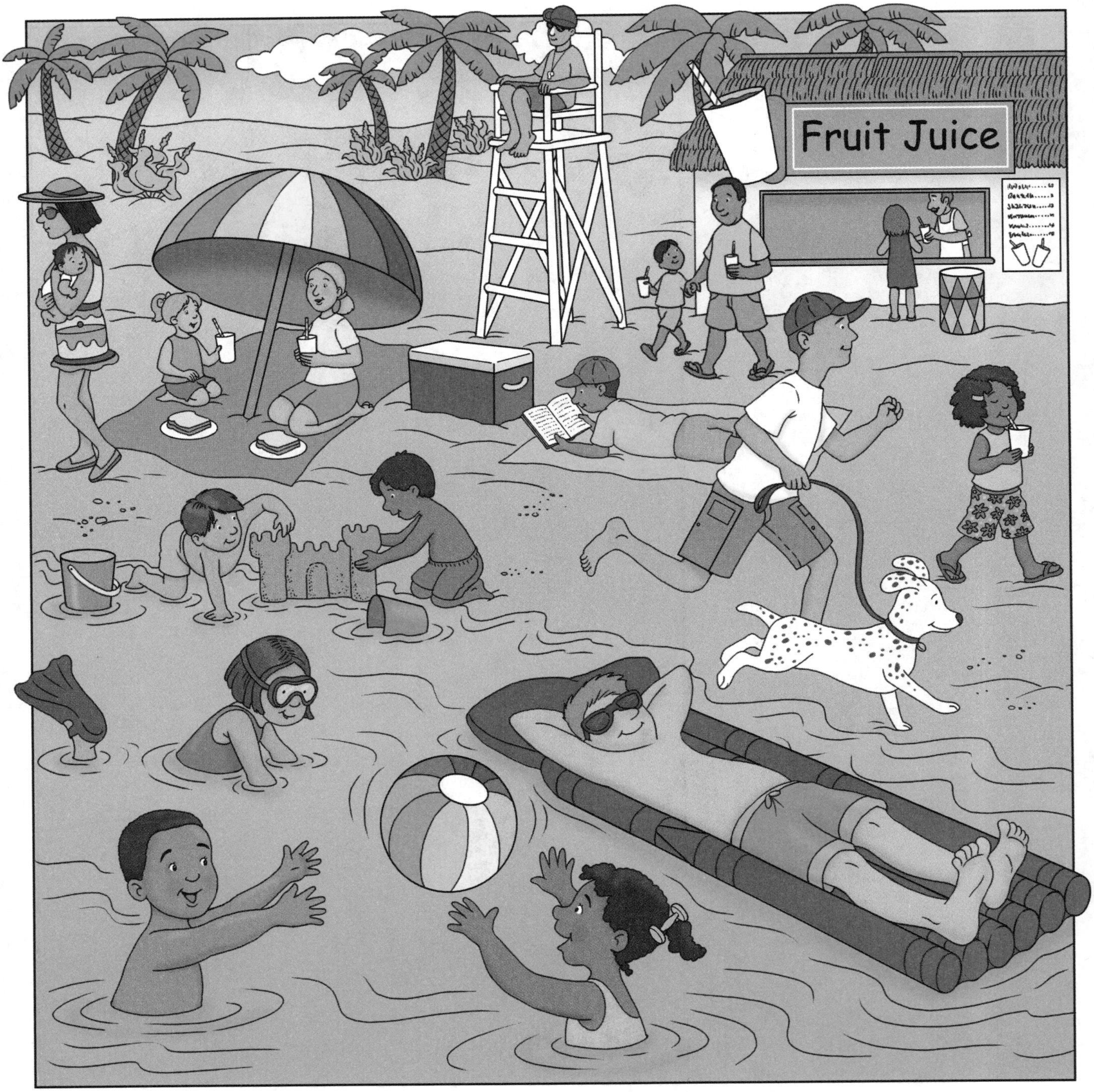

Find and circle the hidden pictures.

crayon

comb

cup

cake

duck

dumbell

drum

door

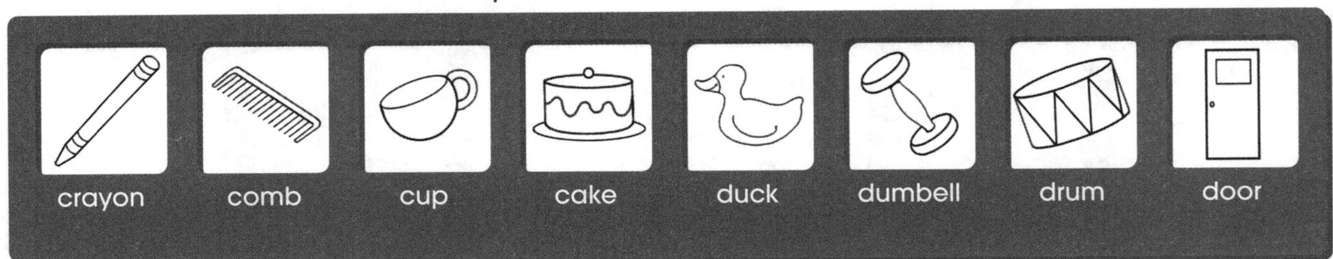

©School Zone Publishing Company

FROM THE FARMERS' MARKET

Find and circle the hidden pictures.

airplane

bird

butterfly

bat

bee

helicopter

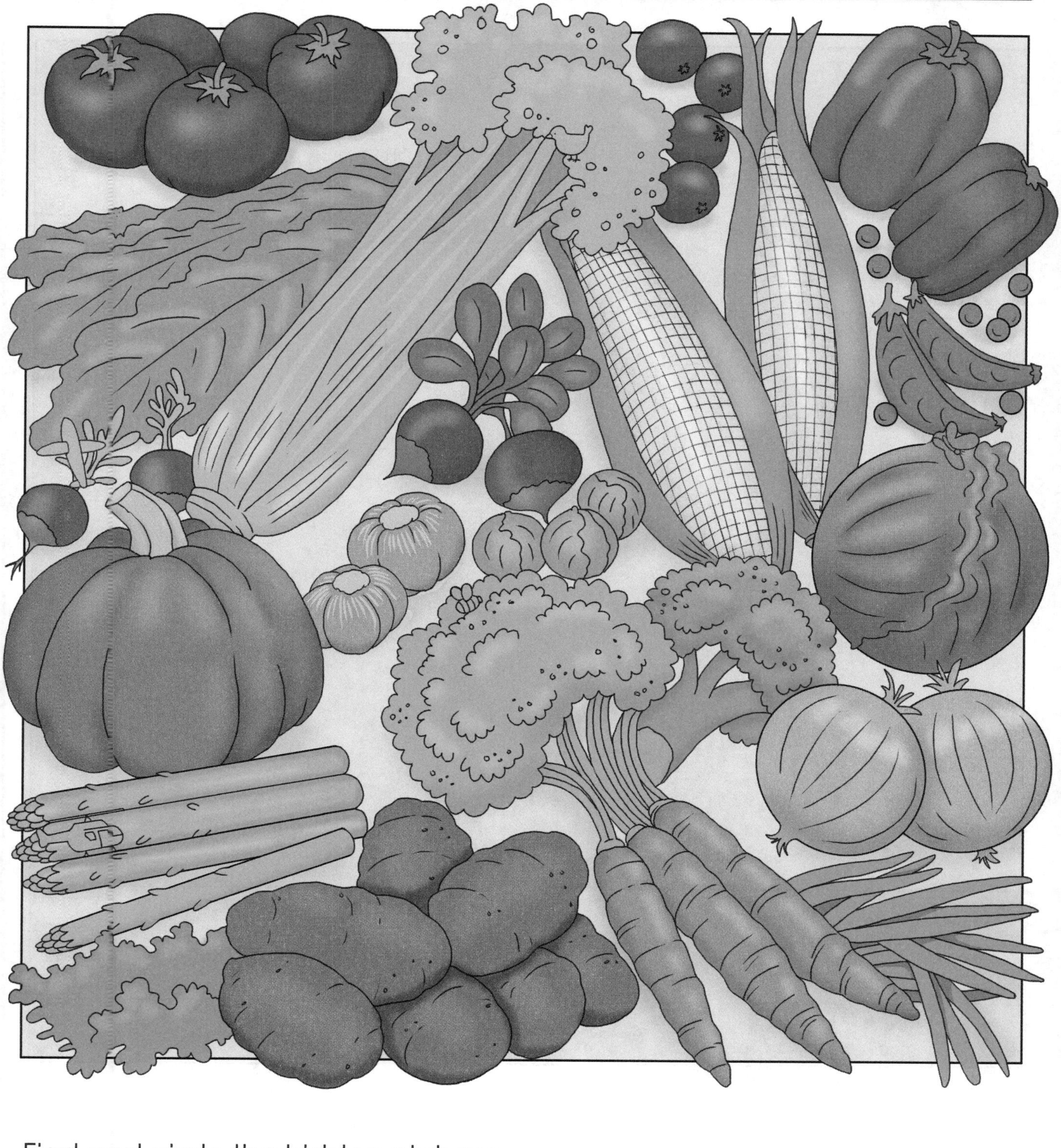

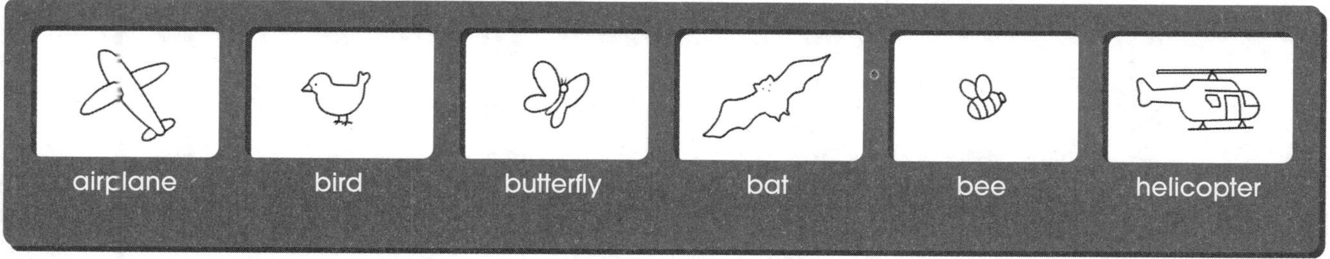

ANIMAL FARM

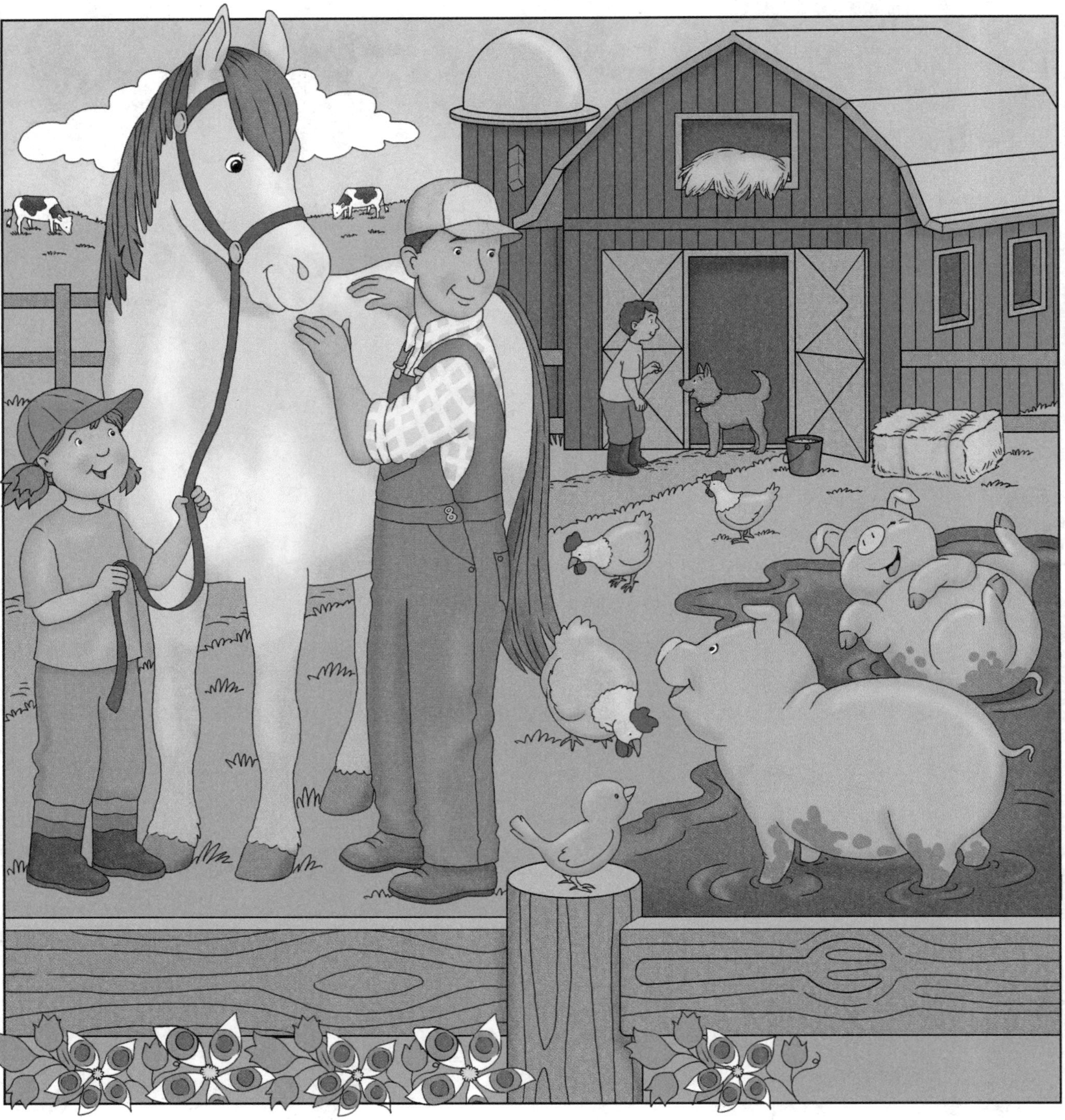

Find and circle the hidden pictures.

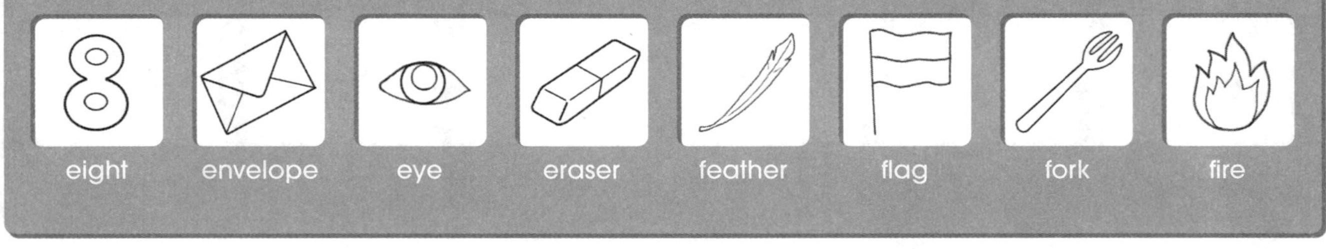

SUMMER FUN

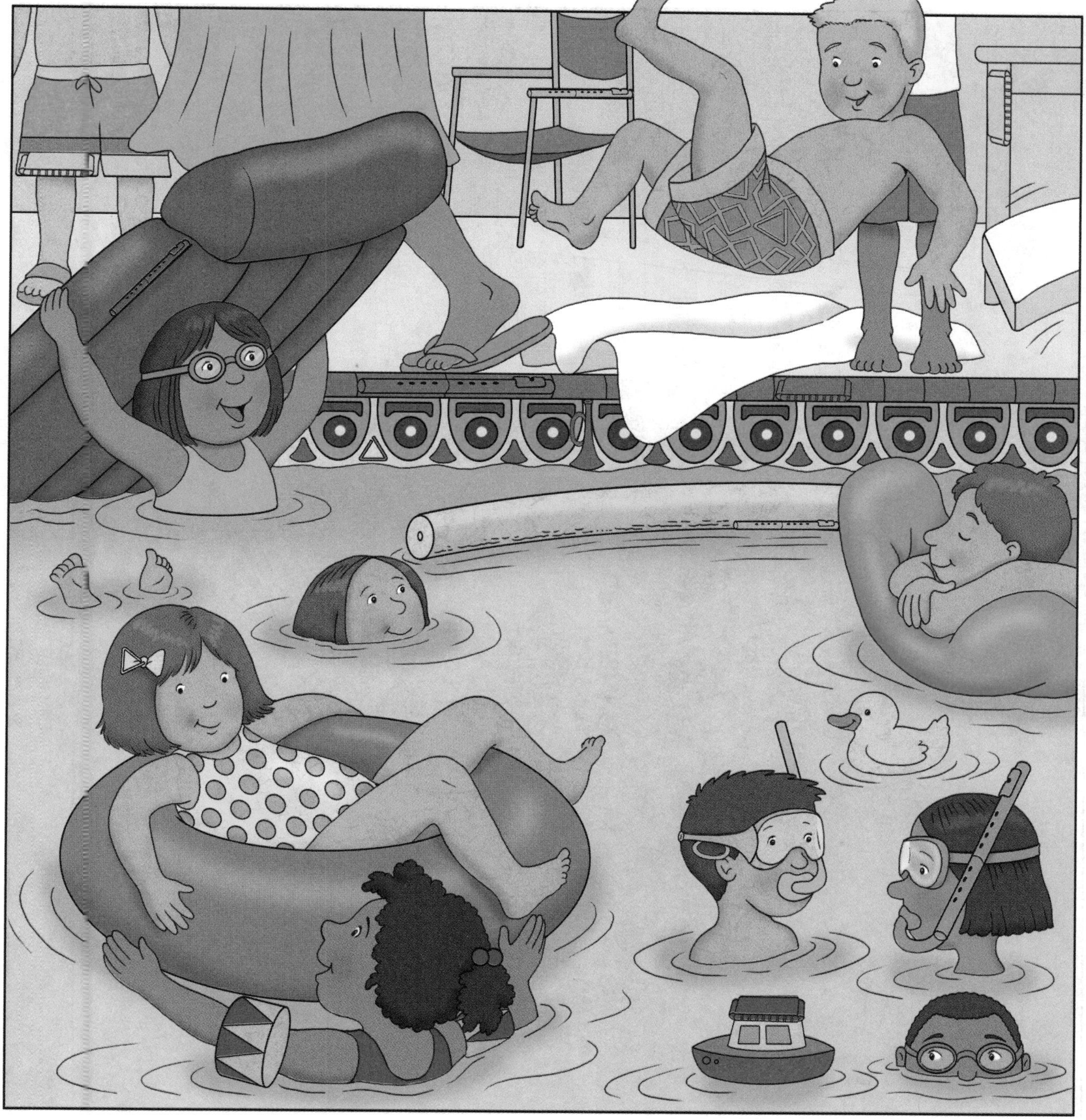

Find and circle the hidden pictures.

Find 1 drum

Find 2 horns

Find 3 triangles

Find 4 harmonicas

Find 5 flutes

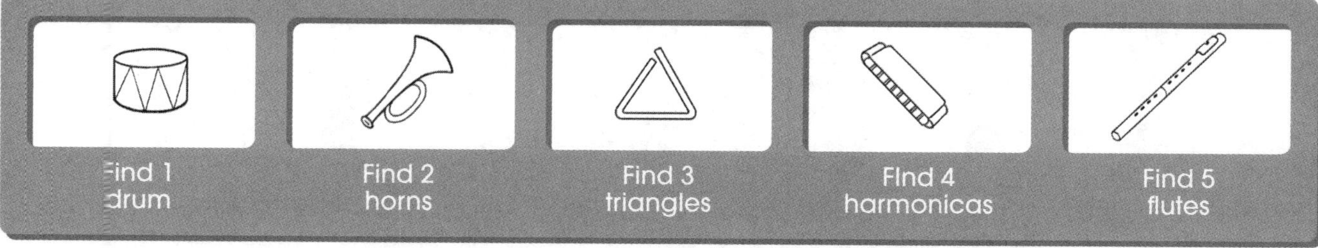

RAKING LEAVES

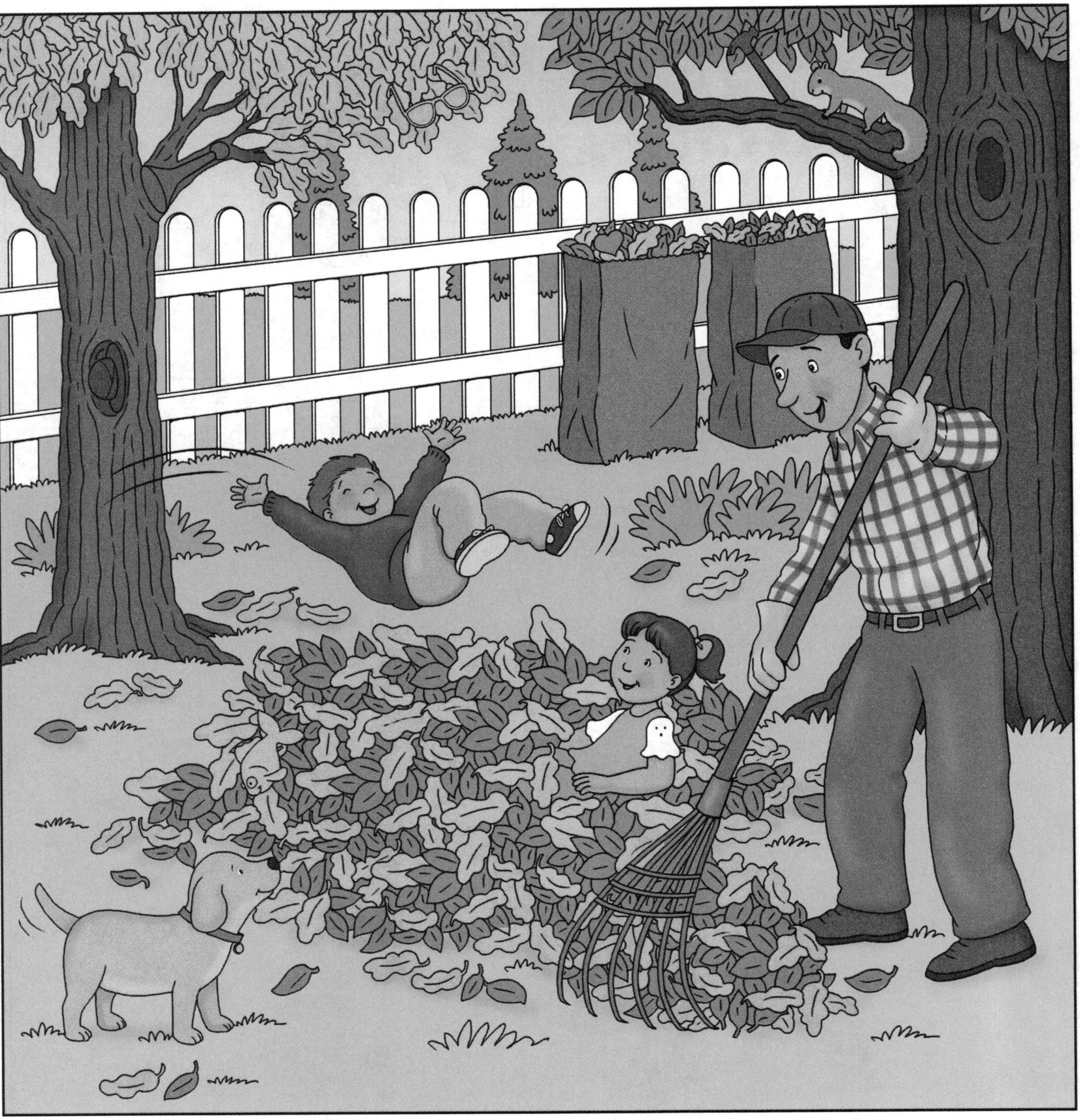

Find and circle the hidden pictures.

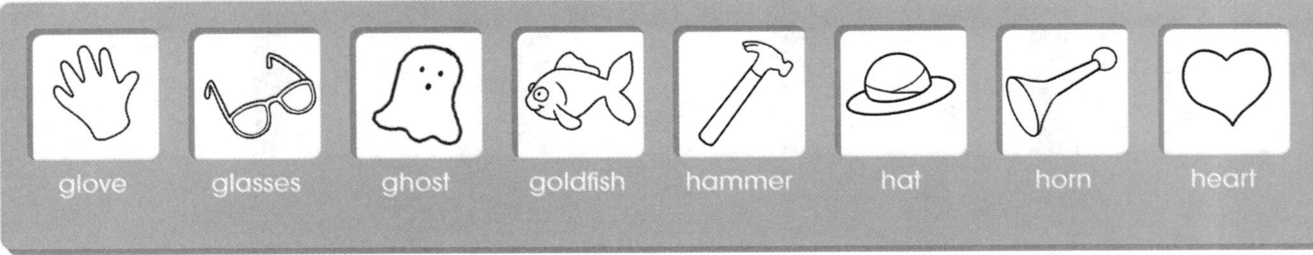

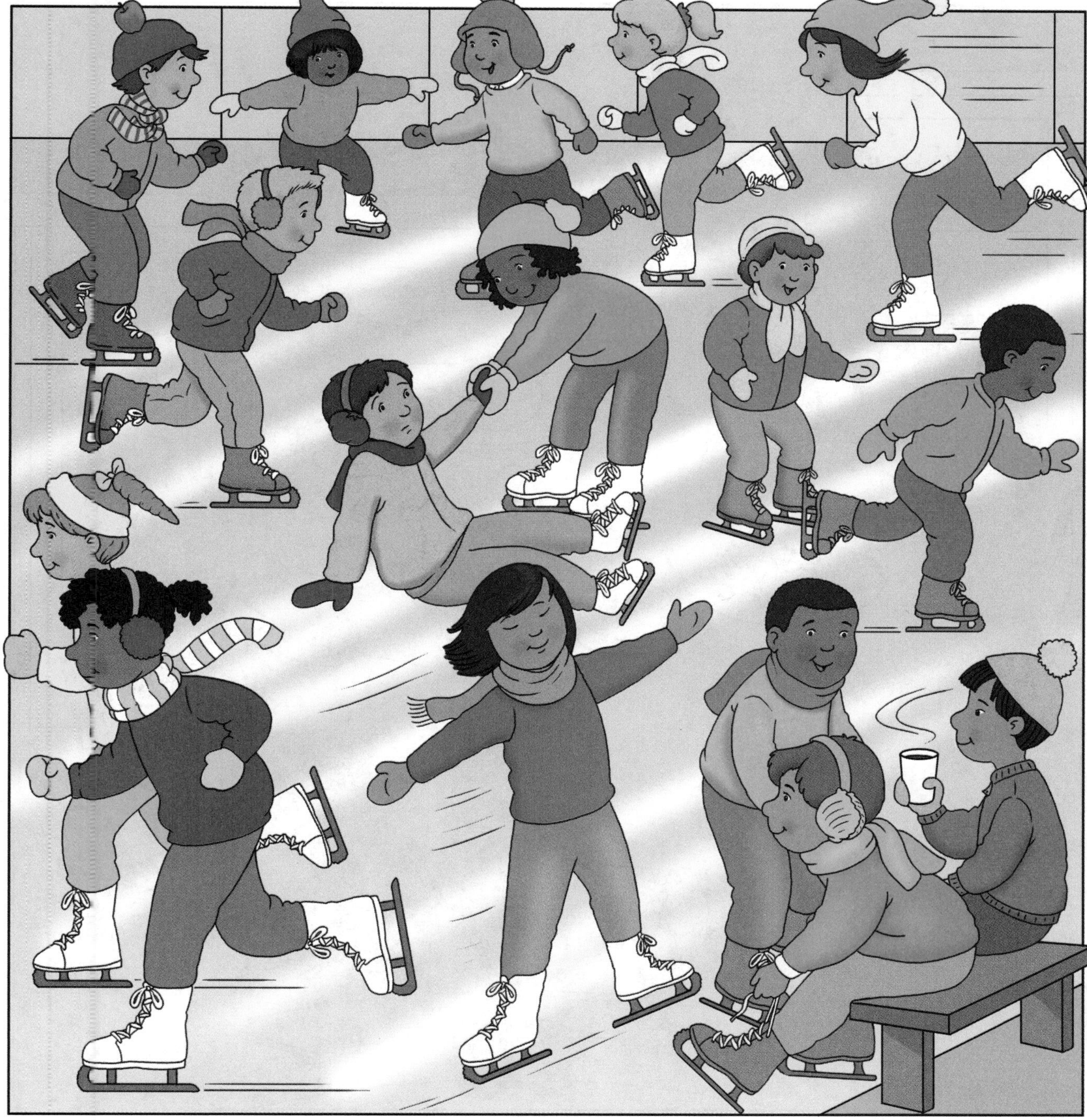

WINTER FUN

Find and circle the hidden pictures.

TEA PARTY

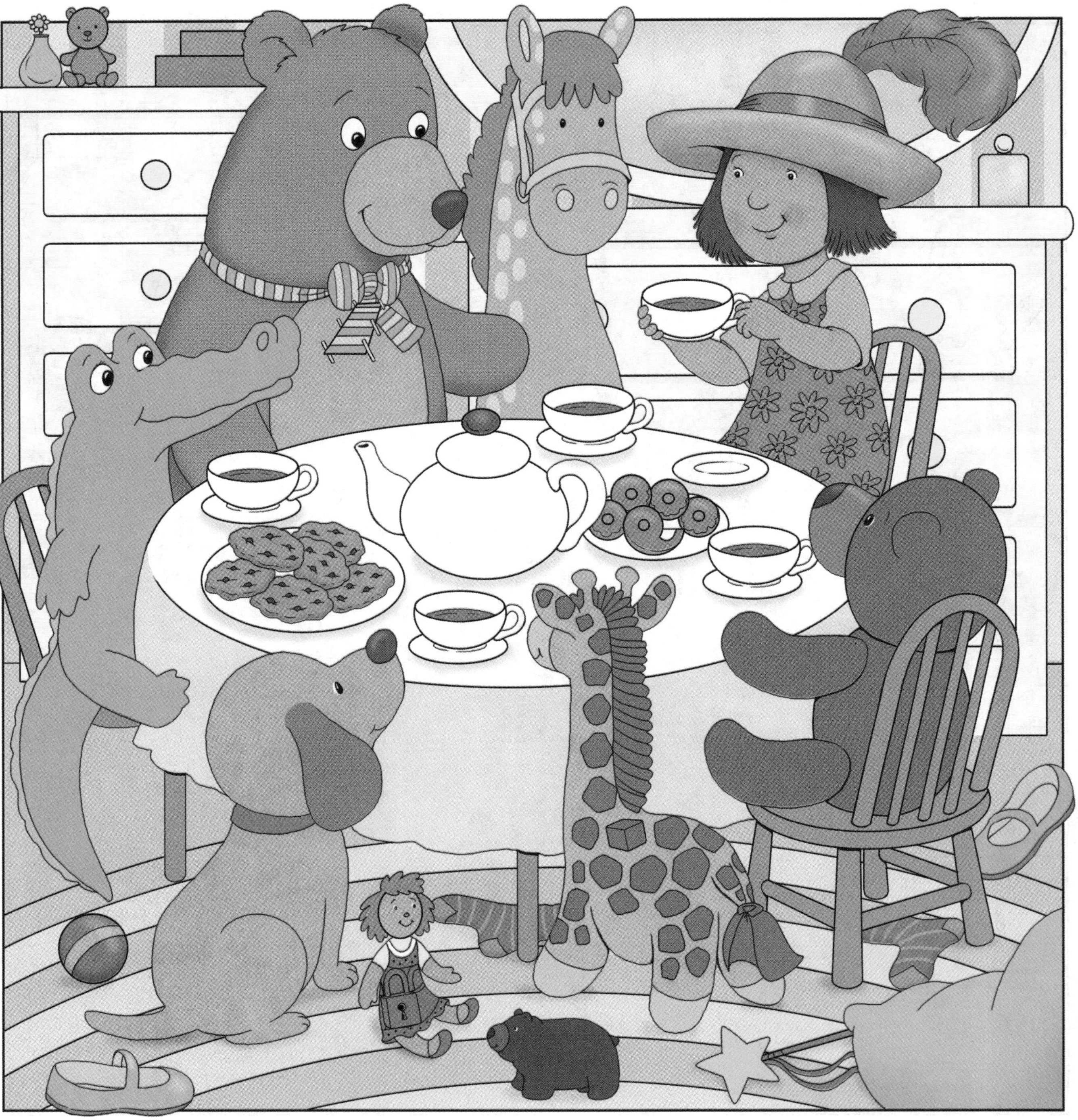

Find and circle the hidden pictures.

grape

tape

cape

lock

dock

block

 ©School Zone Publishing Company

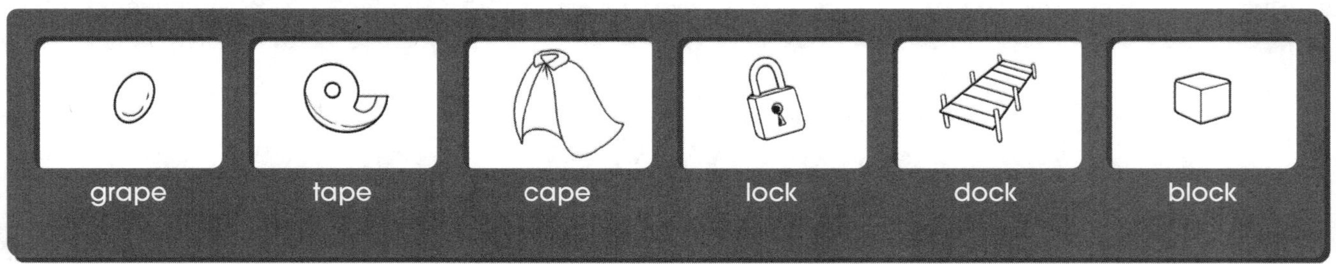

TRY IT BEFORE YOU BUY IT!

Find and circle the hidden pictures.

WHAT'S FOR SALE?

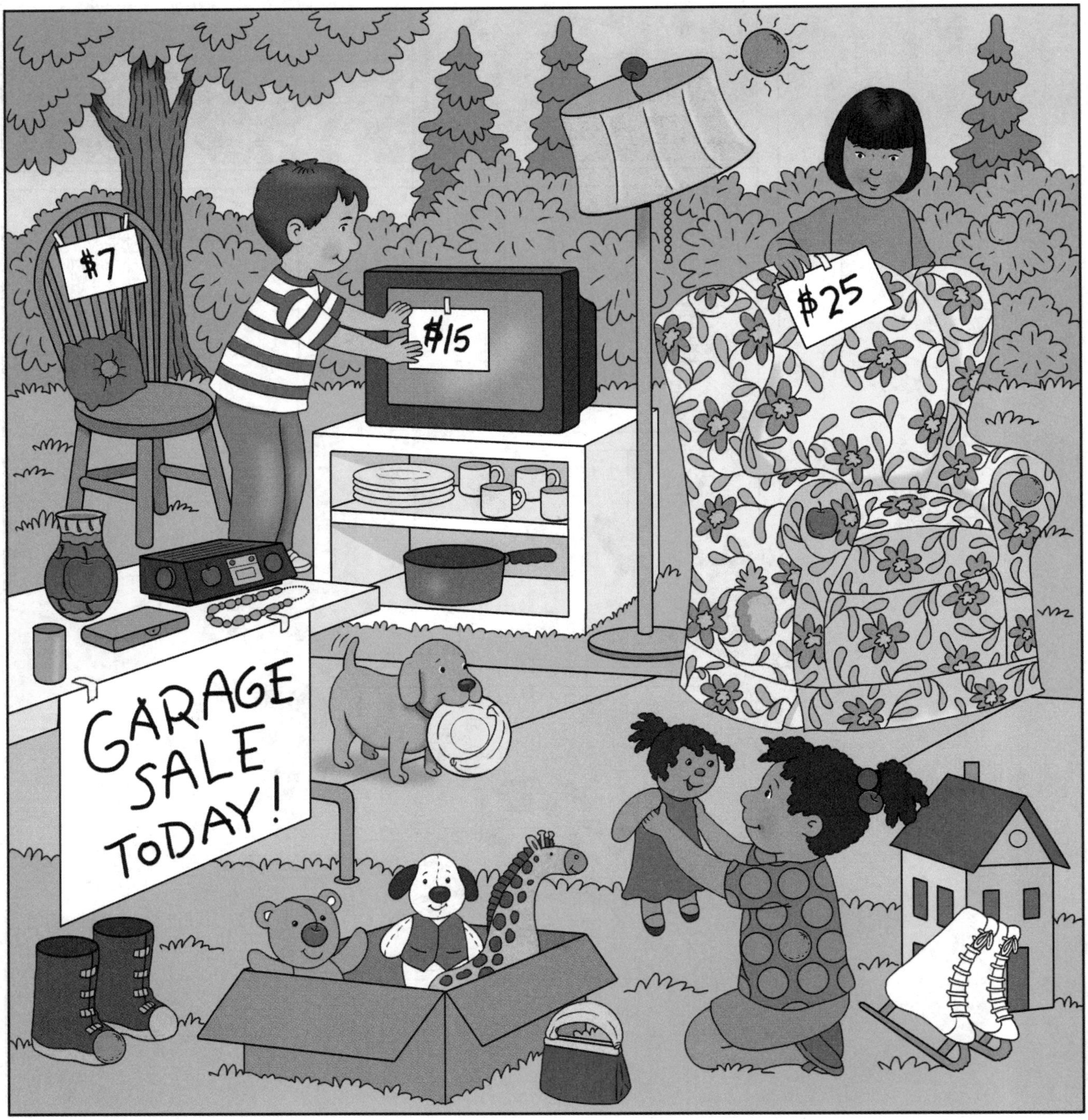

Find and circle the hidden pictures.

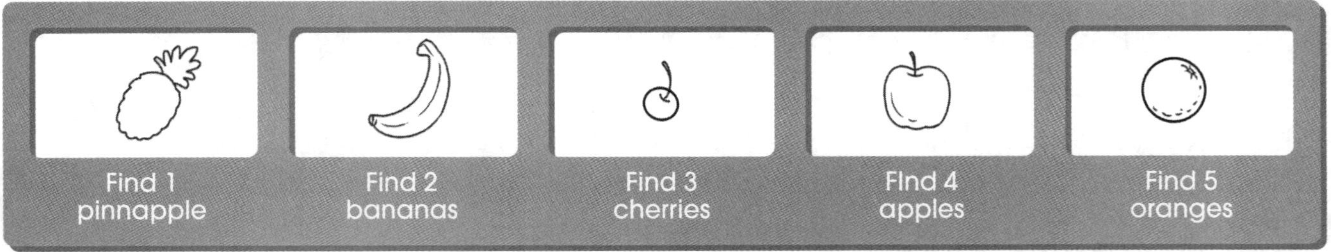

APPLES AND PEARS AND GRAPES, OH MY!

Find and circle the hidden pictures.

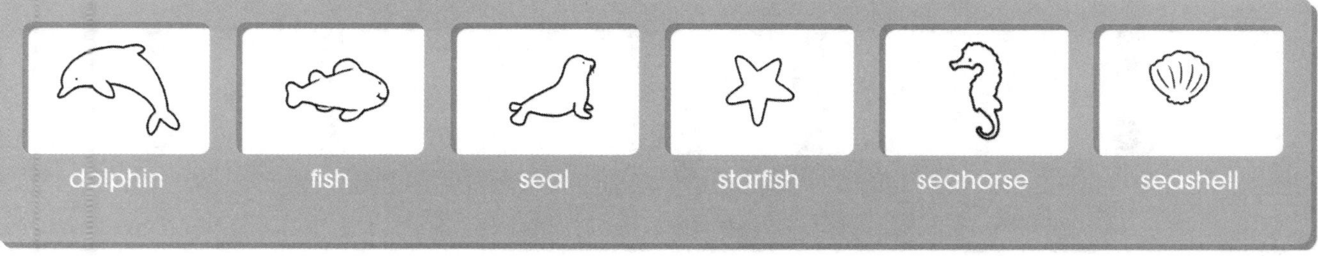

EXPLORING THE JUNGLE

Find and circle the hidden pictures.

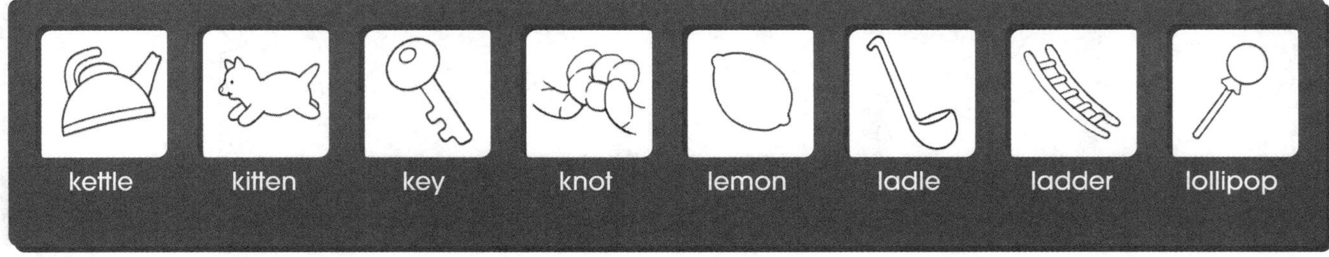

©School Zone Publishing Company

WHAT TO WEAR?

Find and circle the hidden pictures.

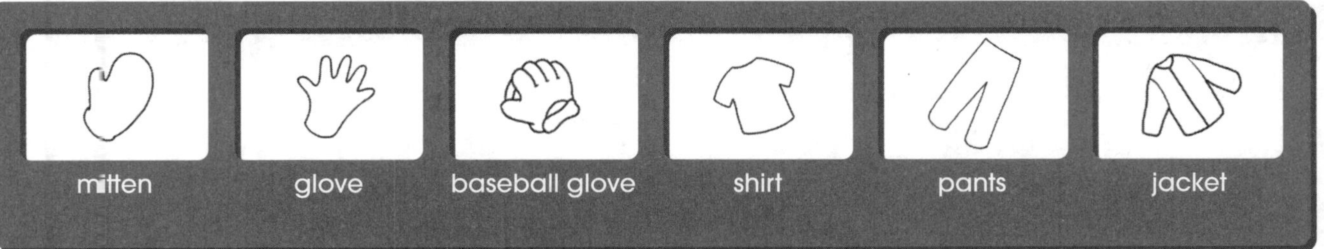

CANOE TRIP

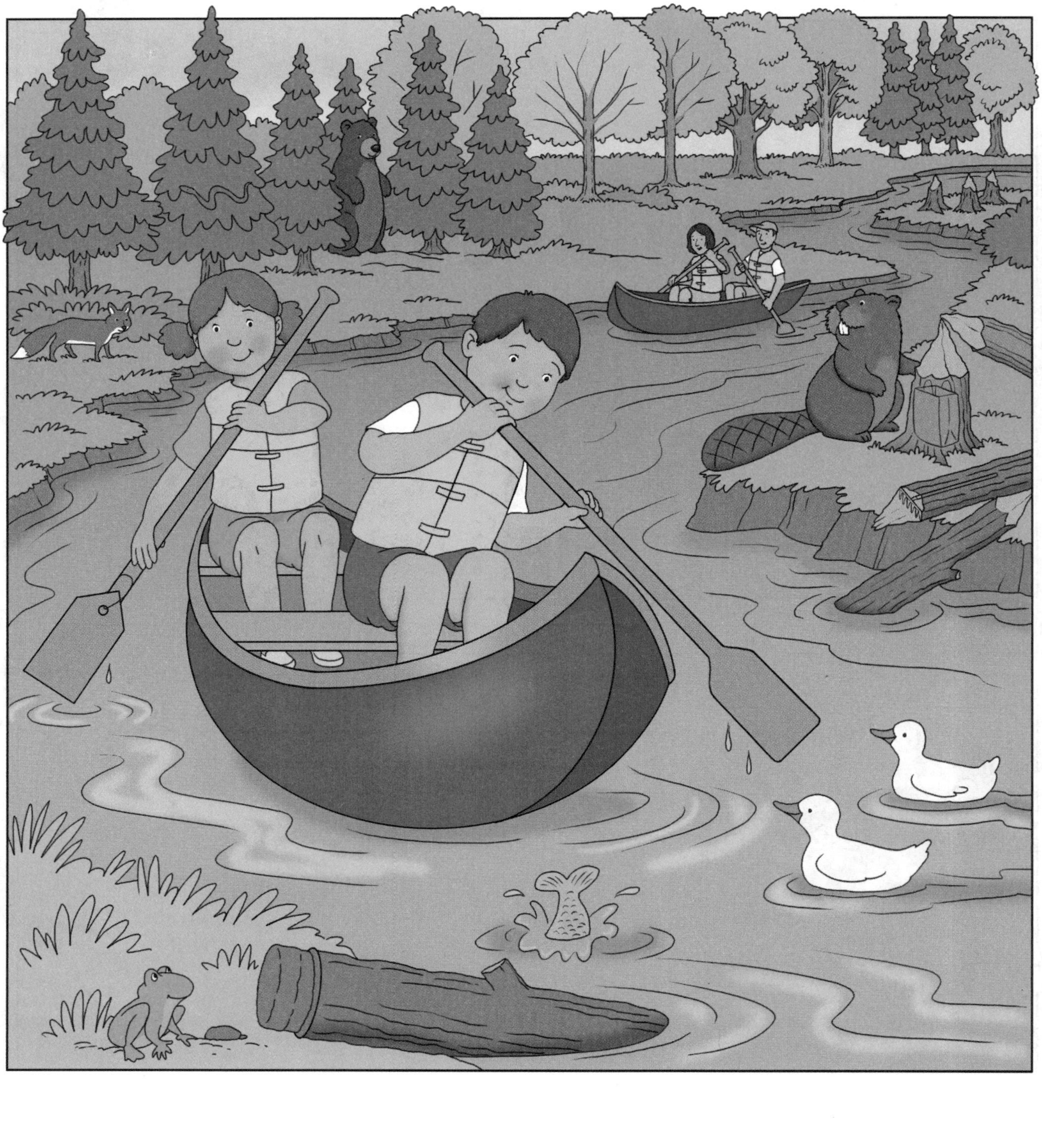

Find and circle the hidden pictures.

flag

tag

bag

cake

rake

snake

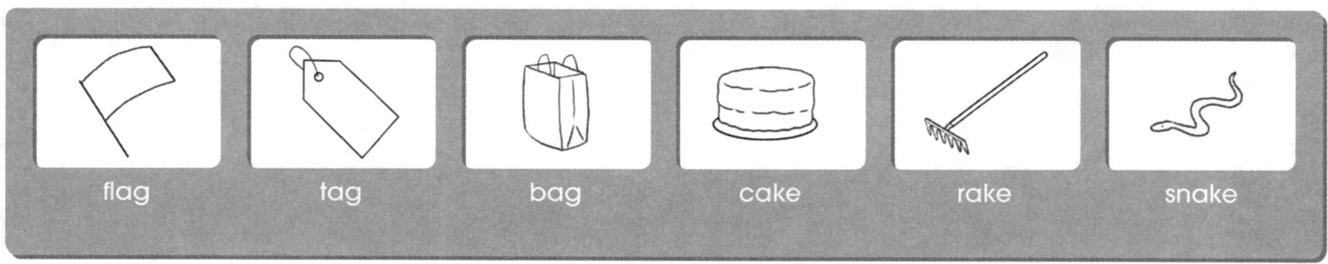

 ©School Zone Publishing Company

A RAINY DAY

Find and circle the hidden pictures.

magnet

magnifying glass

microphone

moon

nail

notebook

nozzle

nut

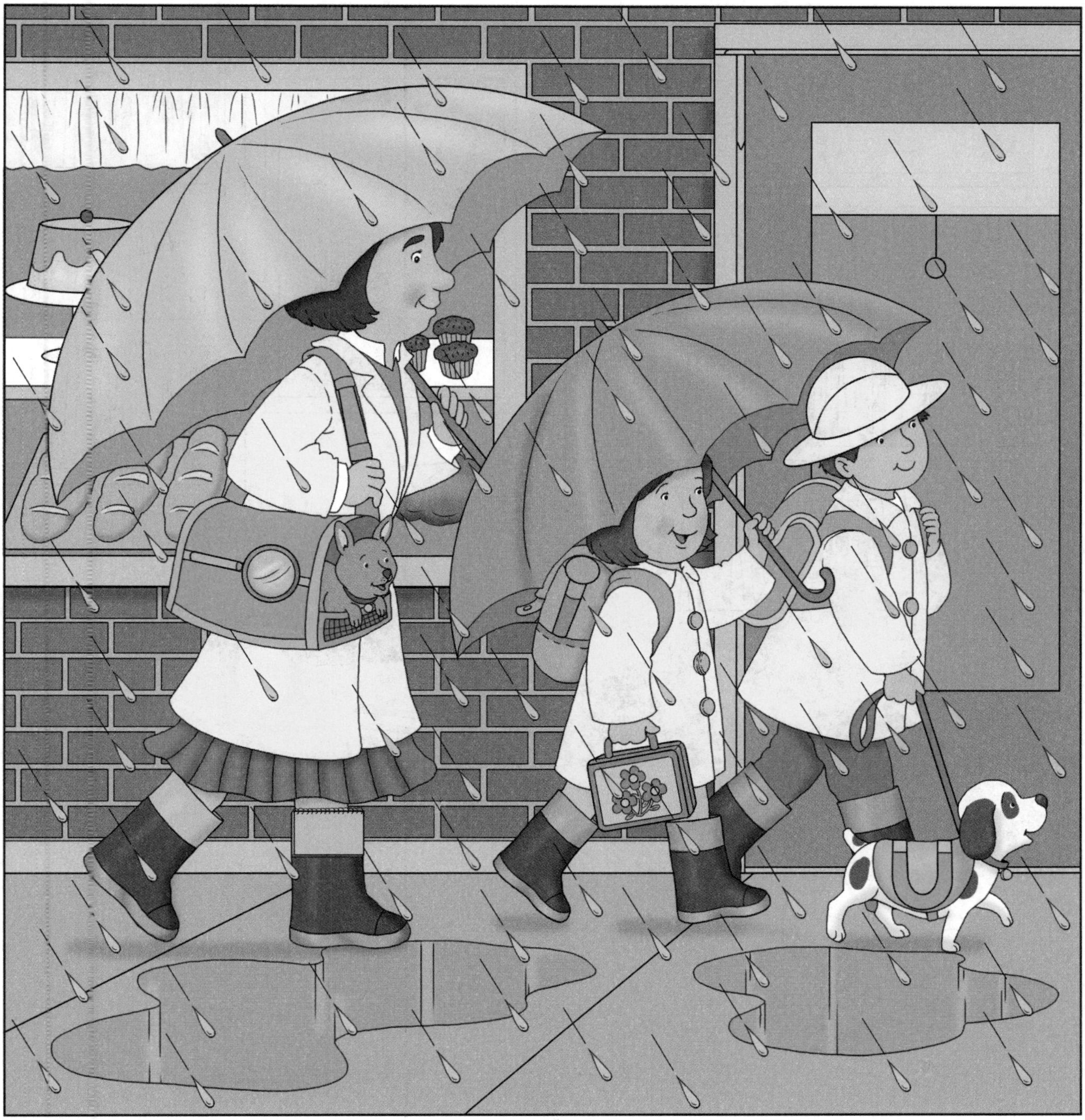

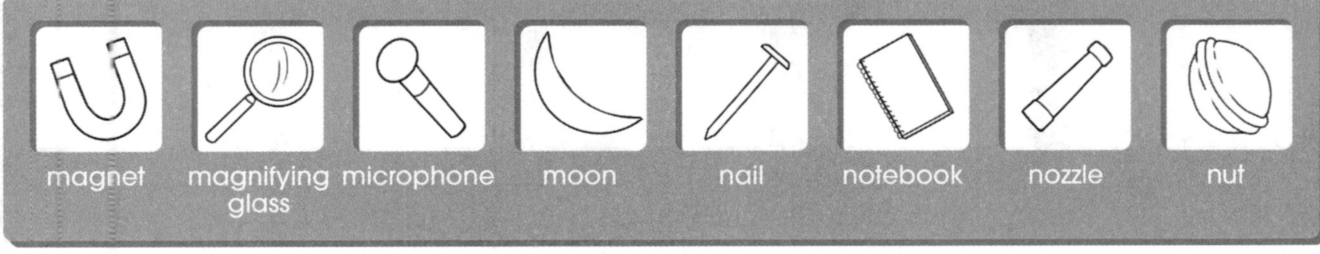

THE READING ROOM

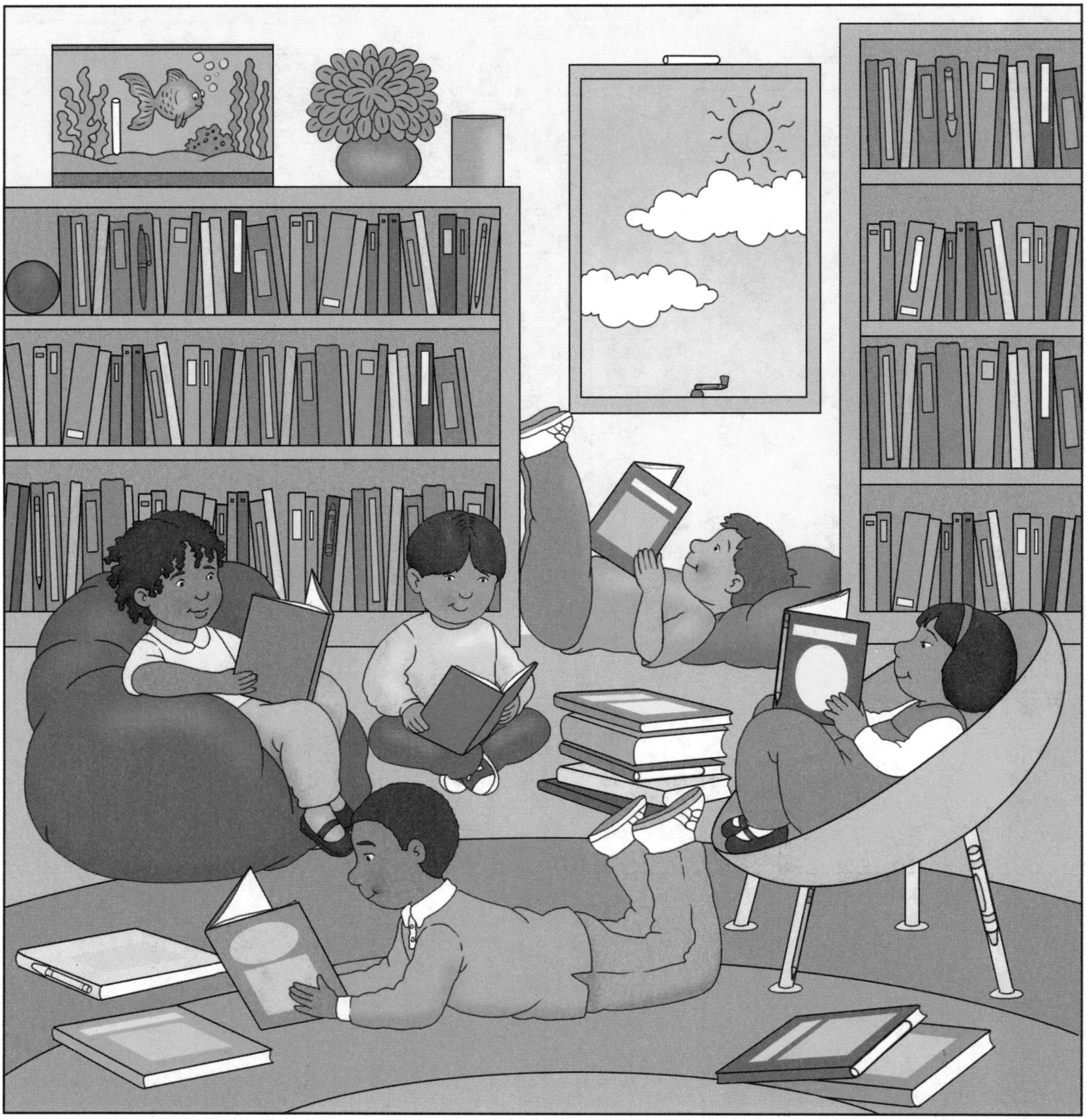

Find and circle the hidden pictures.

Find 1
pen

Find 2
markers

Find 3
crayons

Find 4
pencils

Find 5
pieces of chalk

©School Zone Publishing Company

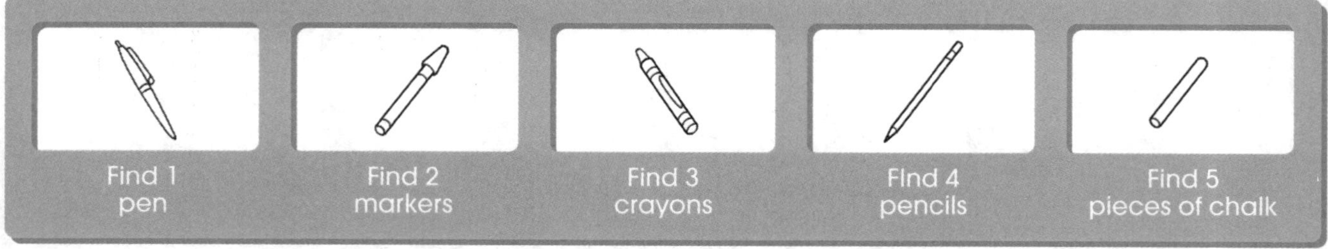

THE SCHOOL PLAY

Find and circle the hidden pictures.

DOES IT GO ON YOUR HEAD OR YOUR FEET?

Find and circle the hidden pictures.

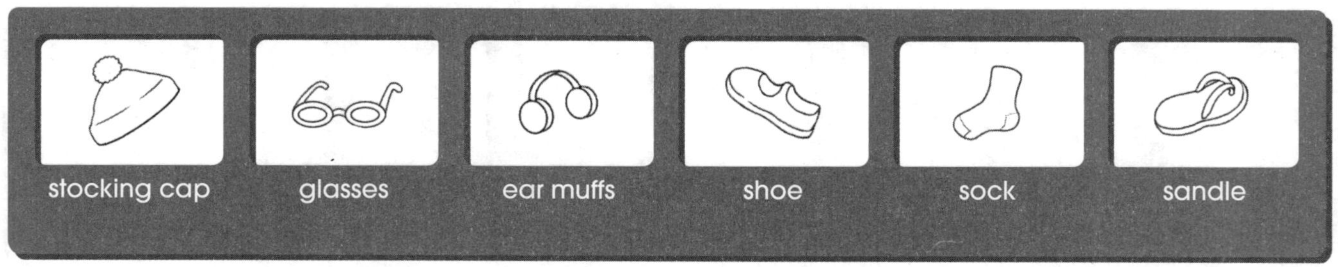

 ©School Zone Publishing Company

TENDING TO THE TOMATOES

Find and circle the hidden pictures.

log frog hog bat rat hat

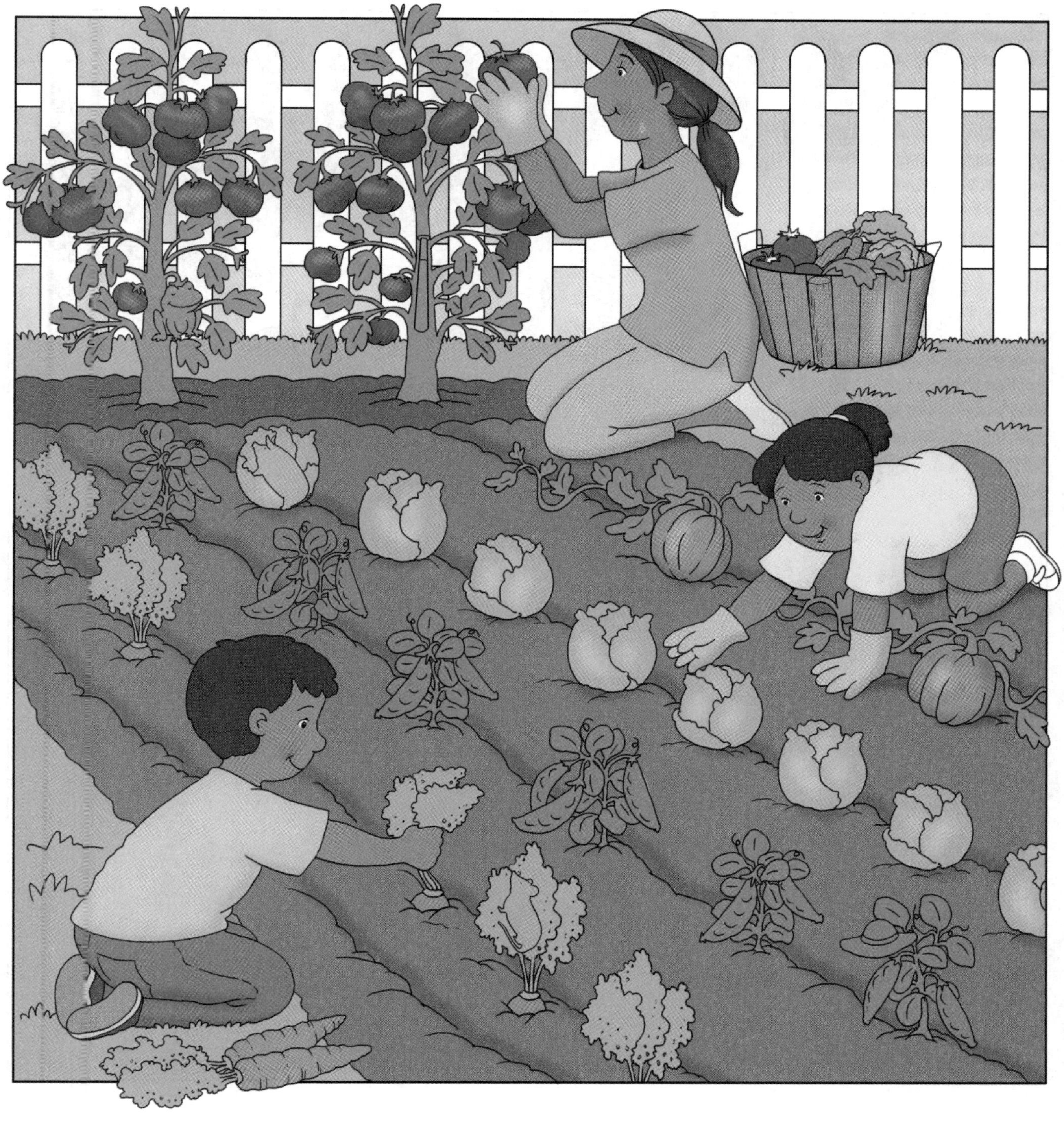

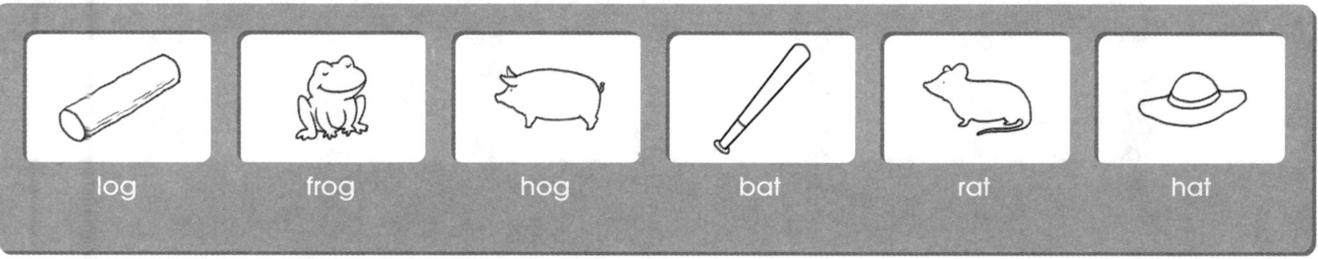

RACE TO THE BOTTOM

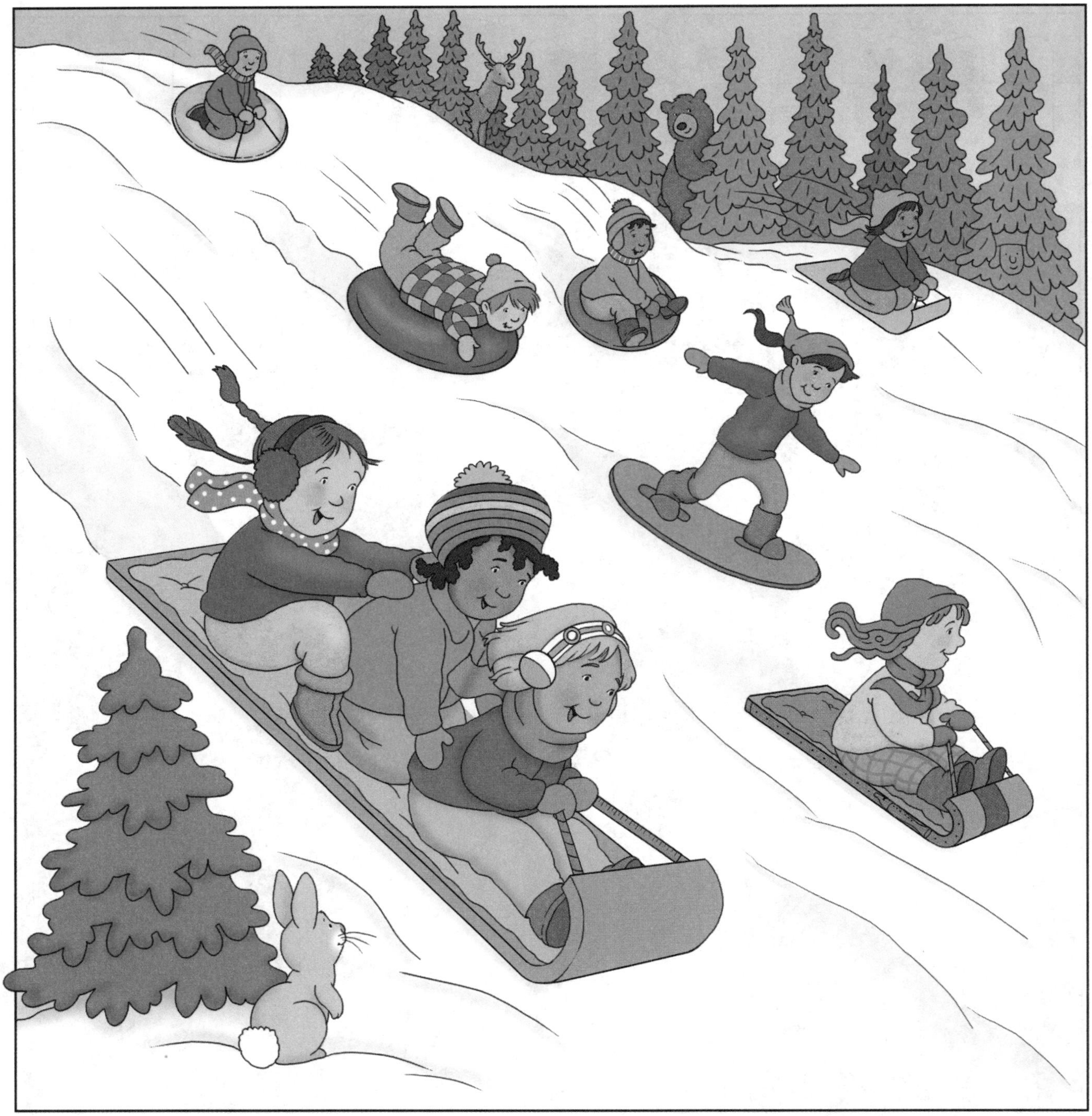

Find and circle the hidden pictures.

question mark

queen

quill

quilt

rattle

ruler

rainbow

recorder

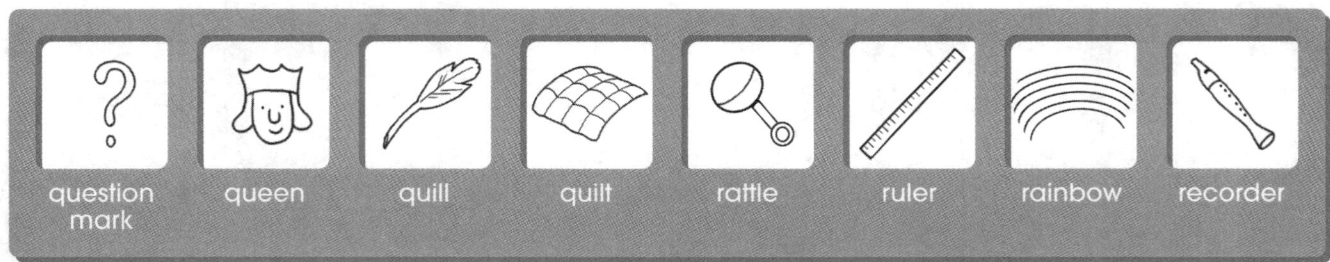

 ©School Zone Publishing Company

HIKING THROUGH THE DESERT

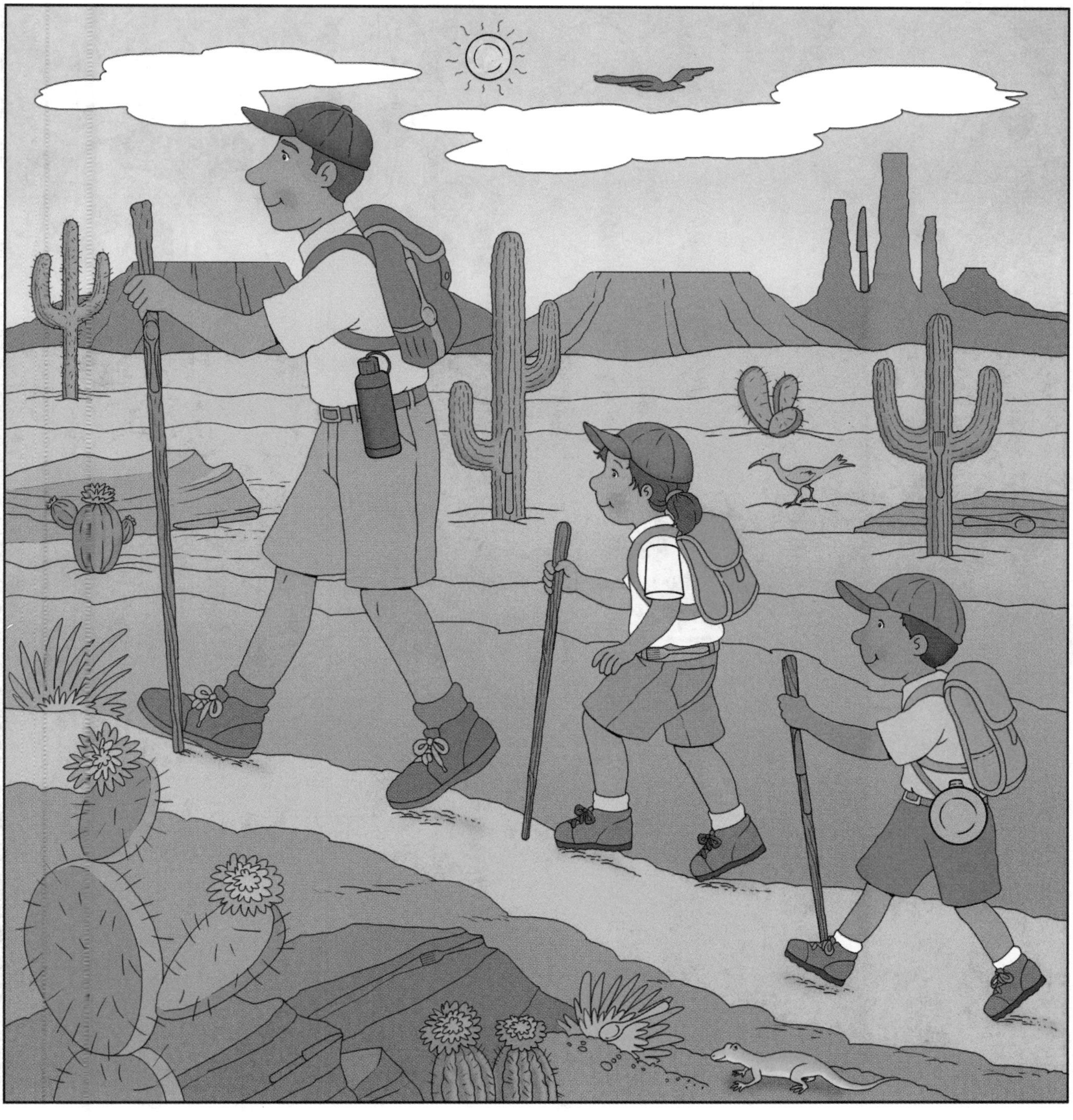

Find and circle the hidden pictures.

Find 1 cup

Find 2 plates

Find 3 forks

Find 4 spoons

Find 5 knives

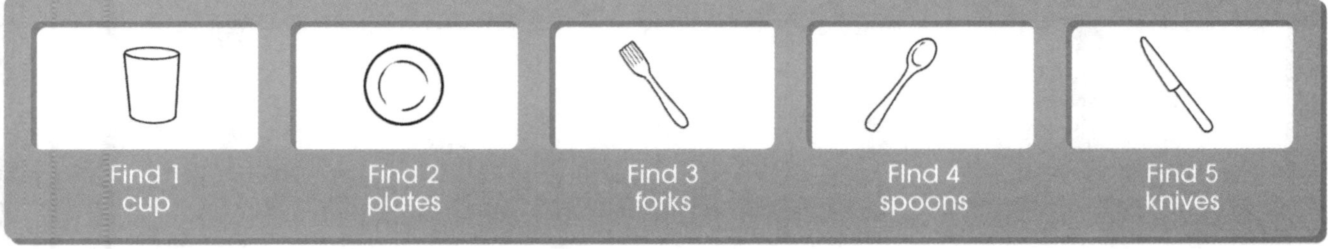

DOG PACK

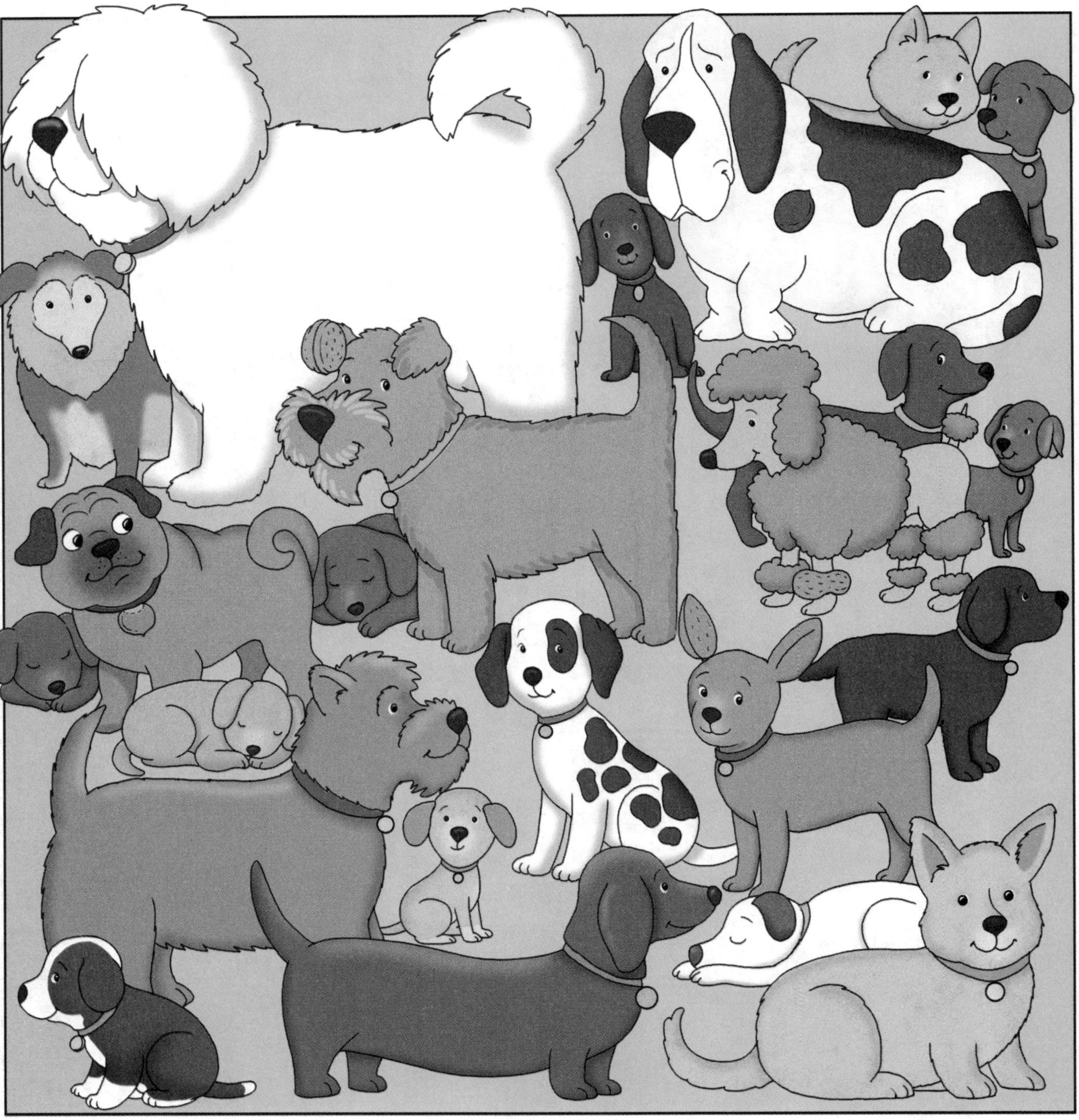

Find and circle the hidden pictures.

pistachio

hazelnut

chestnut

pecan

peanut

walnut

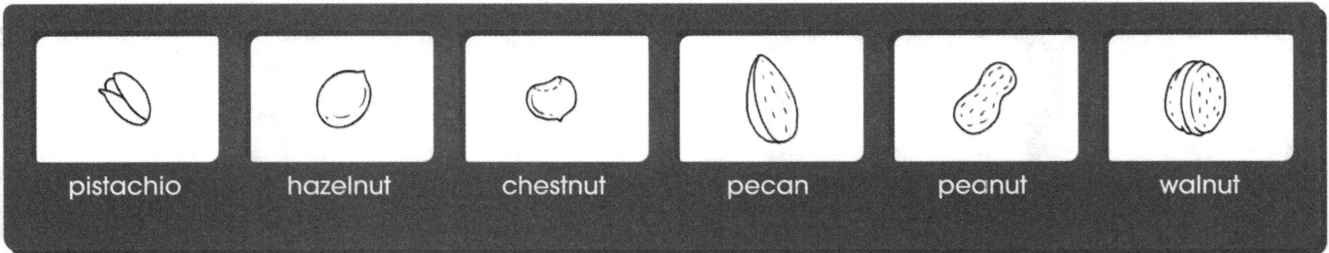

 ©School Zone Publishing Company

BIG FELLOWS

Find and circle the hidden pictures.

sandwich slipper seashell spoon tent toothbrush tomato torch

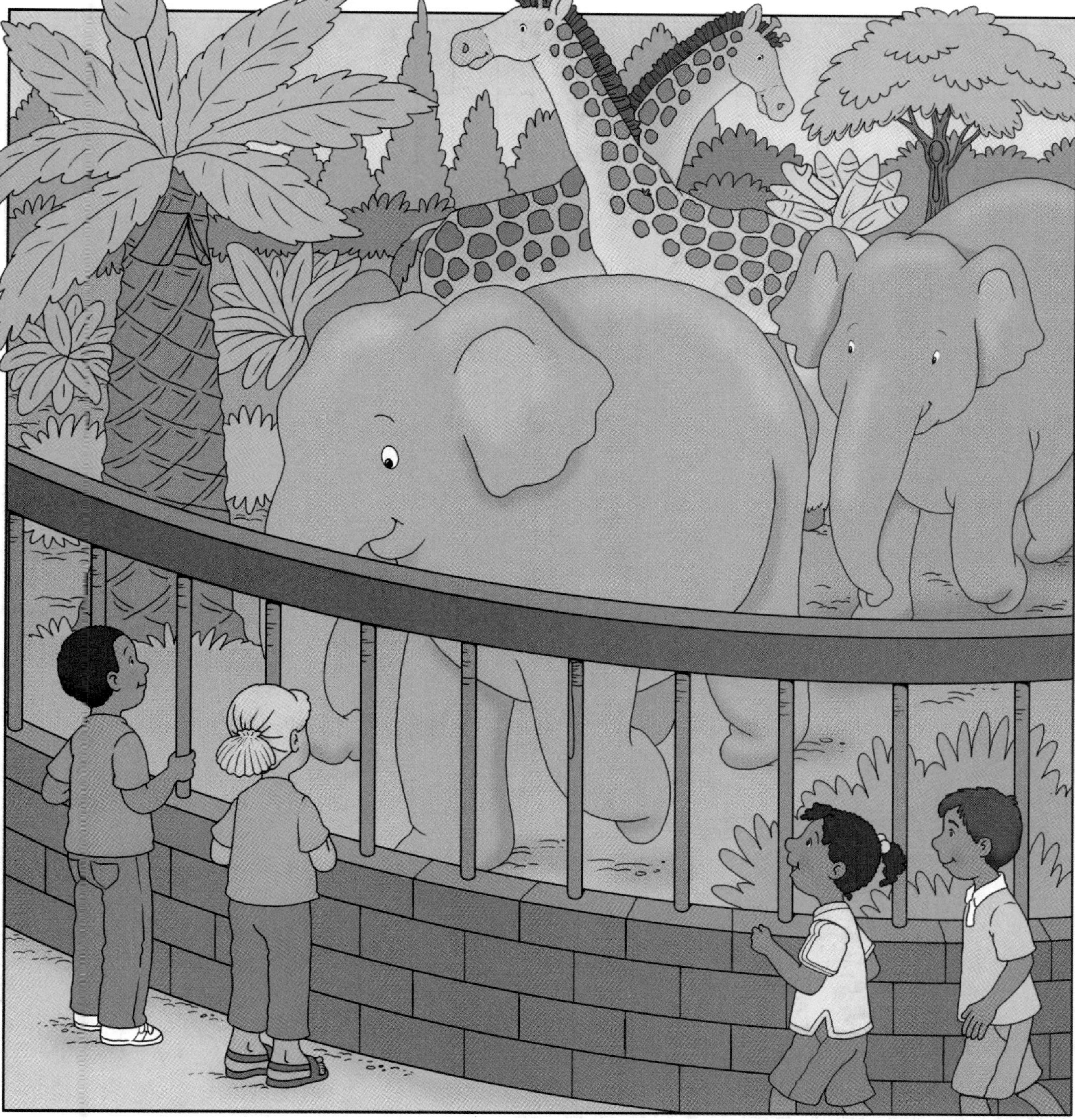

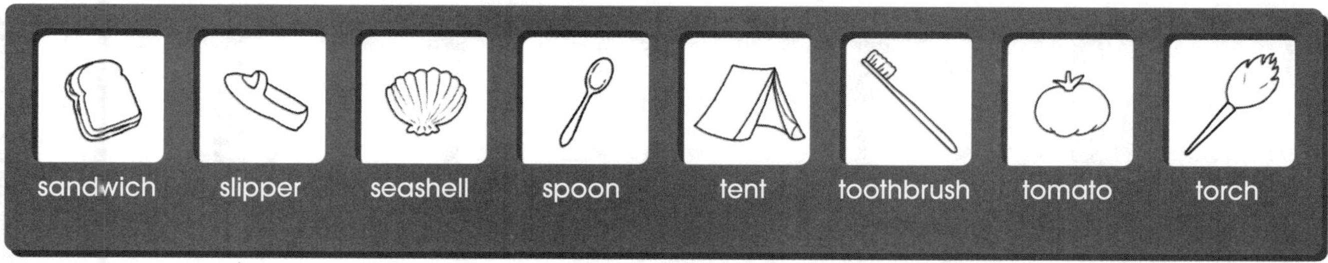

AN AFTERNOON PICNIC

Find and circle the hidden pictures.

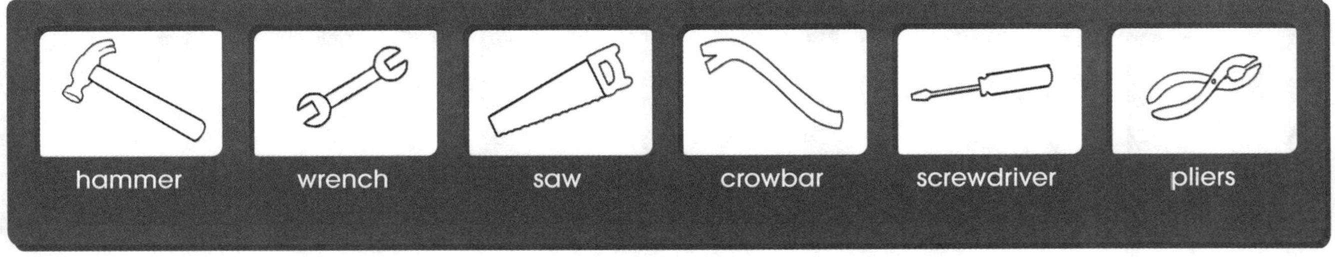

 ©School Zone Publishing Company

BUILDING A TREEHOUSE

Find and circle the hidden pictures.

bone

stone

throne

moon

spoon

balloon

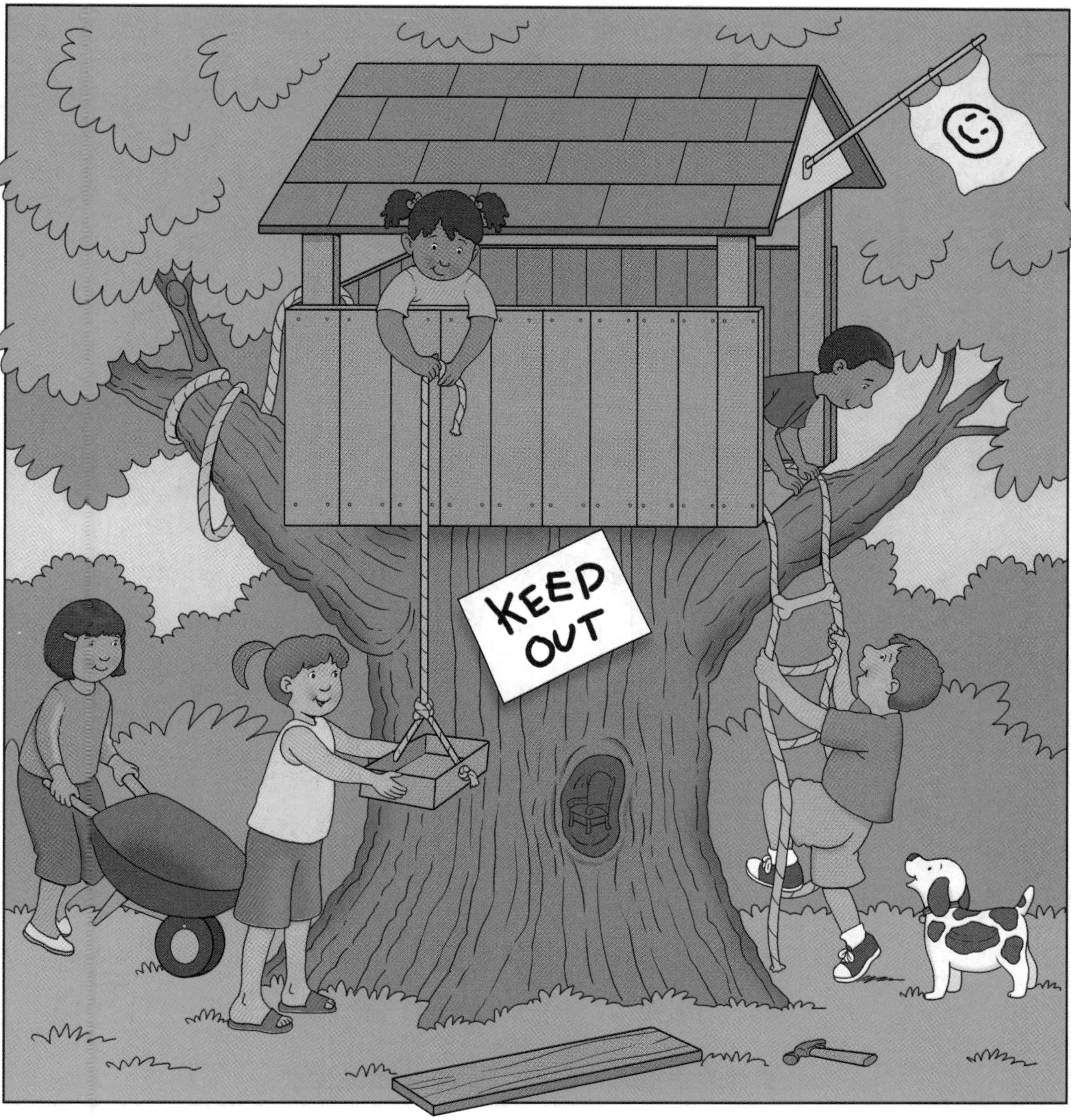

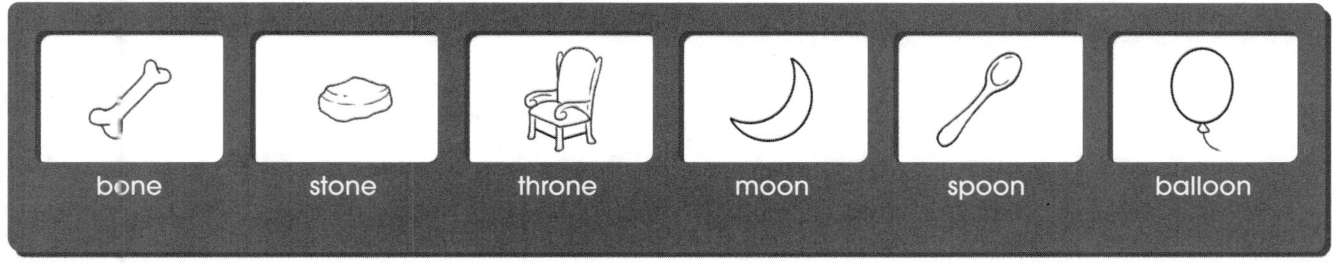

BLOW OUT THE CANDLES

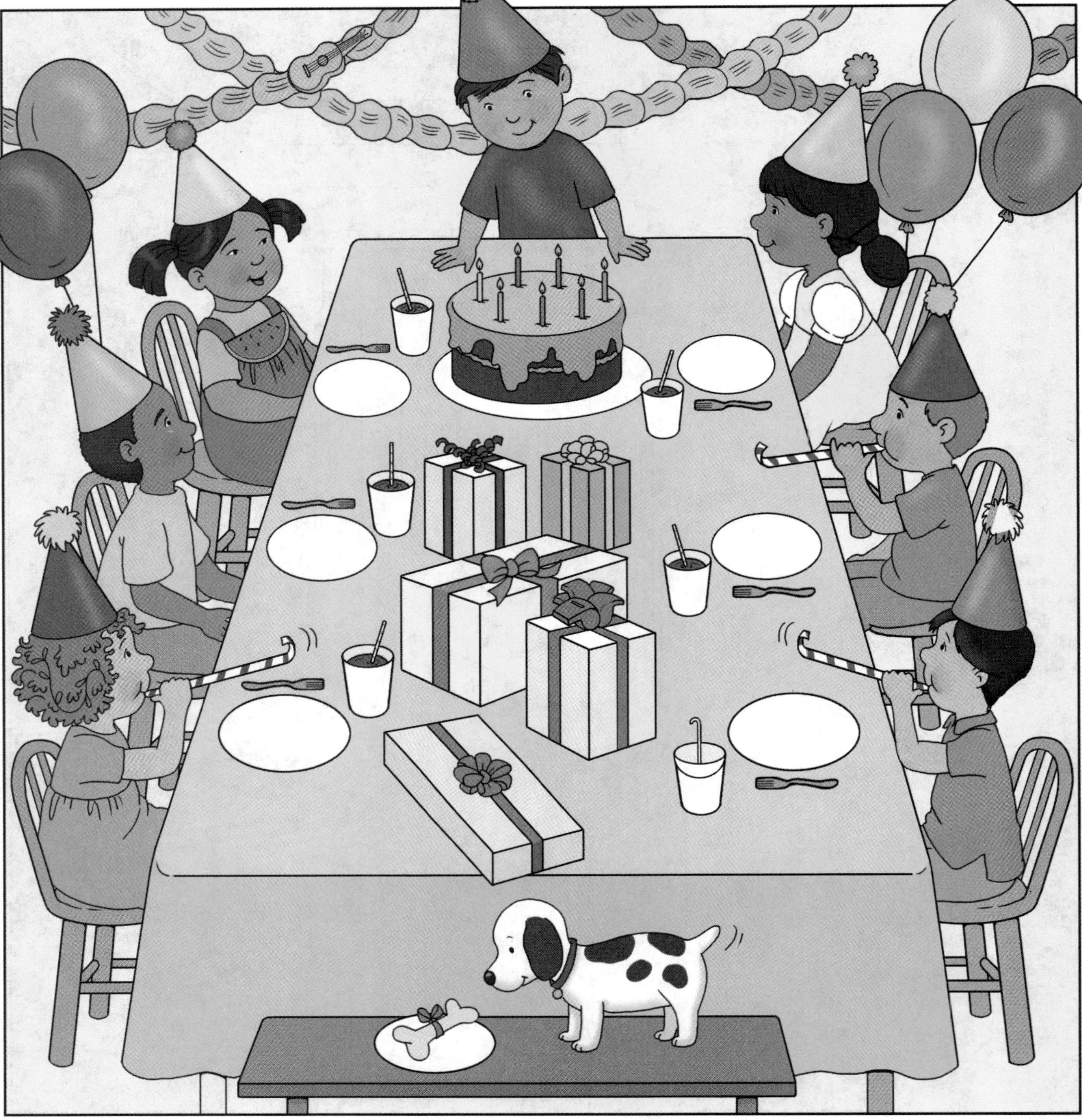

Find and circle the hidden pictures.

umbrella	ukulele	vase	vine	watermelon	whistle

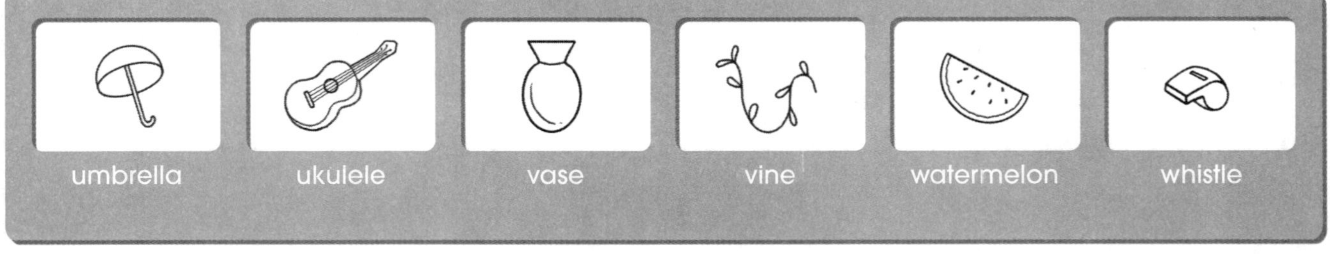

 ©School Zone Publishing Company

MAKING PIZZA

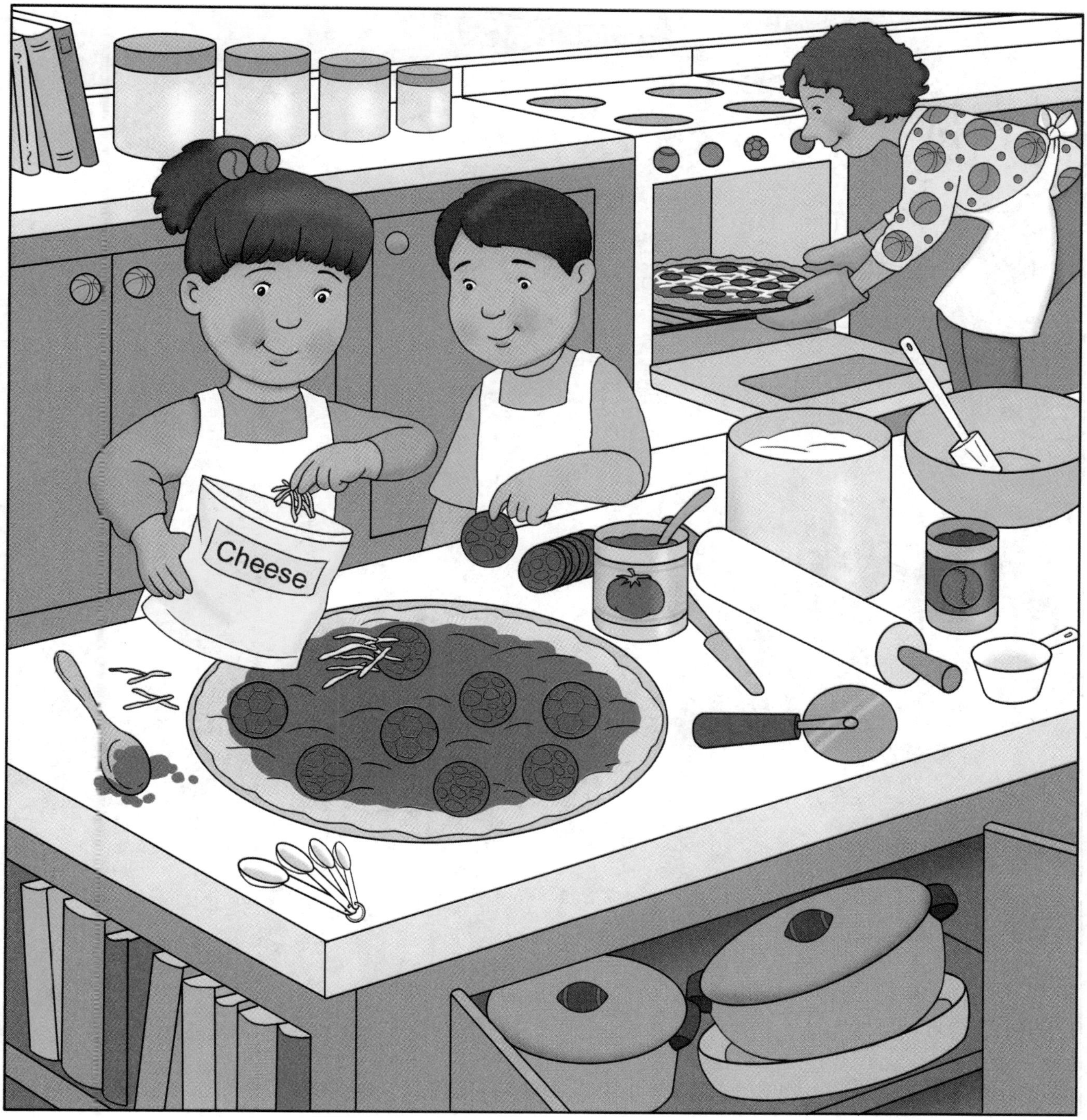

Cheese

Find and circle the hidden pictures.

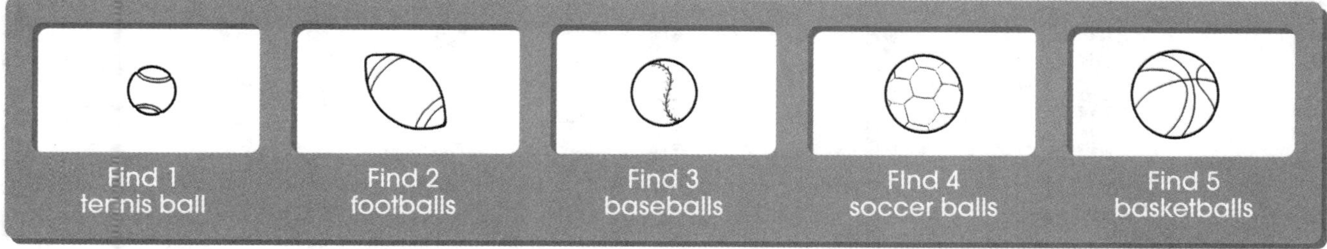

UNDER THE SEA

Find and circle the hidden pictures.

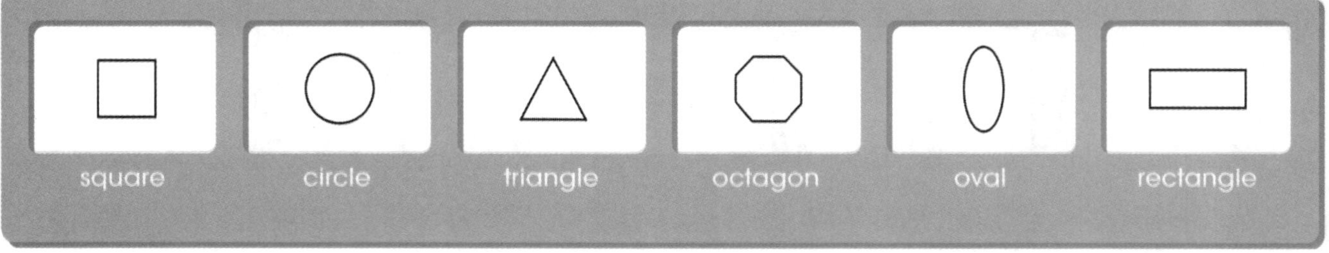

DOWN ON MAIN STREET

Find and circle the hidden pictures.

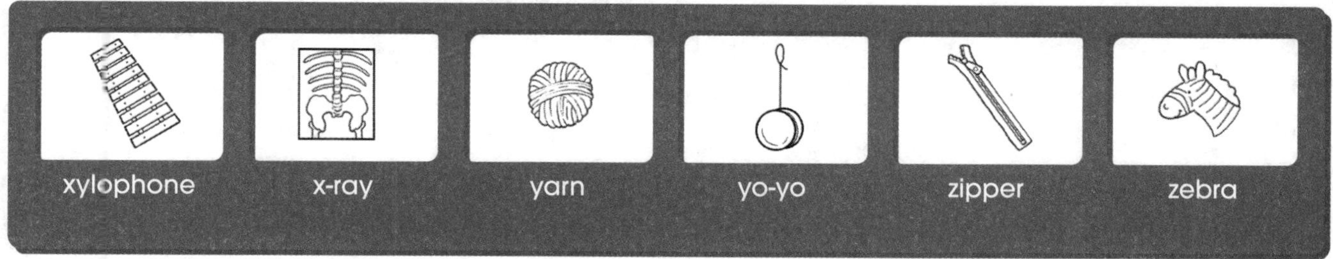

QUITE A COURTYARD

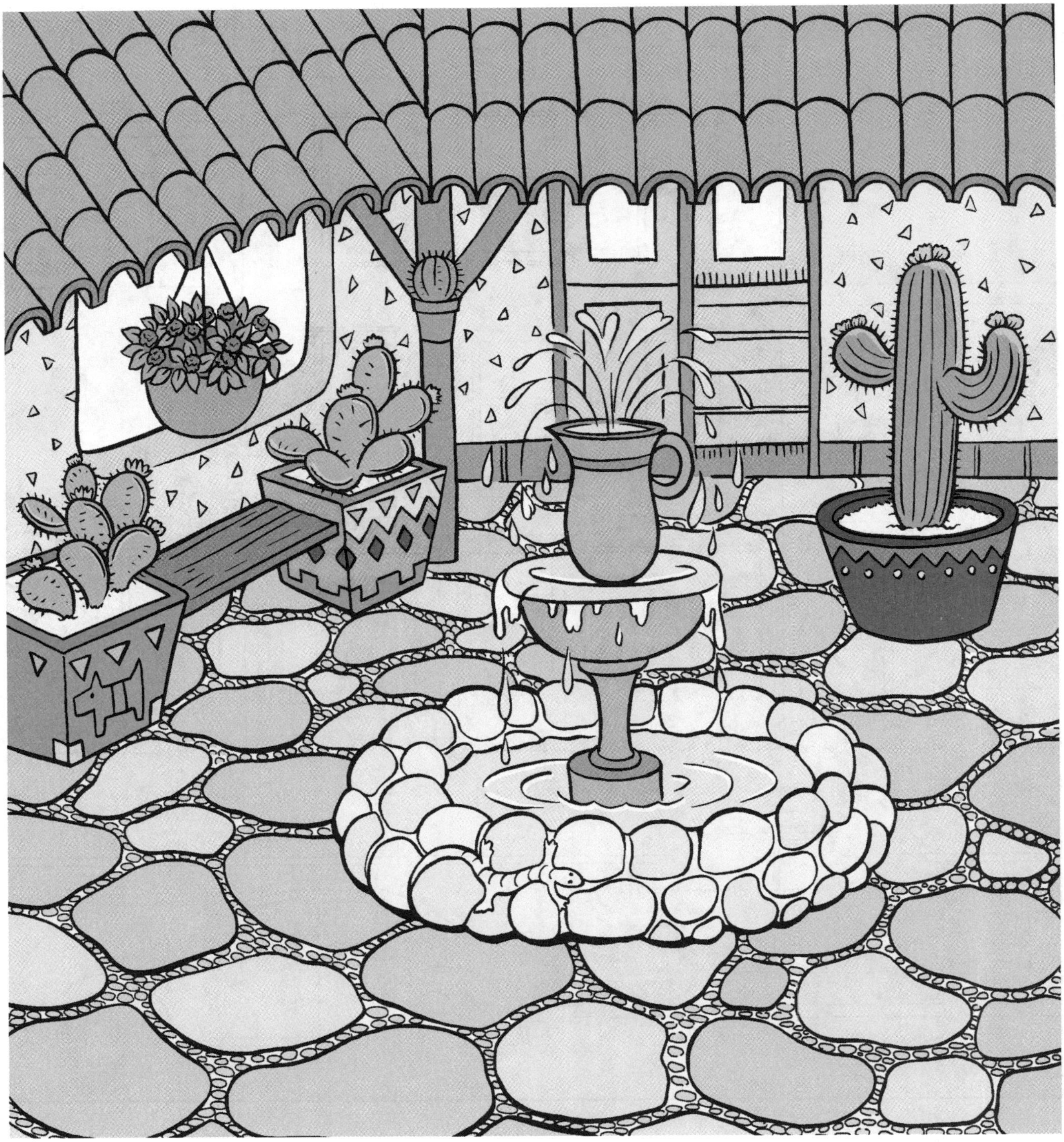

Find and circle the hidden pictures.

cactus

lizard

necklace

dog

rug

pitcher

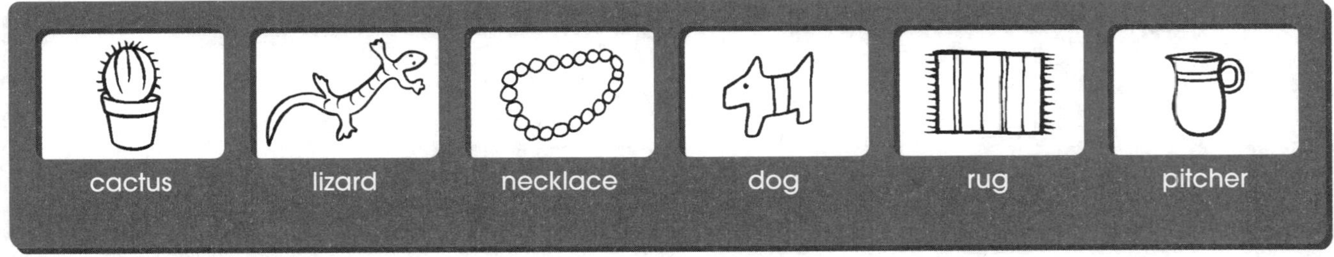

 ©School Zone Publishing Company

DINNER FOR TWO

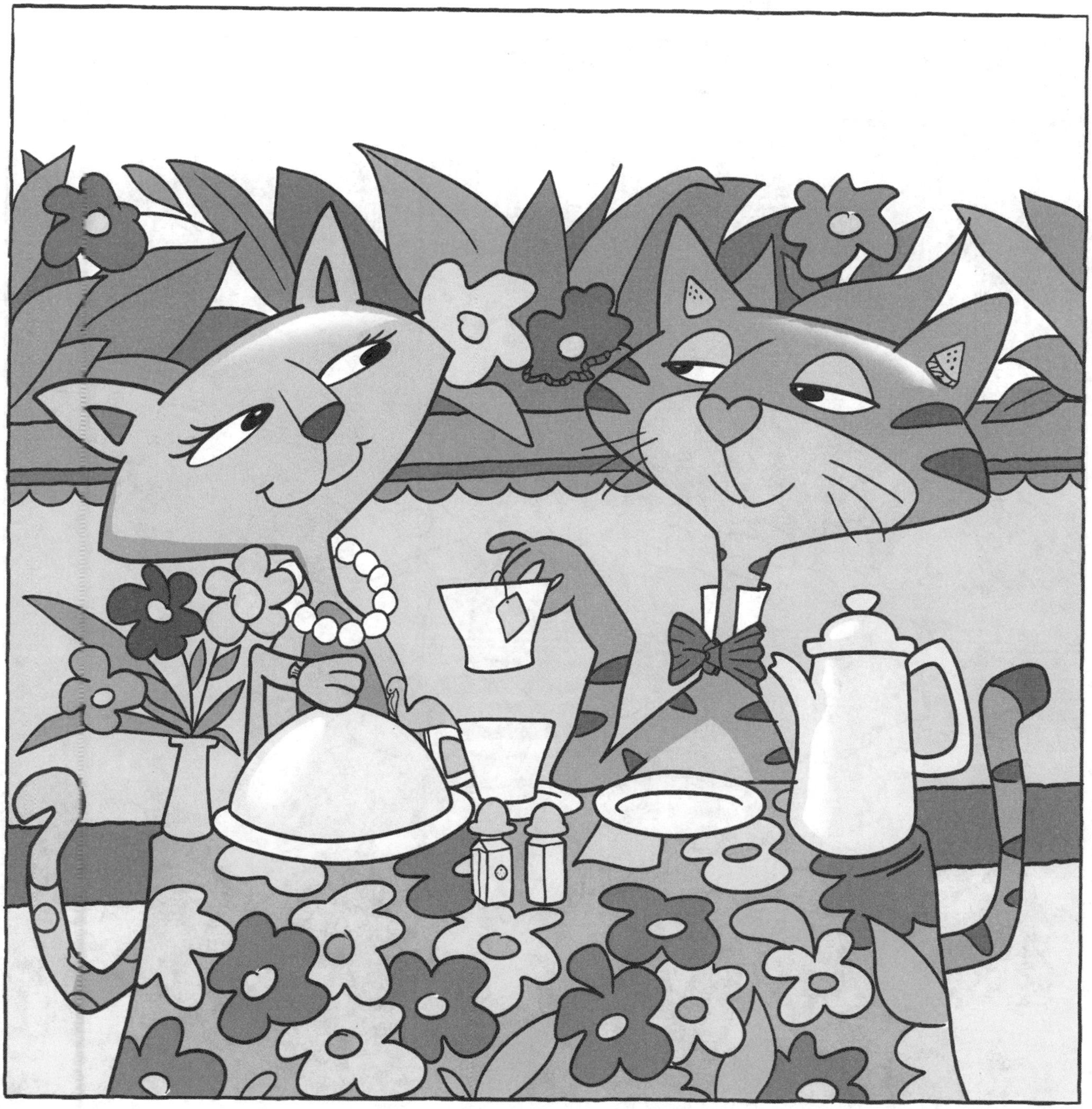

Find and circle the hidden pictures.

juice carton | question mark | heart | watermelon slice | dress | snake | clam | flamingo

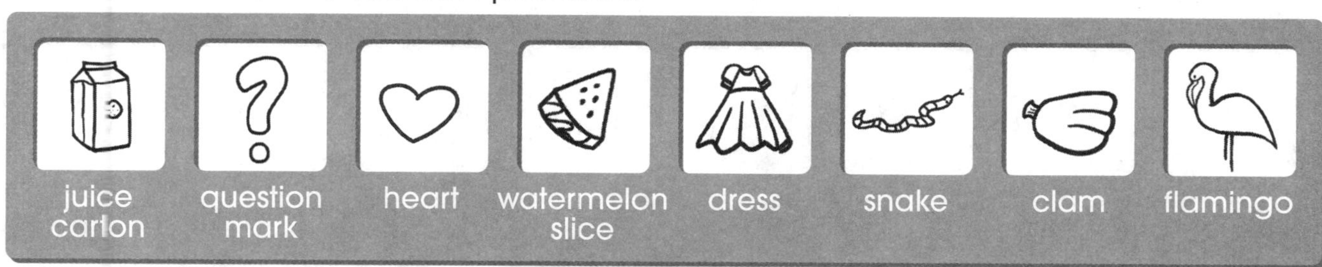

TOASTING MARSHMALLOWS

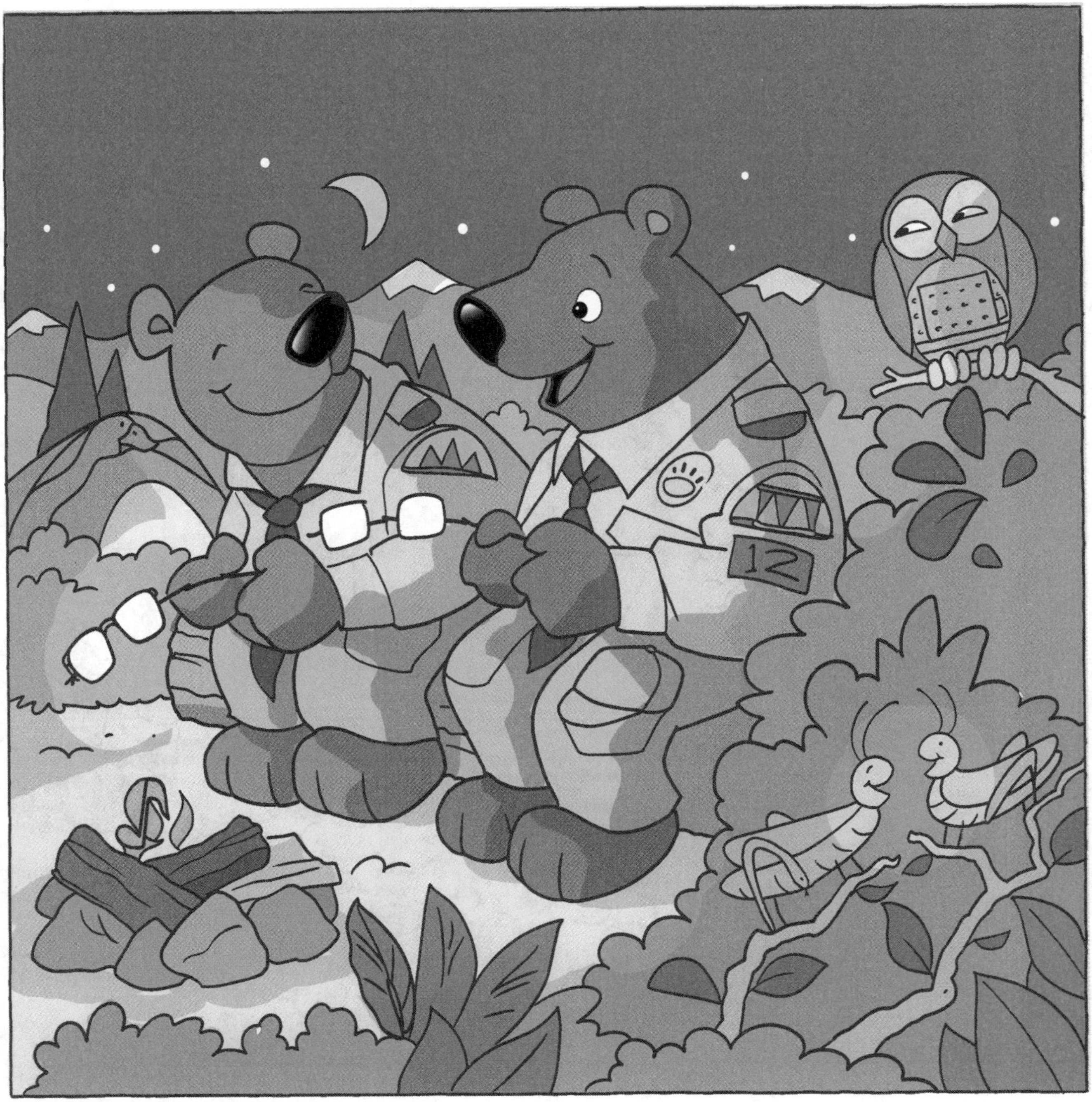

Find and circle the hidden pictures.

goose

glasses

musical note

leaf

building

drum

baseball cap

snake

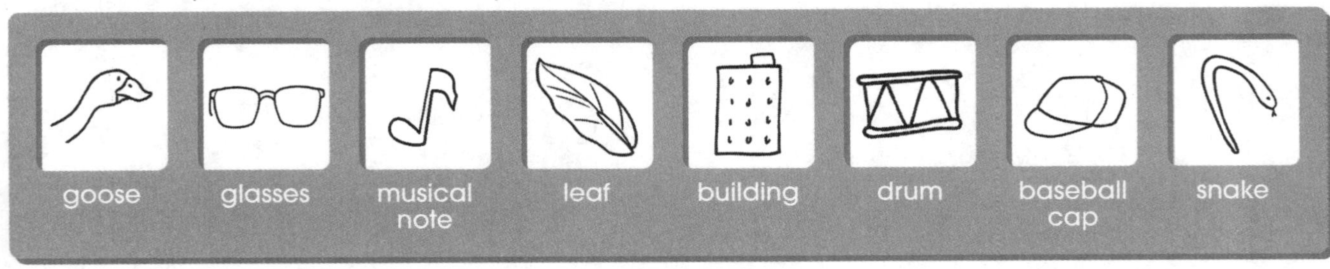

 ©School Zone Publishing Company

TONS OF TOYS

Find and circle the hidden pictures.

doll

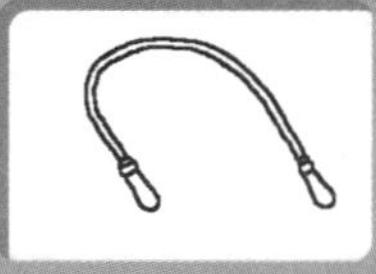

jump rope

bear

toy train

toy soldier

toy car

©School Zone Publishing Company

FUN AT THE FAIR

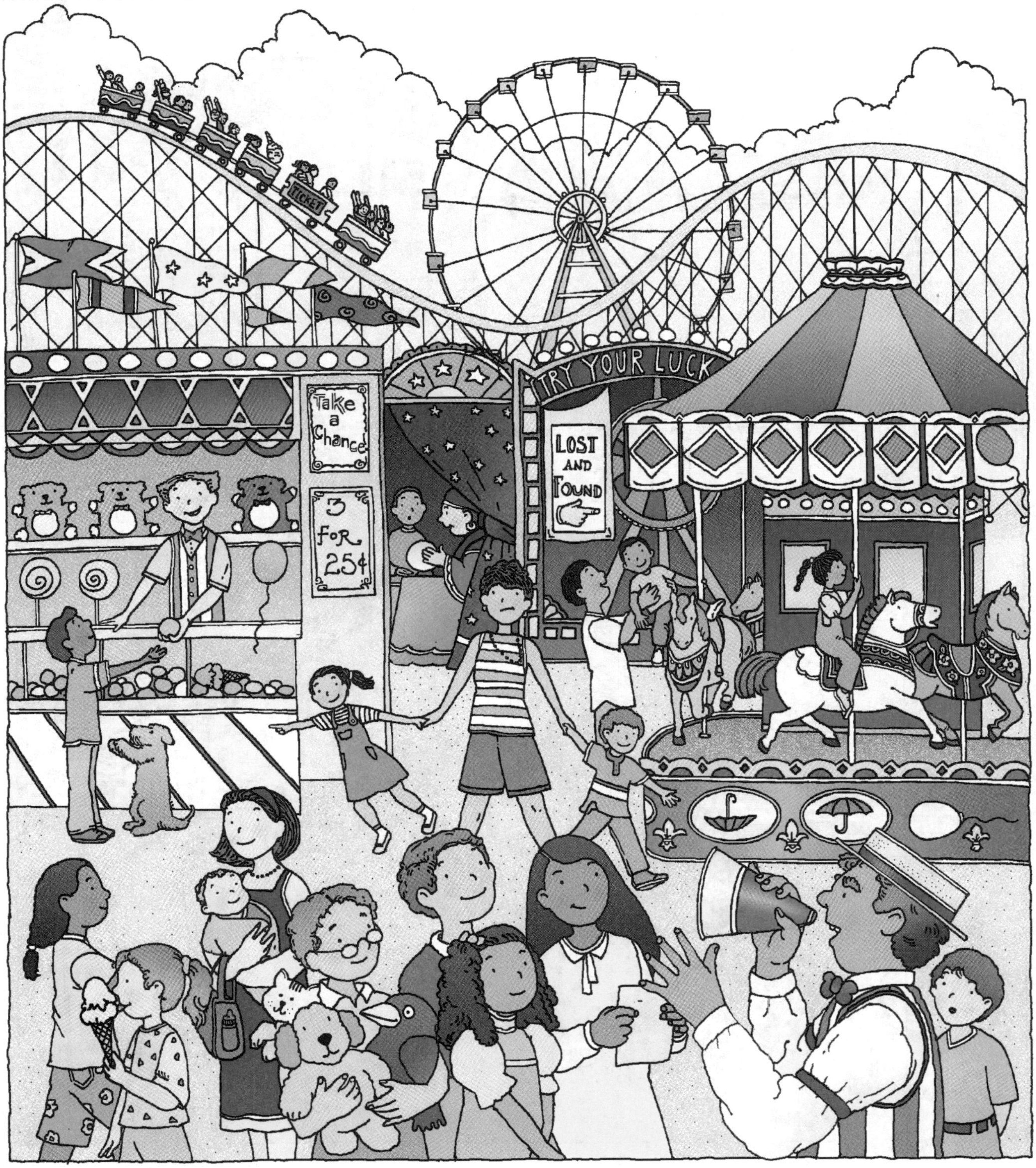

Find and circle the hidden pictures.

1 bottle | 2 ice cream cones | 1 bird | 1 sign | 1 ticket | 3 balloons

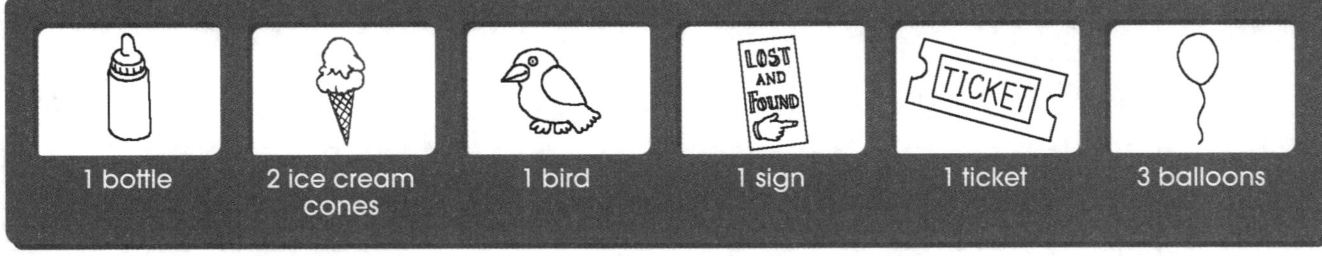

 ©School Zone Publishing Company

SICK DAY

Look at the picture and find:

1 thing you wear on your head

2 things that are the same

3 things that inflate

4 things that roll

5 seashells

6 things that lay eggs

SNOW DAY

Look at the picture and find:

1 thing that is broken

2 things that are wrong

3 cats

4 things to eat

5 things that are circular

6 things that are tied

©School Zone Publishing Company

STUDYING FOR THE TEST

Find cnd circle the hidden pictures.

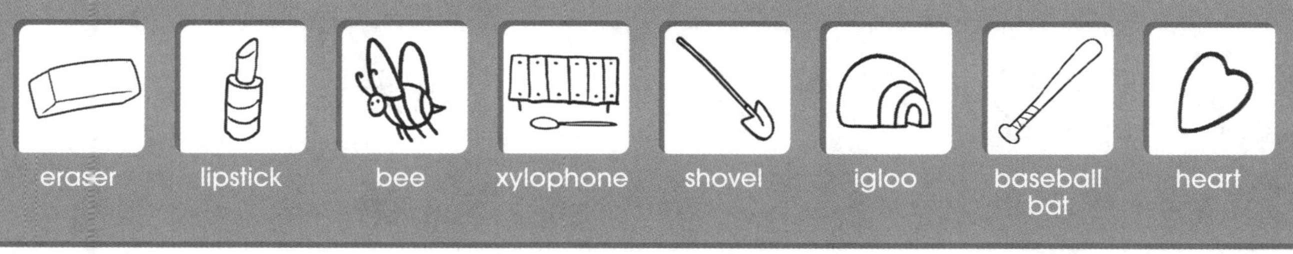

BEDTIME STORY

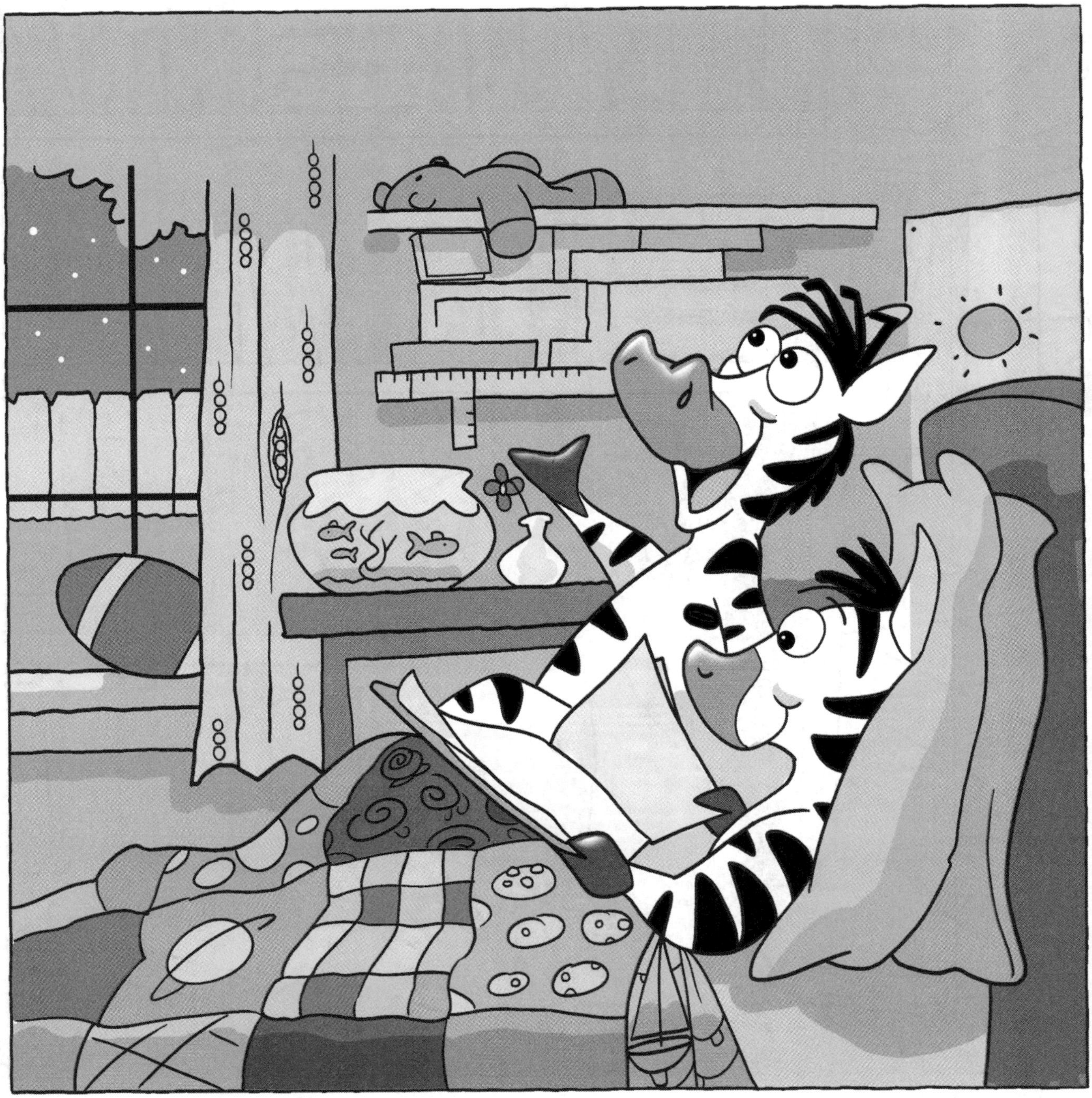

Find and circle the hidden pictures.

seven | cookie | peas | zero | sailboat | rose | square ruler | book

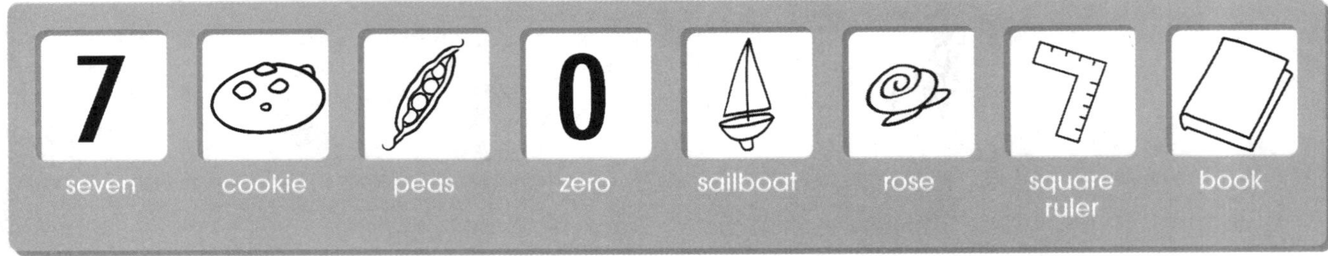

A BOY'S ROOM

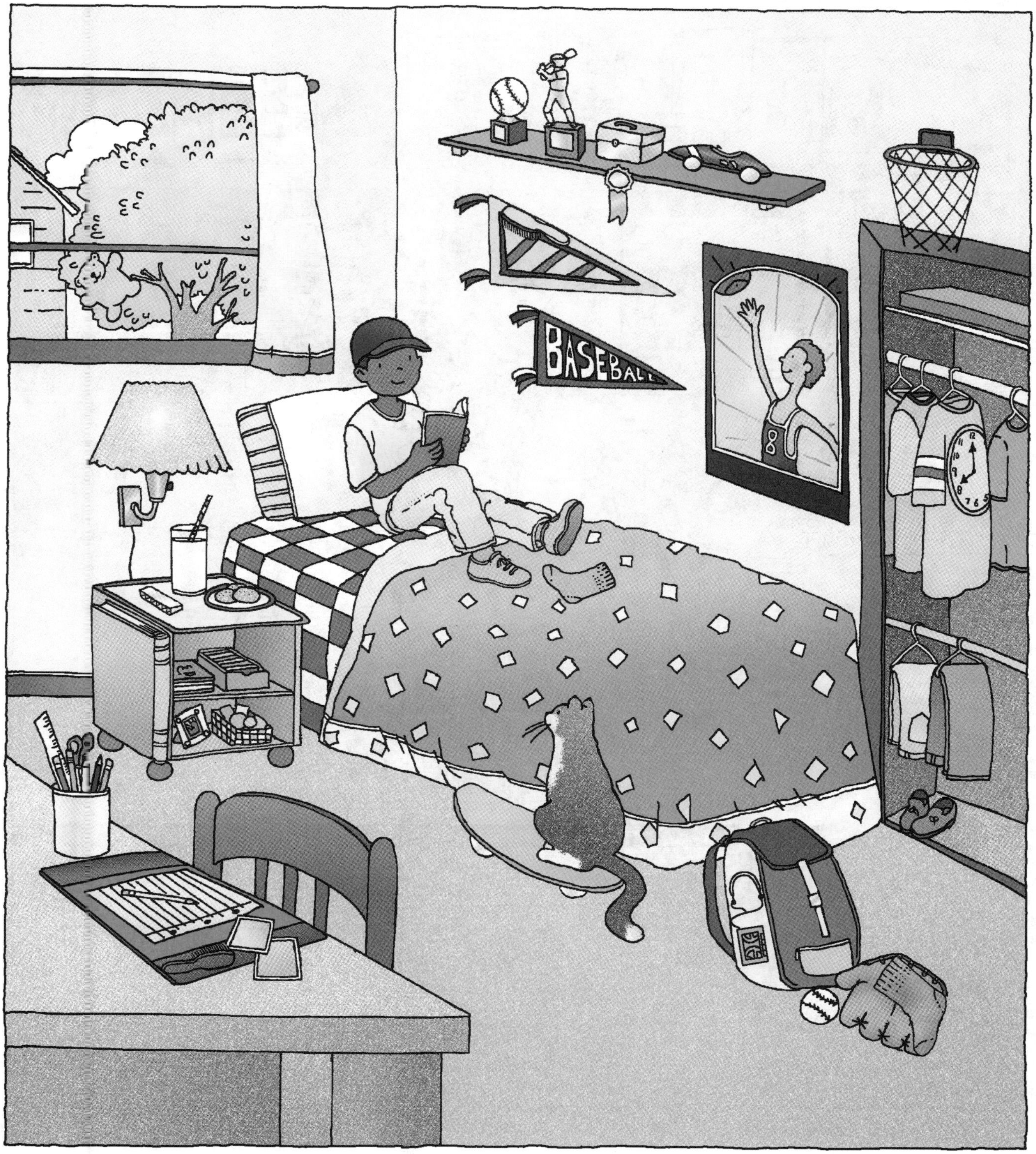

Find and circle the hidden pictures.

2 socks

2 brushes

1 teddy bear

1 music player

1 book

1 clock

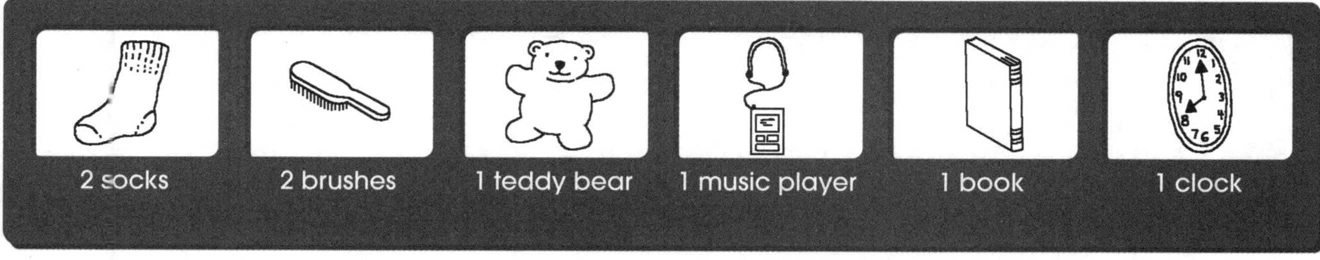

GROCERY SHOPPING

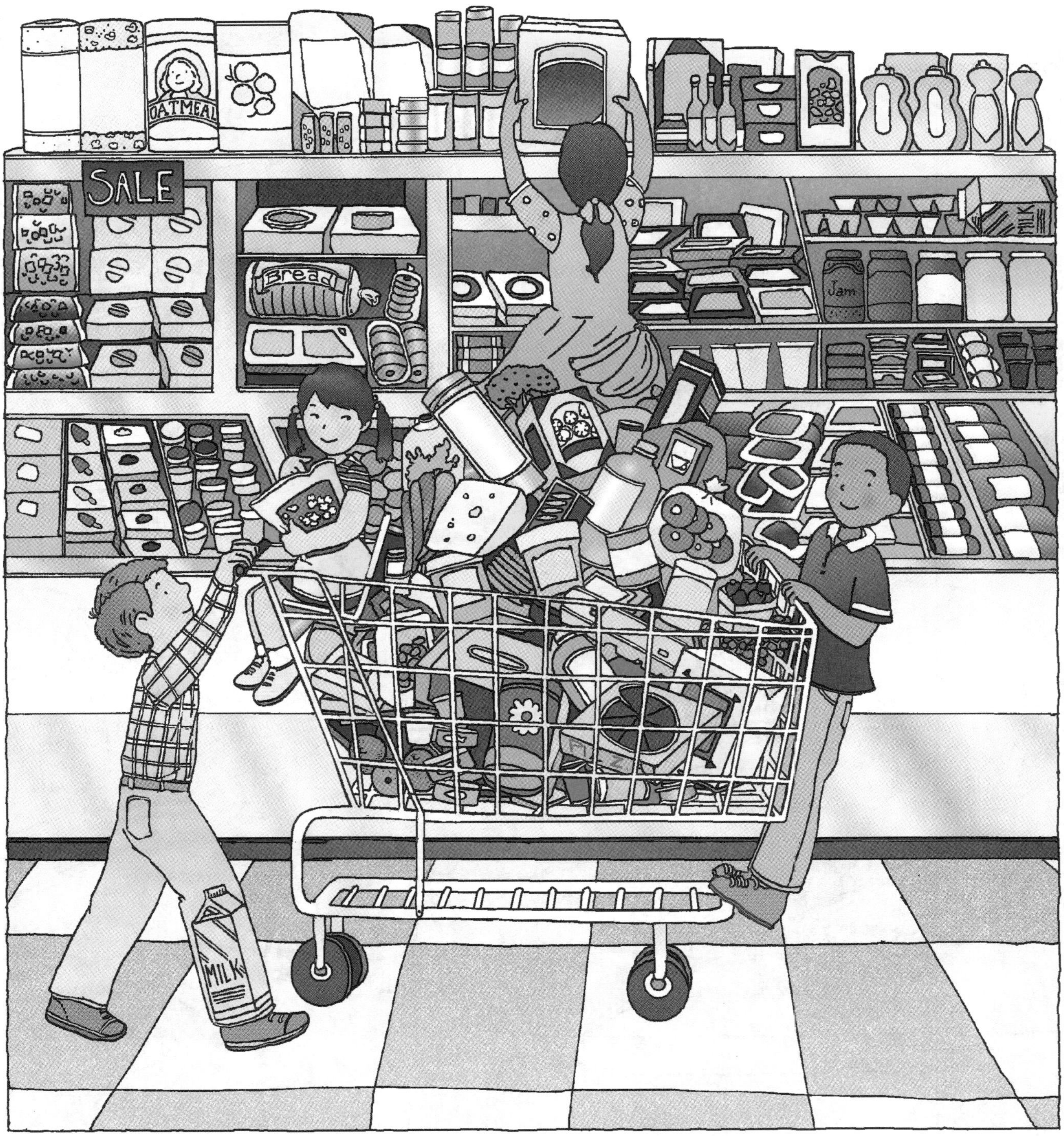

Find and circle the hidden pictures.

2 milk cartons

1 bunch of carrots

1 jar of jam

1 oatmeal container

1 pizza box

1 bunch of bananas

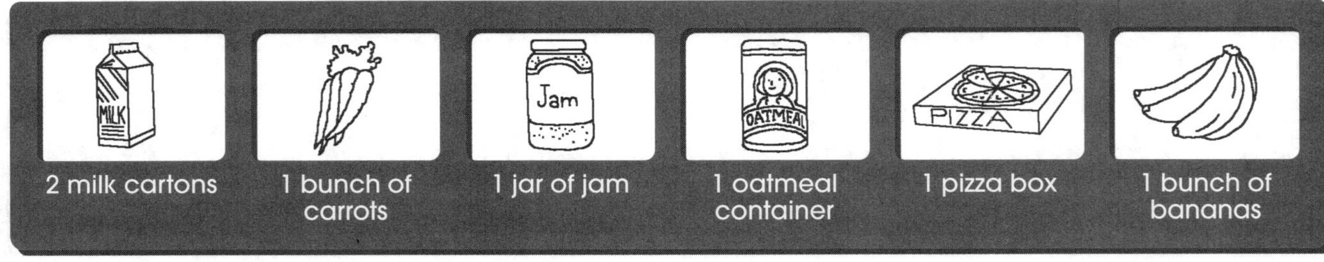

 ©School Zone Publishing Company

BACK TO CLASS

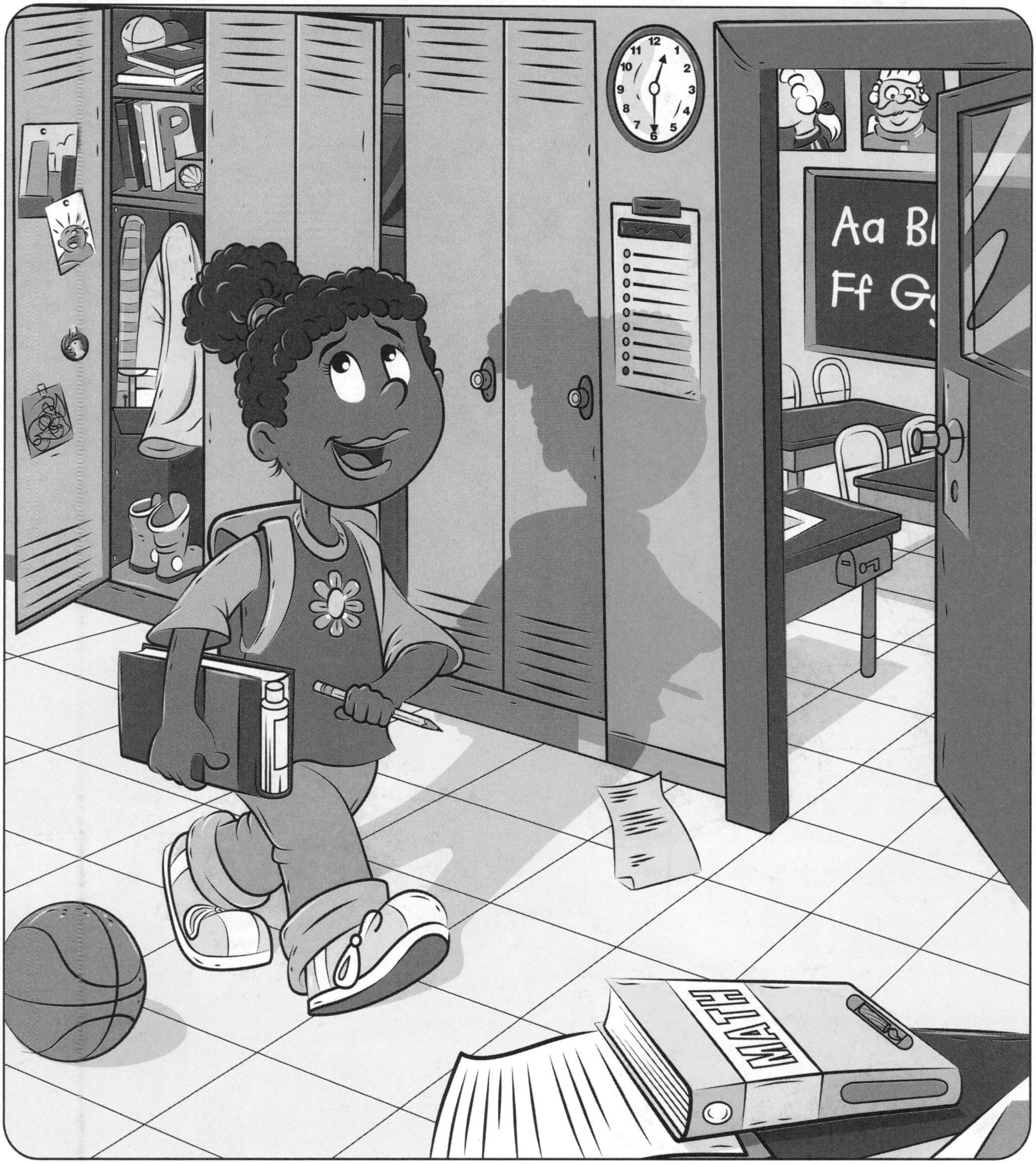

Find and circle the hidden pictures.

shell candle horseshoe bottle pushpin earring lamp mailbox

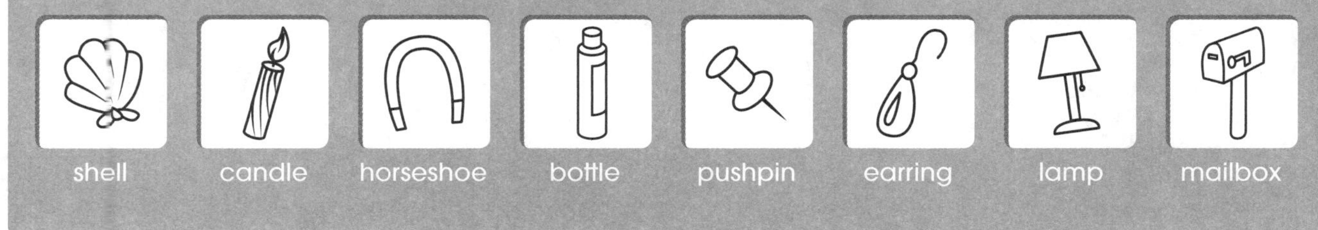

EXPERIMENTS IN THE LAB

Find and circle the hidden pictures.

 ©School Zone Publishing Company

THE BAKERY

Find and circle the hidden pictures.

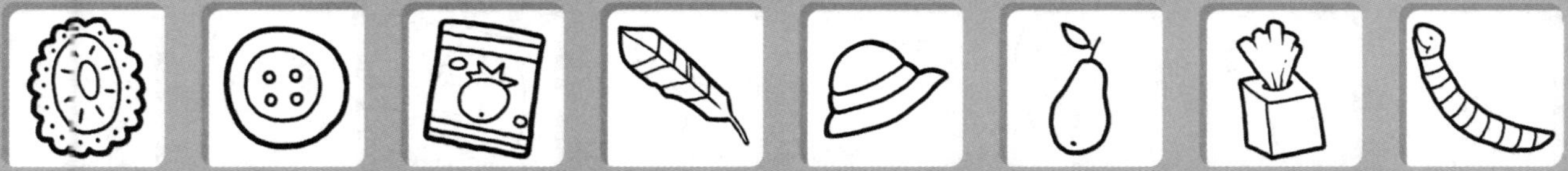

brooch

button

can

feather

hat

pear

tissue box

worm

FRESH PRODUCE

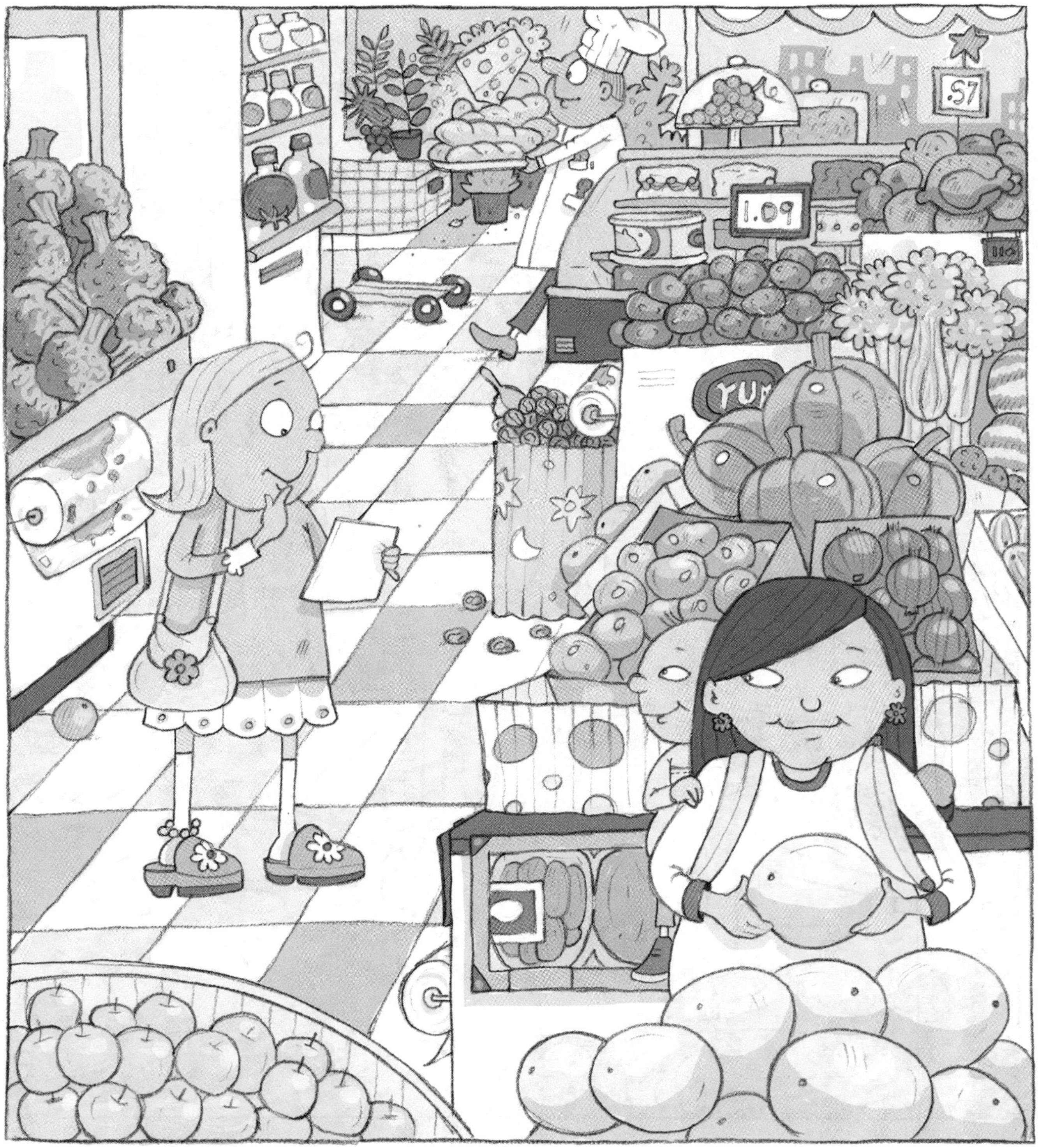

Find and circle the hidden pictures.

banana | celery | cheese | chicken | grapes | pickles | tomato | tuna

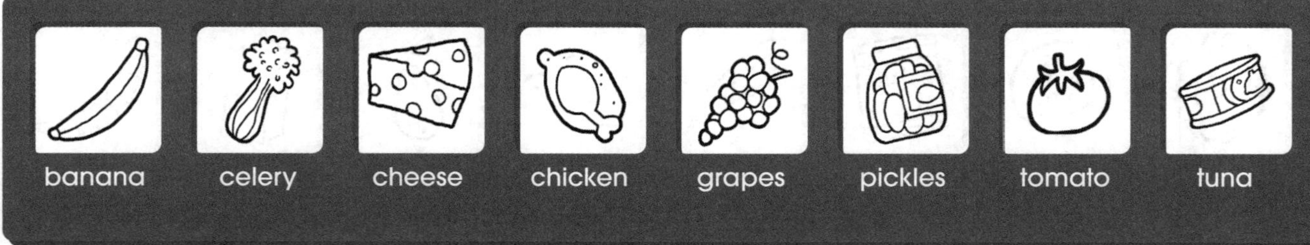

©School Zone Publishing Company

AT THE TOY STORE

Find and circle the hidden pictures.

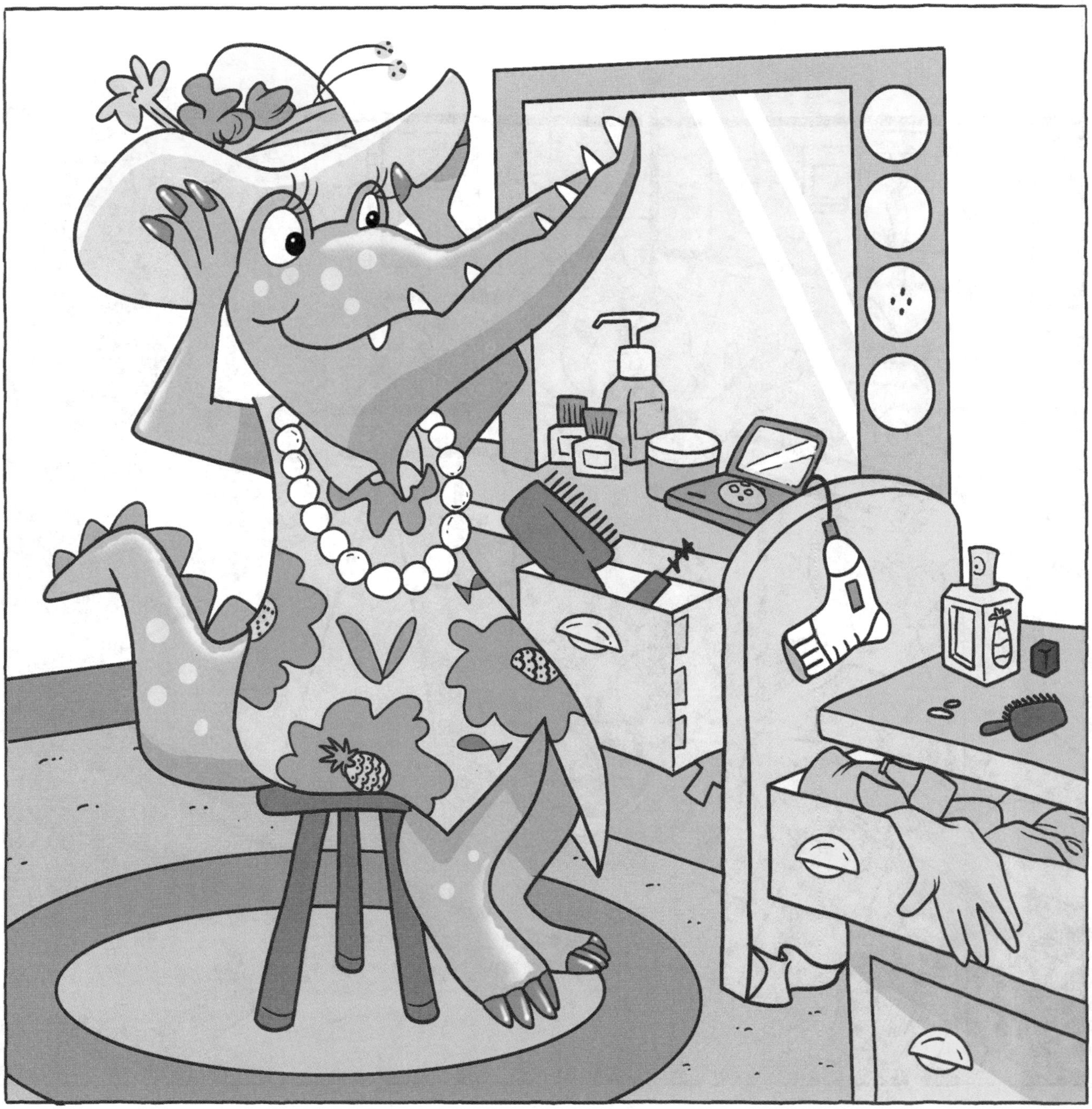

GETTING READY

Find and circle the hidden pictures.

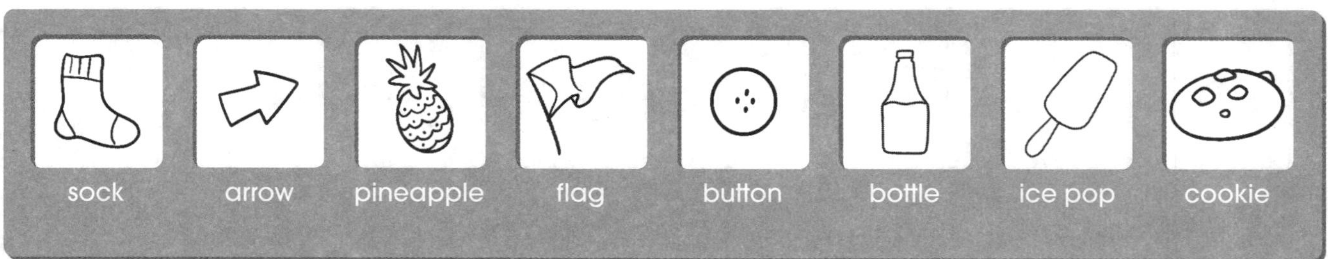

FLY IN THE SKY

Solve each math problem. Find the first answer on the grid. Draw a line to the second answer. Continue drawing lines to connect the answers in order. When you have finished, a picture will be revealed.

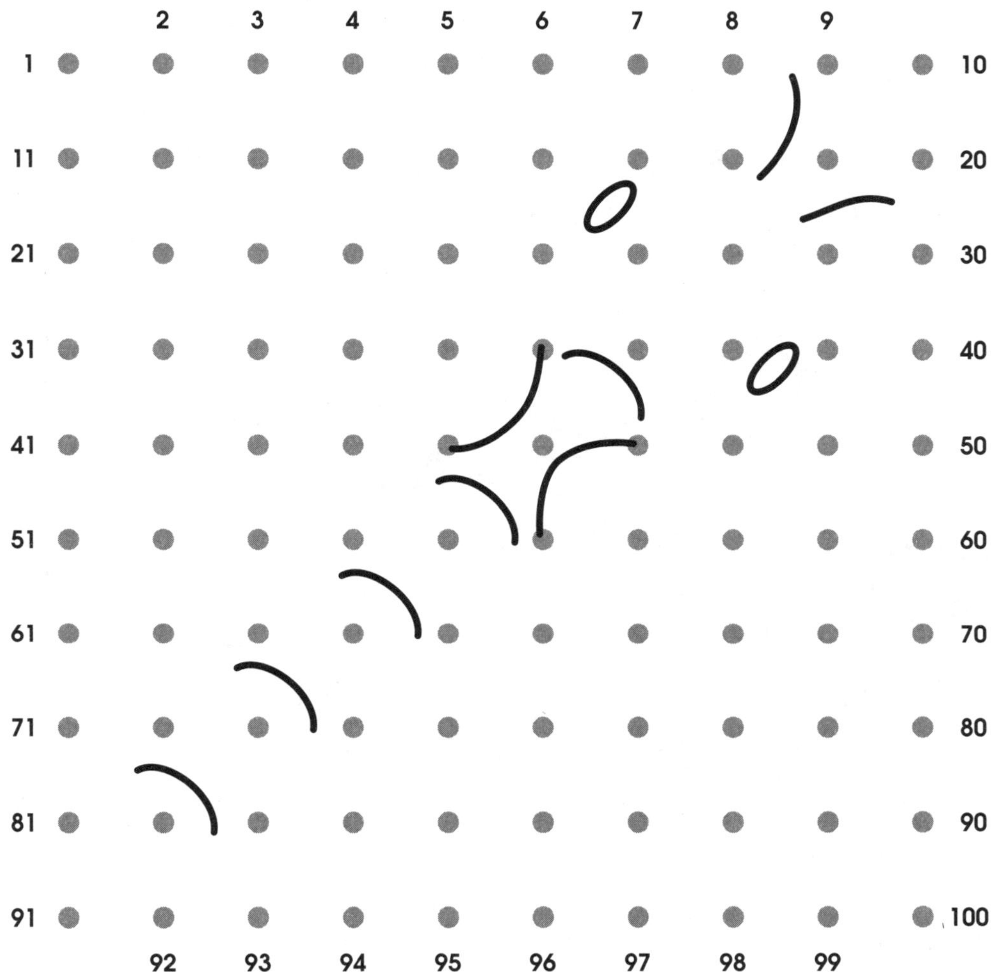

Line 1

1. 25 + 22 = ___

2. 99 – 51 = ___

3. 31 + 8 = ___

4. 45 – 16 = ___

5. 9 + 9 = ___

6. 36 – 19 = ___

7. 13 + 13 = ___

8. 57 – 21 = ___

9. 14 + 11 = ___

10. 20 – 6 = ___

11. 1 + 2 = ___

12. 6 – 4 = ___

13. 6 + 5 = ___

14. 44 – 23 = ___

15. 21 + 11 = ___

16. 88 – 44 = ___

17. 32 + 13 = ___

18. 98 – 44 = ___

19. 38 + 25 = ___

20. 98 – 26 = ___

21. 40 + 41 = ___

22. 100 – 9 = ___

23. 48 + 44 = ___

24. 97 – 14 = ___

25. 61 + 13 = ___

26. 77 – 12 = ___

27. 49 + 7 = ___

28. 96 – 30 = ___

29. 73 + 14 = ___

30. 100 – 2 = ___

31. 76 + 23 = ___

32. 100 – 10 = ___

33. 66 + 14 = ___

34. 87 – 18 = ___

35. 34 + 24 = ___

36. 59 – 12 = ___

SO MANY BUBBLES, SO LITTLE TIME

Follow the maze from start to finish.

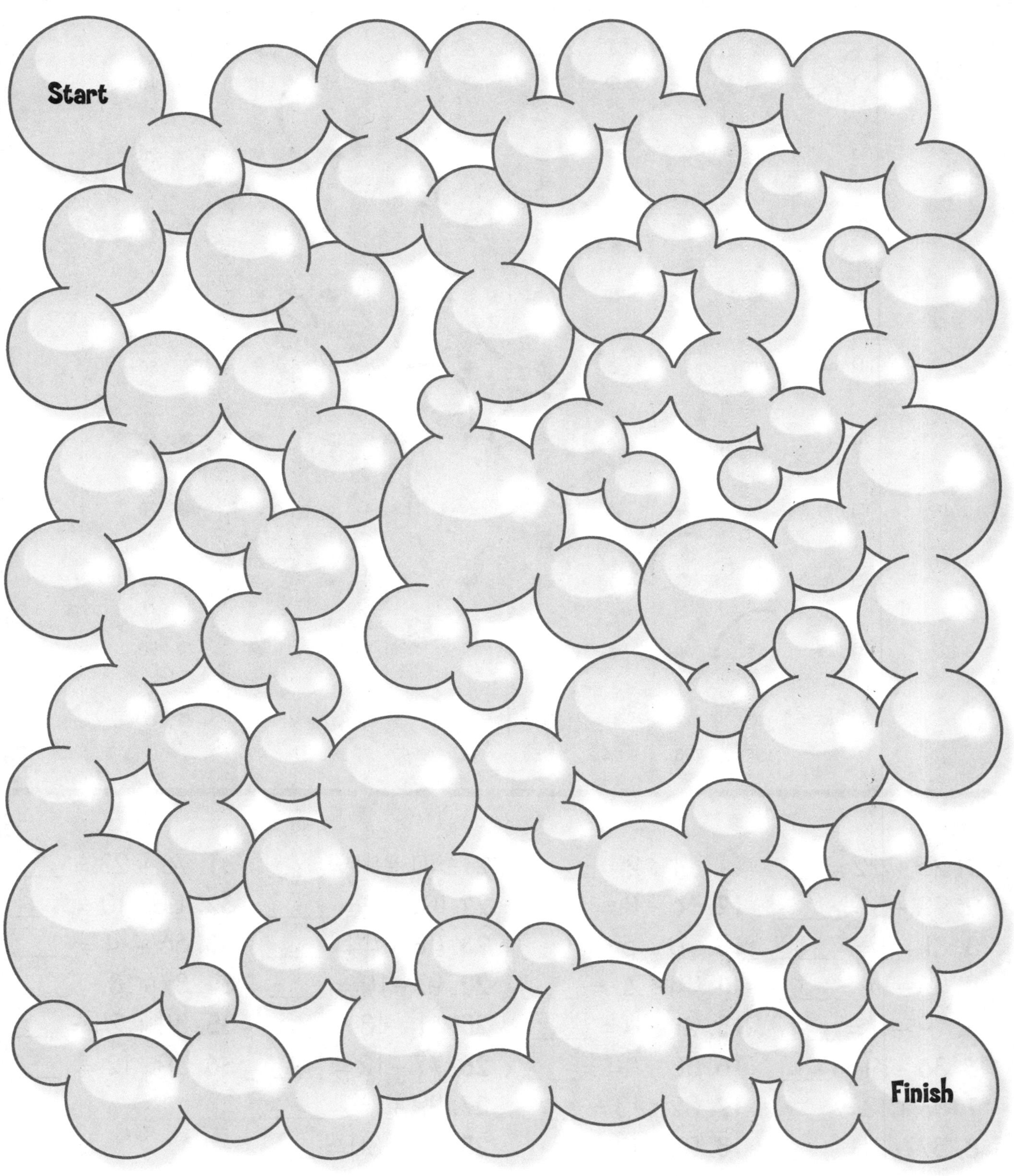

 ©School Zone Publishing Company

PLAY ME A TUNE!

Solve each math problem. Find the first answer on the grid. Draw a line to the second answer. Continue drawing lines to connect the answers in order. When you have finished, a picture will be revealed.

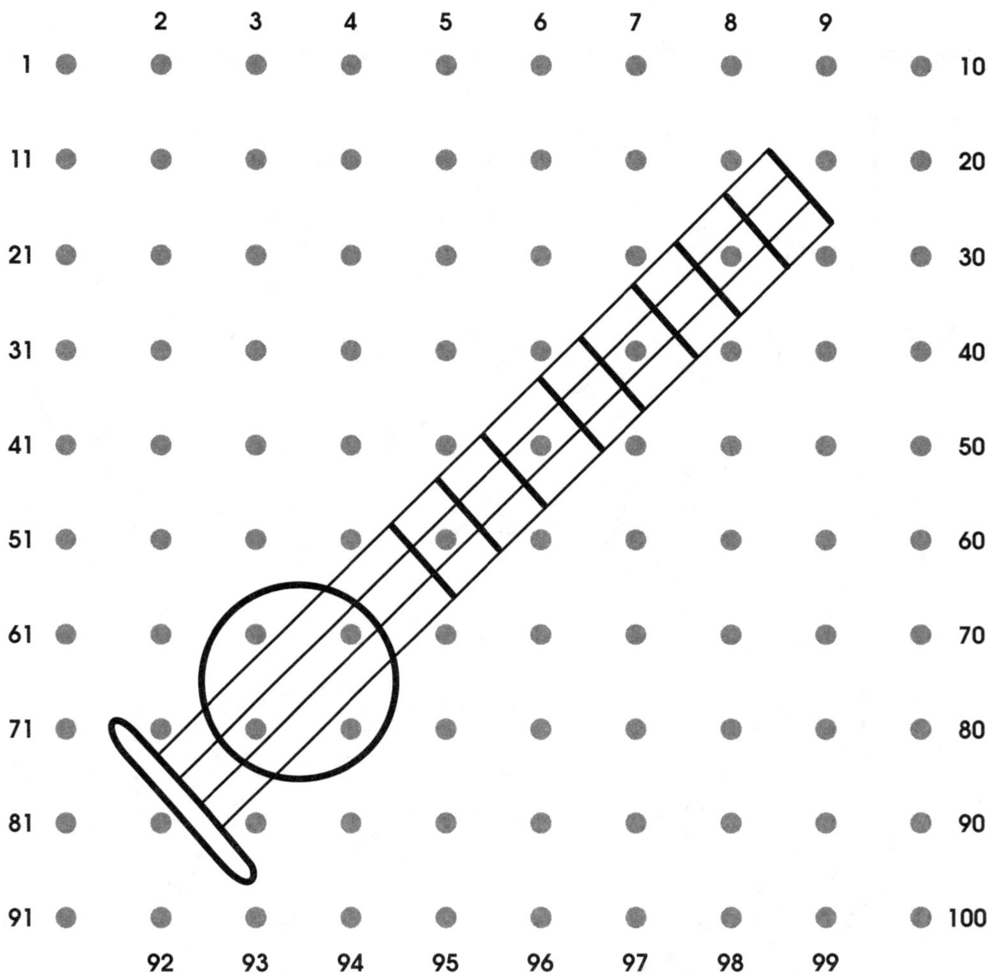

Line 1

1. 4 + 5 = _____
2. 12 − 4 = _____
3. 9 + 9 = _____
4. 57 − 30 = _____
5. 15 + 21 = _____
6. 70 − 35 = _____
7. 22 + 22 = _____
8. 50 − 7 = _____
9. 12 + 30 = _____
10. 25 + 26 = _____
11. 90 − 29 = _____
12. 65 + 6 = _____
13. 90 − 9 = _____
14. 100 − 8 = _____
15. 80 + 13 = _____
16. 81 + 13 = _____
17. 99 − 4 = _____
18. 61 + 25 = _____
19. 100 − 24 = _____
20. 33 + 33 = _____
21. 75 − 18 = _____
22. 40 + 7 = _____
23. 88 − 50 = _____
24. 36 − 7 = _____
25. 60 − 30 = _____
26. 13 + 7 = _____
27. 18 − 9 = _____

Line 2

1. 46 − 10 = _____
2. 40 + 5 = _____
3. 90 − 36 = _____
4. 30 + 35 = _____
5. 48 + 8 = _____
6. 59 − 12 = _____

©School Zone Publishing Company

JUNE BUG

Color the picture below.

1 = yellow 2 = green 3 = yellow green 4 = pink 5 = orange
6 = brown 7 = blue green 8 = red 9 = purple 10 = black 11 = blue

RIBBIT!

Solve each math problem. Find the first answer on the grid. Draw a line to the second answer. Continue drawing lines to connect the answers in order. When you have finished, a picture will be revealed.

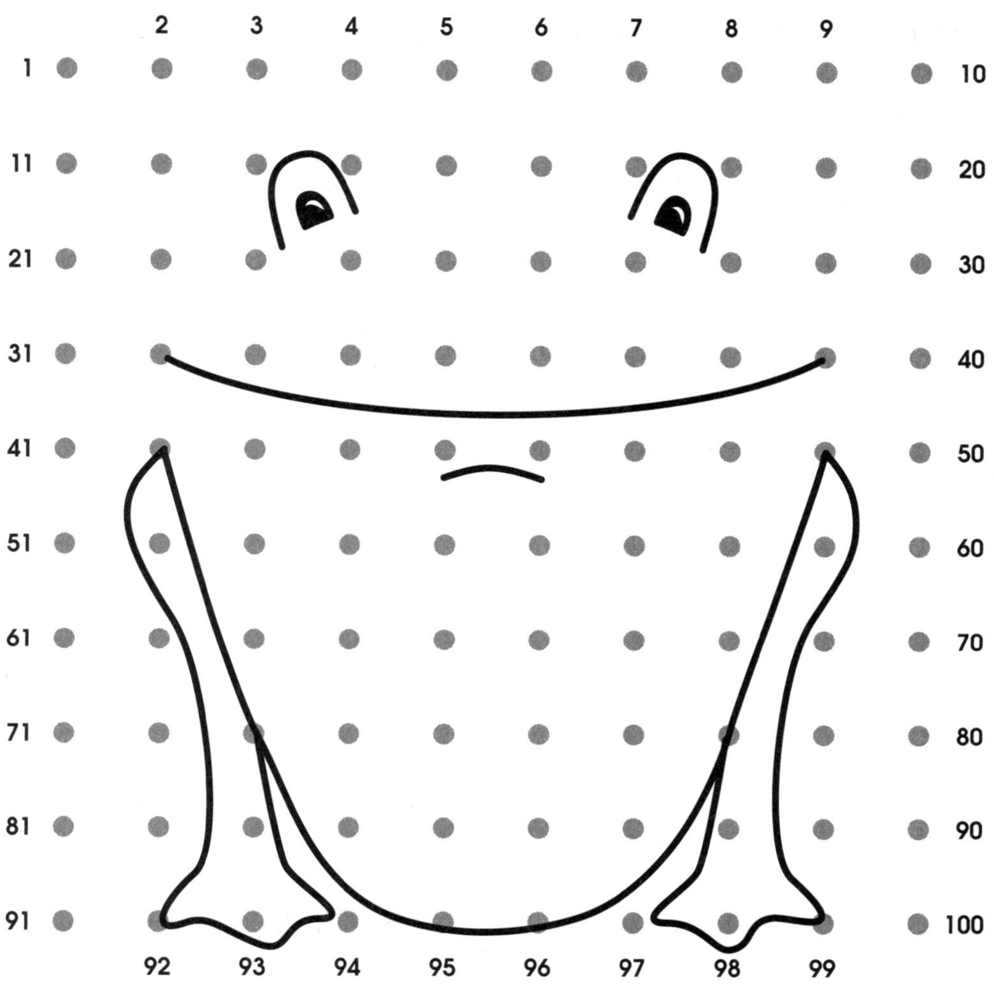

Line 1

1. 100 – 8 = _____
2. 60 + 31 = _____
3. 89 – 8 = _____
4. 40 + 42 = _____
5. 35 + 37 = _____
6. 100 – 49 = _____
7. 20 + 21 = _____
8. 50 – 19 = _____
9. 10 + 32 = _____
10. 15 + 17 = _____
11. 75 – 52 = _____
12. 30 – 15 = _____
13. 8 + 8 = _____
14. 60 – 32 = _____
15. 30 + 9 = _____
16. 100 – 51 = _____
17. 20 + 20 = _____
18. 75 – 25 = _____
19. 77 – 17 = _____
20. 82 – 3 = _____
21. 67 + 22 = _____
22. 45 + 45 = _____
23. 75 + 25 = _____
24. 54 + 45 = _____

©School Zone Publishing Company

WHO'S IN THE CARROT PATCH?

Color the picture below.

1 = **blue** 2 = **yellow** 3 = **green** 4 = **yellow green** 5 = **orange**
6 = **black** 7 = **red** 8 = **pink** 9 = **brown**

2/2	2/2	2/2	2/1	1/9	9/9	1/1	2/1	2/1	1/2	1/1	1/9	9/9	1/1	1/1
2/2	2/2	2/2	2/1	9/9	8/8	9/9	1/1	1/1	1/1	1/9	9/8	9/1	1/1	1/1
2/1	2/1	1/1	1/1	9/9	8/8	8/9	1/1	1/1	1/9	9/8	8/9	9/1	1/1	1/1
1/2	1/1	2/1	1/1	1/1	9/9	8/8	9/9	1/1	9/9	8/9	9/1	1/1	1/1	1/1
1/1	1/1	1/1	2/1	1/1	1/8	8/8	8/8	8/8	8/8	9/1	1/1	1/1	1/1	1/1
1/1	2/1	1/1	1/1	1/1	8/8	6	8/8	8/8	6	8/8	1/1	1/1	1/1	1/1
1/1	1/1	1/1	1/1	1/8	8/8	8/8	8/9	7/9	8/8	8/8	1/1	1/1	1/1	1/1
1/1	1/1	1/1	1/1	9/9	8/8	8/8		9	8	8/8	8/1	1/1	1/1	1/1
1/3	1/1	1/1	1/1	1/1	9/9	8/8	8/8	8/8	8/8	8/1	1/1	1/1	1/1	3/1
1/3	3/1	1		1/8	8					8/8	1/1	1/3	1/3	3/1
3/3	1/1		8	8/8	8/8					8	1/1	1/1	1/1	3/1
3/5	1/1	1/1	8/8	8/8	8/8	8/8				8/8	1/3	1/1	5/5	5/5
5/5	1/1	1/1	8/8	8/9	8/8	8/8			8/8	8/8	1/5	1/1	5/5	5/1
5/5	1/5	1/1	8/8	8/9	8/8	8/8		8/8	8/8	8/8	5/5	1/5	5/5	1/5
5/5	5/8	8/8	8/8	9/9	8/8	8/8	8/8	8/8	4/4	8/8	8/8	1/5	5/5	5/5
4/4	4/4	4/4	4/4	4/4	8/9	8/9	4/4	4/4	4/4	4/4	8/9	8/9	4/4	4/4
4/4	4/4	4/4	4/4	4/4	4/4	4/4	4/4	4/4	4/4	4/4	4/4	4/4	4/4	4/4

©School Zone Publishing Company

CHOO-CHOO!

Solve each math problem. Find the first answer on the grid. Draw a line to the second answer. Continue drawing lines to connect the answers in order. When you have finished, a picture will be revealed.

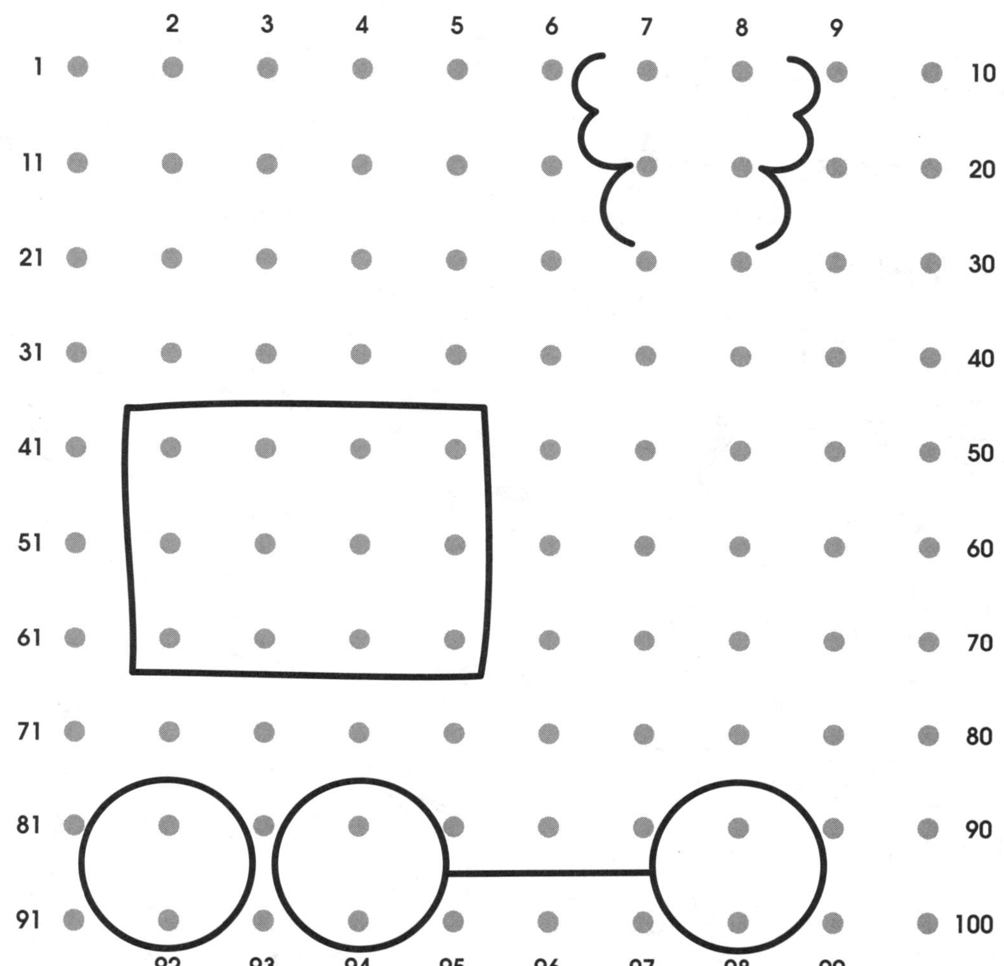

Line 1

1. 45 + 46 = _____
2. 92 − 11 = _____
3. 21 + 50 = _____
4. 73 − 12 = _____
5. 60 − 9 = _____
6. 20 + 21 = _____
7. 75 − 44 = _____
8. 11 + 11 = _____
9. 50 − 27= _____
10. 12 + 12 = _____
11. 20 + 5 = _____
12. 42 − 6 = _____
13. 40 + 6 = _____
14. 25 + 31 = _____
15. 63 − 6 = _____
16. 37 + 10 = _____
17. 40 − 3 = _____
18. 15 + 11 = _____
19. 40 − 13 = _____
20. 14 + 14 = _____
21. 30 − 1 = _____
22. 15 + 23 = _____
23. 24 + 24 = _____
24. 75 − 17 = _____
25. 25 + 34 = _____
26. 90 − 21 = _____
27. 70 + 9 = _____
28. 95 − 6 = _____
29. 80 + 19 = _____
30. 90 + 10 = _____
31. 80 − 11 = _____

Line 2

1. 15 + 16 = _____
2. 30 + 2 = _____
3. 60 − 27 = _____
4. 25 + 9 = _____
5. 70 − 35 = _____
6. 12 + 24 = _____

AMBER LABYRINTH

Follow the maze from start to finish.

 ©School Zone Publishing Company

DINNER FOR TWO

Find and circle the hidden pictures.

1 sword	1 crest	2 keys	2 flags	2 goblets	1 crown

A PEACEFUL PARK

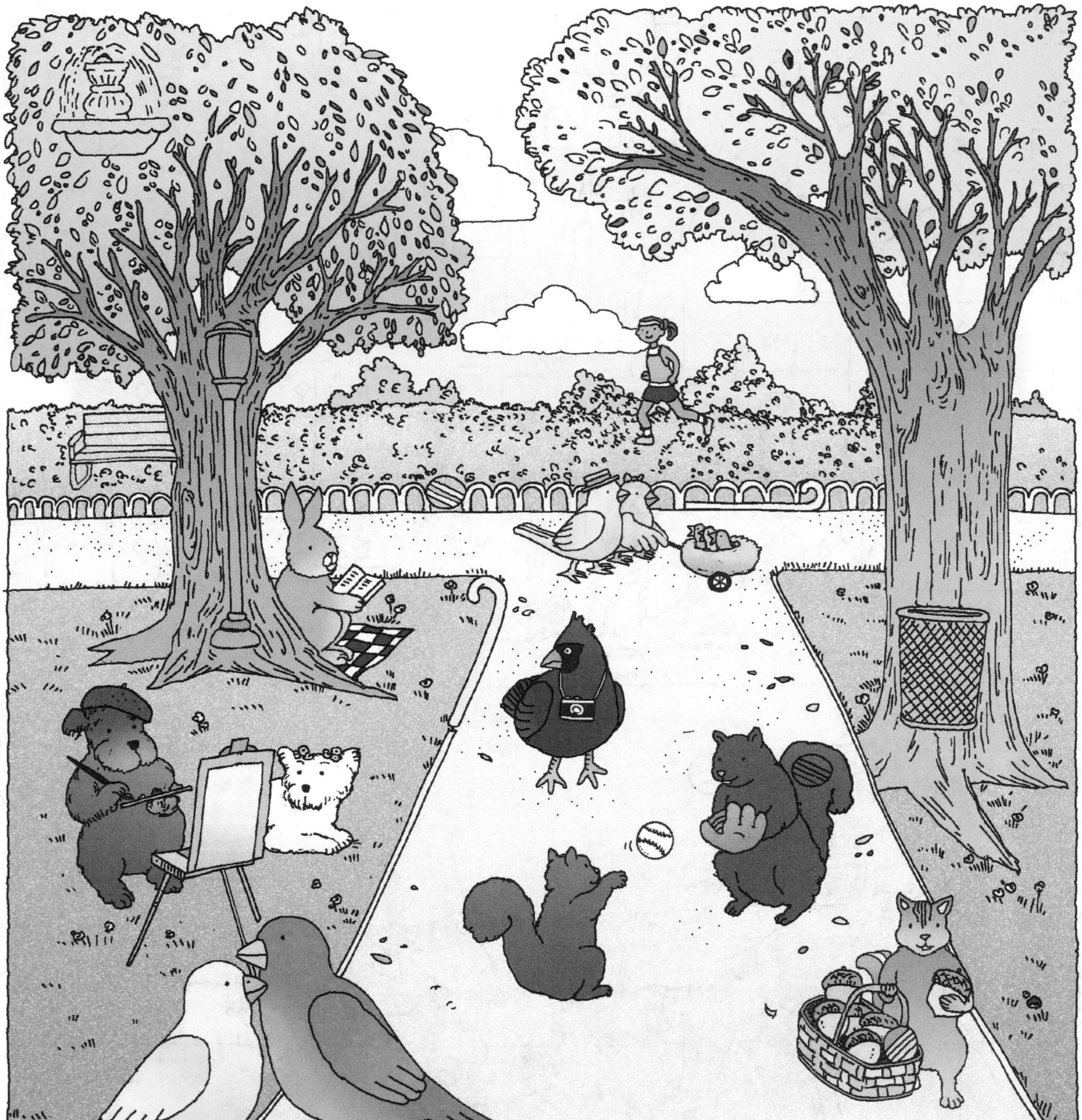

Find and circle the hidden pictures.

1 bench

1 fountain

3 balls

1 trash can

2 canes

1 street light

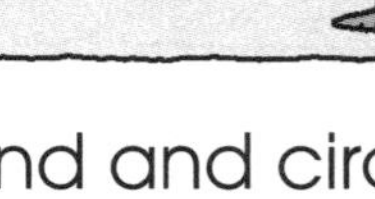

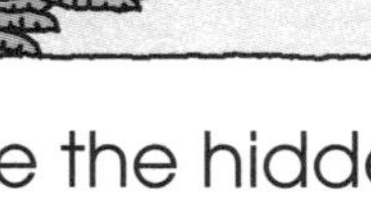

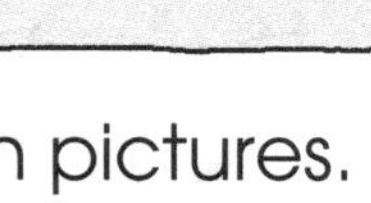

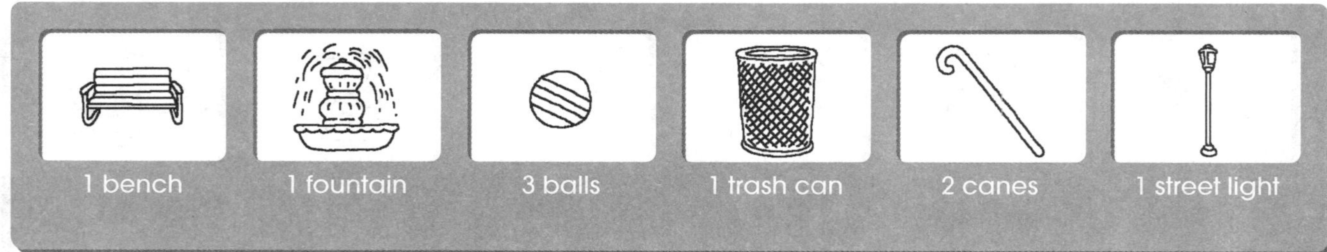

 ©School Zone Publishing Company

THE DINOS IN CONCERT

I ♥ DINOS

Find and circle the hidden pictures.

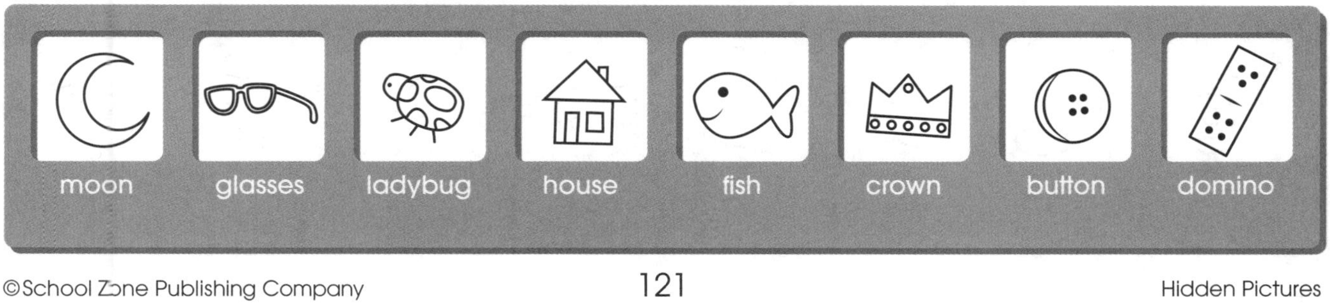

moon

glasses

ladybug

house

fish

crown

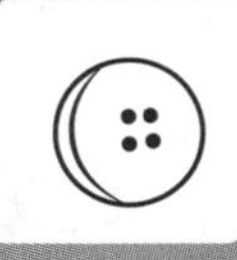
button

domino

A DAY ON THE SLOPES

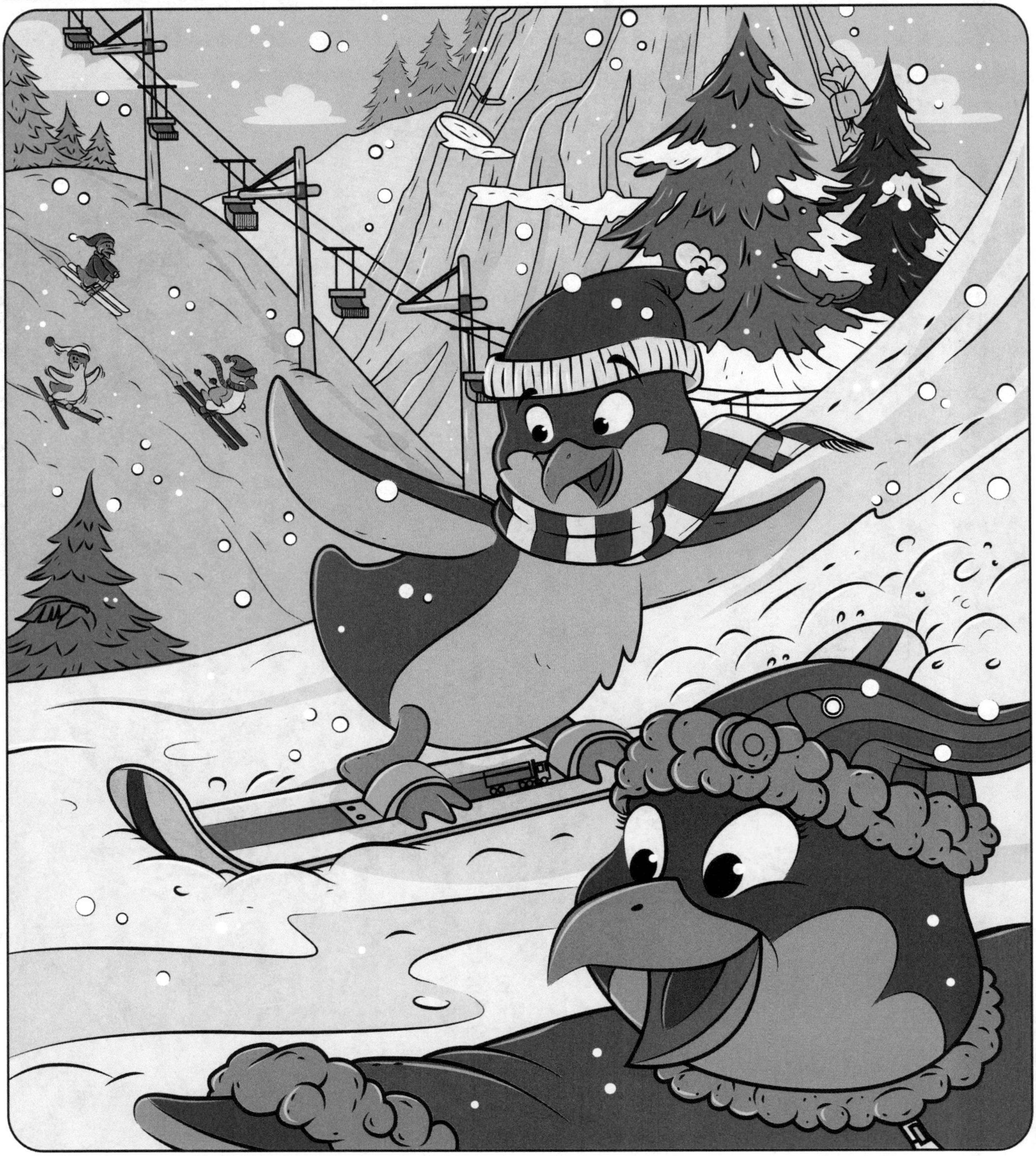

Find and circle the hidden pictures.

CAMPING OUT

Find and circle the hidden pictures.

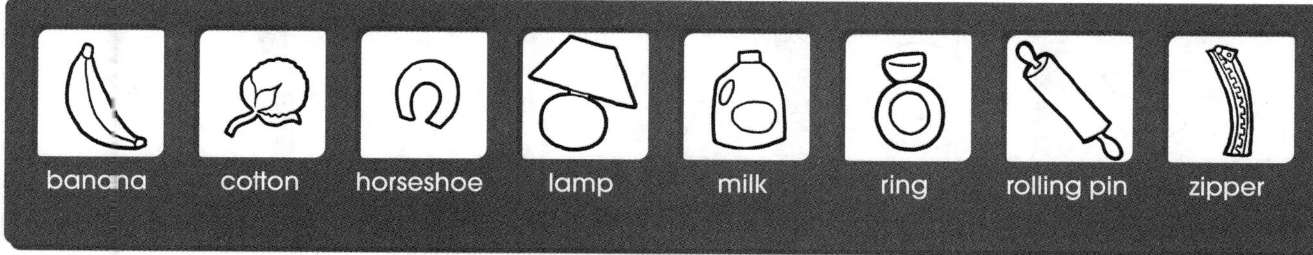

©School Zone Publishing Company

DOG DAY AFTERNOON

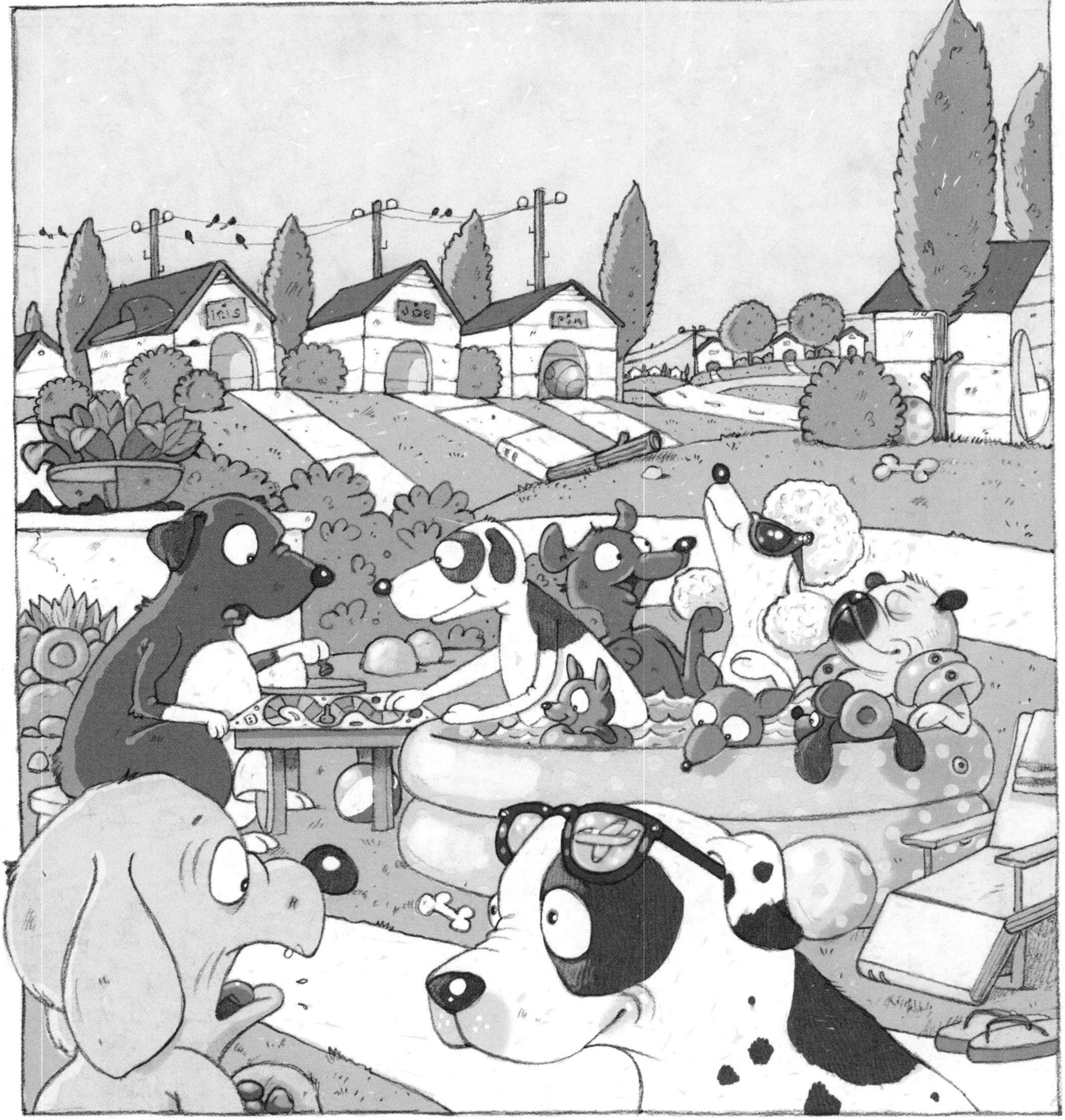

Find and circle the hidden pictures.

Find 1 airplane	Find 2 doughnuts	Find 3 books	Find 4 balls	Find 5 slippers

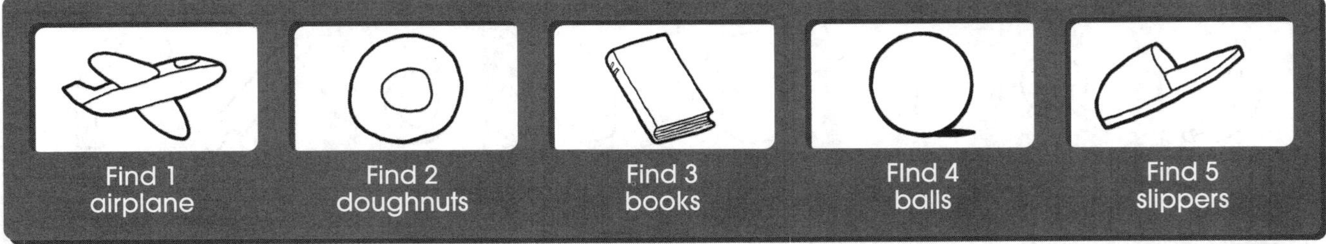

©School Zone Publishing Company

PLAYING IN THE PUMPKIN PATCH

Find and circle the hidden pictures.

TIME TO HARVEST!

Find and circle the hidden pictures.

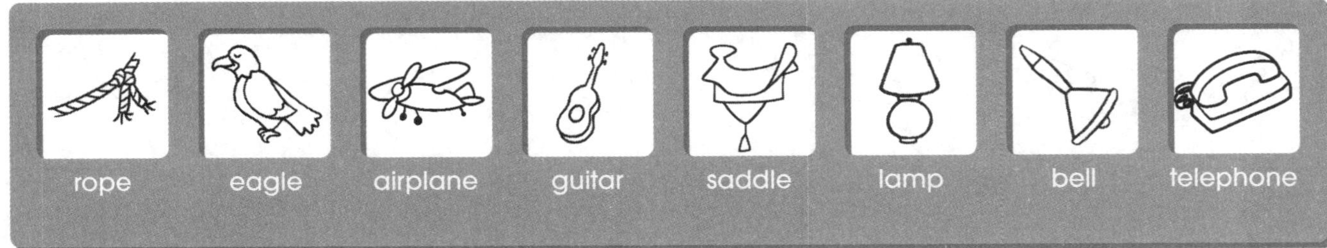

©School Zone Publishing Company

REPORT TIME

Find and circle the hidden pictures.

Find 1
hand shovel

Find 2
bread slices

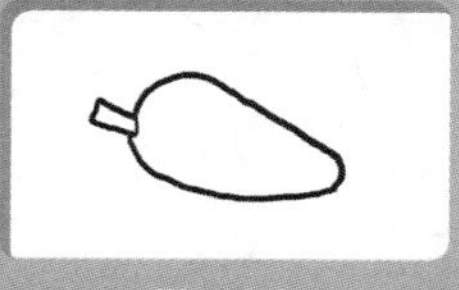

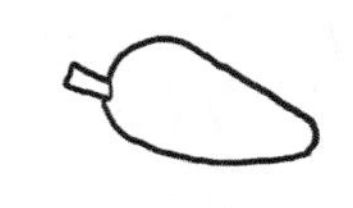
Find 3
peppers

Find 4
keys

Find 5
milk cartons

RATTY'S ADVENTURE

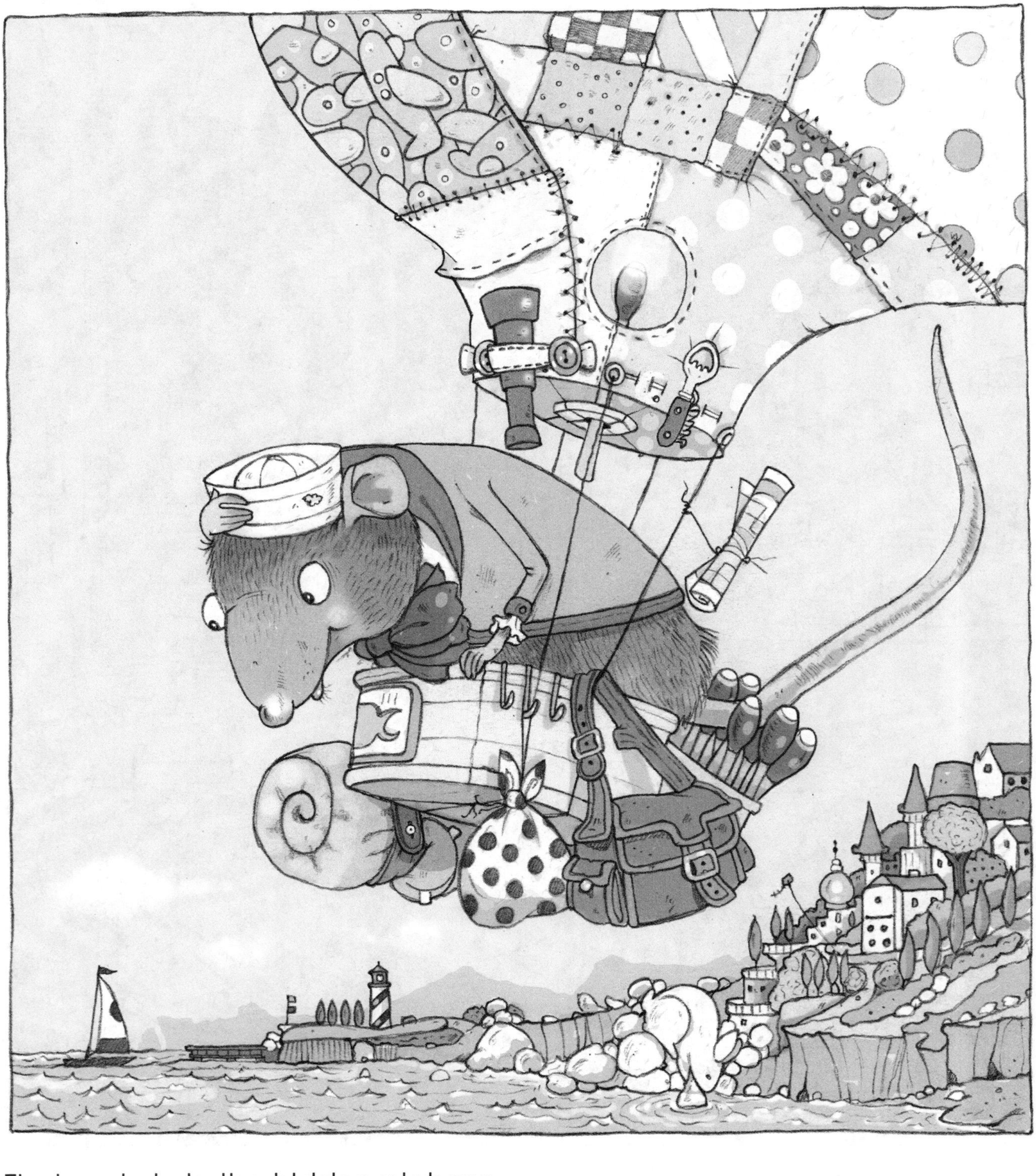

Find and circle the hidden pictures.

brush

bunny

cracker

domino

fortune cookie

plane

plant

stick

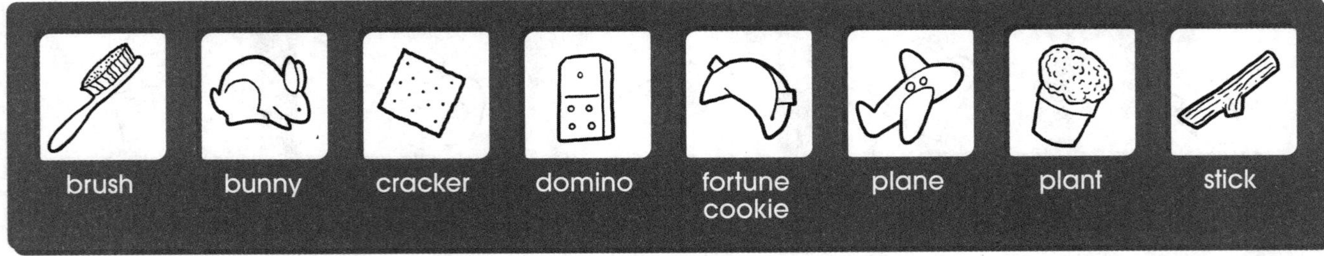

©School Zone Publishing Company

SINK THE PUTT!

Find and circle the hidden pictures.

BOTANICAL GARDENS

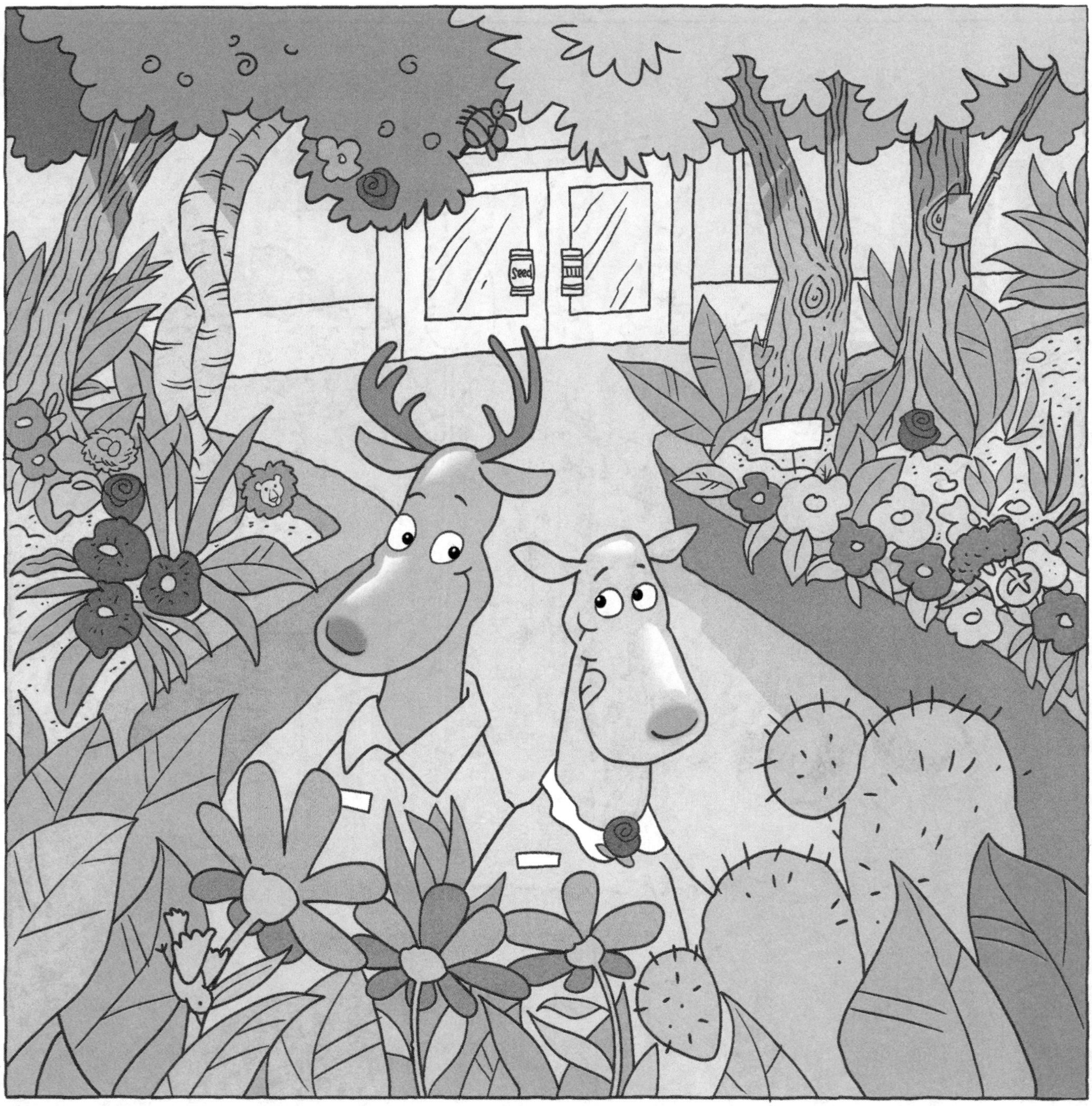

Find and circle the hidden pictures.

lion | bird | vegetables | nest | bee | shovel | watering can | seed packet

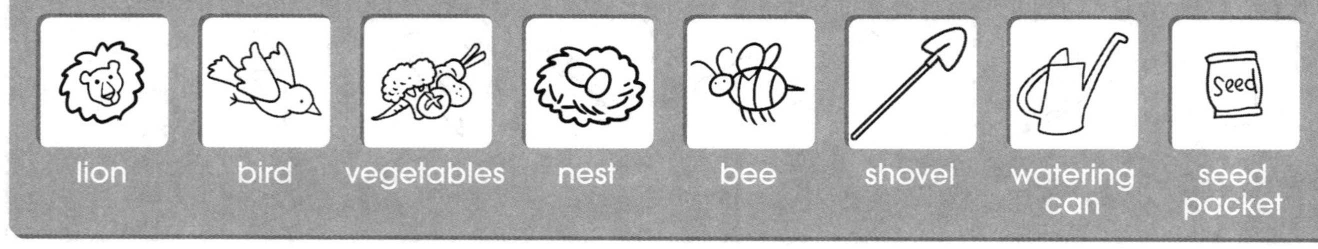

 ©School Zone Publishing Company

WORKS OF ART

Find and circle the hidden pictures.

Find 3 crayons

Find 1 jar of ink

Find 2 paintbrushes

Find 1 painting

Find 3 tubes of paint

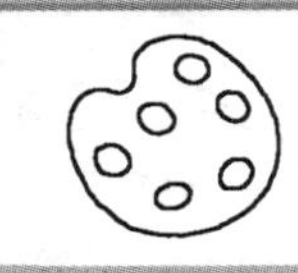
Find 1 palette

FUN AT THE BEACH

Find and circle the hidden pictures.

Find 2 visors

Find 3 pairs of sunglasses

Find 1 bucket

Find 3 sailboats

Find 1 bottle of lotion

Find 1 camera

©School Zone Publishing Company

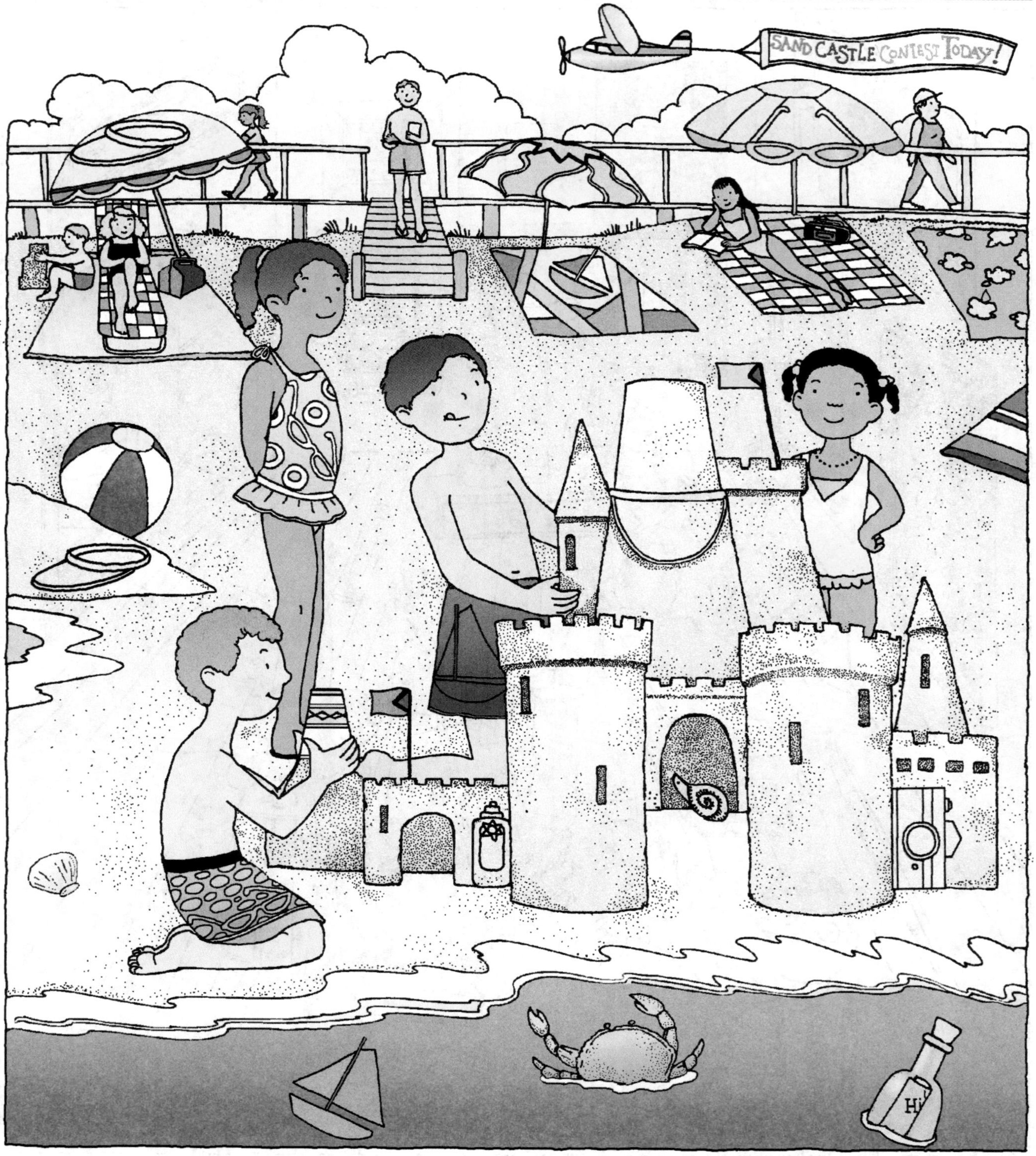

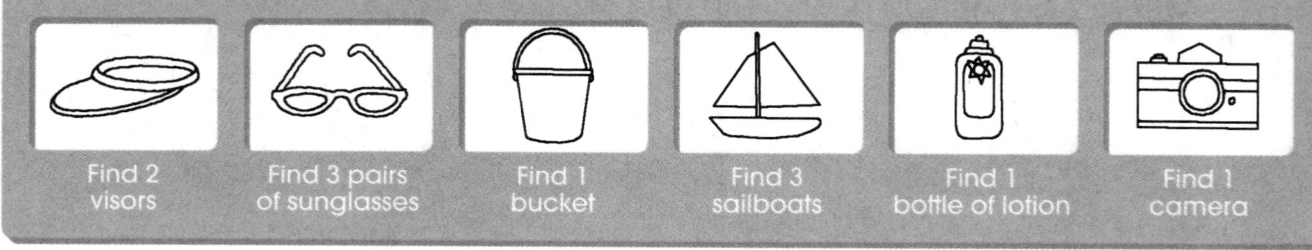

PAINTING FUN

Find and circle the hidden pictures.

©School Zone Publishing Company

A DAY AT THE SALON

Find and circle the hidden pictures.

ball   hot dog   jar   leaf   magnet   mallet   pig   shoe

©School Zone Publishing Company

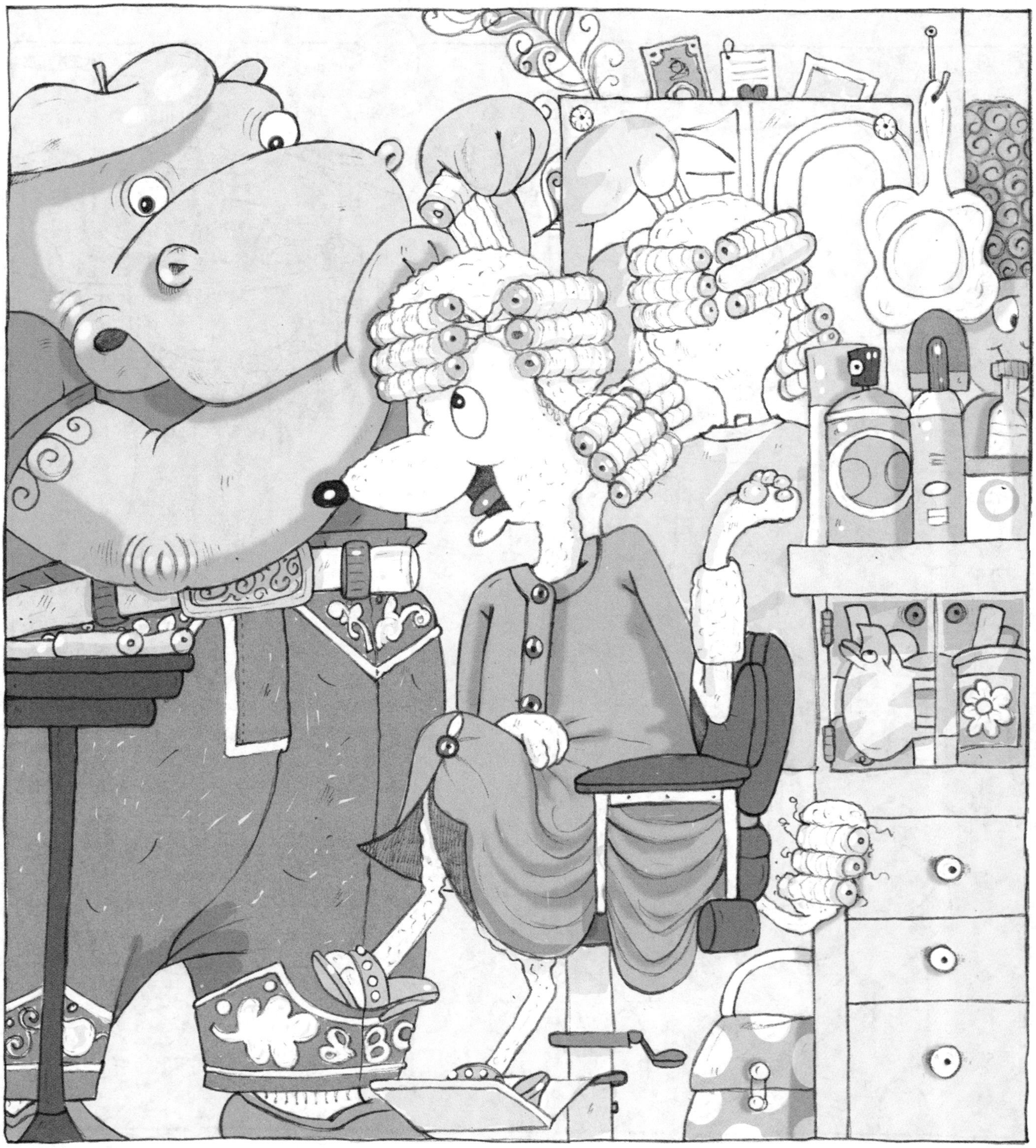

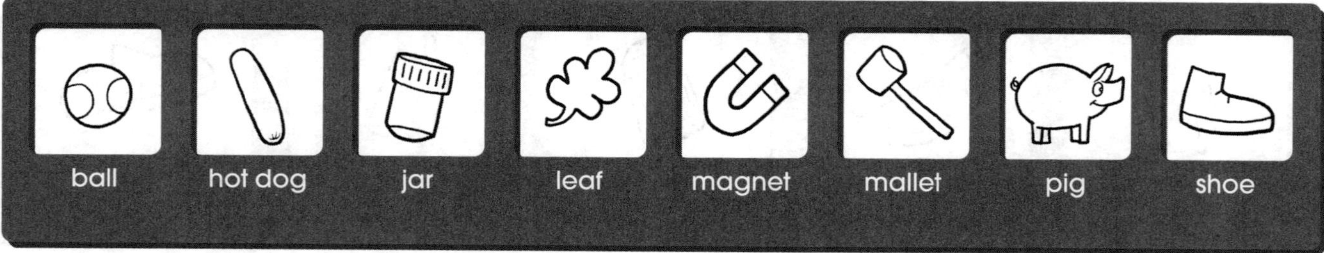

CANNONBALL!

Help Tommy Turtle get to the water.

TANGERINE TRACK

Follow the maze from start to finish.

 ©School Zone Publishing Company

JUST DUCKY

Solve each math problem. Find the first answer on the grid. Draw a line to the second answer. Continue drawing lines to connect the answers in order. When you have finished, a picture will be revealed.

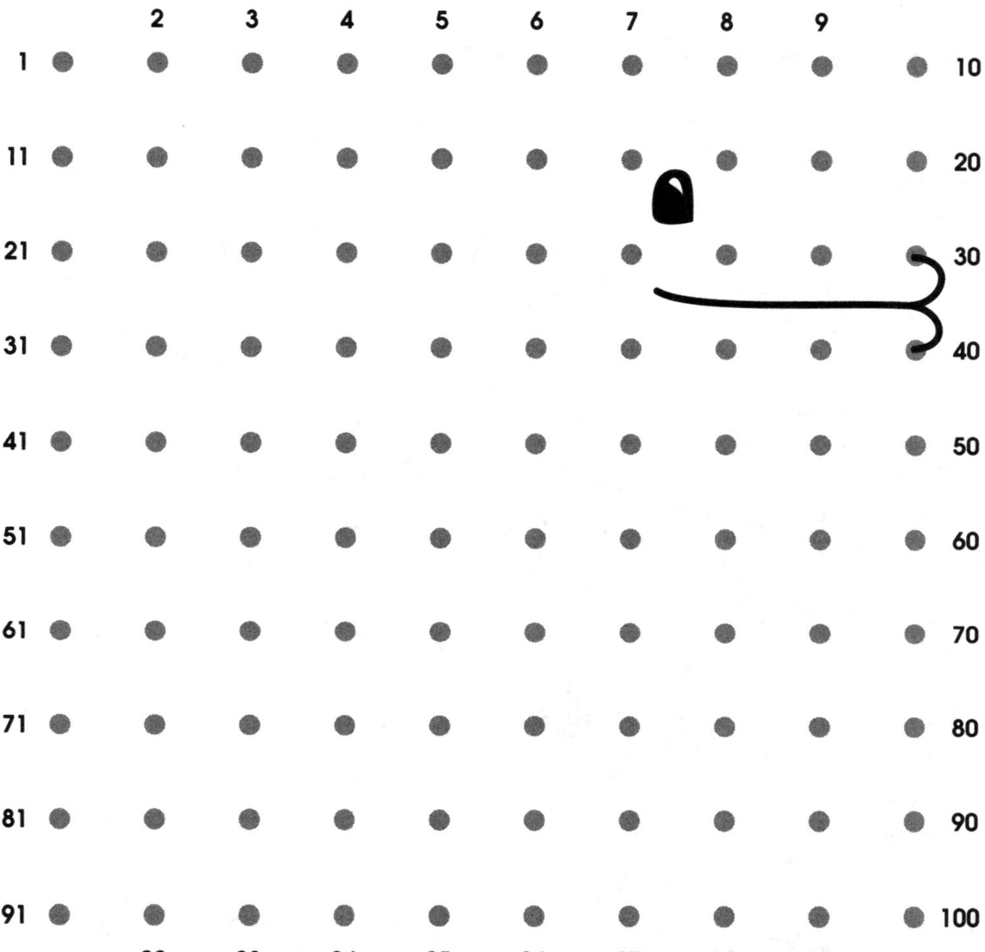

Line 1

1. 15 + 15 = ____
2. 36 − 7 = ____
3. 25 − 6 = ____
4. 4 + 4 = ____
5. 17 − 10 = ____
6. 1 + 5 = ____
7. 30 − 15 = ____
8. 10 + 15 = ____
9. 47 − 12 = ____
10. 17 + 17 = ____
11. 55 − 12 = ____
12. 50 + 2 = ____
13. 20 + 21 = ____
14. 55 − 4 = ____
15. 70 − 9 = ____
16. 32 + 40 = ____
17. 40 + 43 = ____
18. 93 − 9 = ____
19. 35 + 50 = ____
20. 43 + 43 = ____
21. 90 − 3 = ____
22. 100 − 12 = ____
23. 69 + 10 = ____
24. 84 − 15 = ____
25. 25 + 34 = ____
26. 24 + 24 = ____
27. 50 − 12 = ____
28. 27 + 12 = ____
29. 35 + 5 = ____

Line 2

1. 20 + 26 = ____
2. 75 − 30 = ____
3. 22 + 22 = ____
4. 73 − 20 = ____
5. 55 + 7 = ____
6. 85 − 12 = ____
7. 65 + 9 = ____
8. 100 − 25 = ____
9. 87 − 11 = ____
10. 55 + 12 = ____
11. 80 − 23 = ____

HIGH-FLYING HYGIENE

Color the picture below.

1 = pink 2 = green 3 = yellow green 4 = purple 5 = brown
6 = red 7 = blue green 8 = blue 9 = yellow 10 = orange

BLING!

Solve each math problem. Find the first answer on the grid. Draw a line to the second answer. Continue drawing lines to connect the answers in order. When you have finished, a picture will be revealed.

2 3 4 5 6 7 8 9

1 10

11 20

21 30

31 40

41 50

51 60

61 70

71 80

81 90

91 100

92 93 94 95 96 97 98 99

Line 1

1. 13 + 13 = ____
2. 25 − 8 = ____
3. 10 − 4 = ____
4. 25 − 20 = ____
5. 26 − 12 = ____
6. 35 − 10 = ____

Line 2

1. 50 − 25 = ____
2. 12 + 12 = ____
3. 66 − 33 = ____
4. 50 − 8 = ____
5. 25 + 27 = ____
6. 30 + 32 = ____
7. 85 − 13 = ____
8. 75 + 8 = ____
9. 100 − 6 = ____
10. 40 + 55 = ____
11. 80 + 16 = ____
12. 50 + 47 = ____
13. 44 + 44 = ____
14. 95 − 16 = ____
15. 59 + 10 = ____
16. 100 − 41 = ____
17. 40 + 9 = ____
18. 55 − 17 = ____
19. 35 − 8 = ____
20. 13 + 13 = ____

Line 3

1. 40 − 3 = ____
2. 15 + 21 = ____
3. 42 − 7 = ____
4. 15 + 19 = ____
5. 50 − 7 = ____
6. 43 + 10 = ____
7. 75 − 12 = ____
8. 25 + 48 = ____
9. 93 − 9 = ____
10. 65 + 20 = ____
11. 91 − 5 = ____
12. 70 + 17 = ____
13. 85 − 7 = ____
14. 33 + 35 = ____
15. 70 − 12 = ____
16. 24 + 24 = ____
17. 30 + 7 = ____

A BIRD KNOWN FOR ITS COLOR

Color the picture below.

1 = **red** 2 = **green** 3 = **yellow green** 4 = **orange** 5 = **brown**
6 = **pink** 7 = **blue green** 8 = **blue** 9 = **yellow** 10 = **black**

8 / 8	8 / 8	8 / 8	8 / 8	8 / 8	8 / 8	8 / 8	8 / 8	8 / 8	8 / 8	8 / 2	2 / 2	2 / 2	2 / 2	2 / 3
8 / 8	8 / 8	8 / 8	8 / 6	6 / 6	6 / 6	8 / 8	8 / 8	8 / 2	2 / 2	2 / 8	2 / 8	2 / 3	3 / 2	2 / 2
8 / 8	8 / 8	8 / 8	6 / 6	10 / 6	6 / 6	6 / 8	8 / 8	2 / 8	8 / 8	8 / 8	8 / 3	3 / 2	2 / 8	8 / 3
8 / 8	8 / 8	8 /	/	/ 6	6 / 6	6 / 6	8 / 8	8 / 8	8 / 8	8 / 2	3 / 2	2 / 8	3 / 3	2 / 2
8 / 8	8 / 8	10 / 10	/ 8	8 / 8	6 / 6	6 / 8	8 / 8	8 / 8	8 / 2	3 / 2	2 / 8	8 / 3	3 / 2	2 / 8
8 / 8	8 / 8	10 / 8	8 / 8	8 / 6	6 / 8	8 / 8	8 / 8	8 / 8	8 / 8	2 / 8	8 / 8	2 / 8	8 / 8	8 / 2
8 / 8	8 / 8	8 / 8	8 / 6	6 / 6	8 / 8	8 / 8	8 / 8	8 / 8	8 / 8	8 / 8	8 / 8	8 / 8	8 / 8	2 / 2
8 / 8	8 / 8	8 / 8	6 / 6	6 / 8	8 / 8	8 / 6	6 / 6	6 / 6	6 / 6	6 / 6	6 / 6	6 / 8	8 / 8	8 / 8
8 / 8	8 / 8	8 / 8	1 / 6	6 / 6	6 / 6	1 / 1	1 / 1	1 / 1	1 / 1	/	6 / 6	6 / 6	8 / 8	8 / 8
8 / 8	8 / 8	8 / 8	1 / 1	6 / 1	1 / 6	6 / 6	6 / 6	1 / 6	1 / 1	1 / 1	/ 6	6 / 6	6 / 6	8 / 8
8 / 8	8 / 3	8 / 8	8 / 1	1 / 1	1 / 6	6 / 6	6 / 6	6 / 6	6 / 6	1 / 6	6 / 6	6 / 6	6 / 6	8 / 8
8 / 3	8 / 8	8 / 8	8 / 8	1 / 1	1 / 1	6 / 6	6 / 6	6 / 6	6 / 6	6 / 6	6 / 8	8 / 8	6 / 8	8 / 8
2 / 8	8 / 8	8 / 8	8 / 8	8 / 8	1 / 1	1 / 1	1 / 1	1 / 1	1 / 8	8 / 8	8 / 8	8 / 8	8 / 8	8 / 8
2 / 3	3 / 8	8 / 8	8 / 8	8 / 8	8 / 5	5 / 8	5 / 5	8 / 8	8 / 9	8 / 8	9 / 8	8 / 9	8 / 8	8 / 8
3 / 2	8 / 8	2 / 8	8 / 5	5 / 8	8 / 8	8 / 8	5 / 5	8 / 9	8 / 9	9 / 9	9 / 9	9 / 9	9 / 8	8 / 8
2 / 8	8 / 2	2 / 8	8 / 8	5 / 5	8 / 5	8 / 8	5 / 5	8 / 9	9 / 9	9 / 9	9 / 9	9 / 9	8 / 9	8 / 8
7 / 2	2 / 2	7 / 7	7 / 7	7 / 7	7 / 7	5 / 7	5 / 5	4 / 7	4 / 4	4 / 4	4 / 4	4 / 7	4 / 7	7 / 7

©School Zone Publishing Company

EARL GREY, ANYONE?

Solve each math problem. Find the first answer on the grid. Draw a line to the second answer. Continue drawing lines to connect the answers in order. When you have finished, a picture will be revealed.

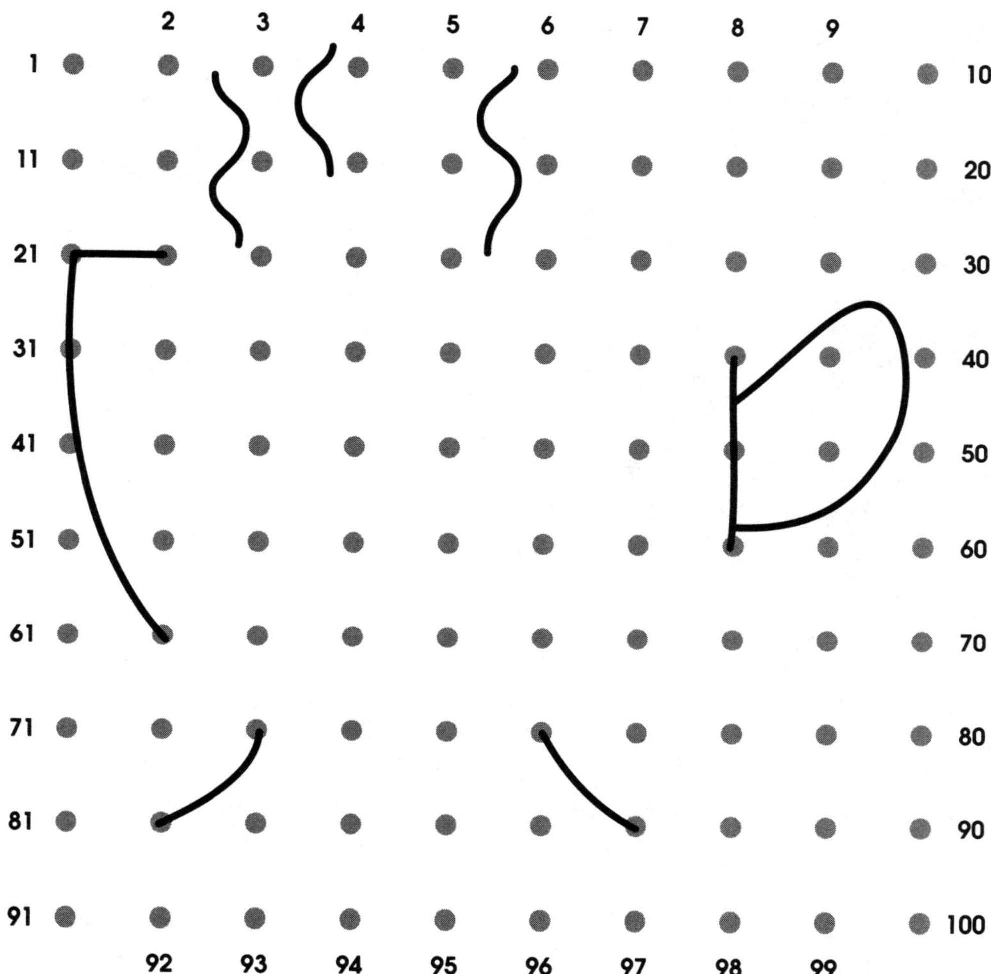

Line 1

1. 20 + 2 = _____
2. 15 + 8 = _____
3. 28 − 4 = _____
4. 30 − 5 = _____
5. 16 + 10 = _____
6. 30 − 3 = _____
7. 29 − 1 = _____
8. 45 − 7 = _____
9. 40 − 11 = _____
10. 15 + 15 = _____
11. 38 + 2 = _____
12. 25 + 25 = _____
13. 49 + 10 = _____
14. 50 + 8 = _____
15. 72 − 5 = _____
16. 69 + 7 = _____
17. 83 − 8 = _____
18. 70 + 4 = _____
19. 85 − 12 = _____
20. 52 + 10 = _____

Line 2

1. 60 + 22 = _____
2. 90 − 7 = _____
3. 70 + 14 = _____
4. 92 − 7 = _____
5. 60 + 26 = _____
6. 90 − 3 = _____

©School Zone Publishing Company

STAR POWER!

Follow the maze from start to finish.

FUN AT THE ARCADE

Find and circle the hidden pictures.

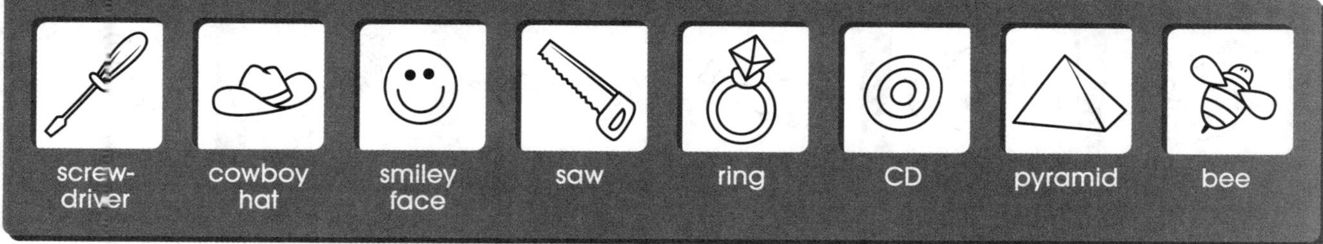

©School Zone Publishing Company

PETS ON THE LOOSE

Find and circle the hidden pictures.

Find 2 mice | Find 2 dogs | Find 1 whale | Find 1 snake | Find 1 brush | Find 1 palm tree

©School Zone Publishing Company

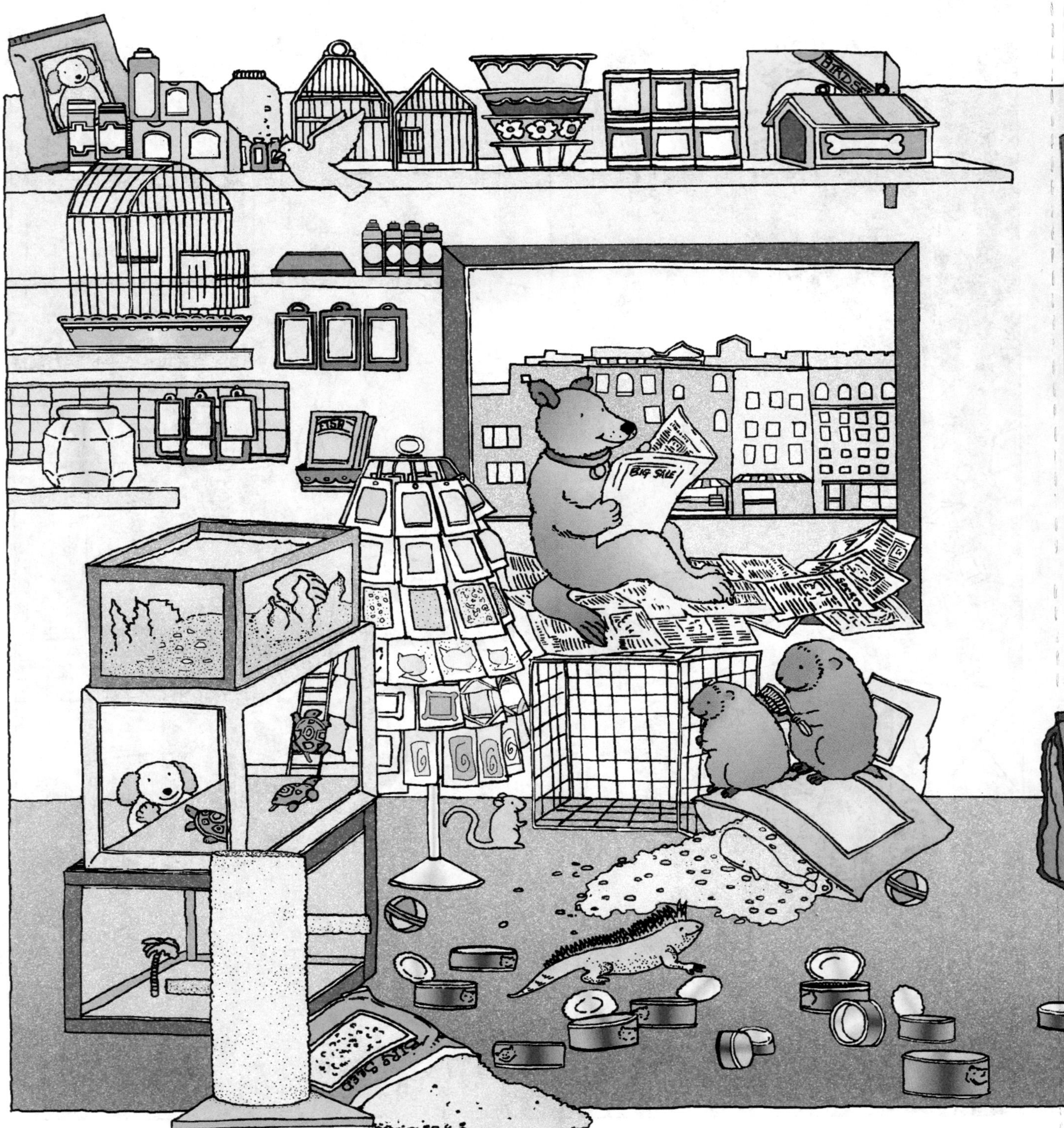

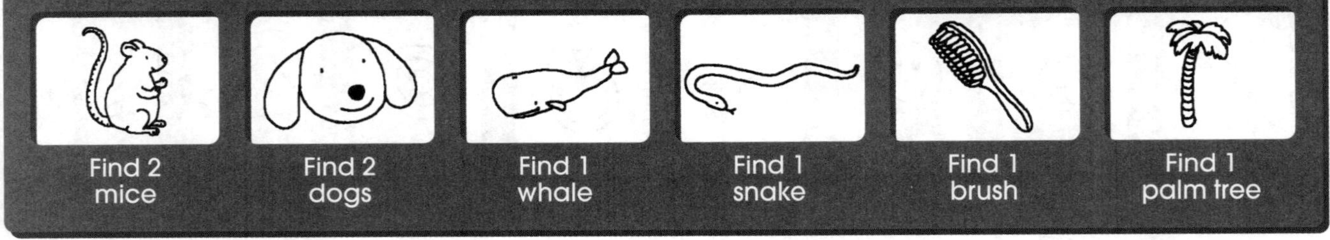

Find and circle the hidden pictures.

- Find 2 bones
- Find 3 birds
- Find 1 lizard
- Find 3 balls
- Find 1 castle
- Find 1 bird feeder

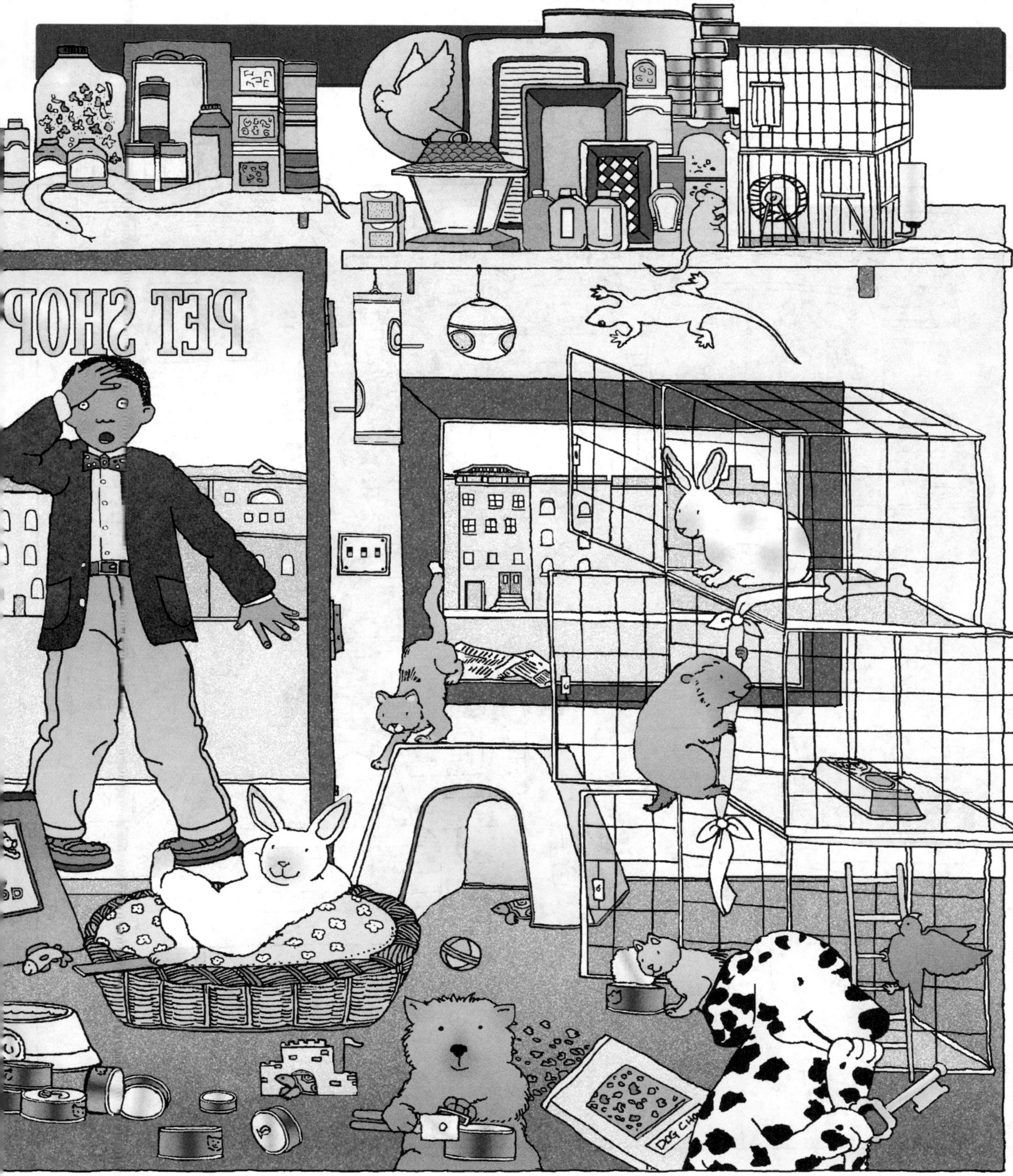

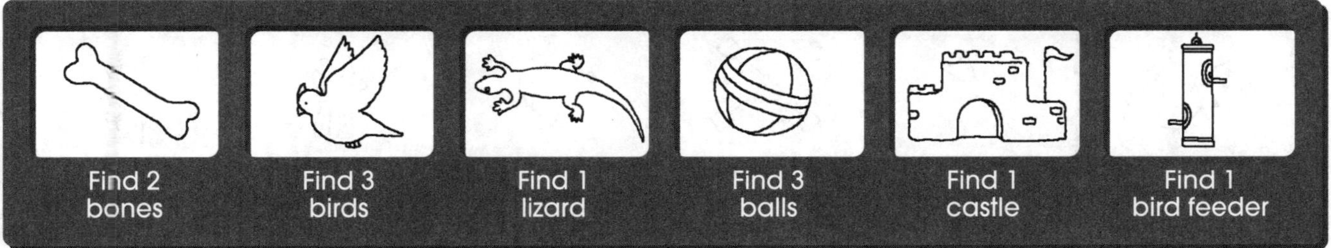

TURTLE CROSSING

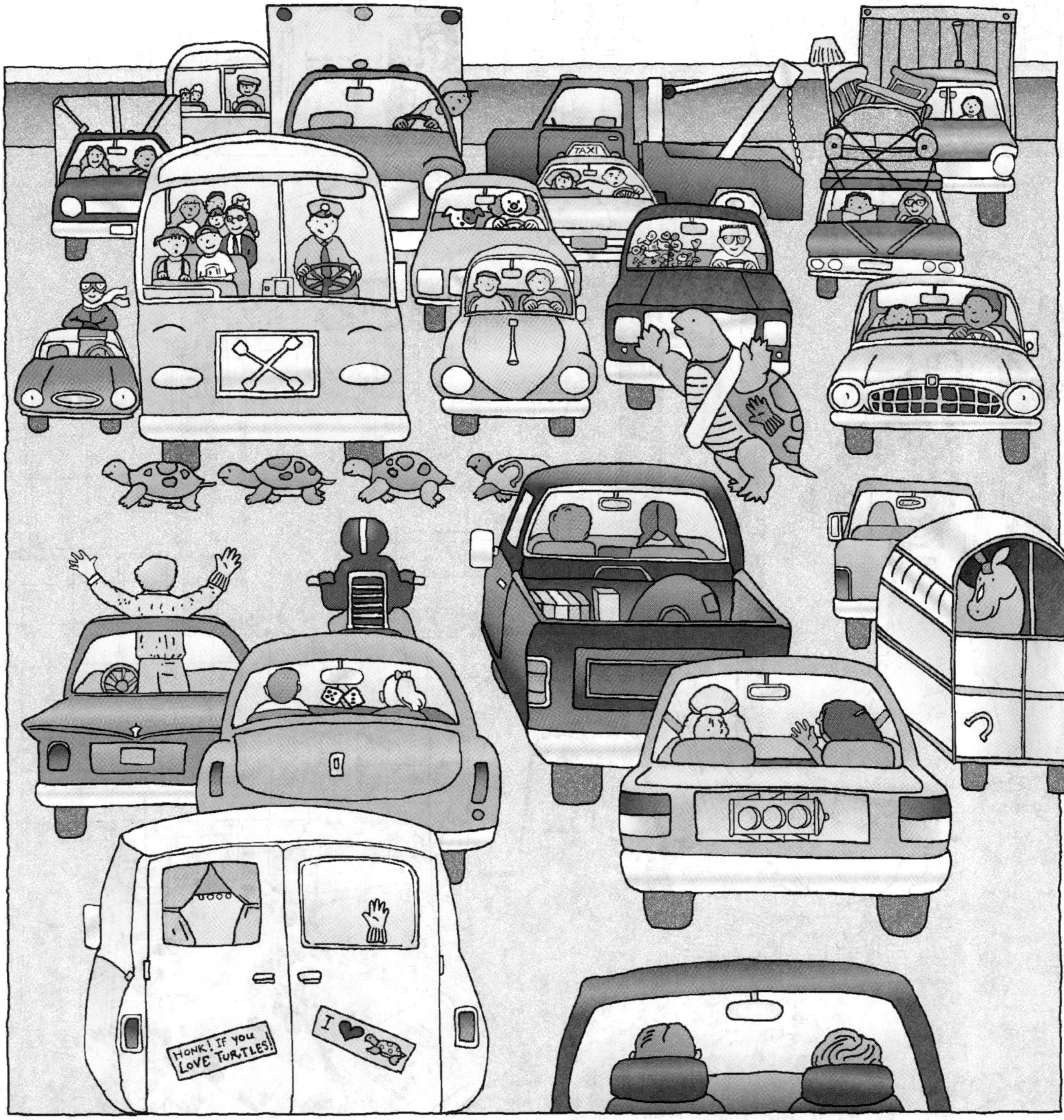

Find and circle the hidden pictures.

Find 1
pair of dice

Find 3
horns

Find 1
tire iron

Find 2
horseshoes

Find 3
gloves

Find 1
traffic light

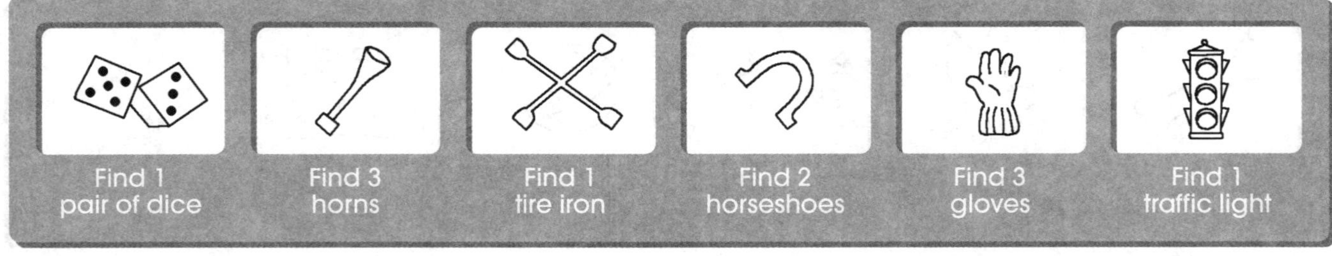

 ©School Zone Publishing Company

DOGGY NAP

Find and circle the hidden pictures.

plate

crayon

hand

peanut

sun

baseball bat

rose

salt shaker

SURF'S UP!

Find and circle the hidden pictures.

 ©School Zone Publishing Company

LIST FOR SANTA

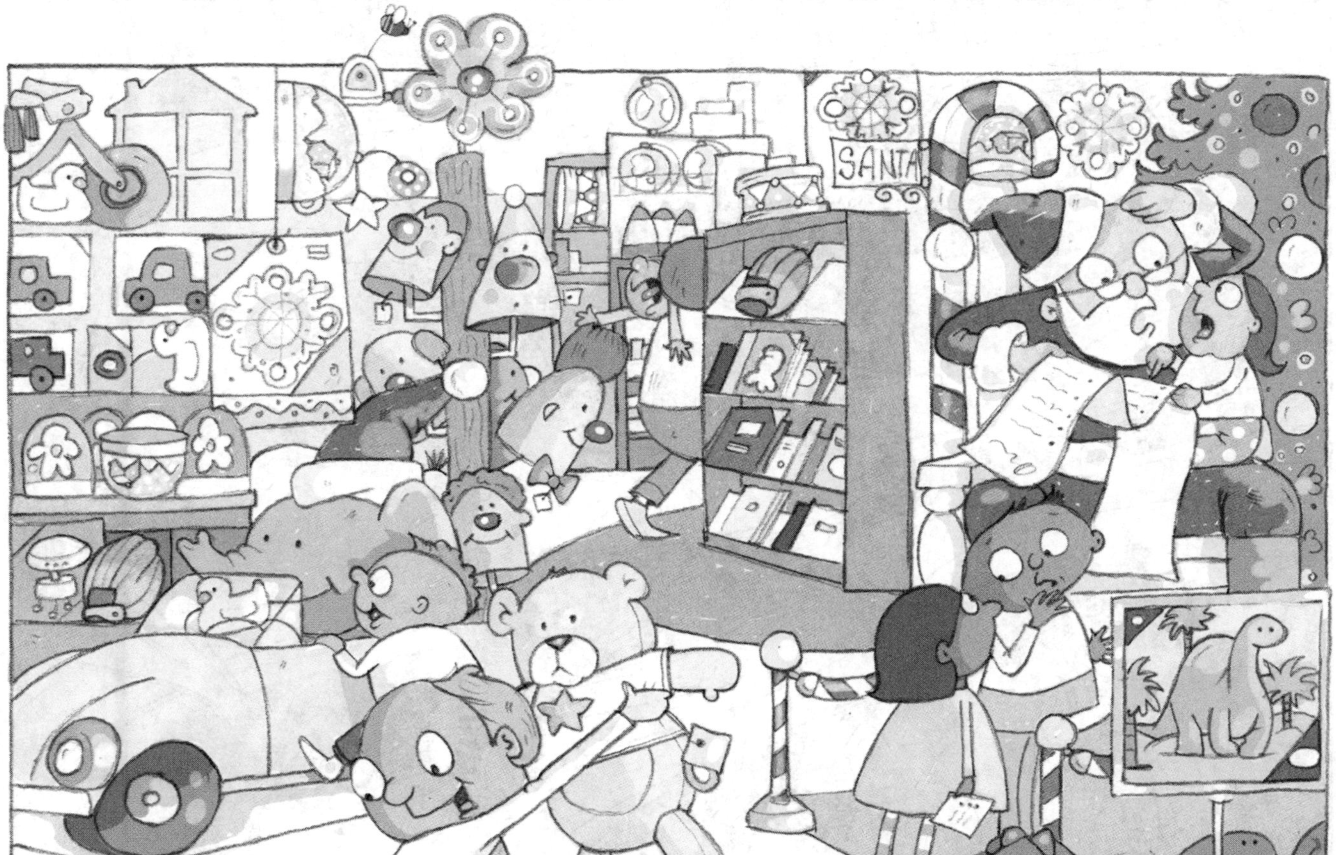

Find and circle the hidden pictures.

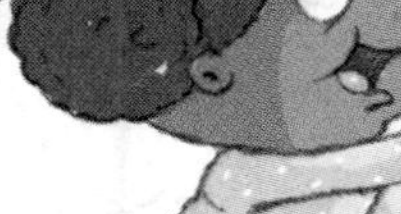
Find 1
turtle

Find 2
catcher's mitts

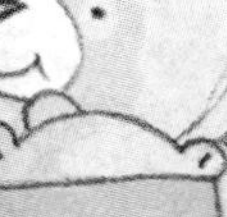
Find 3
drums

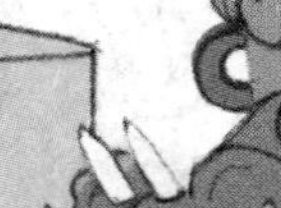
Find 4
ducks

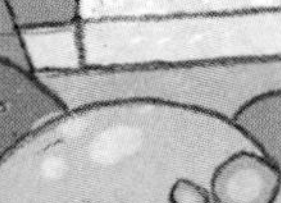
Find 5
snow globes

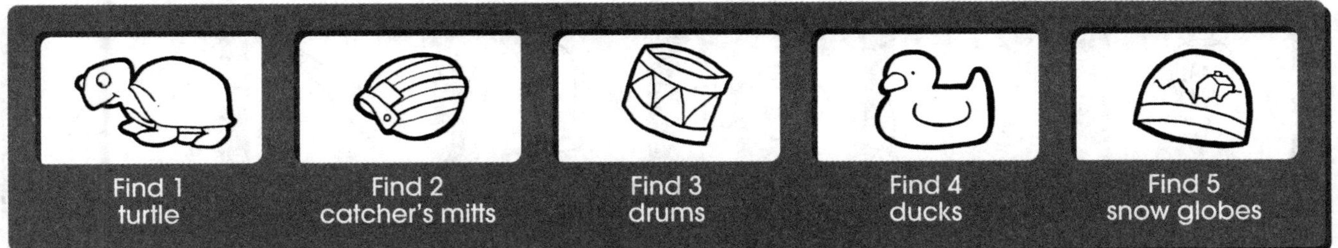

FINAL FRONTIER

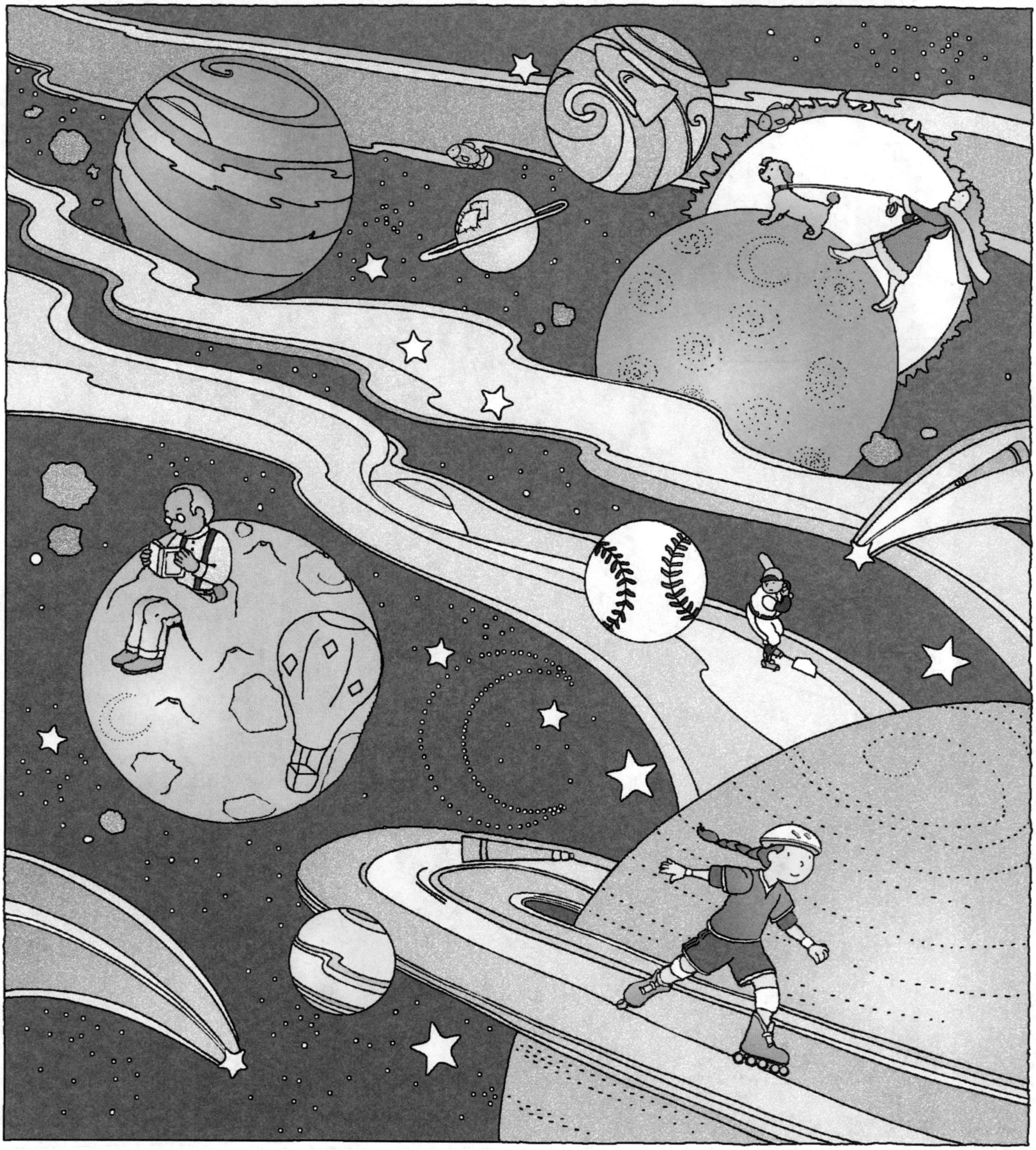

Find and circle the hidden pictures.

Find 1 hot air balloon

Find 3 moons

Find 2 fish

Find 1 space shuttle

Find 2 telescopes

Find 2 spaceships

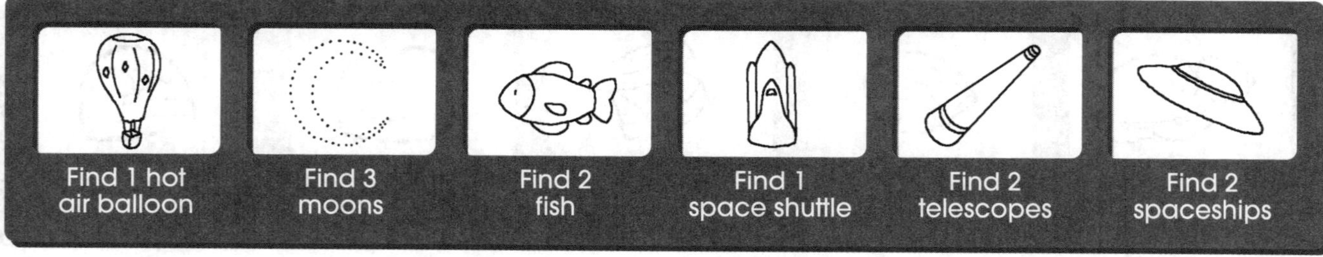

 ©School Zone Publishing Company

ELVES AT WORK

Find and circle the hidden pictures.

Find 3 frogs	Find 1 shovel	Find 1 hose	Find 1 wheelbarrow	Find 1 trowel	Find 2 watering cans

©School Zone Publishing Company

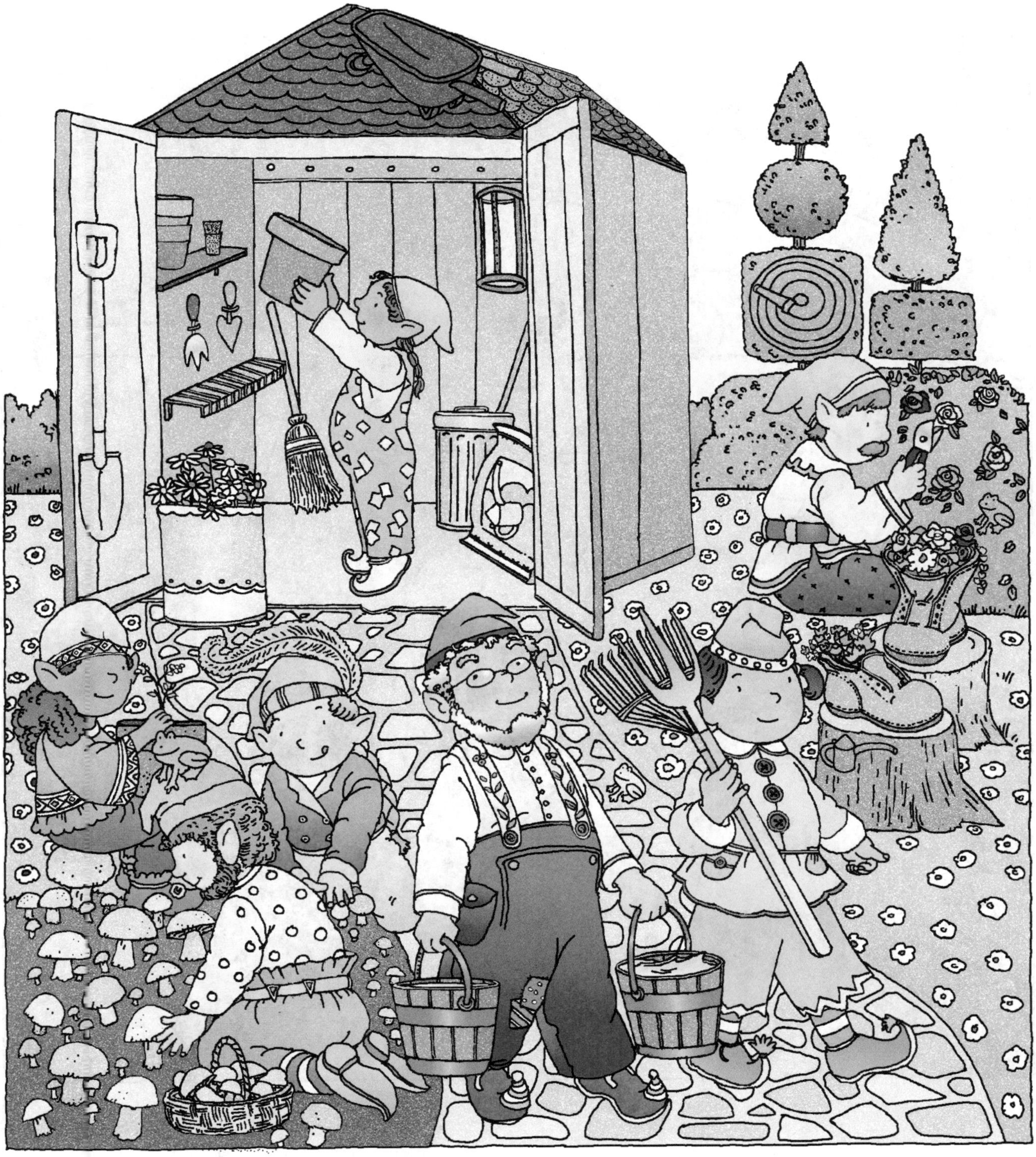

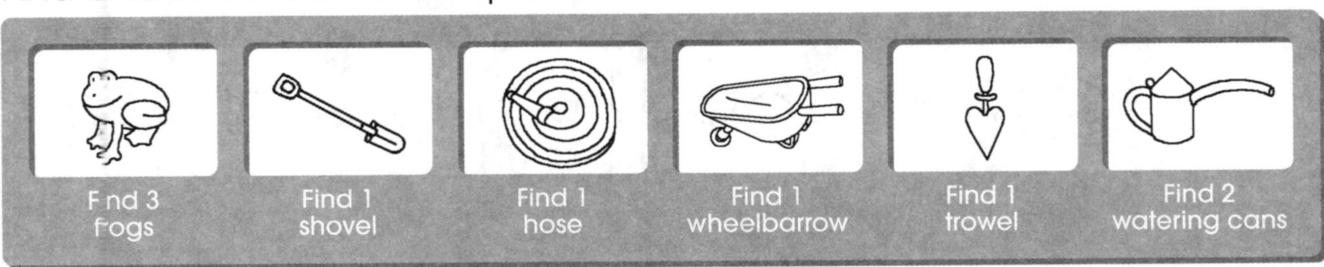

TIME FOR A CHECKUP

Find and circle the hidden pictures.

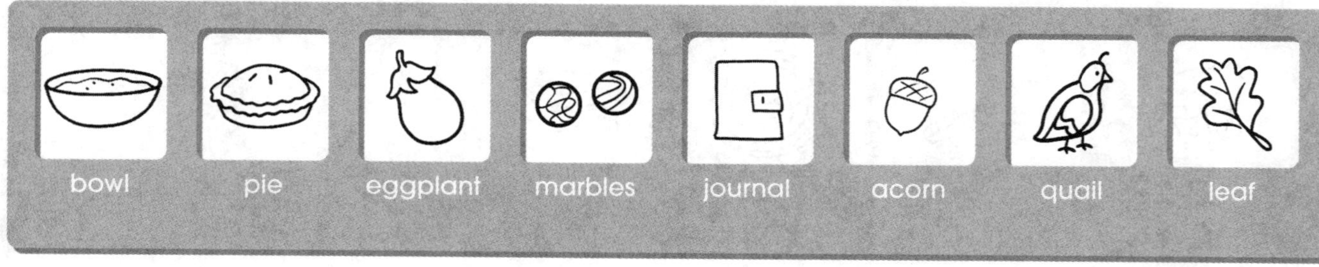

 ©School Zone Publishing Company

IT'S TEATIME!

Find and circle the hidden pictures.

lollipop | pumpkin | hamburger | gift | tape measure | flower | dress | cupcake

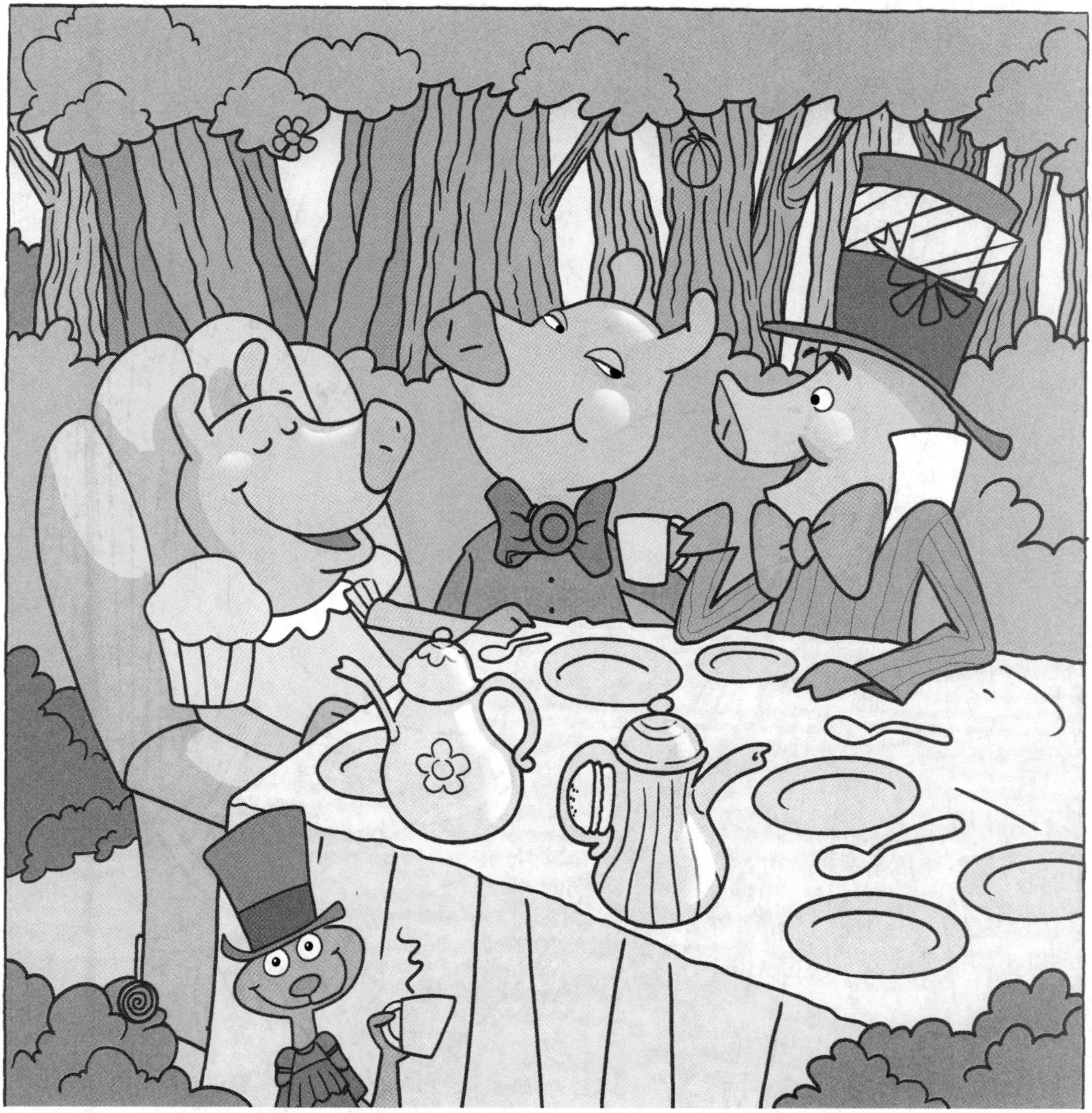

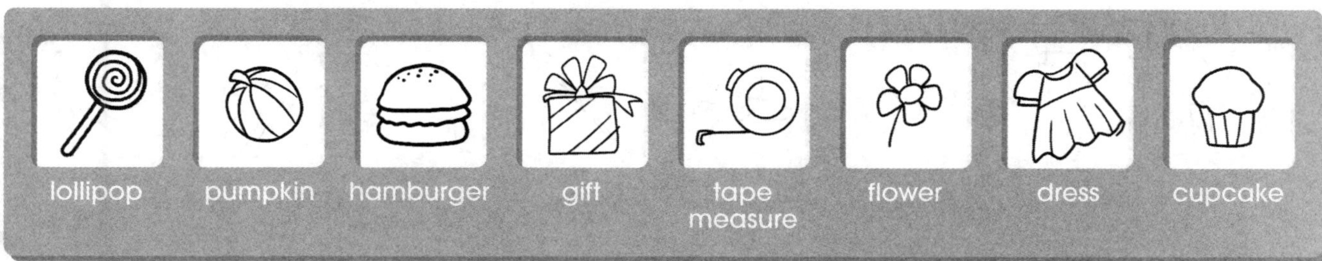

WATCH OUT FOR THAT TREE!

Find and circle the hidden pictures.

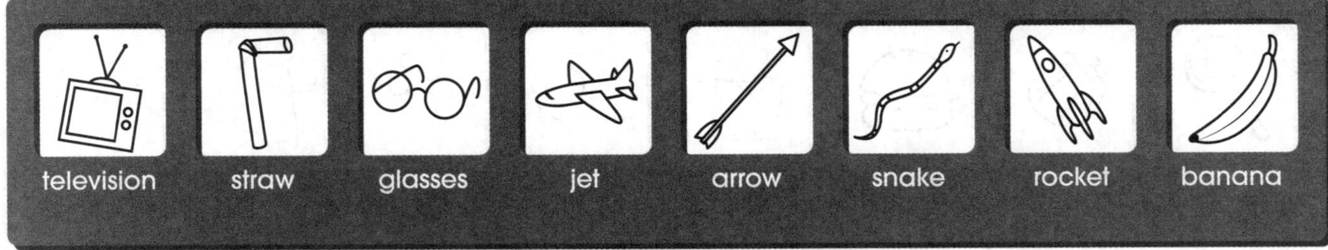

©School Zone Publishing Company

LUNCHTIME

Help the seagull get to the piece of popcorn.

©School Zone Publishing Company

AZTEC DESIGN

Follow the maze from start to finish.

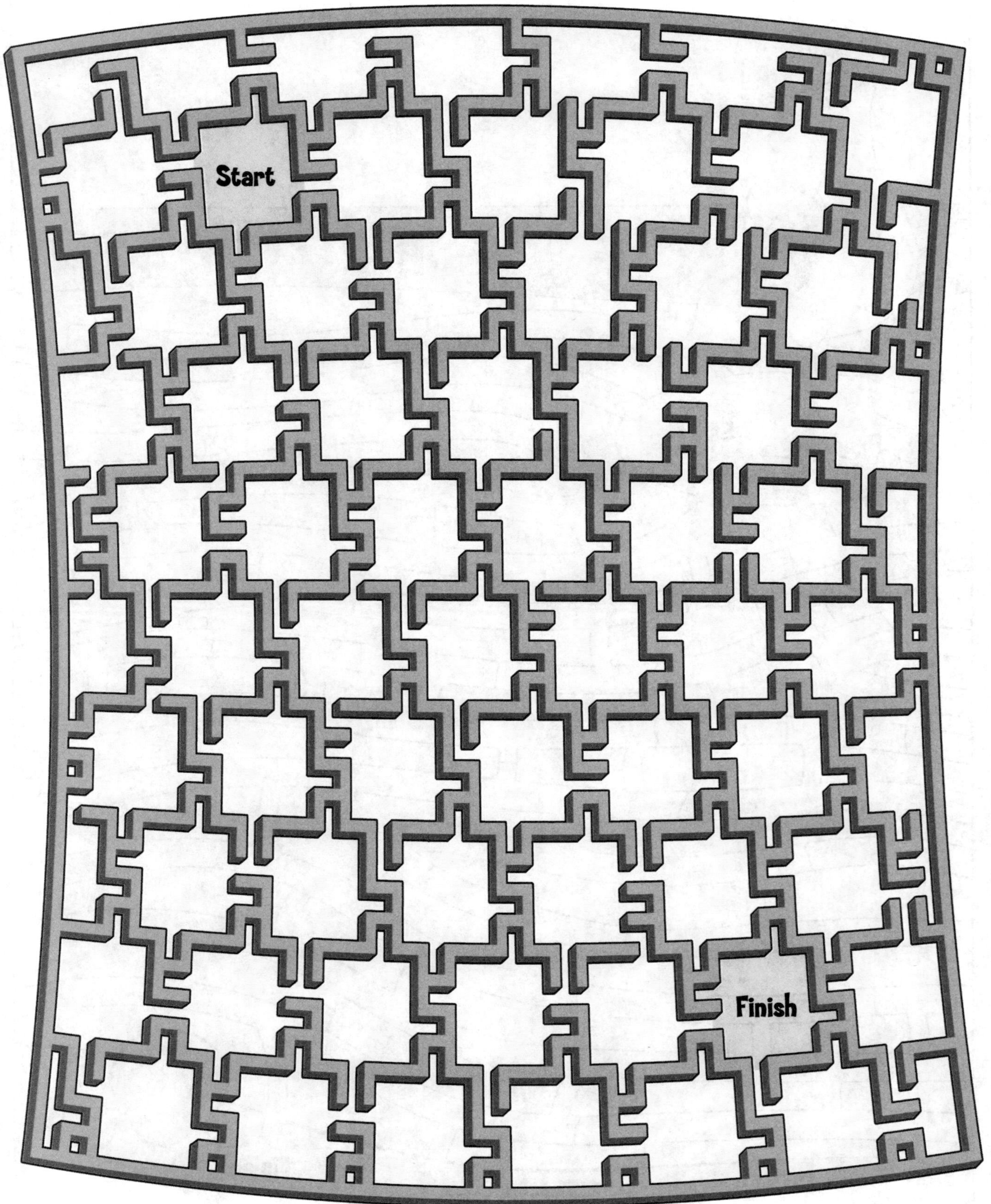

 ©School Zone Publishing Company

SUPERPOWERS, ACTIVATE!

Help the superhero rescue the cat!

RED ROVER'S RUN

Help the dog get to the fire hydrant.

 ©School Zone Publishing Company

WAVES OF WONDER

Follow the maze from start to finish.

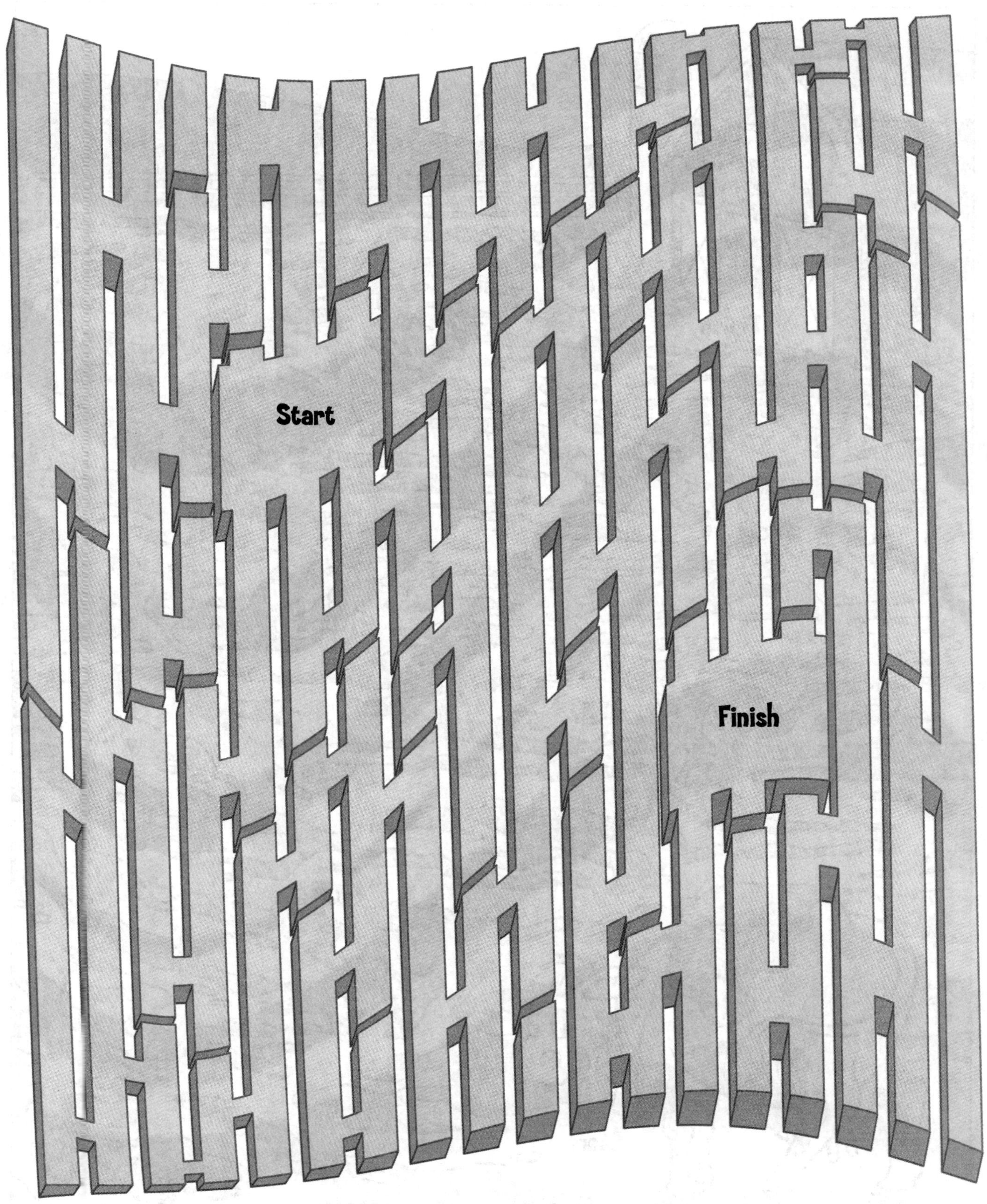

WATCH YOUR STEP!

Help the cow get to the barn.

 ©School Zone Publishing Company

CIRCLE OF FRIENDS

Follow the maze from start to finish.

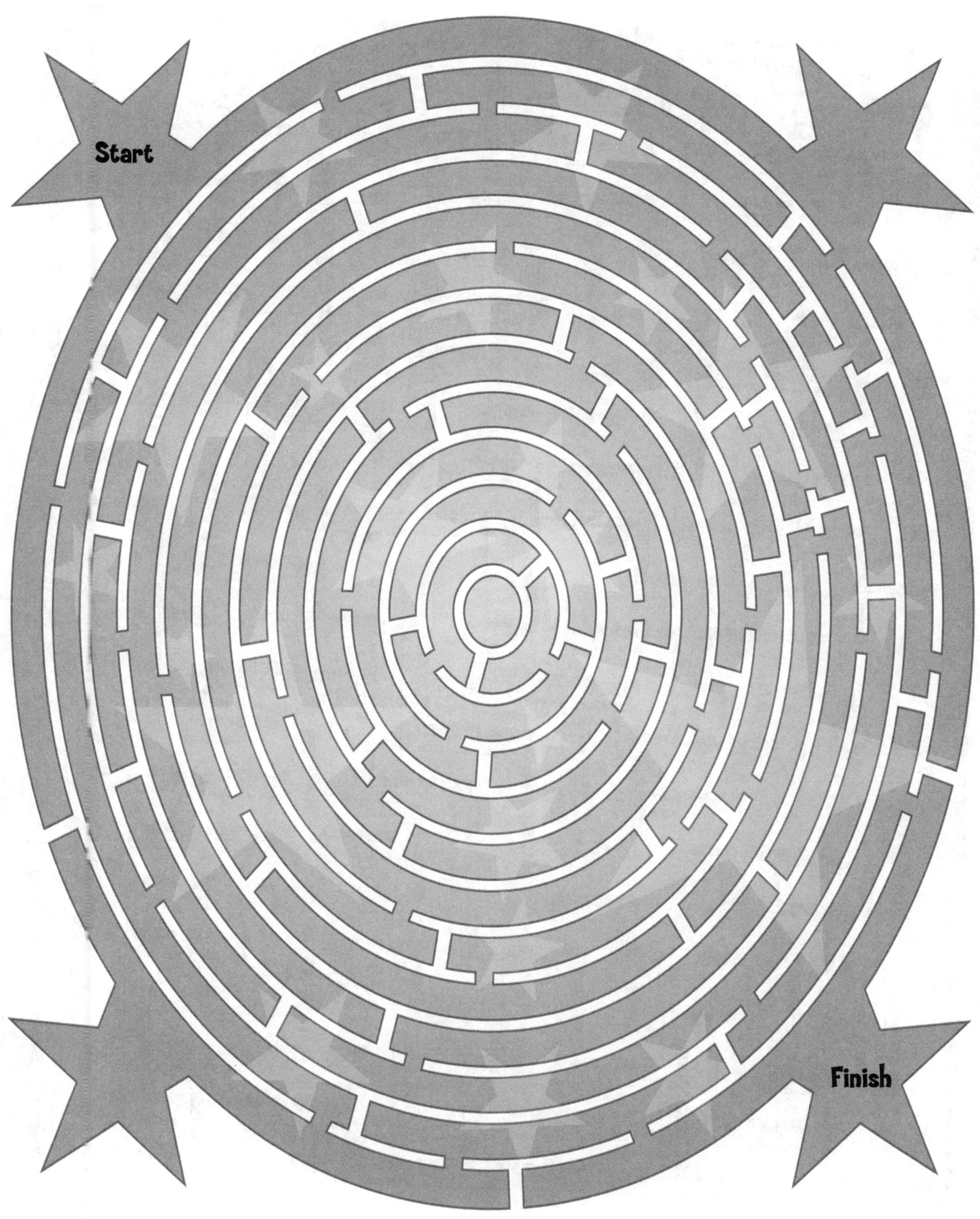

©School Zone Publishing Company

FIELD OF GOLD

Follow the maze from start to finish.

 ©School Zone Publishing Company

ALL ABOARD!

Find and circle the hidden pictures.

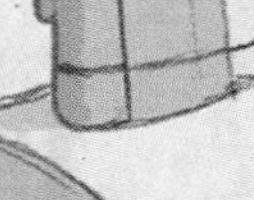

Find 1
cup

Find 2
megaphones

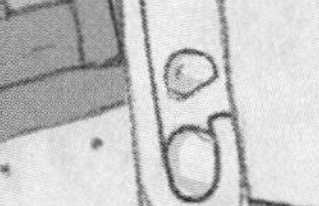

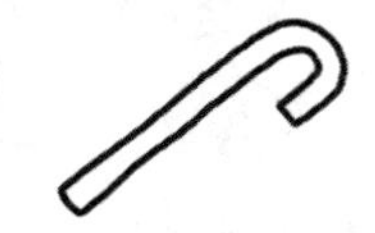
Find 3
canes

Find 4
mushrooms

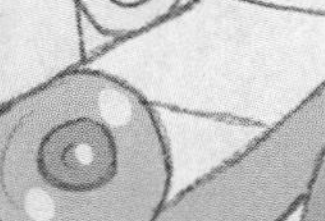

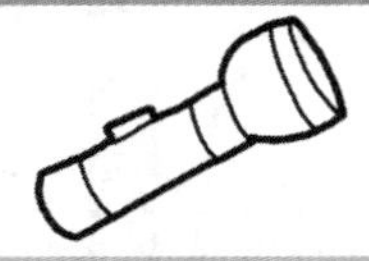
Find 5
flashlights

©School Zone Publishing Company

OPEN WIDE!

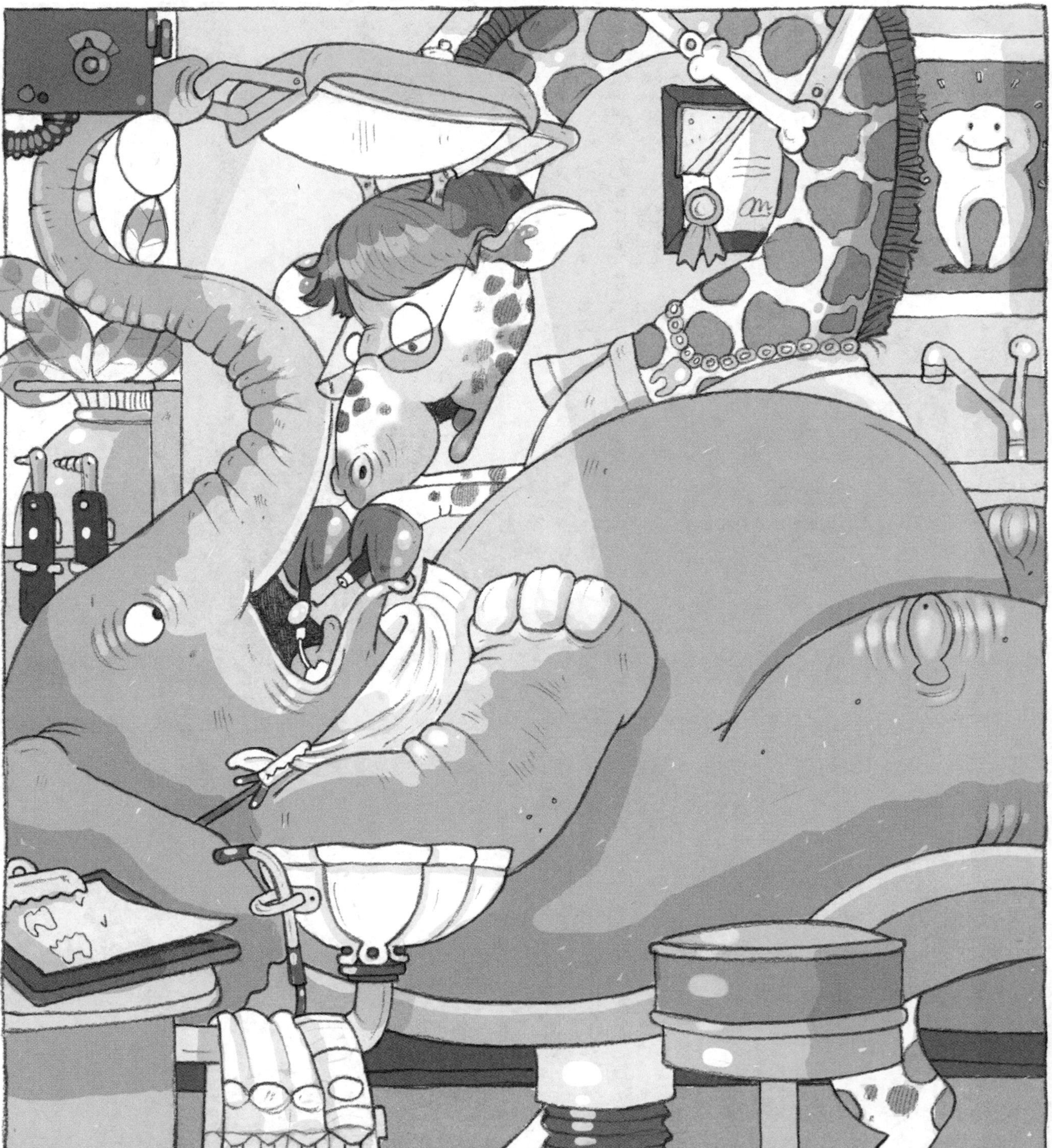

Find and circle the hidden pictures.

bell | bone | canoe | fish | net | sandwich | toothbrush | toothpaste

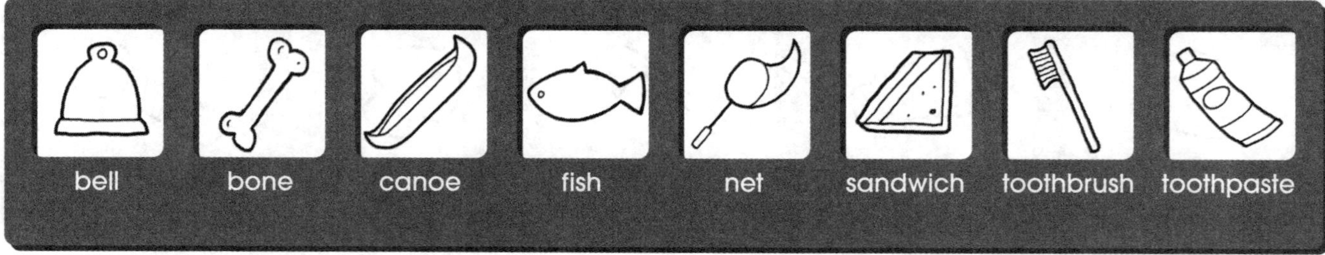

©School Zone Publishing Company

WHO WOULD TRY FLY PIE?

Find and circle the hidden pictures.

jellyfish parachute trophy flute star bowling pin jar flag

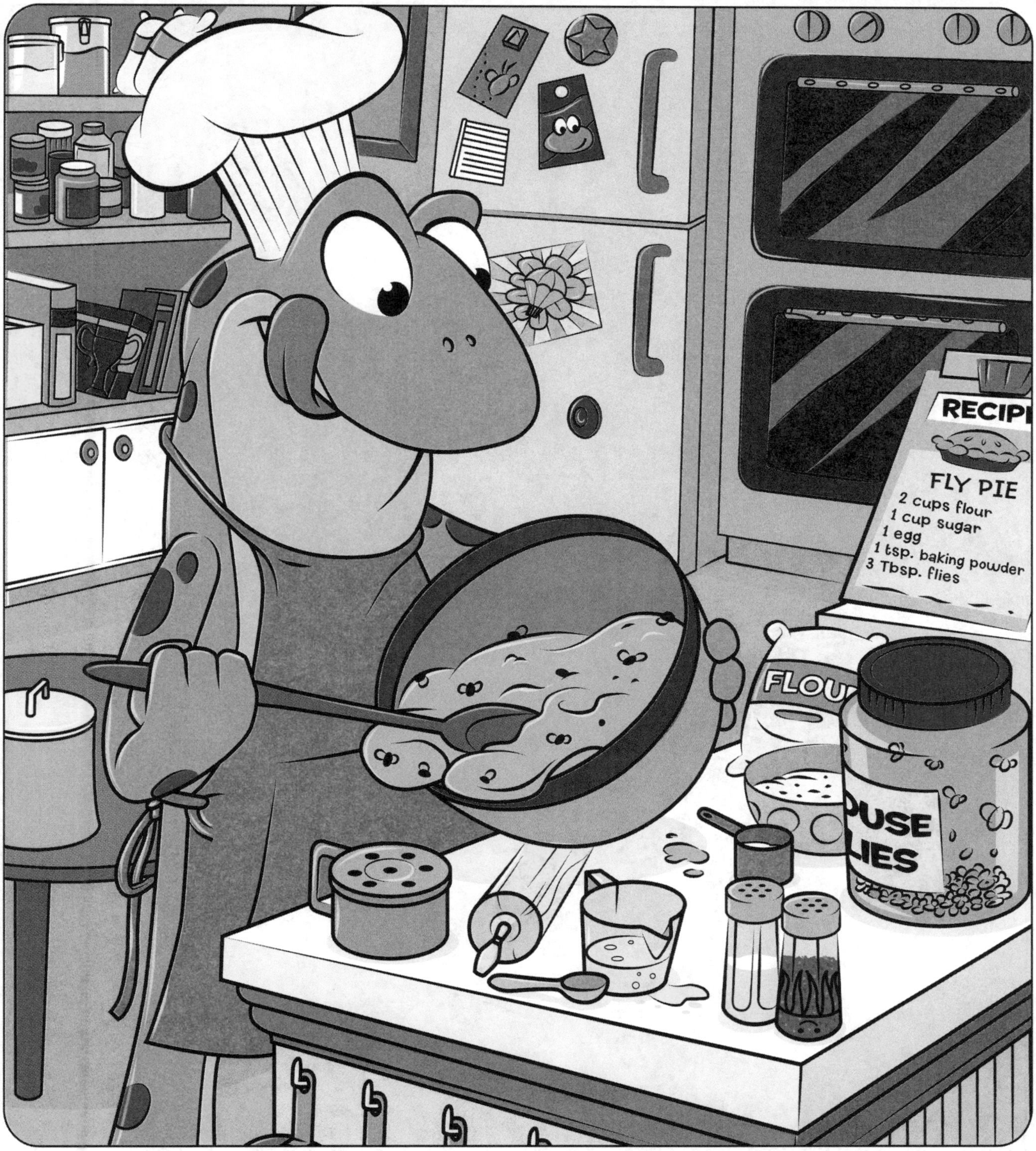

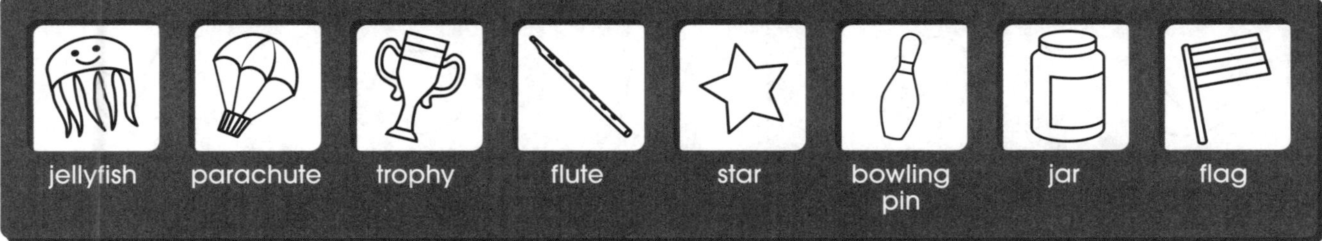

PENGUIN TRIO

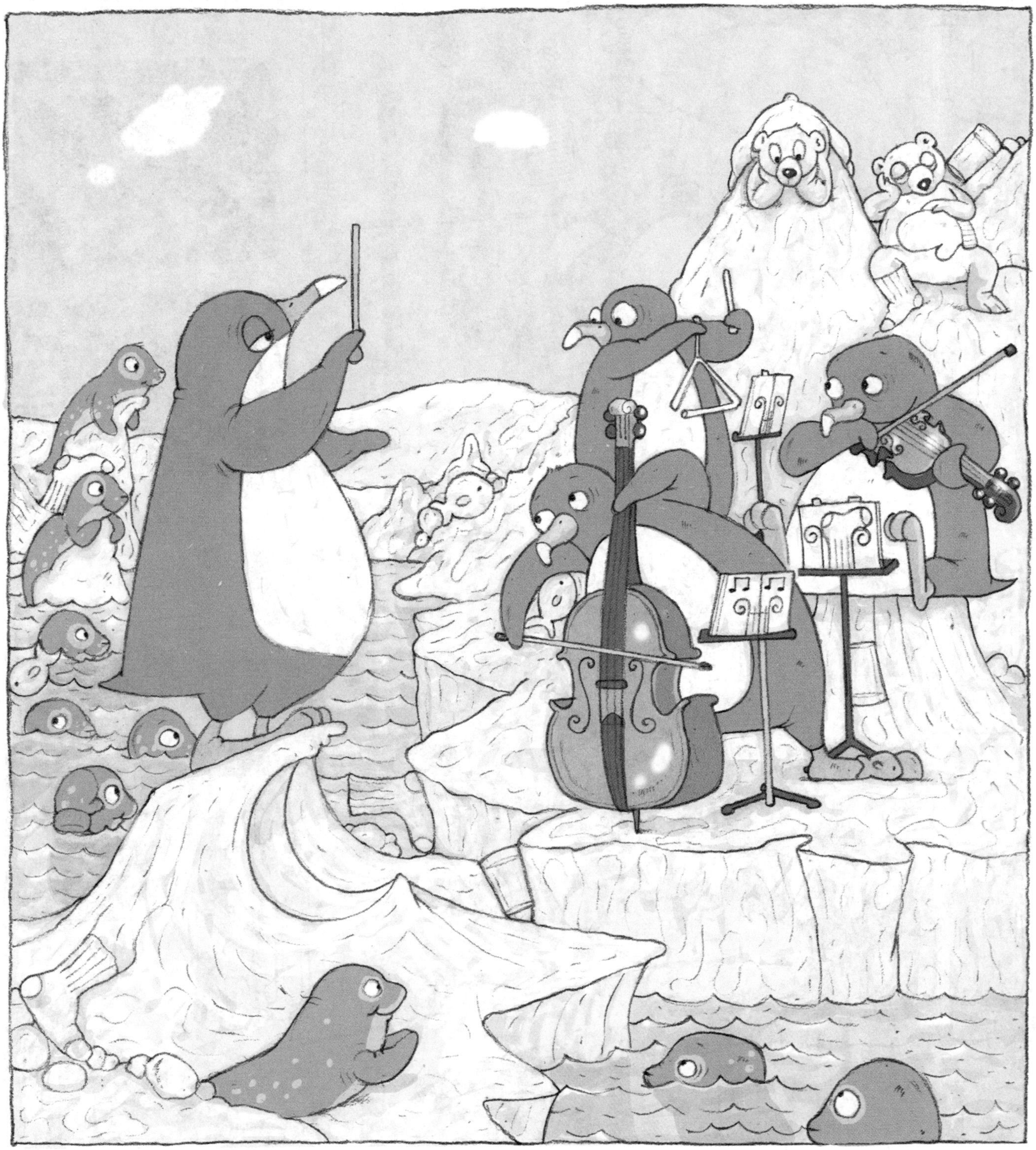

Find and circle the hidden pictures.

Find 1
moon

Find 2
mittens

Find 3
glasses

Find 4
fish

Find 5
socks

 ©School Zone Publishing Company

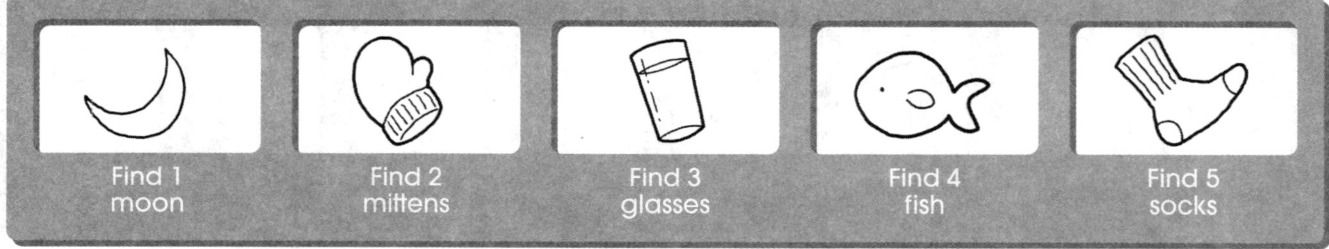

ROCK AND ROLL

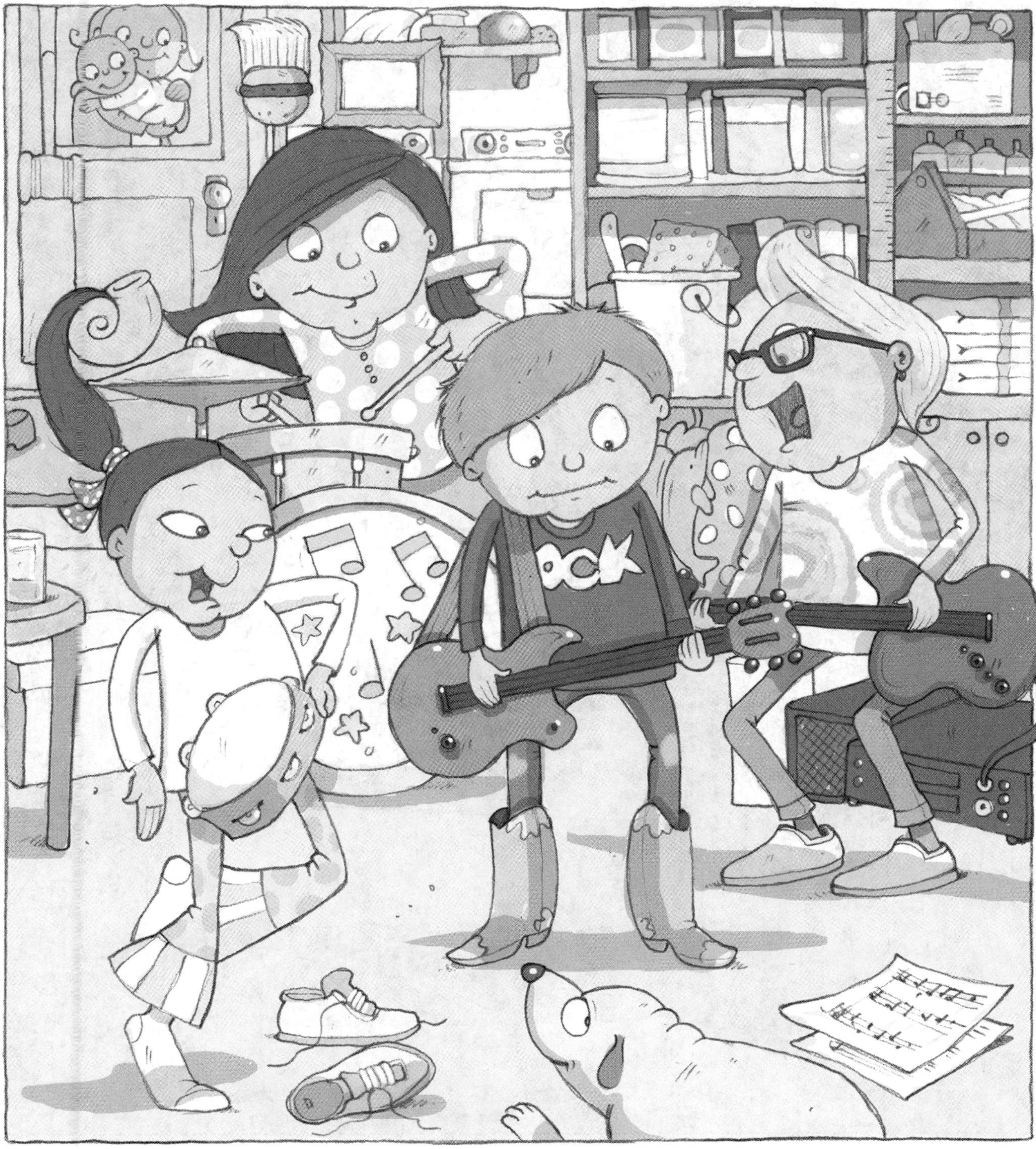

Find and circle the hidden pictures.

burger dolphin frame gavel hat mail ruler shell

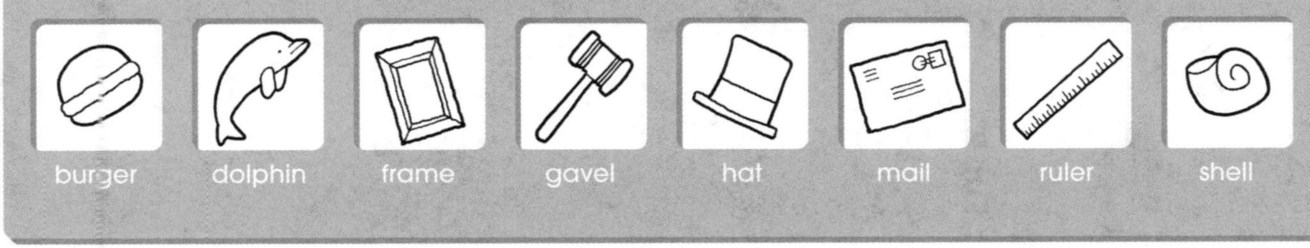

ABRACADABRA!

Find and circle the hidden pictures.

tuna can

magnifying glass

sailboat

pie slice

leaf

lemon

squirrel

pot

©School Zone Publishing Company

WORK ZONE

Find and circle the hidden pictures.

Find 1 paint can

Find 2 hammers

Find 3 paintbrushes

Find 1 box of nails

Find 1 tape measure

Find 3 saws

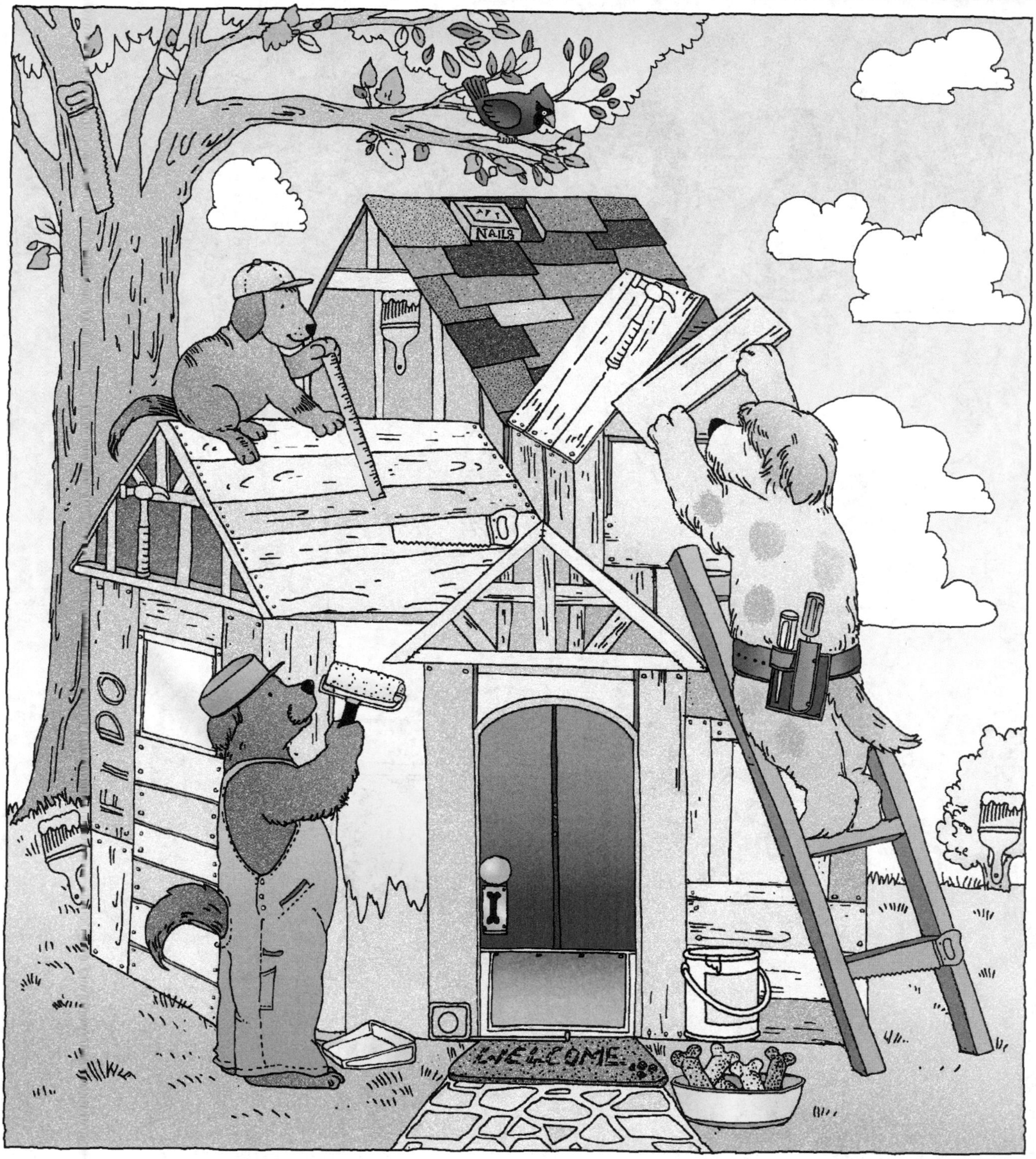

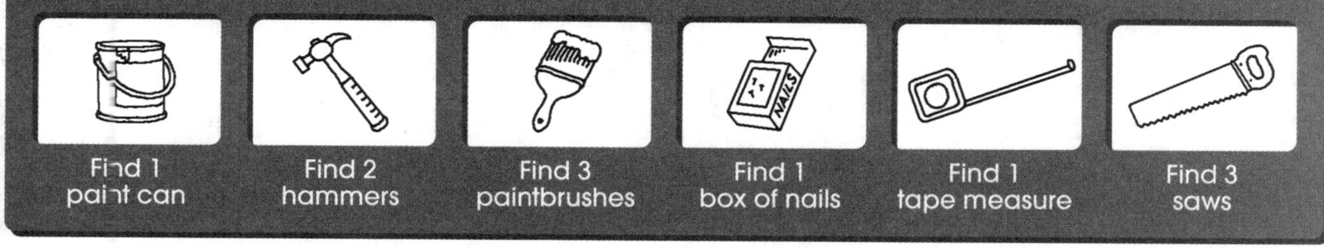

ANYBODY HOME?

Find and circle the hidden pictures.

©School Zone Publishing Company

DINORAMA!

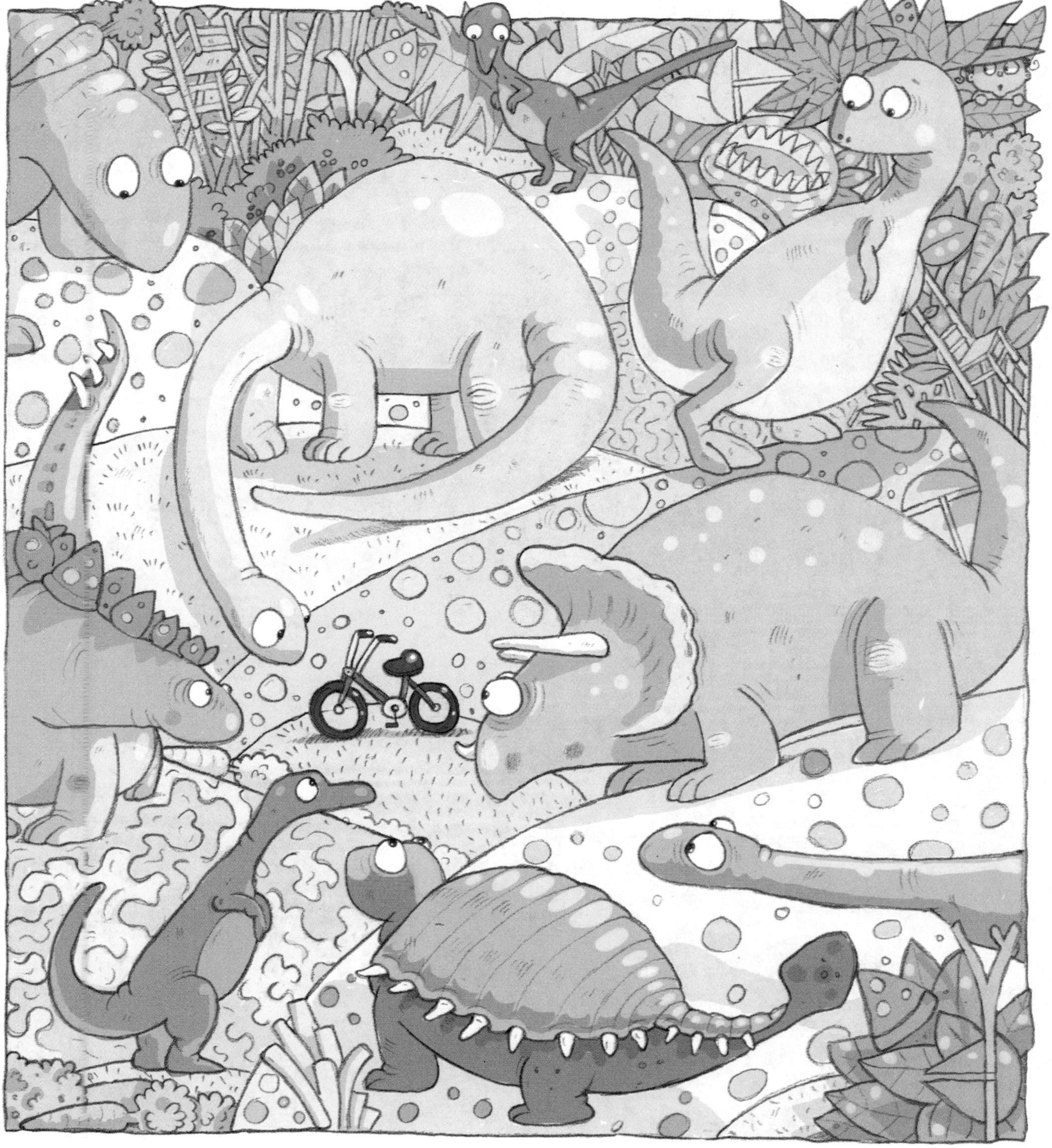

Find and circle the hidden pictures.

Find 1
girl

Find 2
chairs

Find 3
boats

Find 4
carrots

Find 5
pizza slices

9.5

Find and circle the hidden pictures.

©School Zone Publishing Company

WONDERFUL WEDDING

Find and circle the hidden pictures.

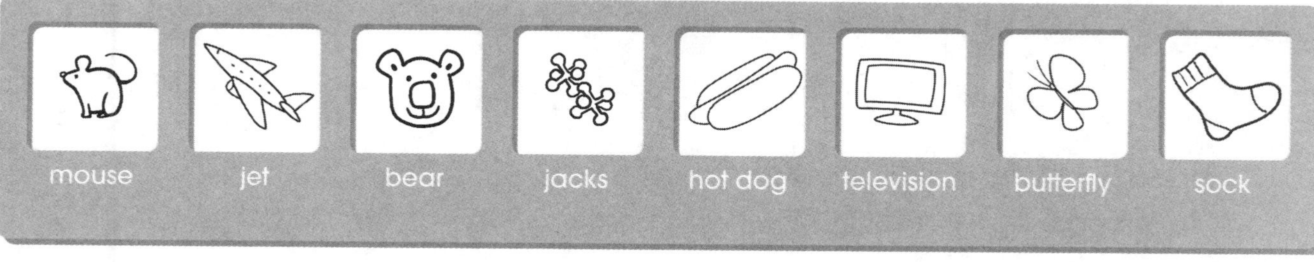

WHAT'S IN THE PICNIC BASKET?

Find and circle the hidden pictures.

©School Zone Publishing Company

TREE FORT

Look at the picture and find:

1 thing that plays music

2 things that you drink from

3 things that tell time

4 things that spin

5 things that fly

6 things that give light

BIRTHDAY PARTY

Find and circle the hidden pictures.

Find 4 candles

Find 2 party hats

Find 1 pair of shoes

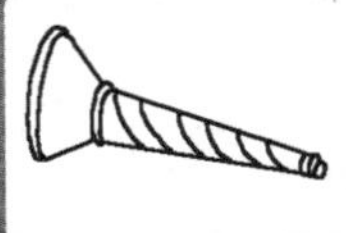

Find 2 horns

Find 1 pair of socks

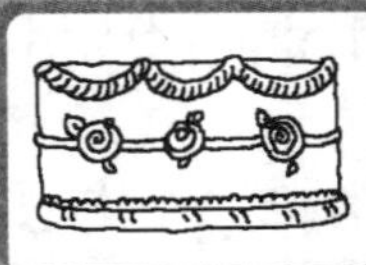

Find 1 cake

©School Zone Publishing Company

DINOSAUR SWAMP

Find and circle the hidden pictures.

Find 2 butterflies

Find 3 dragonflies

Find 1 turtle

Find 1 heron

Find 1 alligator

Find 1 crane

©School Zone Publishing Company

A NEW PERCH

Color the picture below.

1 = orange 2 = green 3 = yellow green 4 = pink 5 = brown
6 = blue green 7 = red 8 = purple 9 = black 10 = yellow

 ©School Zone Publishing Company

THE TALLEST LAND ANIMAL

Color the picture below.

1 = blue green 2 = green 3 = yellow 4 = yellow green
5 = orange 6 = **black** 7 = brown

1 / 1	1 / 1	1 / 1	1 / 1	1 / 7	7 / 7	1 / 1	1 / 1	7 / 7	7 / 1	1 / 1	1 / 1	1 / 1	1 / 1	1 / 1
1 / 7	7 / 7	7 / 7	1 / 1	1 / 1	7 / 7	1 / 1	1 / 7	7 / 7	1 / 1	1 / 1	1 / 7	7 / 7	7 / 7	1 / 1
1 / 1			7 / 7	1 / 3	7 / 7	3 / 3	3 / 3	3 / 3	1 / 7	7 /			7 / 1	1 / 1
1 / 1			/ 3	3 / 3	3 / 7	7 / 7	3 / 3	3 / 3	7 /			/ 1	1 / 1	1 / 1
1 / 1	1 / 1		3 / 3	3 / 7	7 / 7	7 / 3	7 / 7	7 / 7	3 / 3	/ 3	1 / 1	1 / 1	1 / 1	1 / 1
1 / 1	1 / 1	1 / 6	6 / 6	3 / 3	7 / 3	3 / 3	7 / 3	3 / 6	6 / 3	3 / 3	1 / 1	1 / 1	1 / 1	1 / 1
1 / 1	1 / 1	3 / 3	6 / 6	3 / 3	3 / 3	3 / 3	3 / 3	6 / 6	6 / 3	3 / 3	1 / 1	1 / 1	1 / 1	1 / 1
1 / 1	1 / 1	3 / 3	6 / 3	3 / 7	3 / 3	3 / 3	3 / 3	3 / 3	3 / 3	3 / 1	1 / 1	1 / 1	1 / 1	1 / 1
1 / 1	1 / 1	1 / 1	3 / 3	7 / 7	3 / 3	3 / 3	3 / 7	3 / 3	3 / 3	3 / 7	1 / 1	1 / 1	1 / 1	1 / 1
1 / 1	4 / 1	1 / 1	1 / 1	7 / 7	7 / 7	3 / 3	7 / 7	3 / 3	3 / 3	7 / 7	7 / 1	1 / 1	1 / 1	1 / 1
1 / 4	1 / 1	1 / 1	1 / 1	3 / 3	7 / 3	3 / 3	3 / 3	7 / 3	3 / 3	3 / 3	3 / 7	7 / 1	1 / 1	1 / 1
4 / 2	4 / 1	1 / 1	1 / 1	6 / 6	3 / 3	3 / 3	6 / 6	3 / 3	3 / 7	7 / 3	3 / 7	7 / 7	7 / 1	1 / 1
2 / 1	1 / 1	4 / 1	1 / 1	7 / 3	3 / 3	3 / 3	3 / 3	3 / 3	3 / 7	3 / 3	7 / 7	7 / 7	7 / 1	1 / 1
1 / 4	4 / 4	1 / 1	1 / 1	7 / 7	7 / 7	7 / 7	7 / 7	7 / 7	7 / 3	3 / 3	3 / 3	3 / 3	3 / 3	7 / 1
4 / 2	2 / 4	4 / 1	1 / 1	1 / 1	5 / 5	5 / 5	5 / 5	5 / 1	3 / 7	7 / 7	7 / 7	3 / 3	3 / 3	3 / 7
2 / 2	4 / 4	4 / 1	1 / 4	1 / 1	1 / 1	1 / 1	1 / 1	1 / 1	1 / 1	7 / 7	7 / 7	3 / 3	3 / 7	3 / 7
2 / 2	2 / 4	2 / 4	2 / 2	2 / 1	1 / 4	4 / 1	1 / 1	4 / 2	1 / 1	7 / 7	7 / 3	3 / 3	7 / 7	7 / 7

WAVE RIDER

Color the picture below.

1 = yellow 2 = **green** 3 = yellow green 4 = pink 5 = orange
6 = **brown** 7 = blue green 8 = **red** 9 = **purple** 10 = **blue**

HIGH-FLYING FUN

Color the picture below.

1 = **purple** 2 = **green** 3 = **blue**
4 = **red** 5 = **yellow** 6 = **orange**

3/3	3/3	3/3	3/3	3/3	3/3	3/3	3/3	3/3	3/3	3/3	3/3	3/3	3/3	3/3
3/3	3/3	5/5	5/4	4/4	4/4	4/2	4/4	4/4	4/3	4/3	4/3	3/3	3/3	3/3
3/3	3/3	5/4	1/1	1/1	1/2	2/2	4/4	4/3	3/3	3/3	3/3	3/3	3/3	3/3
3/3	3/3	4/4	1/1	1/2	2/2	2/2	4/4	3/3	3/3	3/3	3/3	3/3	3/3	3/3
3/3	3/3	4/4	1/2	2/2	2/2	2/2	4/4	4/3	4/3	4/3	3/3	3/3	3/3	3/3
3/3	3/3	4/2	2/2	2/2	2/2	2/2	4/4	3/3	3/3	3/6	3/3	3/3	3/3	3/3
3/3	3/3	4/4	4/4	4/4	4/4	4/3	4/4	4/4	4/3	4/3	6/3	6/3	3/3	3/3
3/3	3/3	4/4	4/3	3/3	4/3	3/3	3/3	3/3	3/3	3/3	3/3	6/3	6/3	3/3
3/3	3/3	4/3	3/3	3/3	4/3	4/3	3/3	3/3	3/3	3/3	3/3	3/3	6/3	3/3
3/3	3/3	4/3	3/3	3/3	3/3	3/3	3/3	3/3	3/3	3/3	3/3	3/6	3/3	3/3
	3/3	4/3	3/3	3/3	3/3	3/6	6/3	6/3	6/3	6/3	6/3	3/3	3/3	3/3
		/3	3/3	3/6	6/3	3/3	3/3	3/3	3/3	3/3	3/3	3/		
			3/3	3/6	3/3	3/3	3/3	3/3	3/					
			3/3	3/3	6/6	3/								
				3/	3/	6/	6/6							
								6/6	/6					
										6/				

MANATEE UNDER THE SEA

Color the picture below.

1 = **red** 2 = **green** 3 = **yellow green** 4 = **pink** 5 = **orange**
6 = **brown** 7 = **blue green** 8 = **blue** 9 = **purple**

 ©School Zone Publishing Company

ONE ROUGH REPTILE

Color the picture below.

1 = yellow green 2 = orange 3 = yellow
4 = **brown** 5 = green 6 = **black**

4/4	4/4	4/4	5/1	1/1	1/4	4/4	4/4	1/1	5/1	1/1	4/4	4/4	4/4	2/4
4/4	4/4	5/1	1/4	4/4	4/4	4/4	4/1	1/5	1/1	5/4	4/4	2/2	4/4	4/4
4/4	5/1	1/4	4/4	4/4	4/4	4/1	1/5	1/1	5/1	4/4	4/4	4/4	4/4	4/4
4/4	1/4	4/4	4/1	1/1	1/1	1/5	1/1	1/1	5/1	4/1	1/1	1/1	4/4	4/4
4/4	4/4	4/4	1/1	1/5	1/5	1/5	1/1	1/1	5/1	1/1	1/5	1/5	1/1	6/4
4/4	4/4	4/1	1/5	5/4	1/5	1/5	1/1	1/1	5/1	5/1	4/4	4/4	5/5	6/4
2/2	4/4	6/4	6/4	4/4	1/5	1/5	1/1	1/1	5/1	5/1	1/1	4/4	4/4	4/2
2/2	4/4	4/4	4/4	4/4	1/5	1/5	1/1	1/1	5/1	5/1	1/1	4/4	4/2	2/2
2/2	2/2	4/4	4/1	1/1	1/1	1/5	1/1	1/1	5/1	5/1	1/1	4/4	4/4	2/2
2/2	2/4	4/4	1/1	5/5	5/5	5/1	1/1	1/1	5/1	1/5	1/1	1/1	4/4	4/4
2/4	4/6	1/1	5/4	4/4	5/1	1/1	1/1	1/1	1/1	1/1	5/5	1/5	1/1	6/4
4/4	4/6	5/4	4/4	4/4	5/5	1/1	3/3	1/1	3/3	1/1	5/4	4/4	5/5	6/4
4/4	4/4	4/4	4/4	4/4	4/4	5/5	1/1	1/1	1/1	1/4	4/4	4/4	4/4	4/4
4/4	4/4	2/4	2/2	4/4	4/4	5/	1/1	1/1	1/1	4/4	4/4	4/2	4/4	2/2
2/4	4/4	4/4	4/2	4/4	4/4	5/	1/6	1/1	1/6	4/4	4/4	4/2	4/2	2/2
2/2	4/4	4/4	2/2	4/4	4/4	5/	1/1	1/1	1/1	4/4	4/2	2/2	2/2	2/4
2/2	2/2	4/4	2/2	2/2	4/4	4/4	/4	/4	/4	4/2	2/2	2/4	2/4	2/2

HIPPO TALK

Color the picture below.

1 = pink   2 = green   3 = yellow green   4 = orange   5 = brown
6 = blue green   7 = red   8 = purple   9 = yellow   10 = blue

©School Zone Publishing Company

LITTLE BUZZER

Color the picture below.

1 = blue green 2 = green 3 = yellow 4 = yellow green
5 = blue 6 = **black** 7 = pink

4/4	4/4	4/2	4/4	4/	4/4	4/2	2/4	4/4	4/2	2/4	4/4	4/4	4/4	4/4
4/4	2/2	4/4	4/	/	/	4/4	4/4	4/2	4/4	4/4	4/6	4/4	4/4	4/2
2/2	4/4	4/4	/	/	/	4/	/	4/4	4/4	4/6	6/6	4/4	4/2	2/4
2/4	4/4	4/4	/	/	/	/	/4	4/6	6/3	3/3	6/6	4/4	2/4	4/4
4/4	4/4	2/4	/	/	/	/3	3/3	3/3	3/3	3/3	3/	/	/	/
4/2	4/2	4/4	4/4	/	/	3/6	3/6	3/6	3/	/	/	/	/	/
2/2	2/4	4/4	4/4	4/4	/	6/6	6/6	6/	/	/	/	/	/	/4
2/4	4/4	4/4	4/4	4/6	6/6	6/3	6/3	6/	/	/6	3/3	6/6	4/4	4/4
4/4	4/4	4/4	4/6	3/3	3/3	3/3	3/3	/3	6/6	6/6	6/4	4/4	6/4	4/4
4/4	4/6	6/4	4/4	3/6	3/6	3/6	3/3	3/3	3/3	6/6	6/6	4/4	4/4	4/4
4/4	6/4	4/4	4/1	6/6	6/6	6/6	6/6	3/3	3/4	4/4	4/4	6/6	4/4	4/4
4/4	6/4	4/4	5/6	6/6	6/1	1/1	6/6	6/6	6/6	4/4	4/4	6/4	4/4	4/2
4/4	4/4	4/4	6/6	6/6	5/5	1/6	6/6	4/4	4/4	6/6	4/4	4/4	4/2	2/4
4/4	4/2	4/4	6/6	6/6	6/6	6/7	6/6	4/4	4/4	4/4	6/6	4/2	4/4	4/2
4/2	2/2	4/4	4/4	4/4	7/7	7/6	6/4	4/4	2/4	4/4	6/4	4/4	4/2	2/2
4/2	2/4	4/4	4/4	4/4	4/4	4/4	4/2	2/4	4/4	4/4	4/4	4/2	2/2	2/2
2/4	4/4	4/4	4/4	4/2	4/4	4/2	2/4	4/4	4/4	4/4	4/2	2/4	4/4	4/4

CHRISTMAS DAY

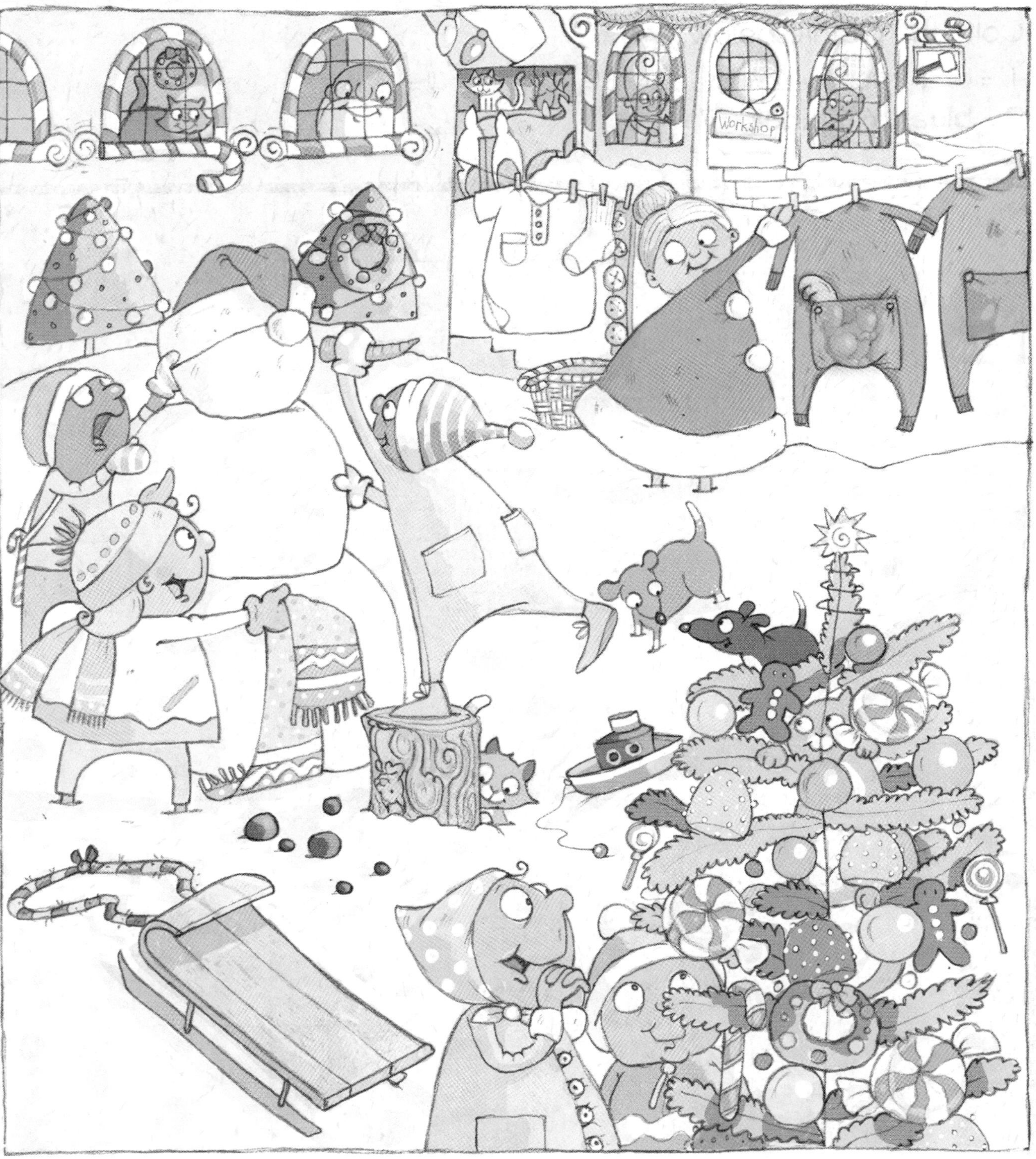

Find and circle the hidden pictures.

Find 1
sock

Find 2
squirrels

Find 3
wreaths

Find 4
cats

Find 5
candy canes

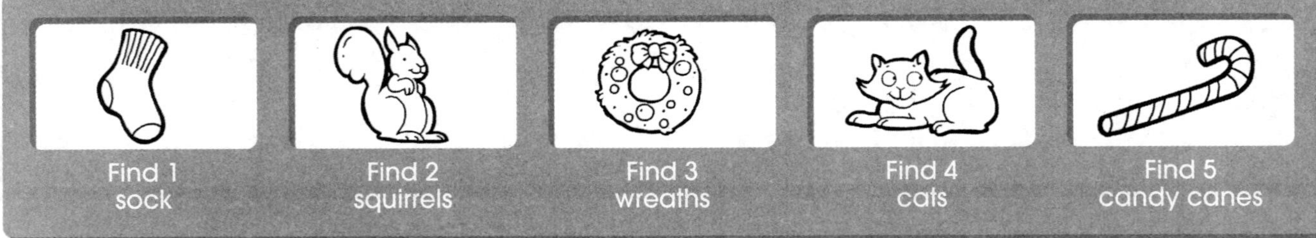

 ©School Zone Publishing Company

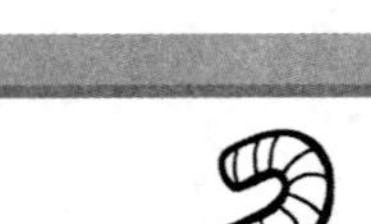

FUMBLE

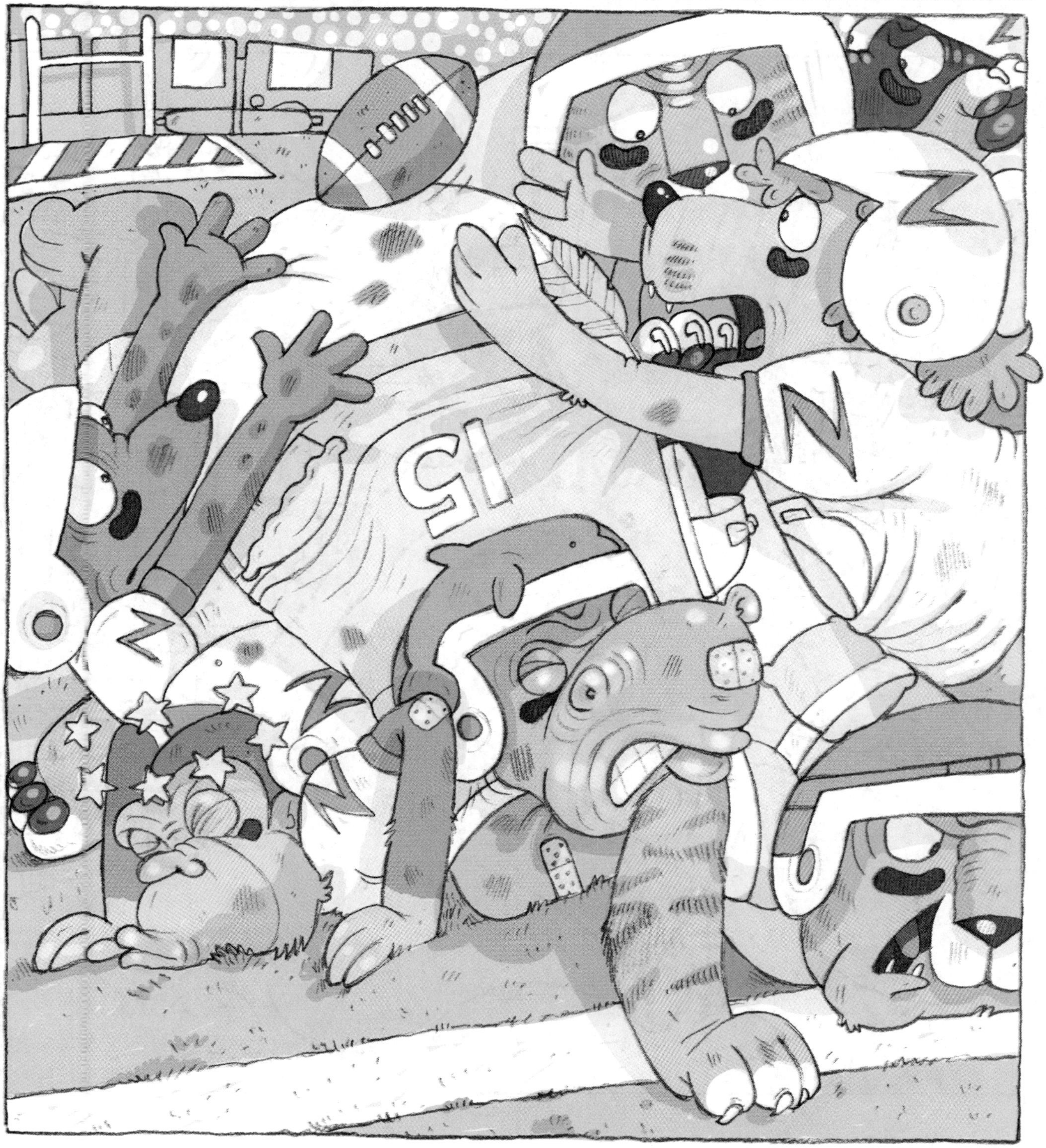

Find and circle the hidden pictures.

cup | dolphin | feather | hockey stick | pen | pie | pillow | slipper

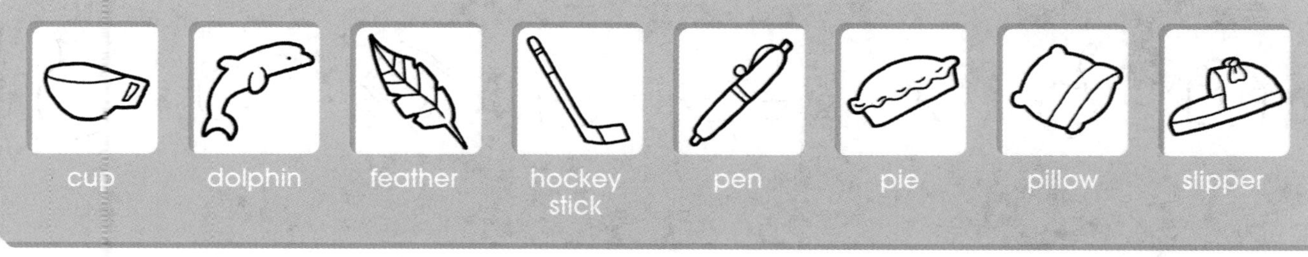

WHAT'S IN THE OVEN?

Find and circle the hidden pictures.

milk carton

ornament

fishing pole

ship

measuring cup

quilt

pet bed

jump rope

 ©School Zone Publishing Company

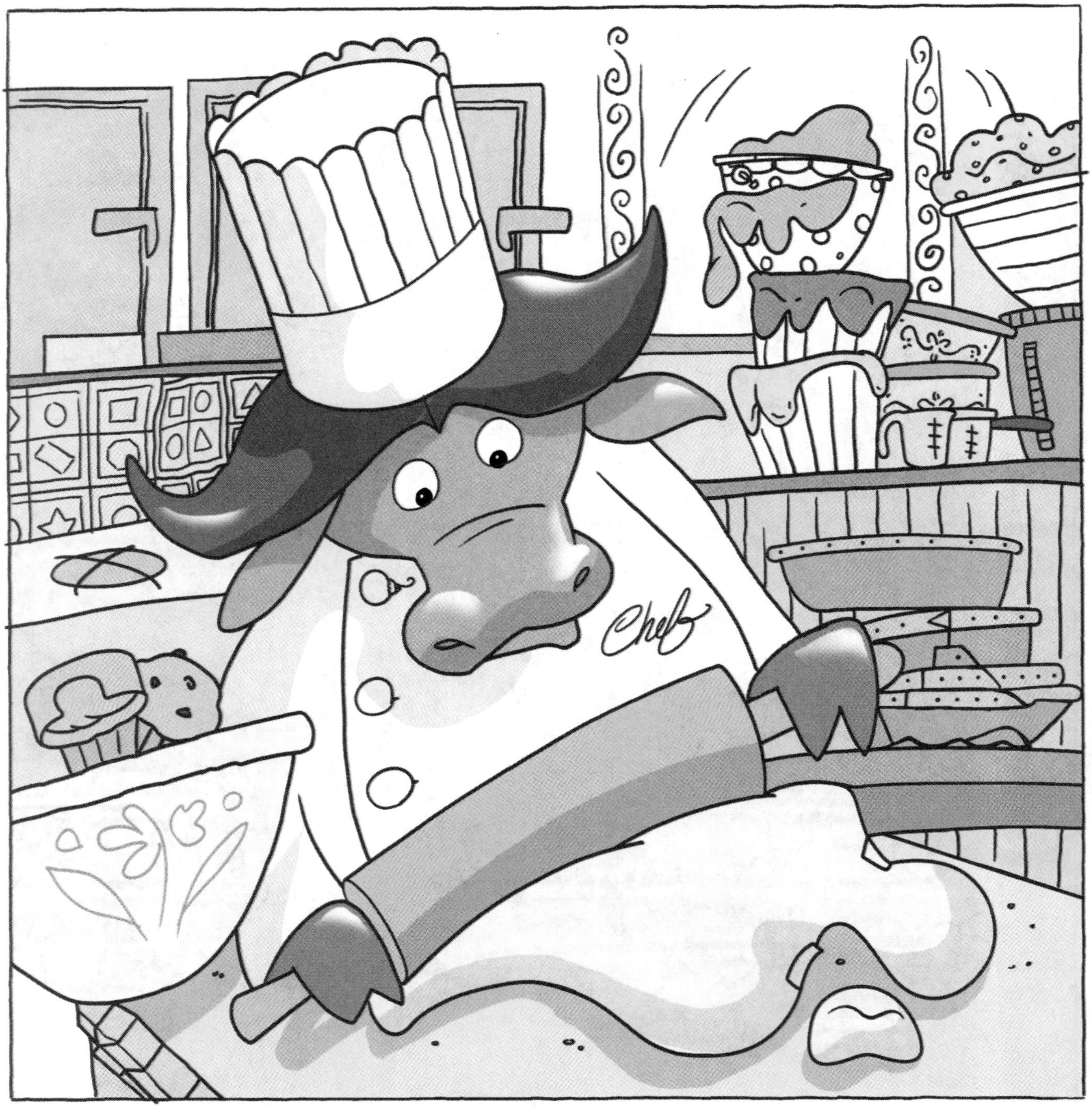

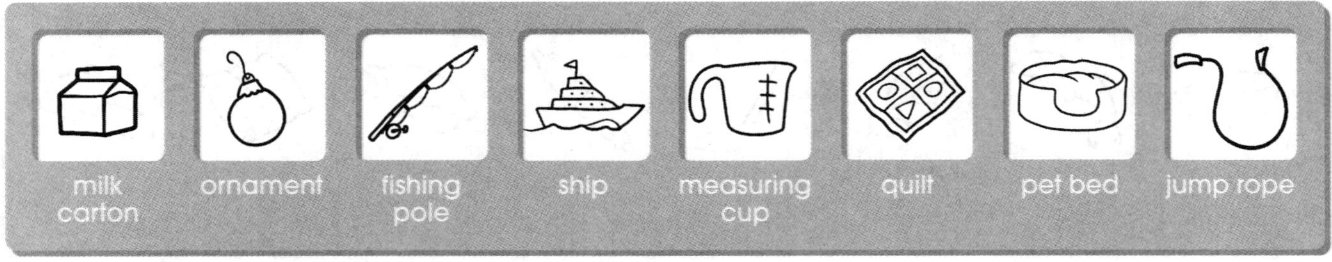

FOLLOW THE TRAIL!

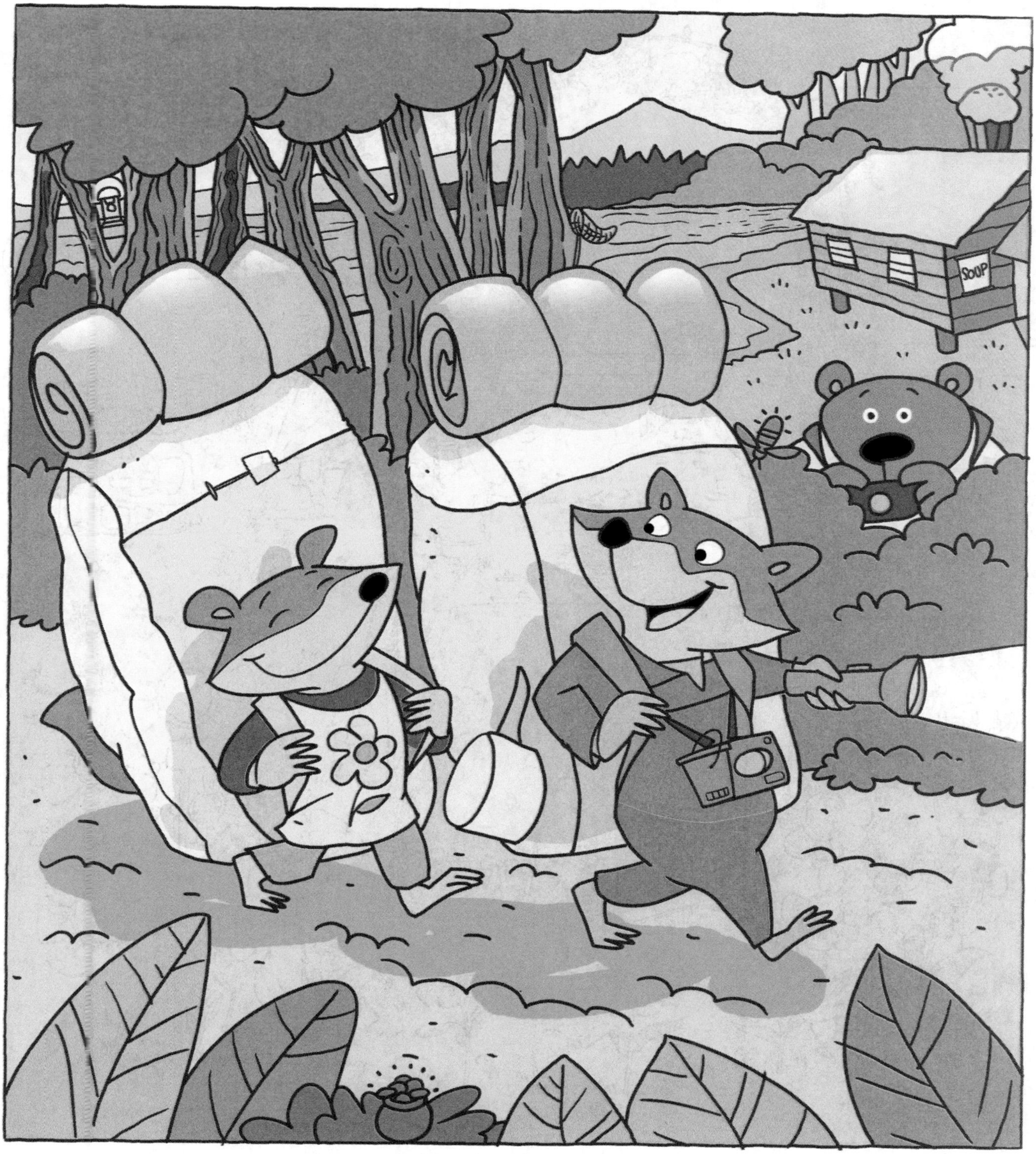

Find and circle the hidden pictures.

net | lamp | bucket | muffin | lightning bug | gold | soup can | lantern

©School Zone Publishing Company

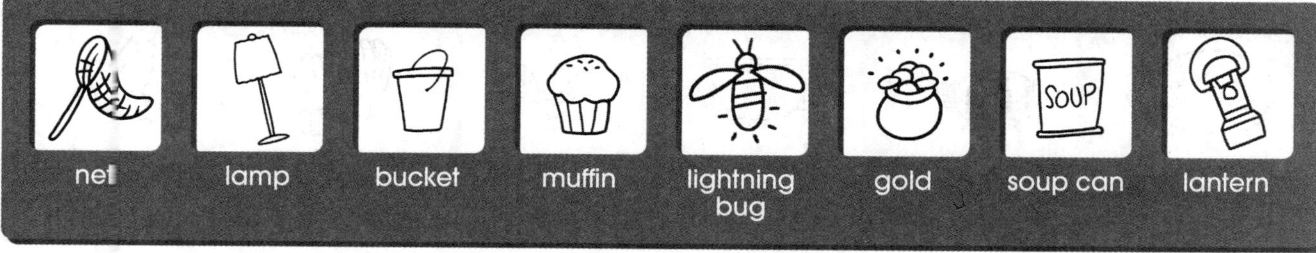

AFTERNOON TEA

Find and circle the hidden pictures.

Find 1 hedgehog	Find 4 bees	Find 2 teacups	Find 2 tulips	Find 1 pair of gloves	Find 1 bird

©School Zone Publishing Company

THE BUSY CITY

Find and circle the hidden pictures.

Find 3 chimneys	Find 2 pigeons	Find 1 cab	Find 1 statue	Find 4 whistles	Find 2 fire hydrants

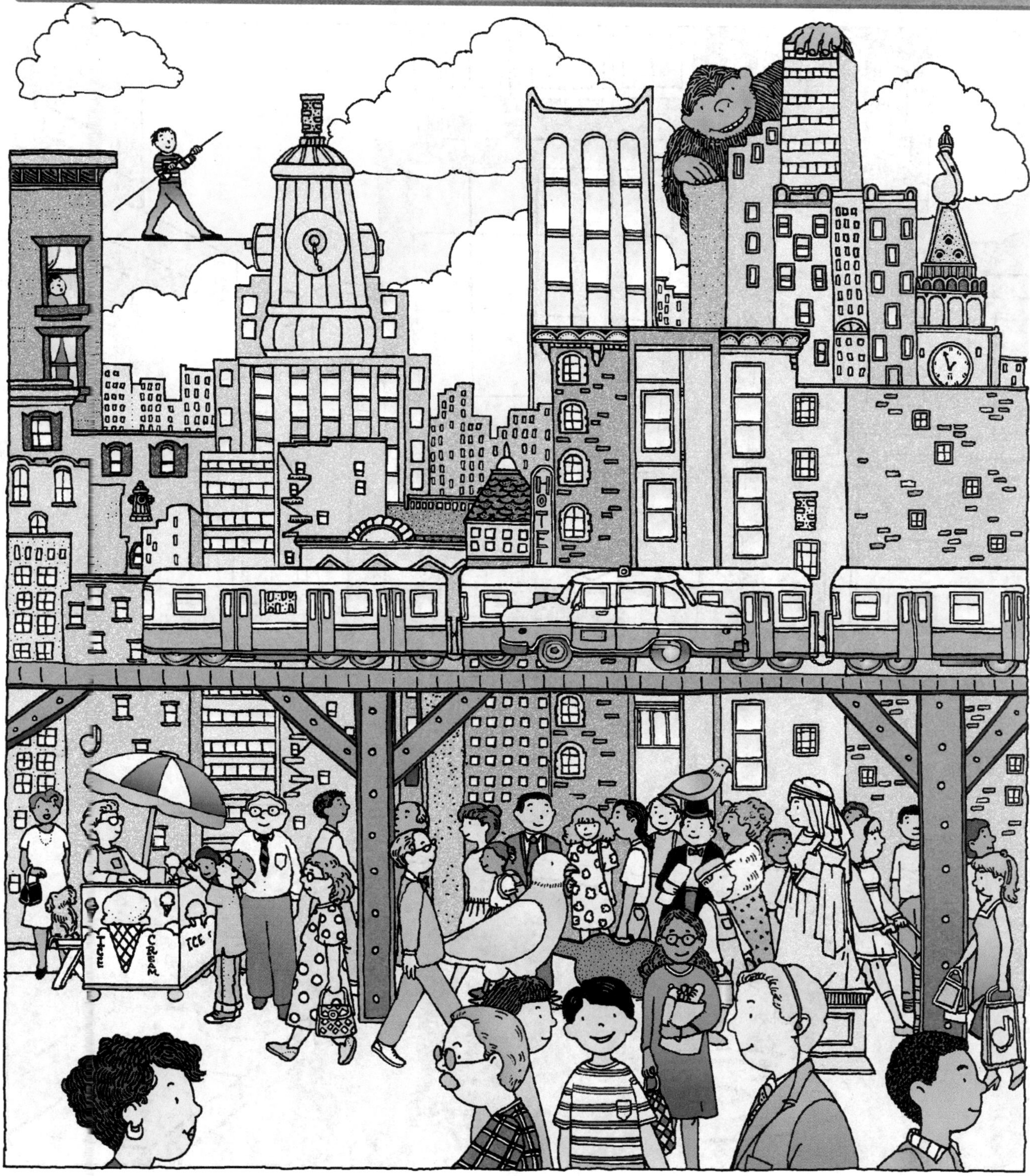

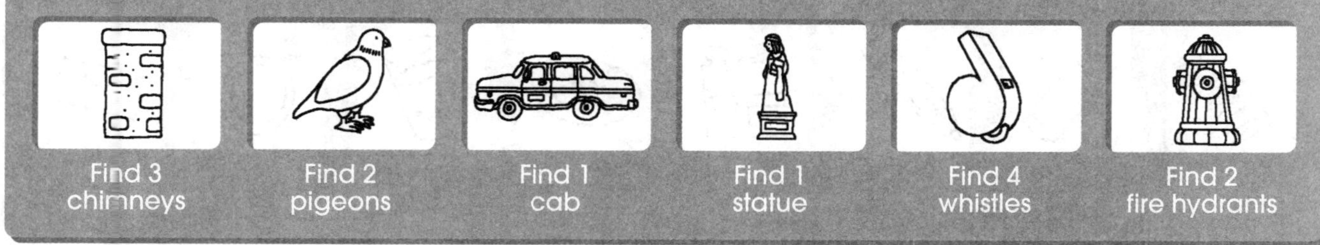

CITY STREETS

Find and circle the hidden pictures.

©School Zone Publishing Company

SUMMER PICNIC

Find and circle the hidden pictures.

Find 2 dandelions

Find 1 can opener

Find 3 cameras

Find 1 container

Find 2 kites

Find 1 stereo

DRIVING ALONG

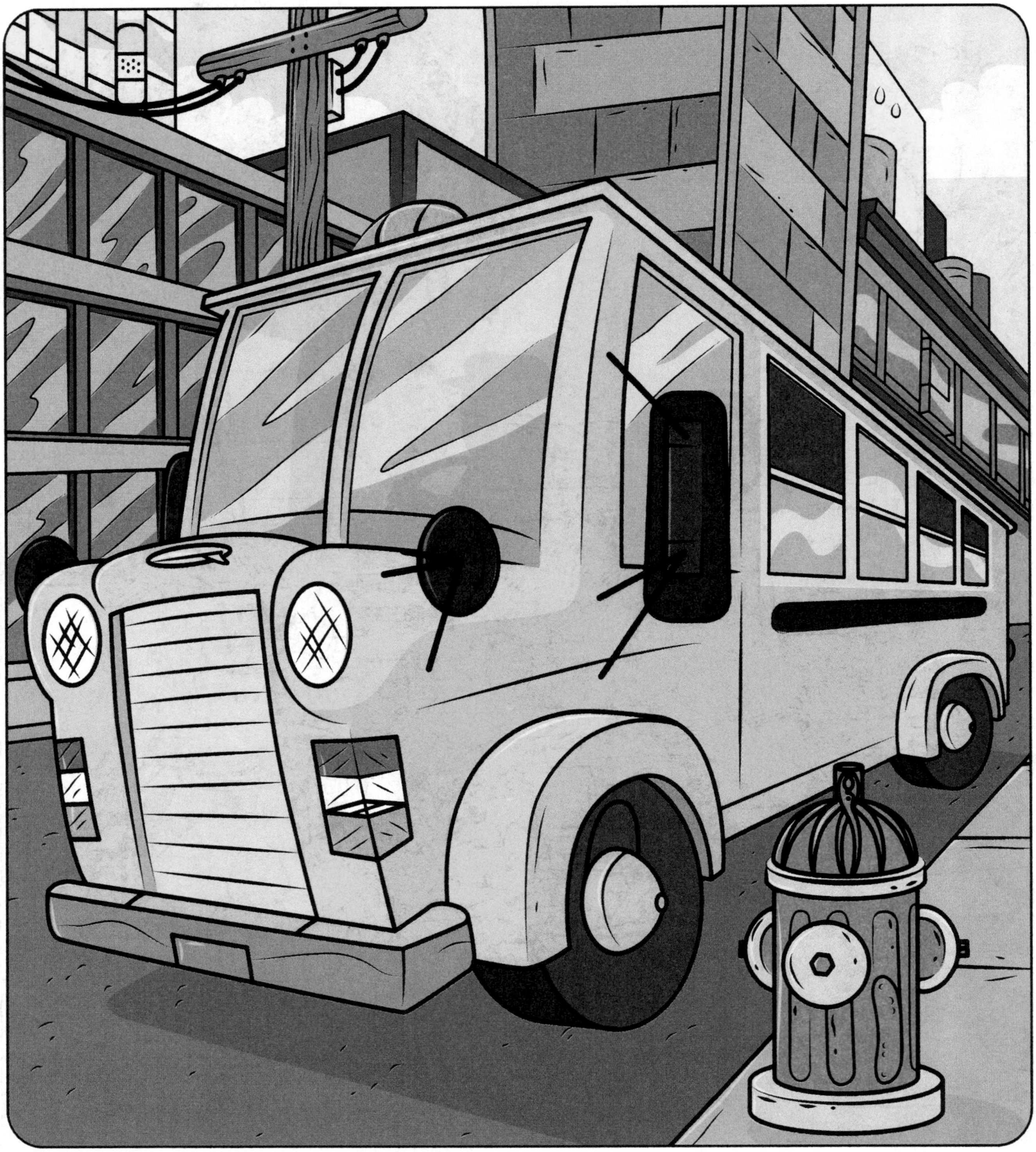

Find and circle the hidden pictures.

hat

cucumber

pliers

book

surfboard

bandage

hockey stick

box

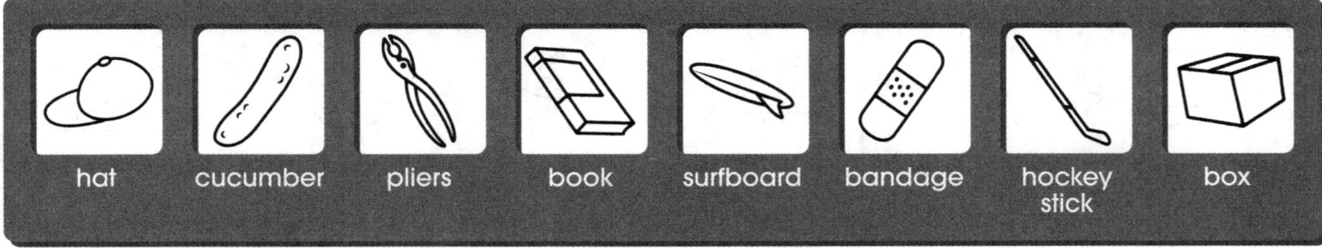

©School Zone Publishing Company

DINING OUT

Find and circle the hidden pictures.

Find 1 cardinal

Find 2 nests

Find 3 doves

Find 1 birdbath

Find 1 birdcage

Find 1 birdhouse

©School Zone Publishing Company

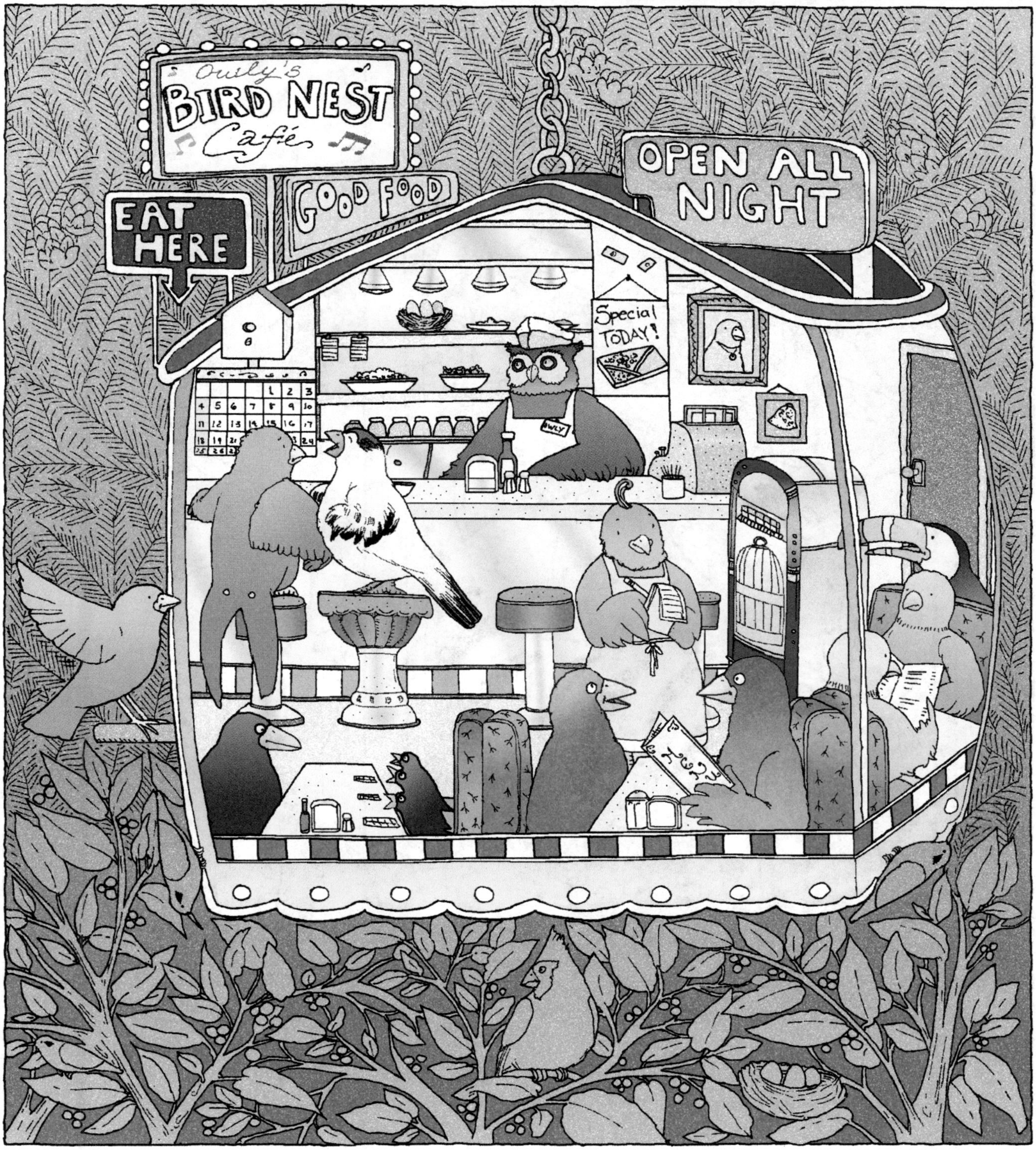

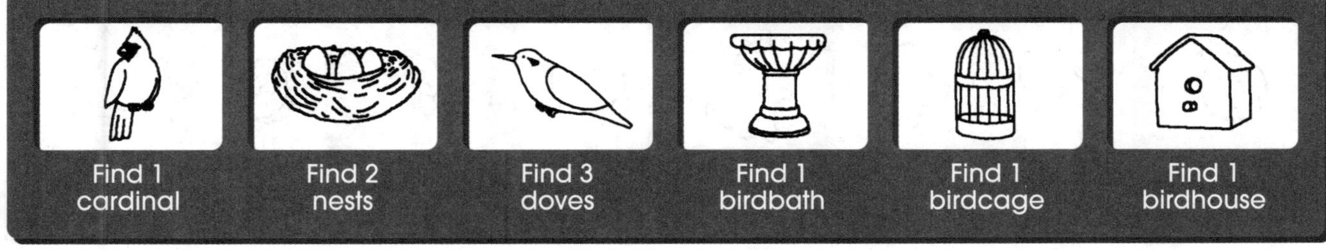

WHICH WAY TO THE PENGUINS?

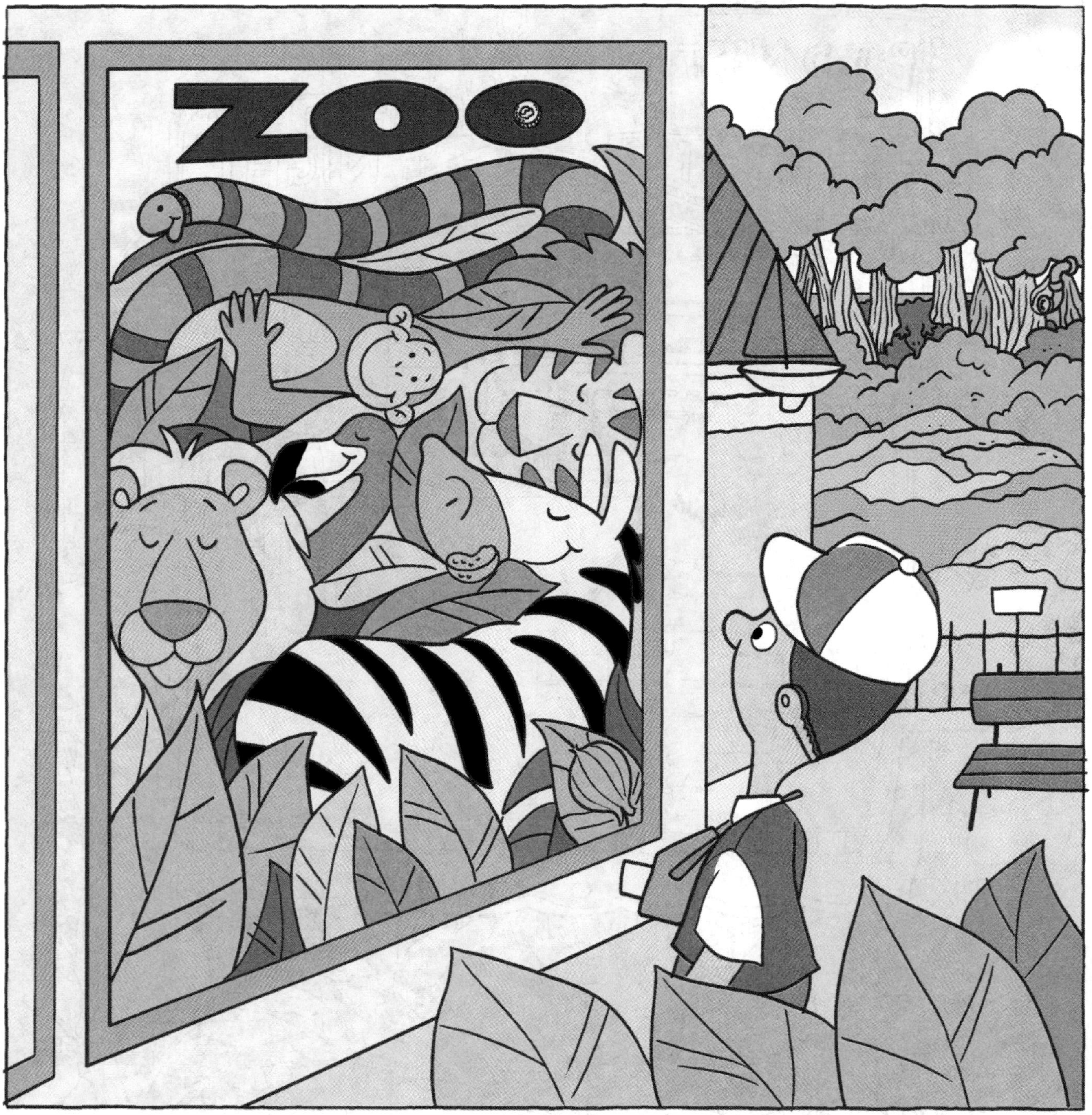

Find and circle the hidden pictures.

onion key mitten ghost peanut pipe quarter sailboat

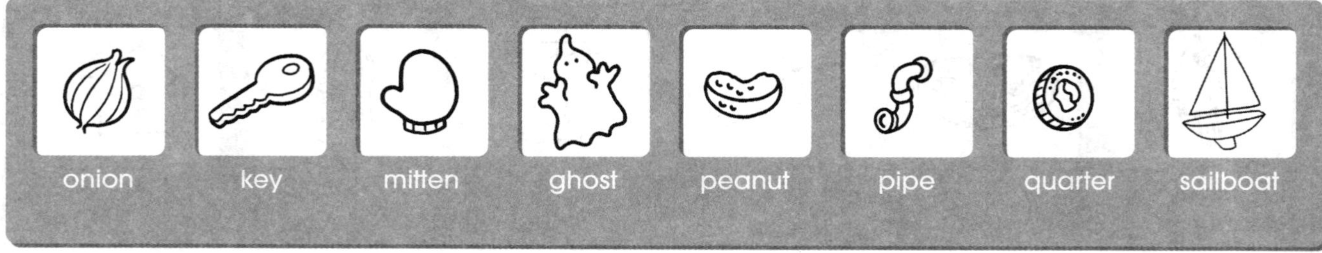

 ©School Zone Publishing Company

UNDER THE SEA

Find and circle the hidden pictures.

flowers | rocket | lobster | mushroom | pear | goggles | lettuce | pretzel

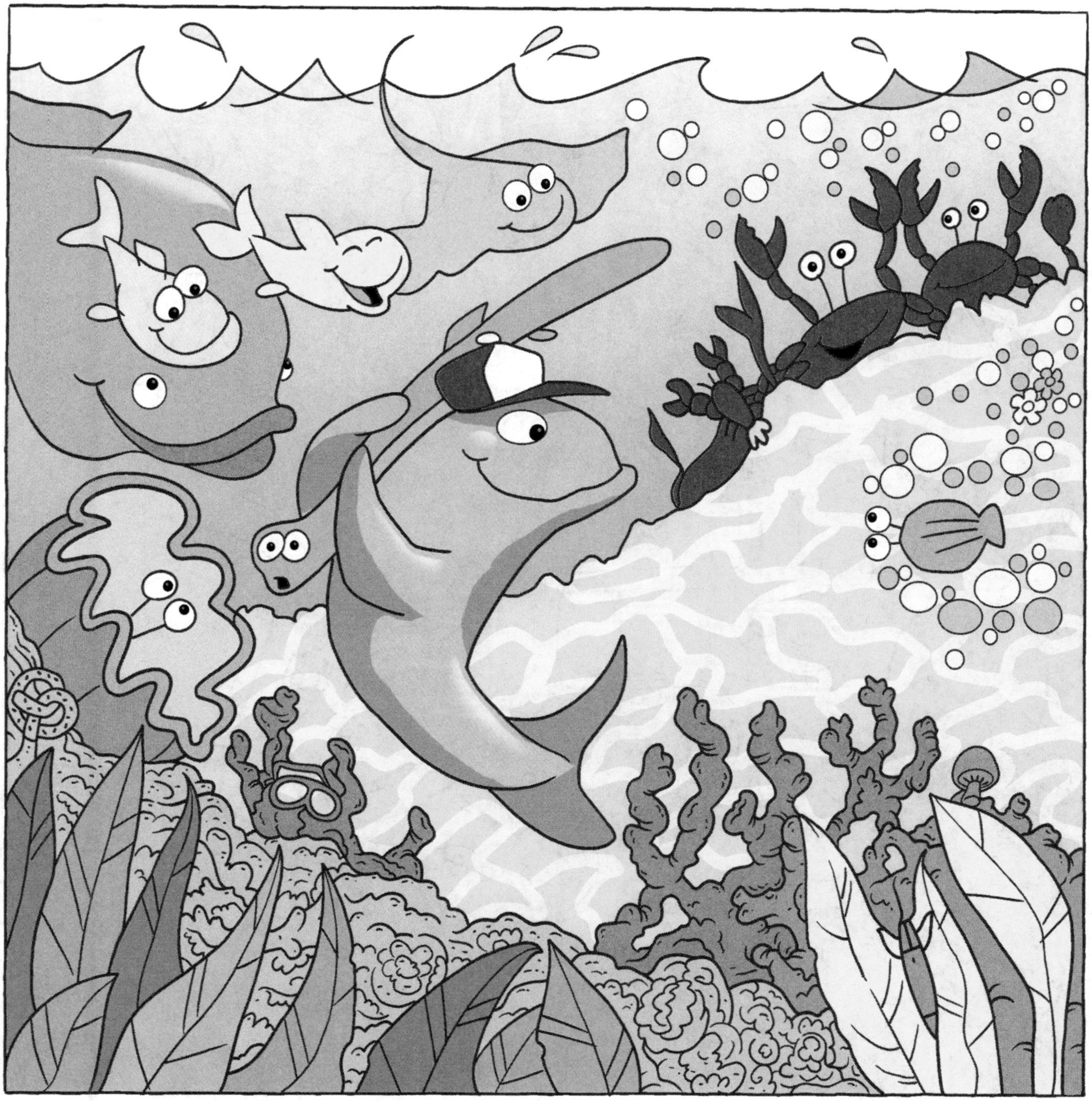

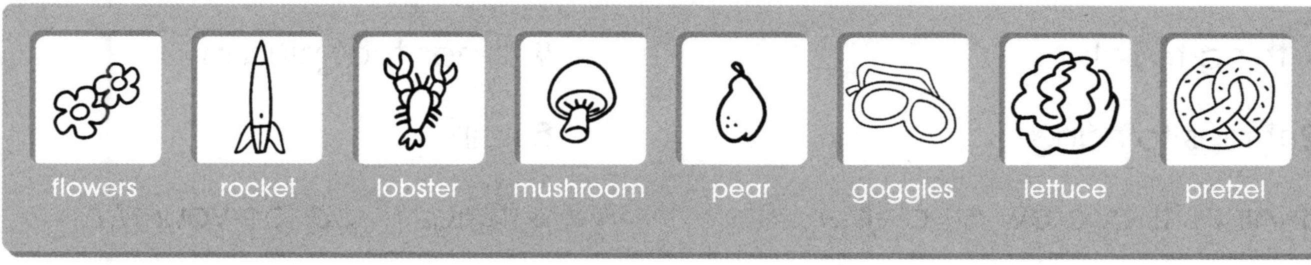

HODGEPODGE 1

Look at the picture and find:

1 thing to lick

2 things to hang

3 things that grow on a vine

4 things that plug in

5 balls

6 things to put on your feet

 ©School Zone Publishing Company

HODGEPODGE 2

Look at the picture and find:

1 thing with humps

2 things that jump

3 things with wings

4 things that ring

5 things from a tree

6 things from the sea

©School Zone Publishing Company

CLOWN SCHOOL

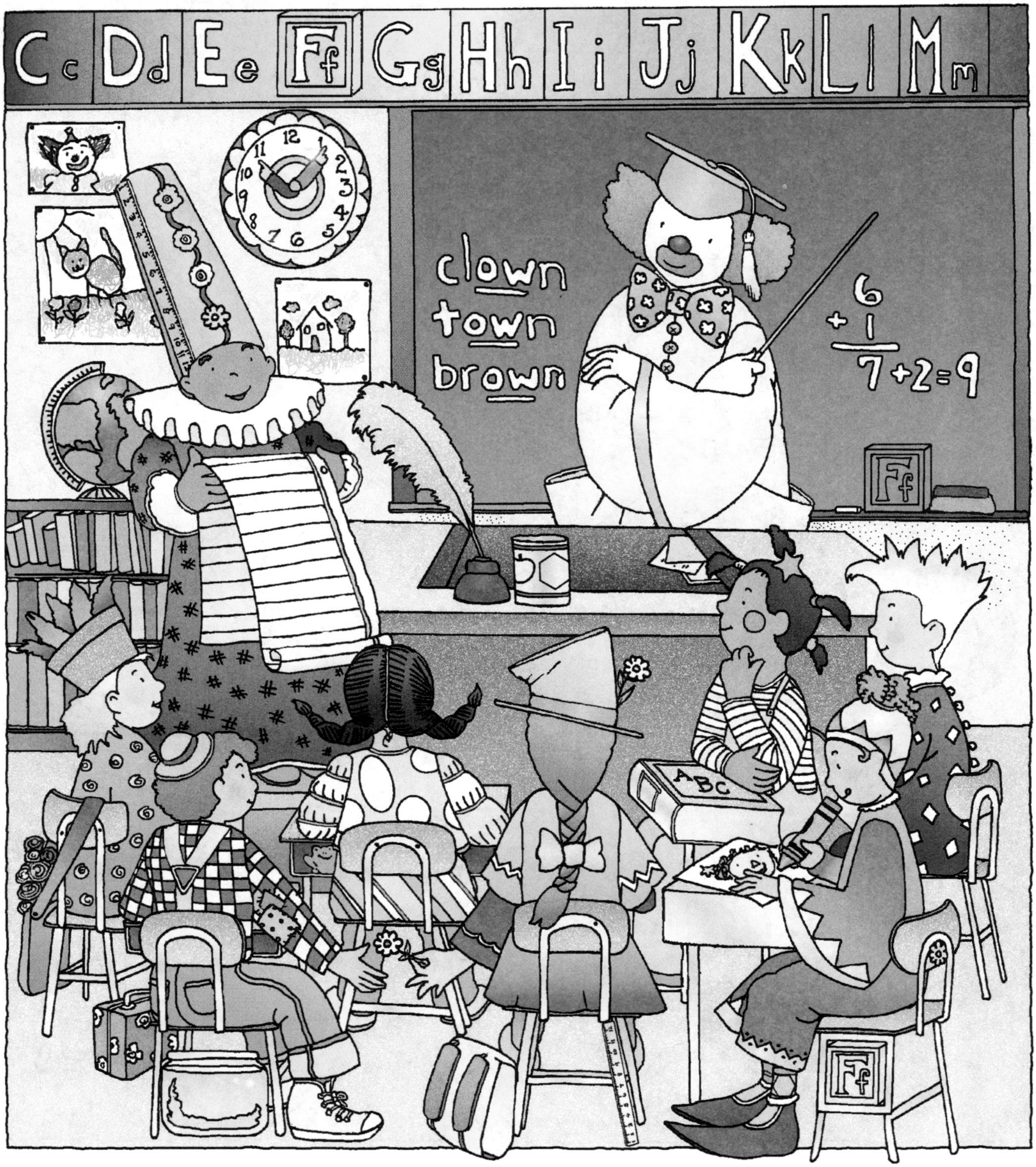

Find and circle the hidden pictures.

Find 2 hexagons

Find 1 crayon

Find 3 letter blocks

Find 1 plant

Find 2 rulers

Find 4 flowers

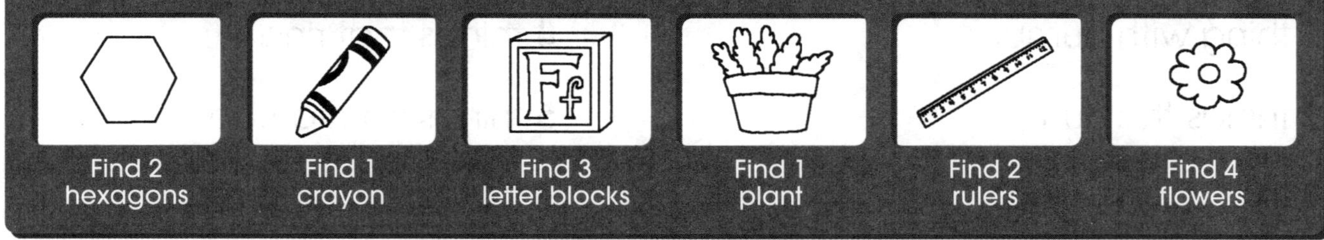

 ©School Zone Publishing Company

BAKING AT HOME

HONEY

Find and circle the hidden pictures.

Find 1
teacup

Find 3
cookie cutters

Find 1
muffin

Find 3
jars

Find 2
spoons

©School Zone Publishing Company

MADAME INSECT

Solve each math problem. Find the first answer on the grid. Draw a line to the second answer. Continue drawing lines to connect the answers in order. When you have finished, a picture will be revealed.

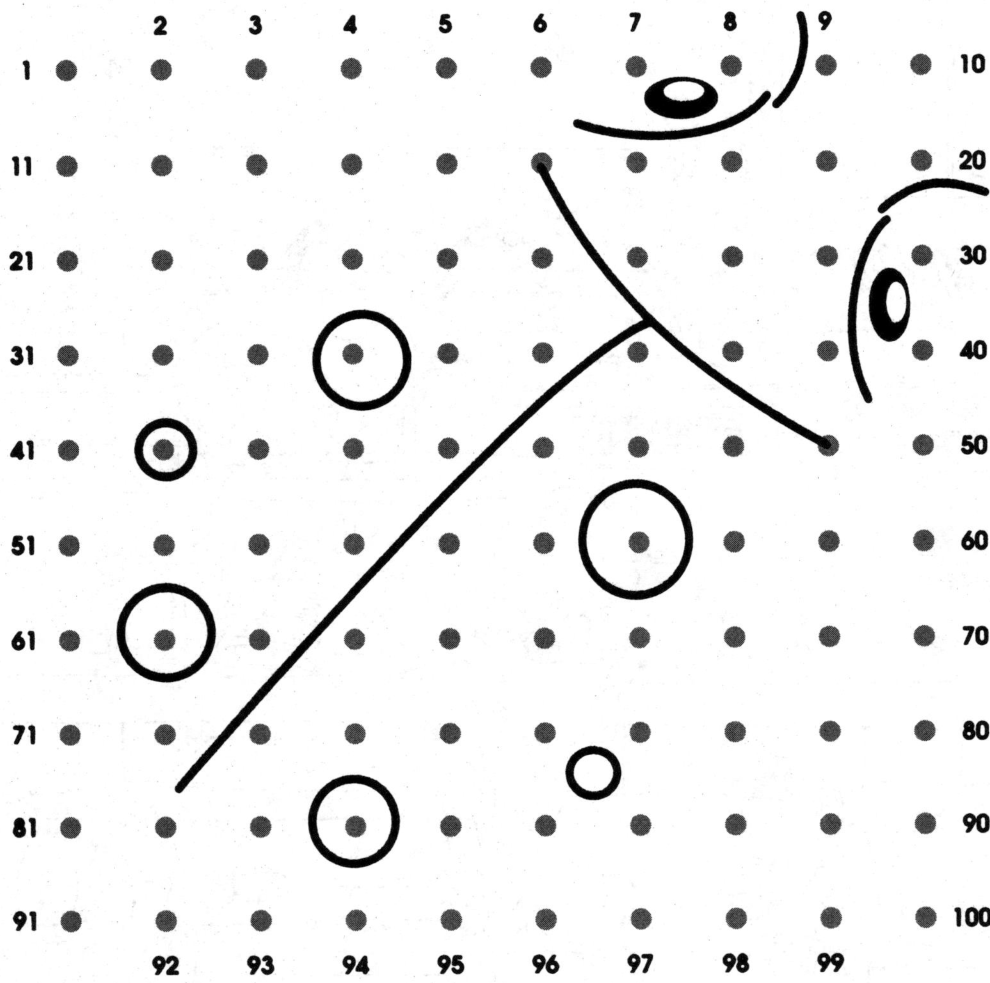

Line 1

1. 6 + 2 = ____
2. 10 – 3 = ____
3. 8 + 8 = ____
4. 30 – 15 = ____
5. 10 + 4 = ____
6. 55 – 32 = ____
7. 18 + 14 = ____
8. 66 – 25 = ____
9. 40 + 11 = ____
10. 87 – 26 = ____
11. 36 + 35 = ____
12. 98 – 16 = ____
13. 77 + 16 = ____
14. 99 – 5 = ____
15. 49 + 46 = ____
16. 99 – 3 = ____
17. 75 + 12 = ____
18. 91 – 13 = ____
19. 50 + 19 = ____
20. 68 – 9 = ____
21. 44 + 5 = ____
22. 69 – 29 = ____
23. 15 + 15 = ____
24. 29 – 10 = ____
25. 7 + 1 = ____

 ©School Zone Publishing Company

A-MAZING GREEN

Follow the maze from start to finish.

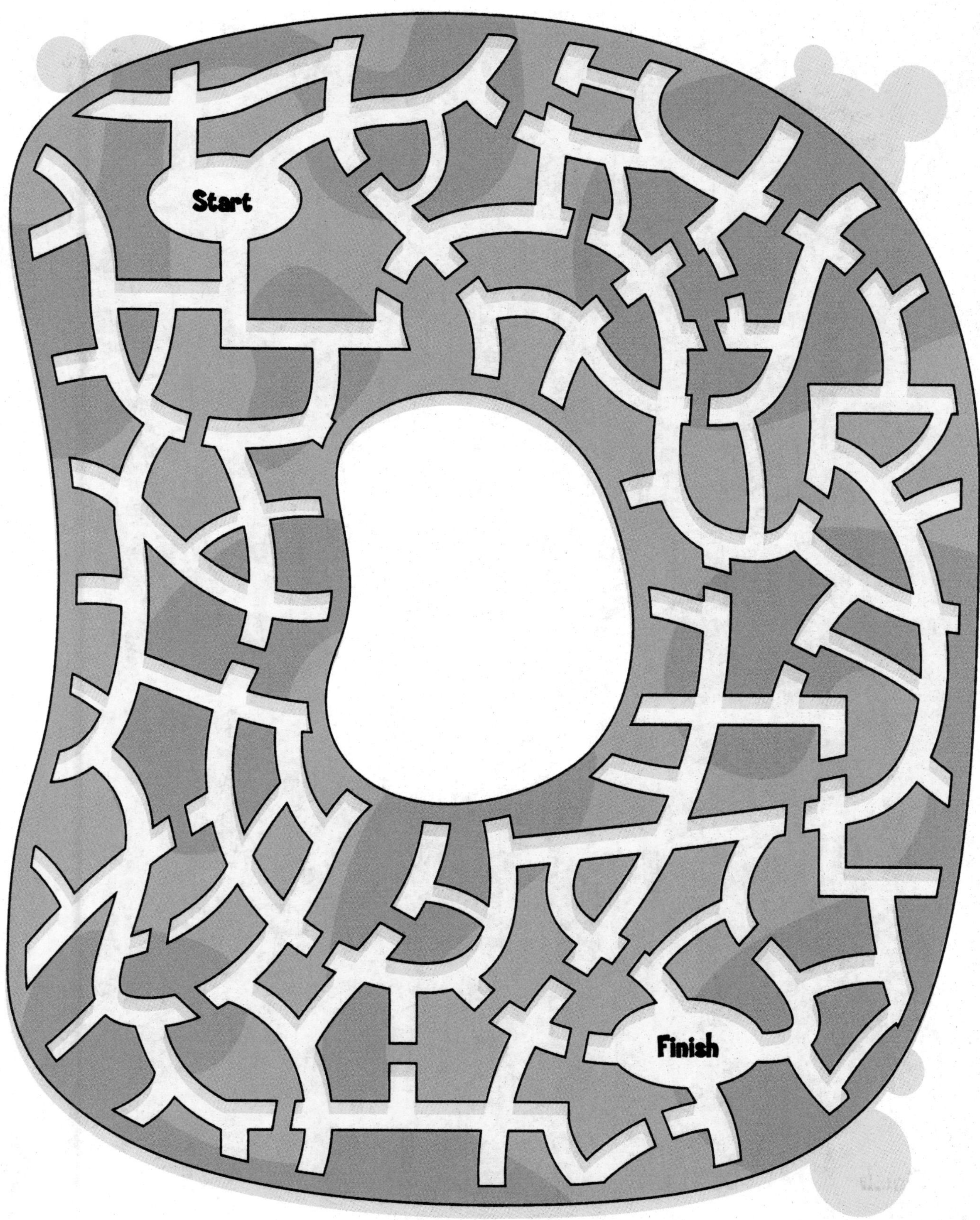

HOURGLASS

Follow the maze from start to finish.

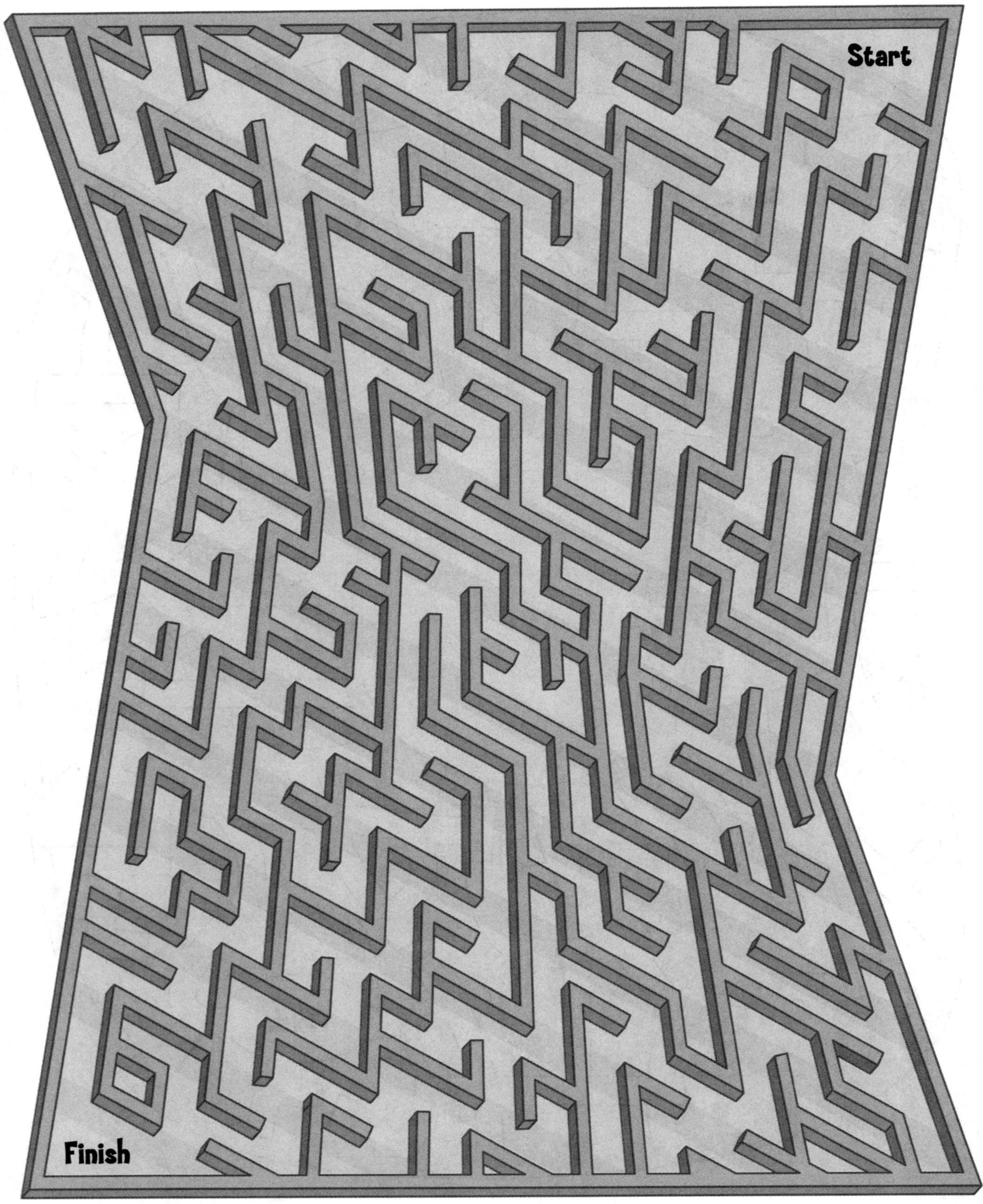

 ©School Zone Publishing Company

INTO THE MACHINE

Follow the maze from start to finish.

TIC-TAC-TOE

Choose which player will be X and which player will be O. Take turns drawing an X or an O in each section of the grid. Play until there are three Xs or three Os in a row horizontally, vertically, or diagonally or until the grid is filled. Whoever gets three in a row first wins!

©School Zone Publishing Company

TIC-TAC-TOE

Extra Playing Page: Directions can be found on page 206.

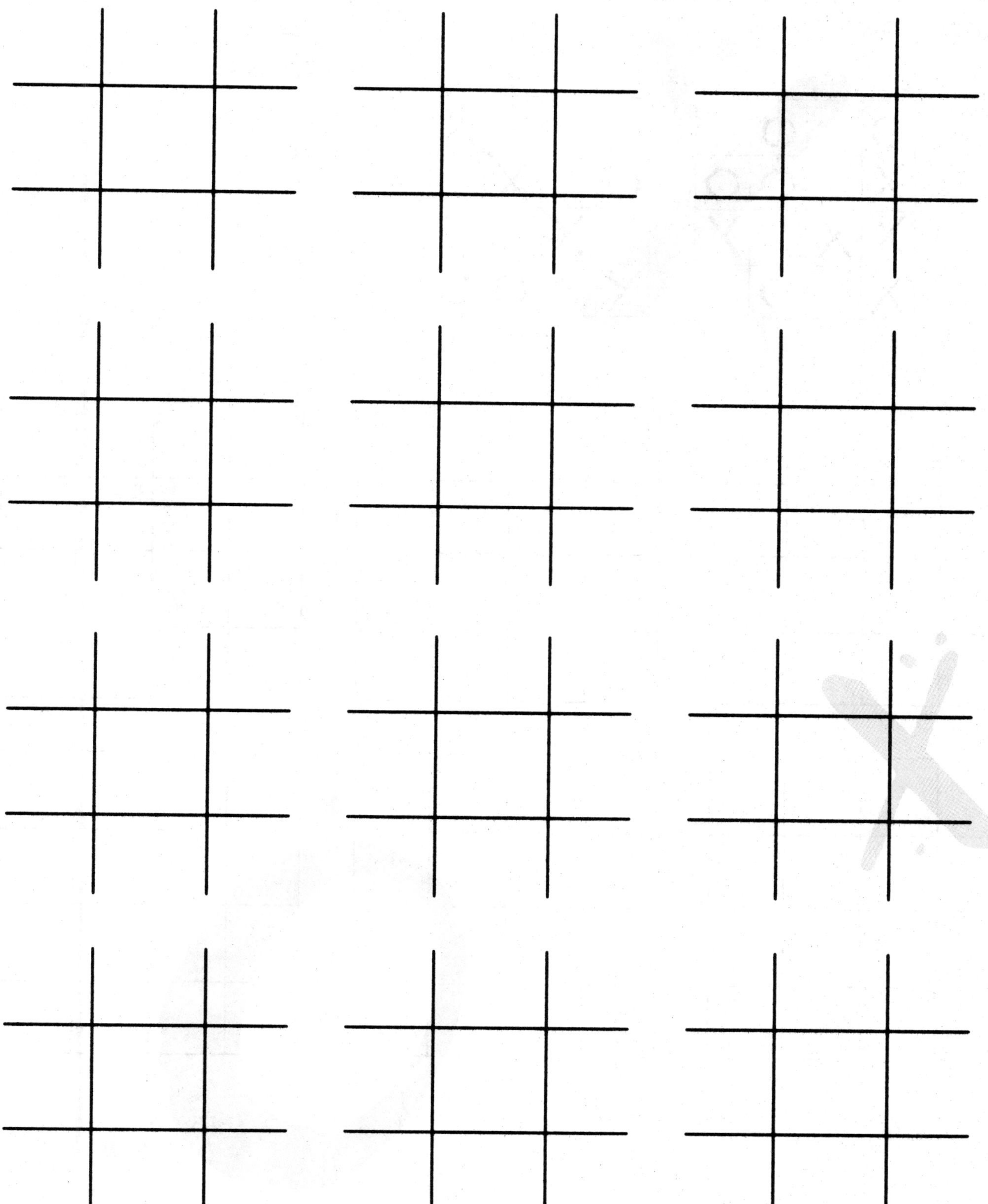

TIC-TAC-TOE VARIATION

Choose which player will be X and which player will be O. Take turns drawing an X or an O at each intersection. Play until there are four Xs or four Os in a row horizontally, vertically, or diagonally or until the grid is filled. Whoever gets four in a row first wins!

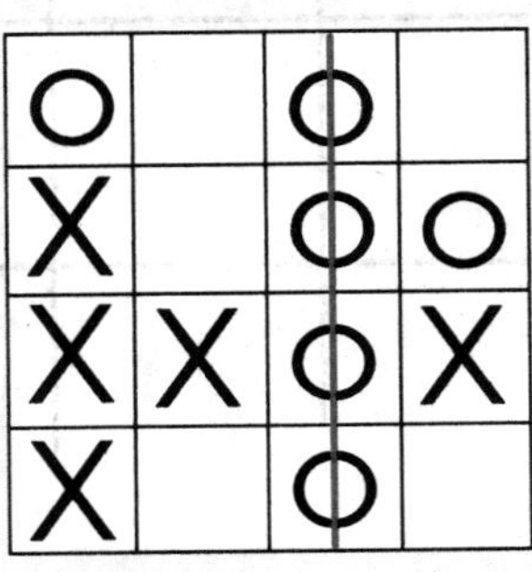

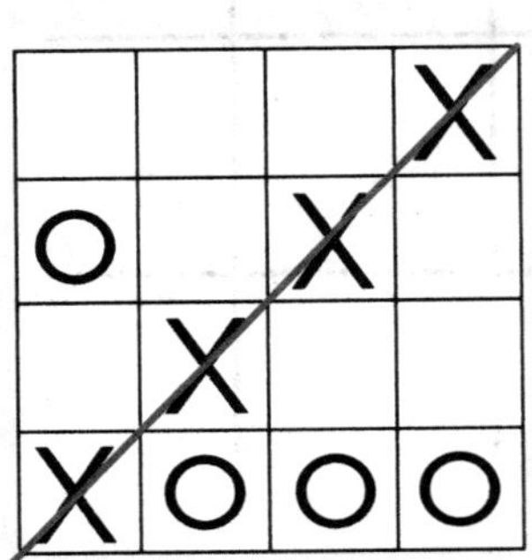

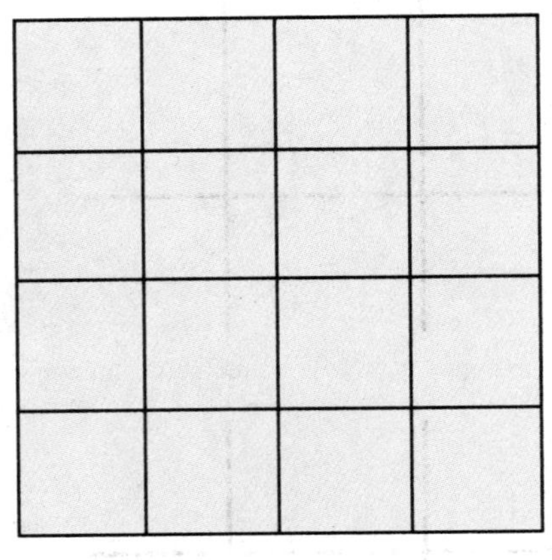

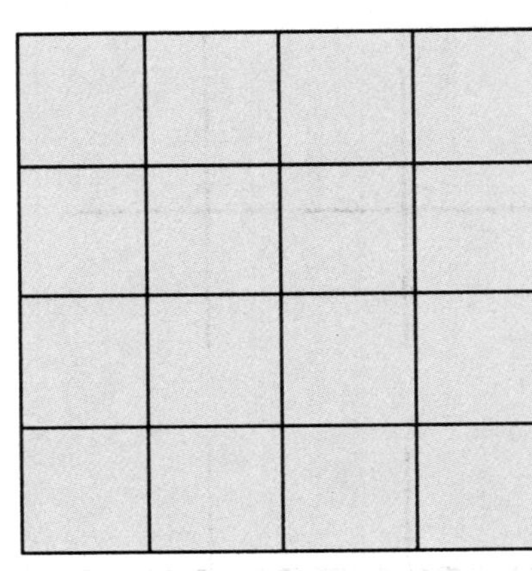

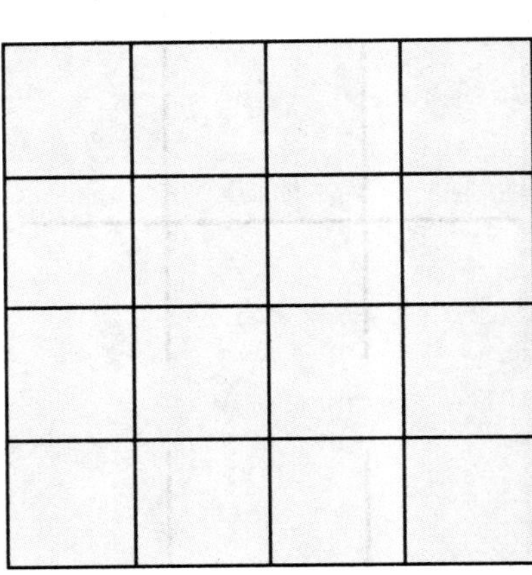

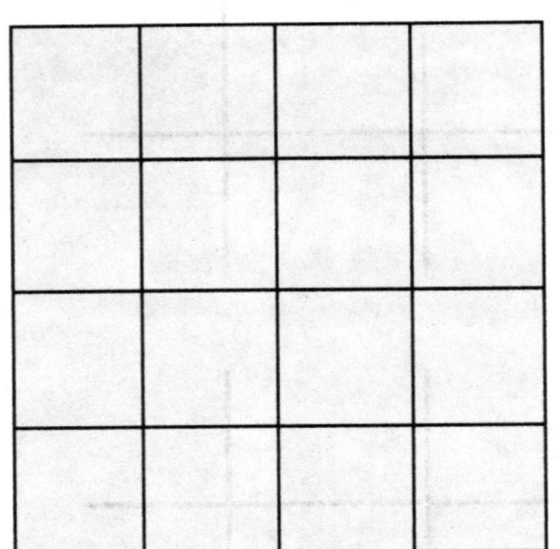

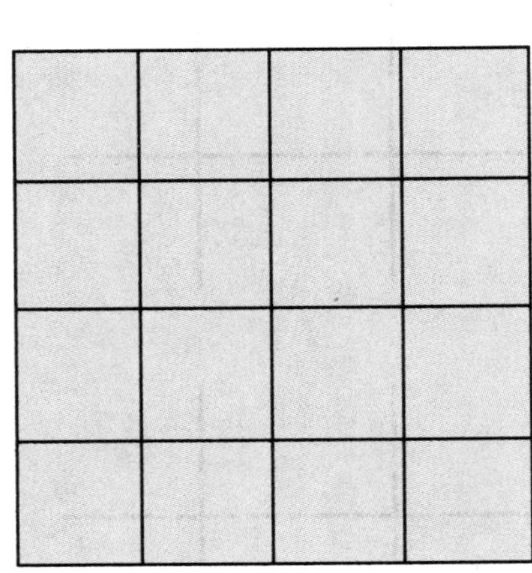

©School Zone Publishing Company

TIC-TAC-TOE VARIATION

Extra Playing Page: Directions can be found on page 208.

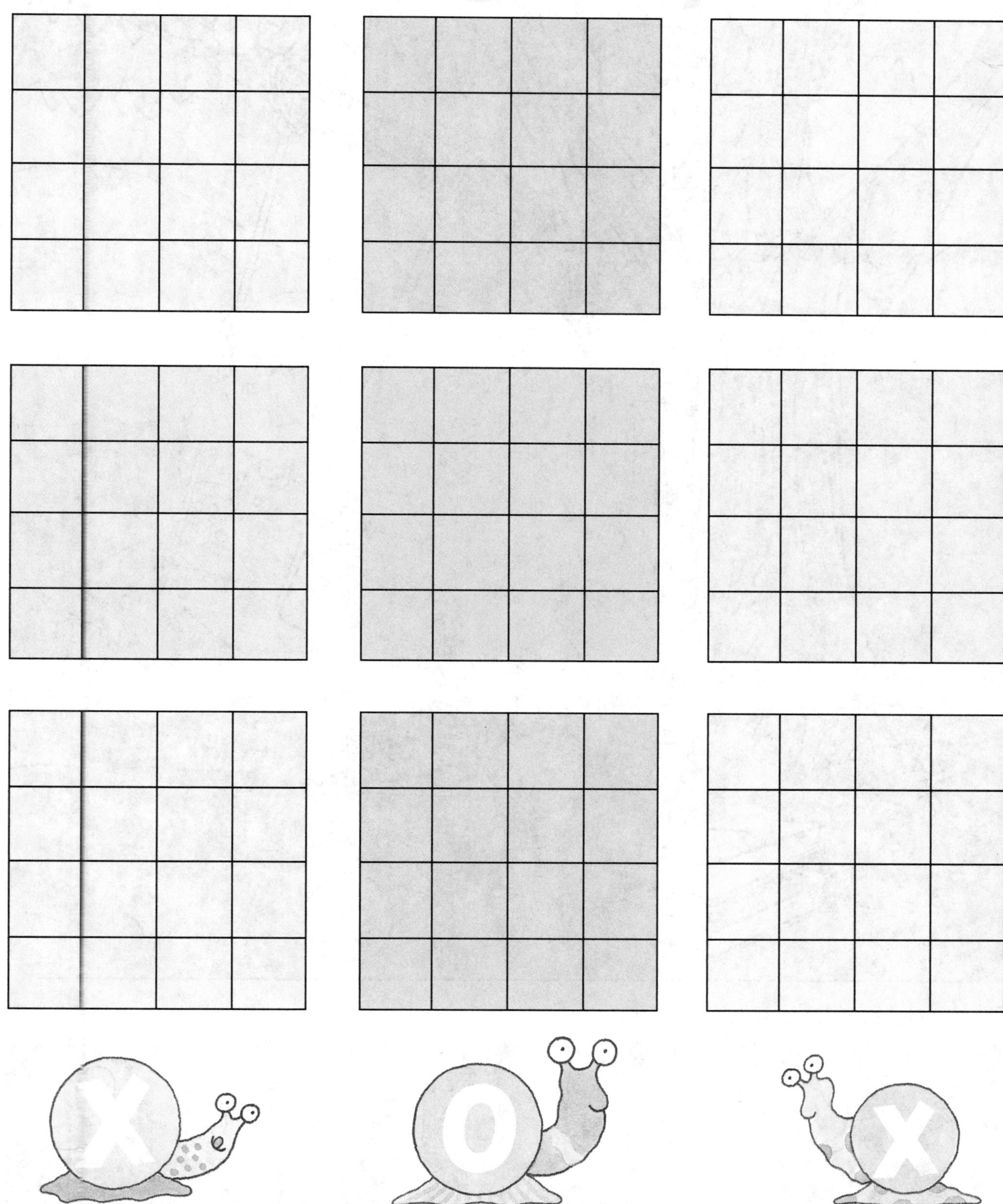

FALL FUN

Find and circle the hidden pictures.

©School Zone Publishing Company

GONE FISHING

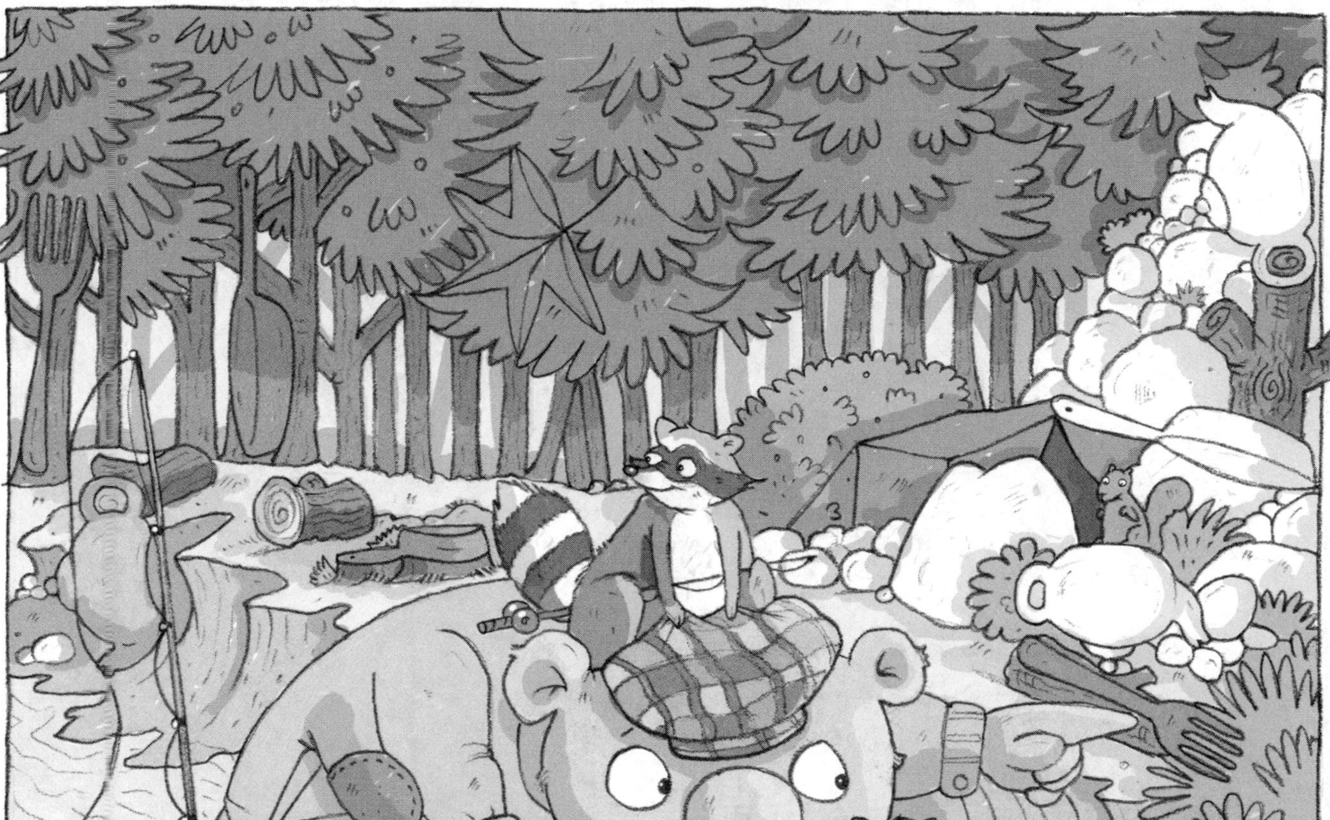

Find and circle the hidden pictures.

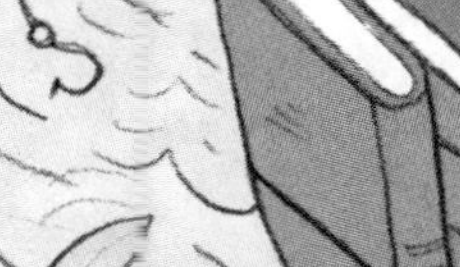

Find 1
book

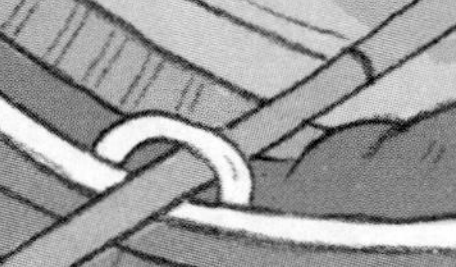

Find 2
leaves

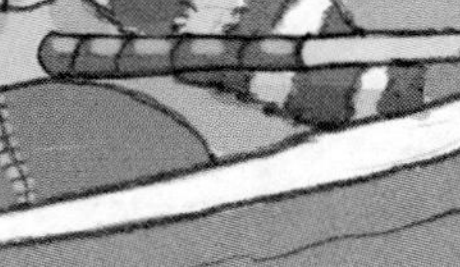

Find 3
teapots

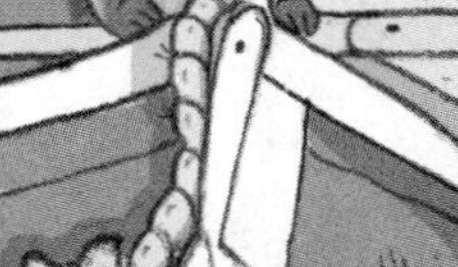

Find 4
forks

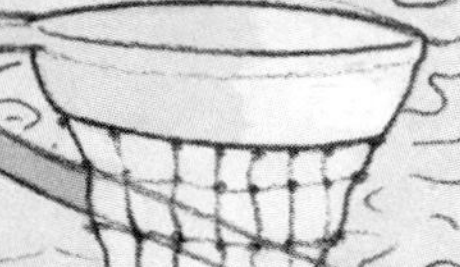

Find 5
pans

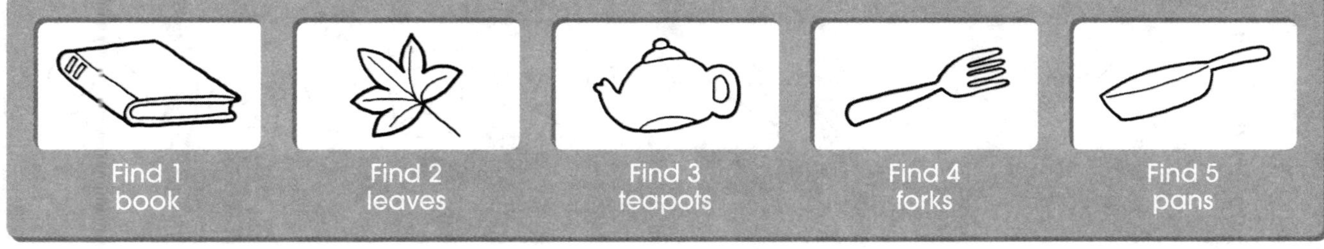

THE OFFICE

Find and circle the hidden pictures.

 ©School Zone Publishing Company

SPRING'S FIRST FLOWER

Find and circle the hidden pictures.

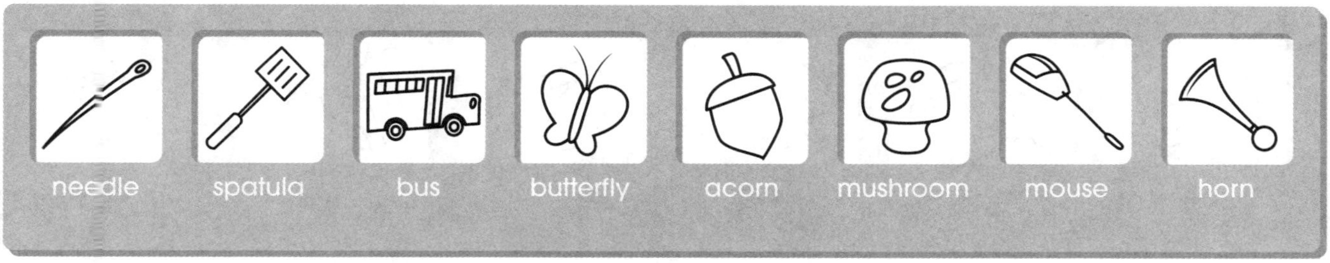

needle

spatula

bus

butterfly

acorn

mushroom

mouse

horn

IN THE TREETOPS

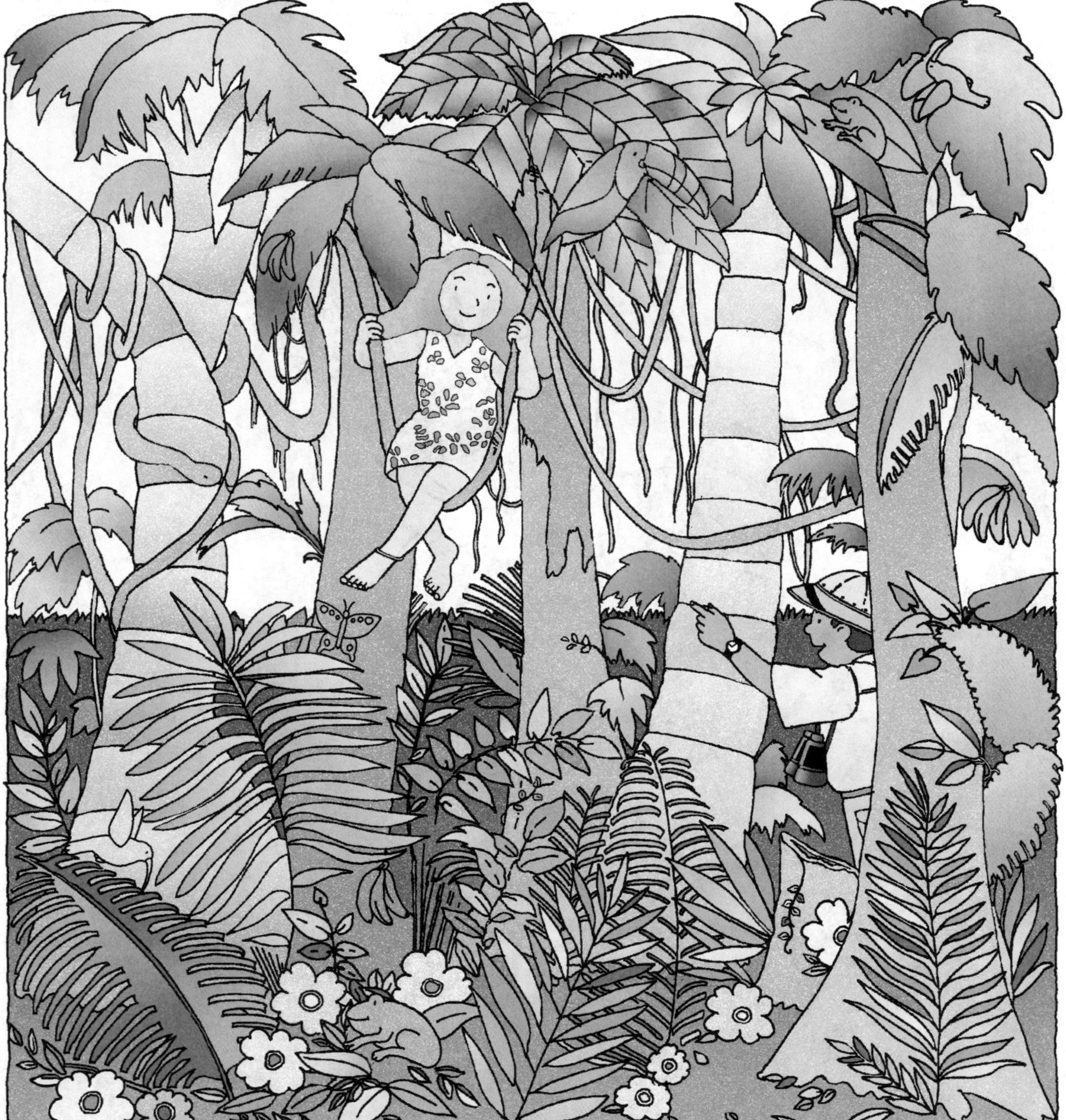

Find and circle the hidden pictures.

Find 1 snake

Find 1 toucan

Find 2 frogs

Find 3 bunches of bananas

Find 2 hummingbirds

Find 1 butterfly

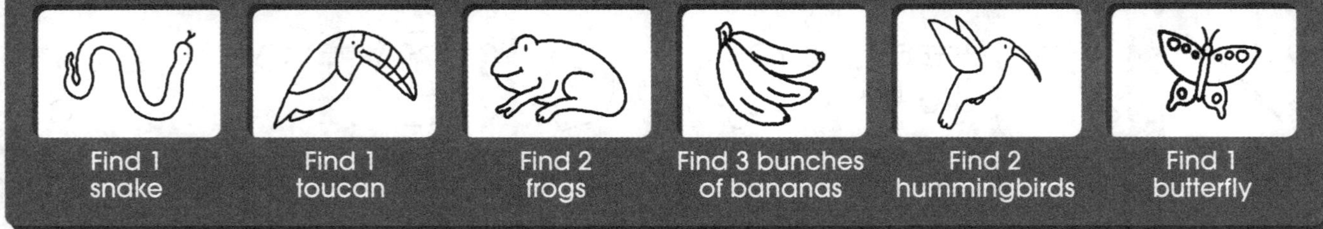

©School Zone Publishing Company

GARDEN FRIENDS

Find and circle the hidden pictures.

Find 1
seed package

Find 2
tomatoes

Find 3
snails

Find 1
head of lettuce

Find 3
butterflies

Find 2
frogs

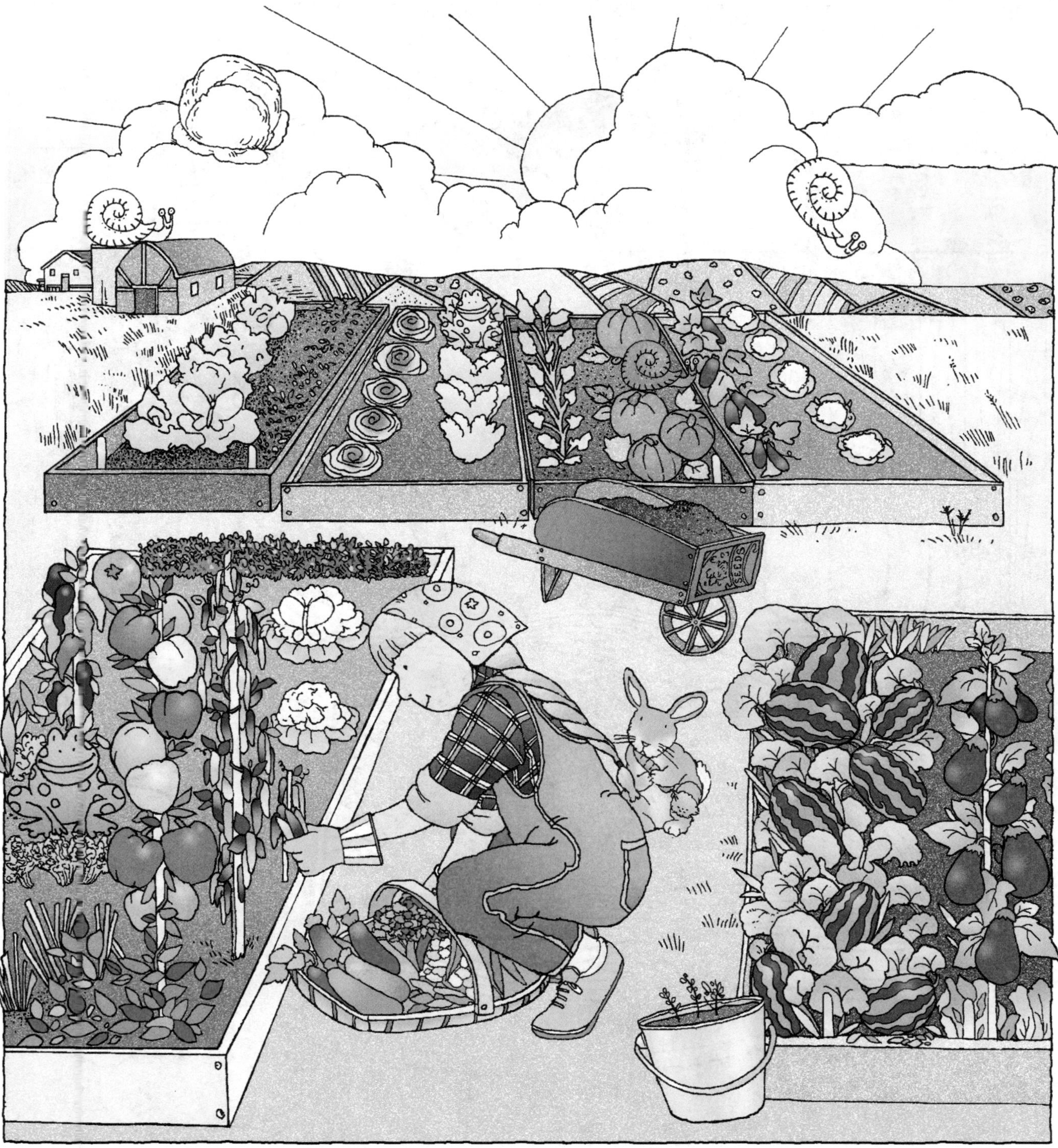

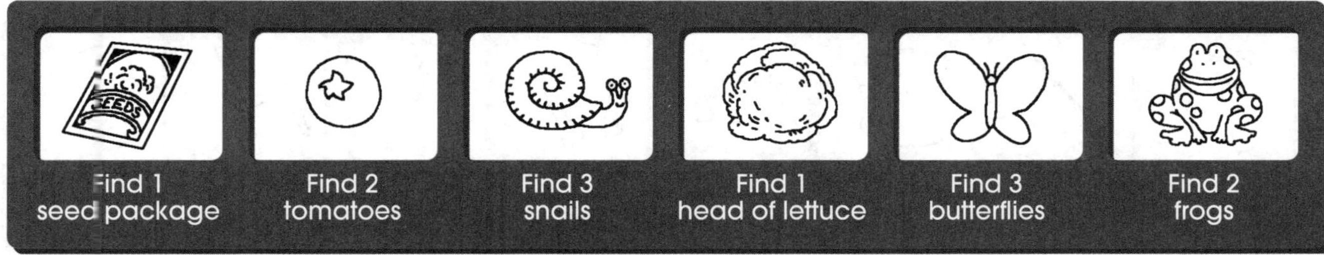

GOOD AND MESSY

Find and circle the hidden pictures.

flowers

fishing pole

bucket

igloo

horseshoe

hammer

chair

ice cream cone

 ©School Zone Publishing Company

READING IS FUN!

Find and circle the hidden pictures.

Find 1 microscope

Find 2 binoculars

Find 3 telescopes

Find 4 glasses

Find 5 magnifying glasses

DEPARTMENT STORE

Find and circle the hidden pictures.

blender

earmuffs

gloves

hat

ring

slippers

tie

watch

©School Zone Publishing Company

MUD BATH

Find and circle the hidden pictures.

MOVIE NIGHT

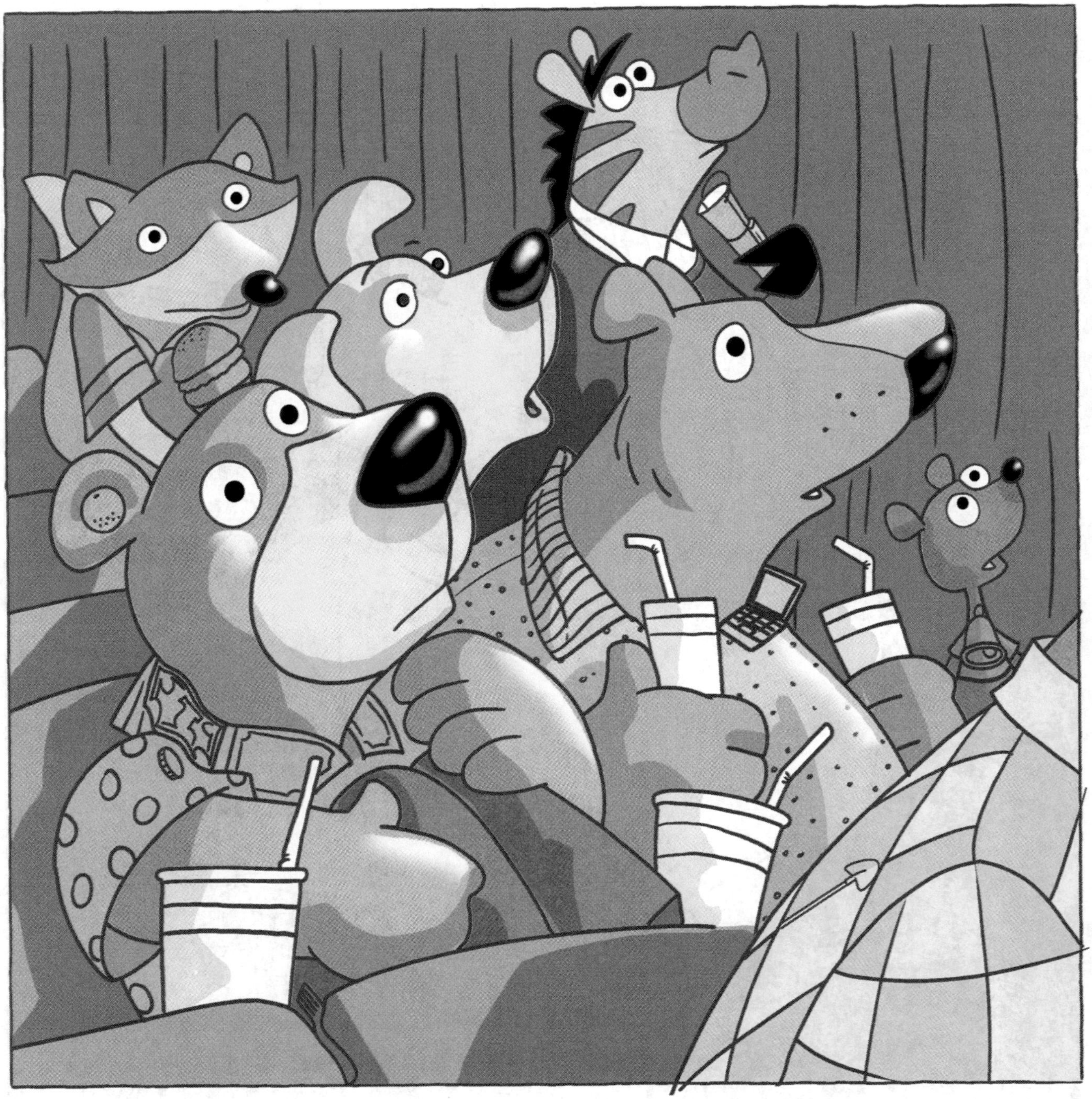

Find and circle the hidden pictures.

orange bell money hamburger shovel laptop bucket fork

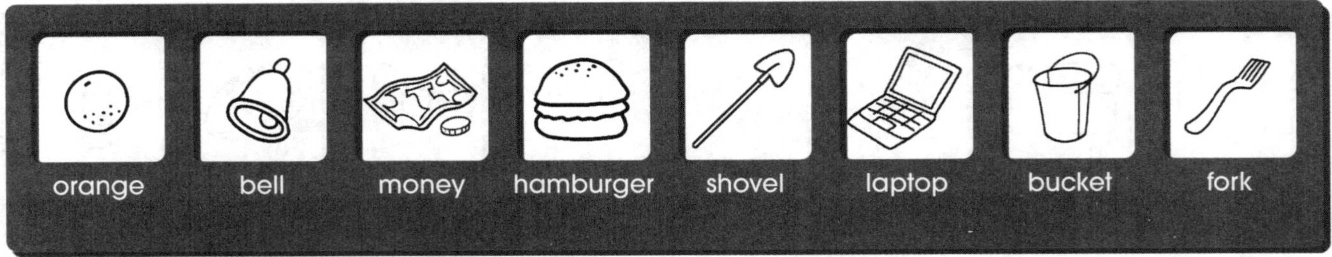

 ©School Zone Publishing Company

DAY AT THE CIRCUS

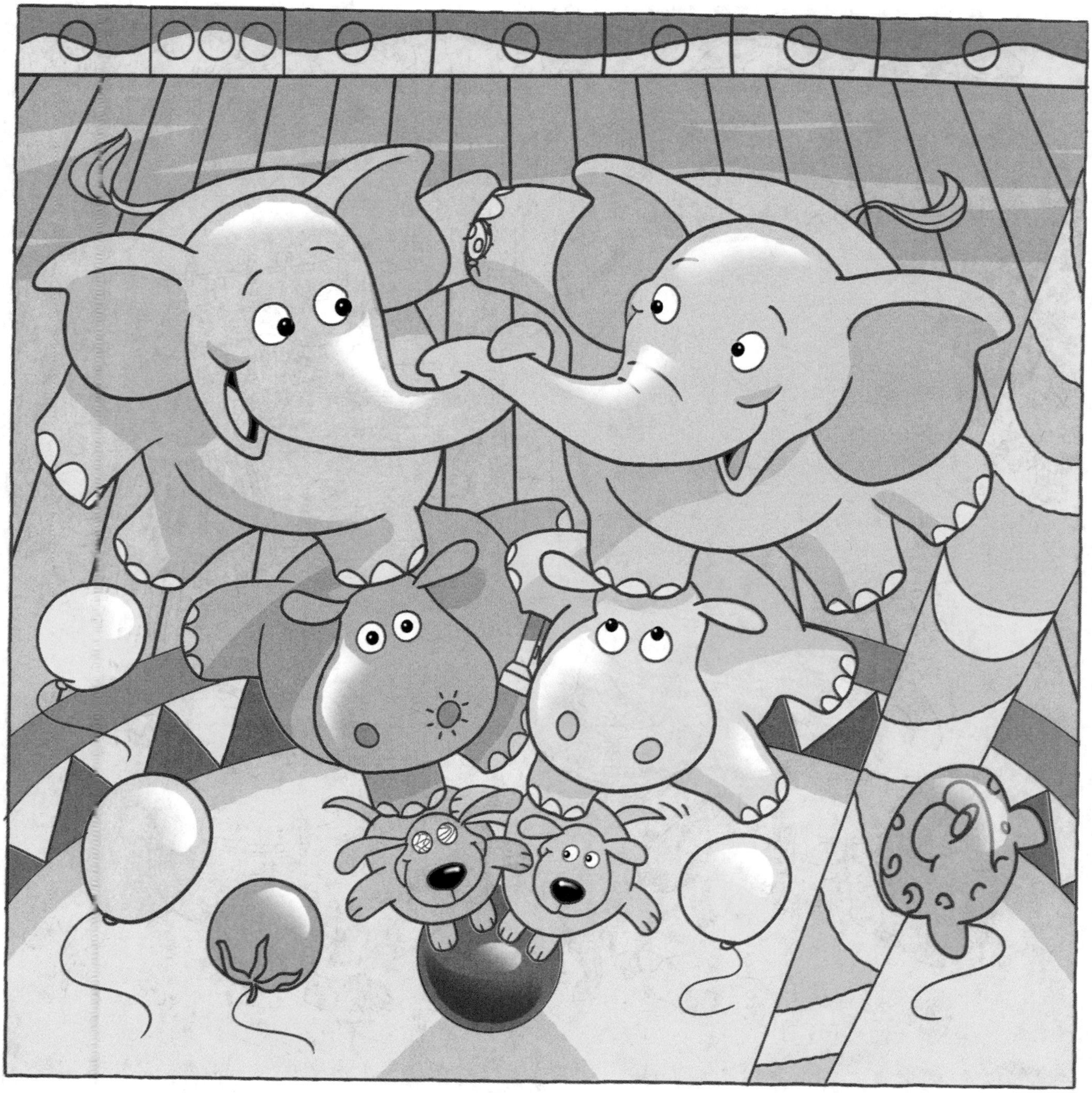

Find and circle the hidden pictures.

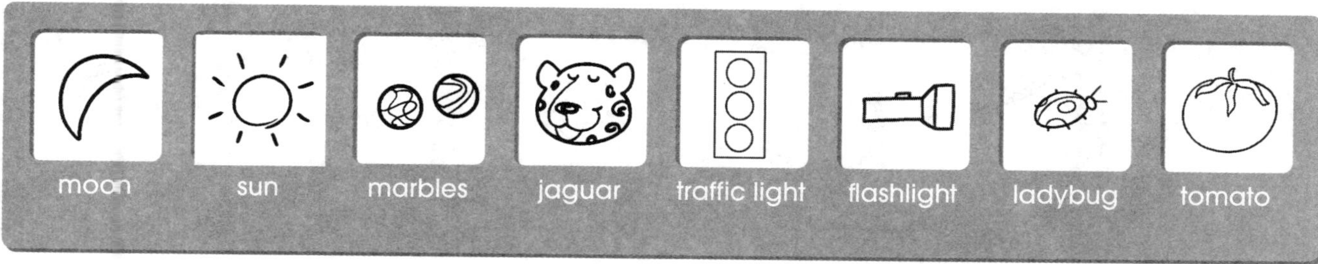

CAMPING OUT

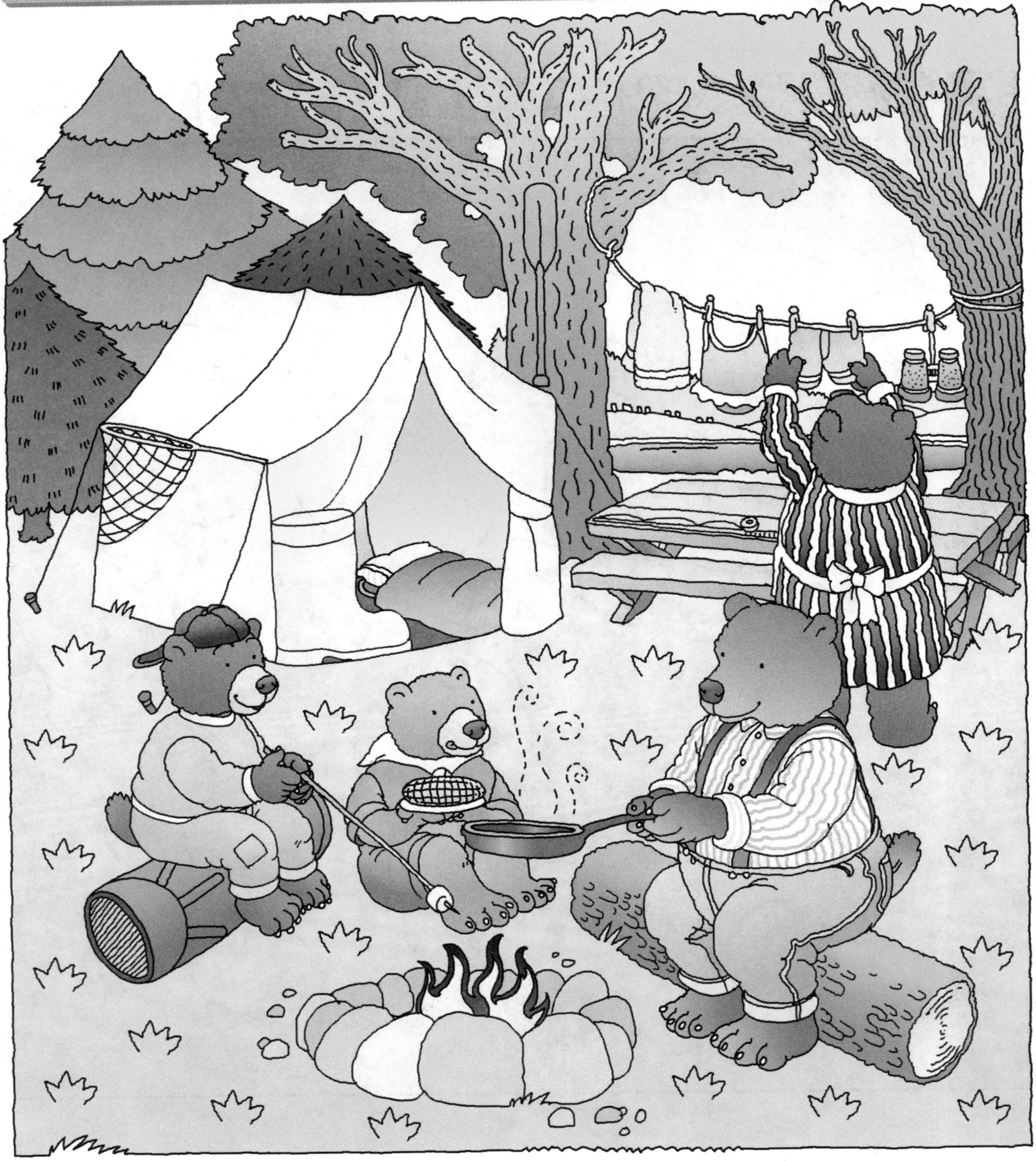

Find and circle the hidden pictures.

oar

fishing pole

boot

binoculars

grill

net

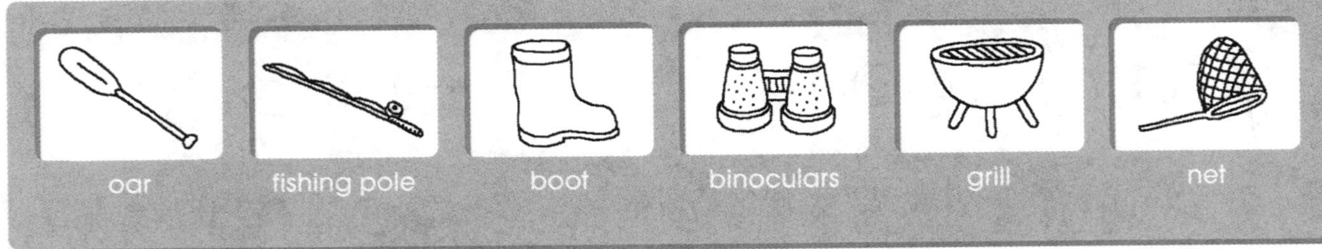

©School Zone Publishing Company

FARM JAMBOREE

Find and circle the hidden pictures.

STORY TIME

Look at the picture and find:

1 thing that rhymes with **tassel**

2 things that rhyme with **man**

3 things that rhyme with **camp**

4 things that rhyme with **far**

5 things that rhyme with **cool**

6 things that rhyme with **low**

©School Zone Publishing Company

SWIMMING HOLE

Look at the picture and find:

1 thing that rhymes with **spoon**

2 things that rhyme with **dog**

3 things that rhyme with **black**

4 things that rhyme with **sat**

5 things that rhyme with **see**

6 things that rhyme with **smock**

DON'T GET LOST!

Follow the maze from start to finish.

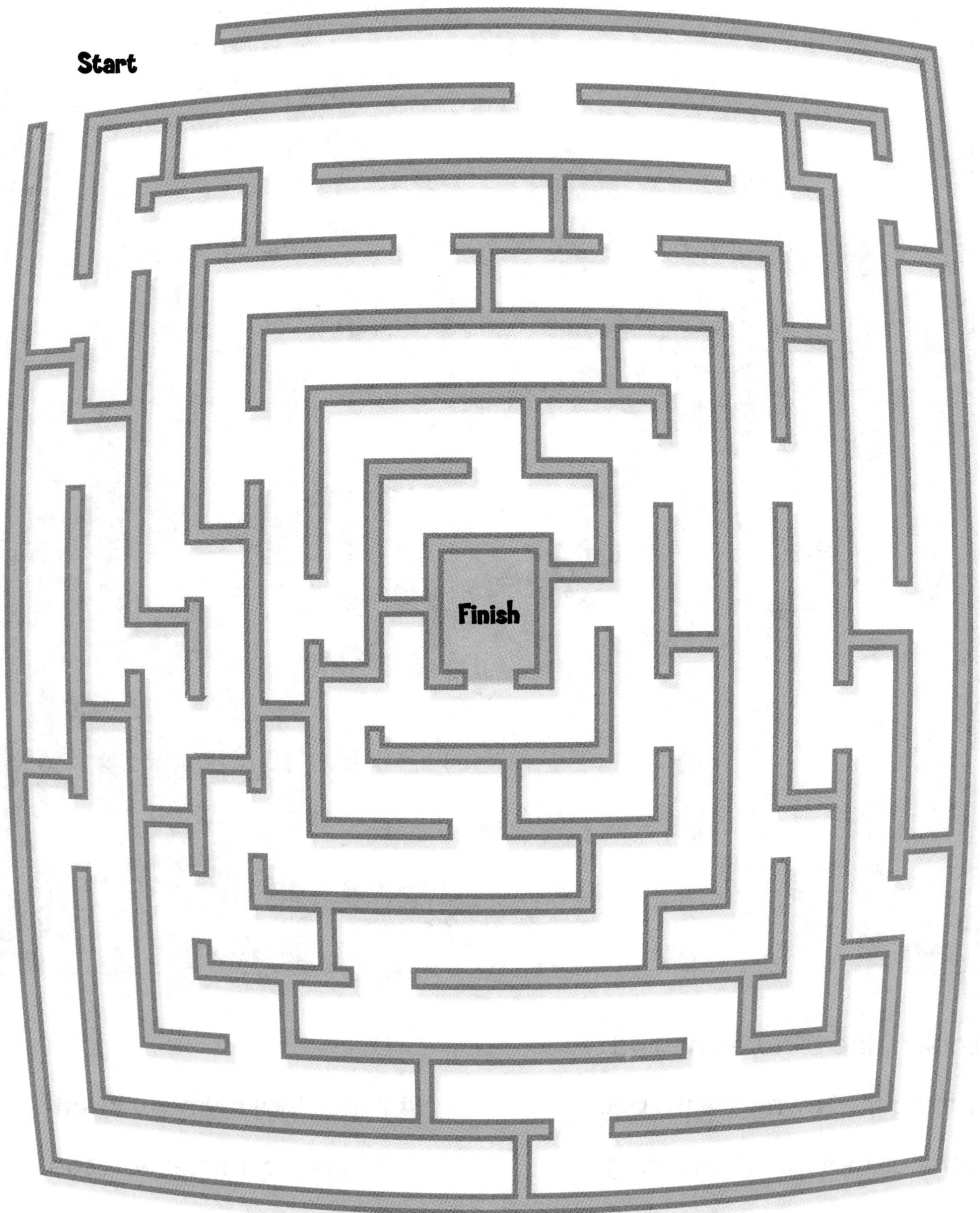

 ©School Zone Publishing Company

Follow the maze from start to finish.

OCEAN BLUE

Follow the maze from start to finish.

 ©School Zone Publishing Company

ROUND AND ROUND

Follow the maze from start to finish.

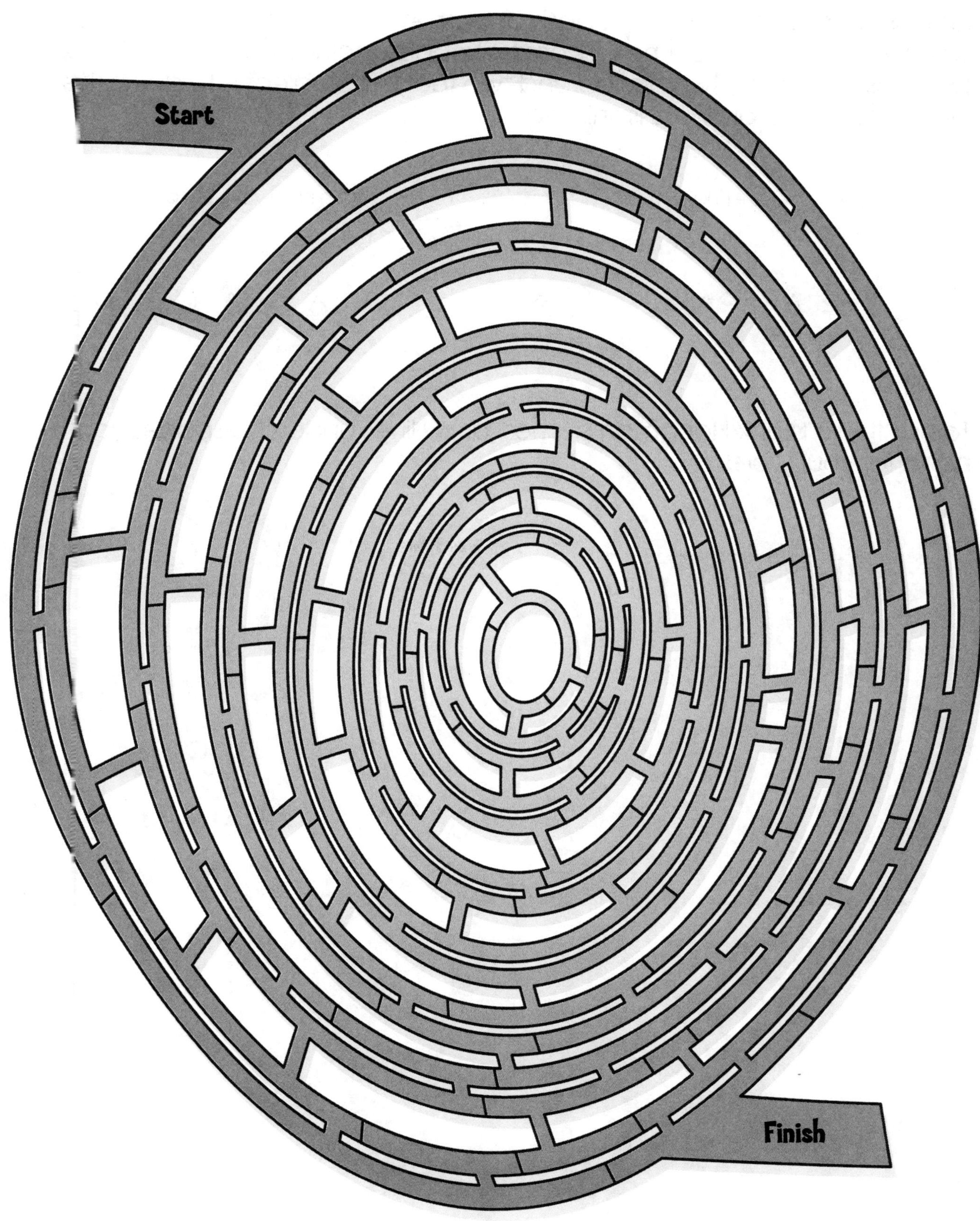

HANGMAN

One person thinks of a word and draws the same number of dashes as letters in the word. The other player guesses the letters. If a guess is right, the letter is written on the correct dash or dashes. If the guess is wrong, a body is drawn one part at a time (a complete body includes a head, a torso, two legs, two arms, two hands, and two feet). The object is to guess the word before the drawing is finished.

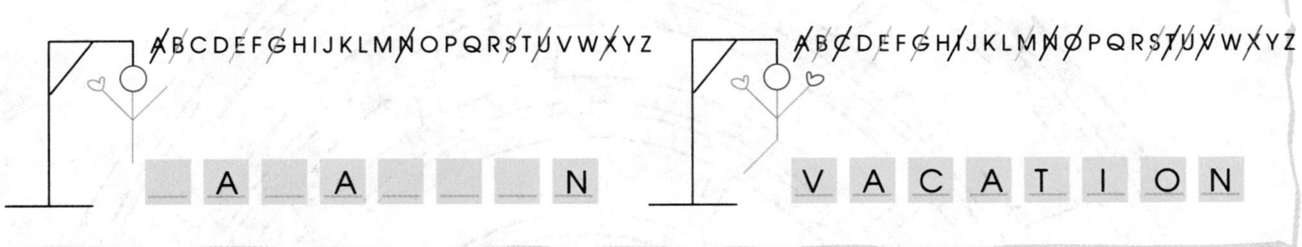

To use these blank Hangman games, draw lines under the spaces you need for your word.

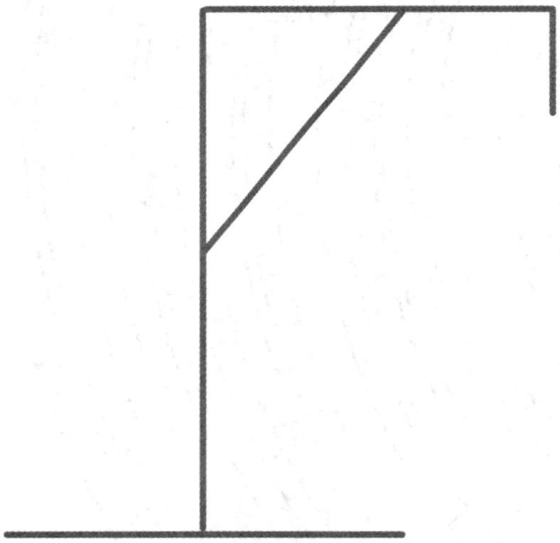

2 players

A B C D E F G H
I J K L M N O P Q
R S T U V W X Y Z

©School Zone Publishing Company

HANGMAN

Extra Playing Page: Directions can be found on page 230.

Challenge!
To make this game harder, you can choose long words, phrases, or movie titles.

A B C D E F G H
I J K L M N O P Q
R S T U V W X Y Z

A B C D E F G H
I J K L M N O P Q
R S T U V W X Y Z

HANGMAN

Extra Playing Page: Directions can be found on page 230.

A B C D E F G H
I J K L M N O P Q
R S T U V W X Y Z

A B C D E F G H
I J K L M N O P Q
R S T U V W X Y Z

 ©School Zone Publishing Company

HANGMAN

Extra Playing Page: Directions can be found on page 230.

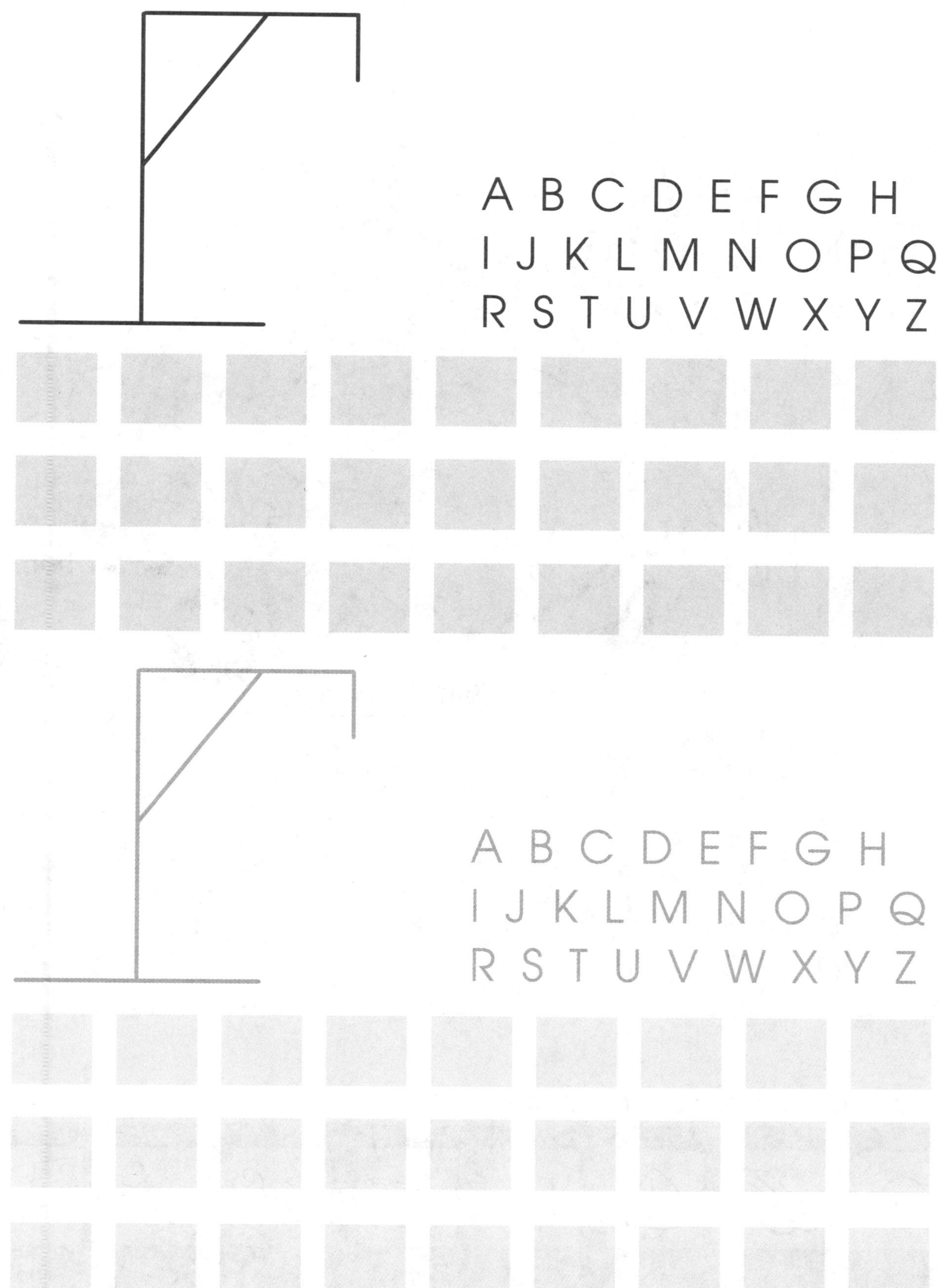

SOMEBODY'S CRABBY!

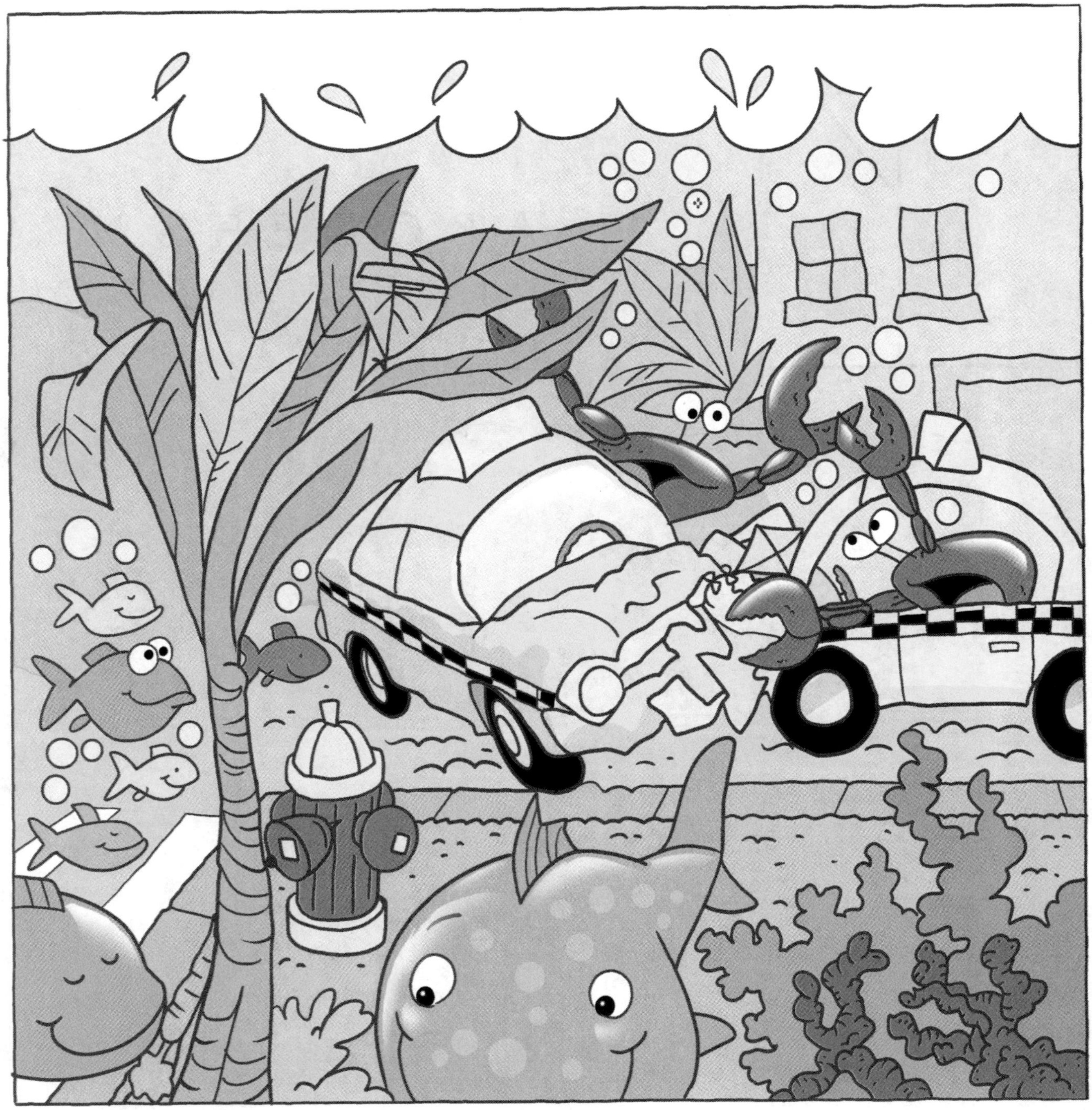

Find and circle the hidden pictures.

button hot dog sailboat top plate worm carrot kite

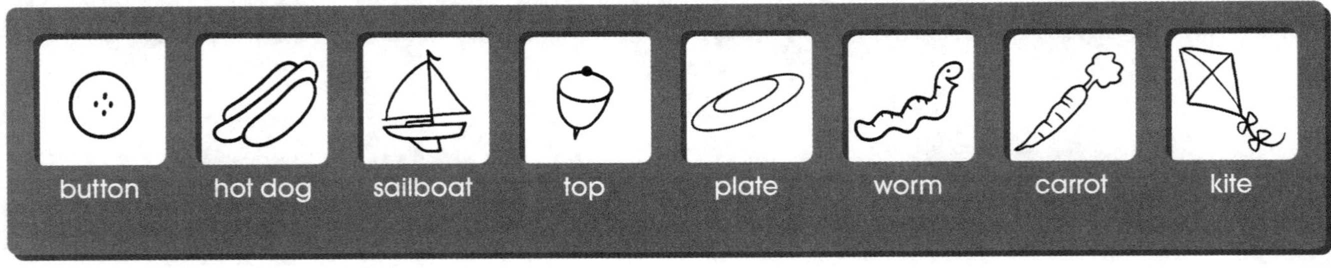

©School Zone Publishing Company

DOWN ON THE FARM

Find and circle the hidden pictures.

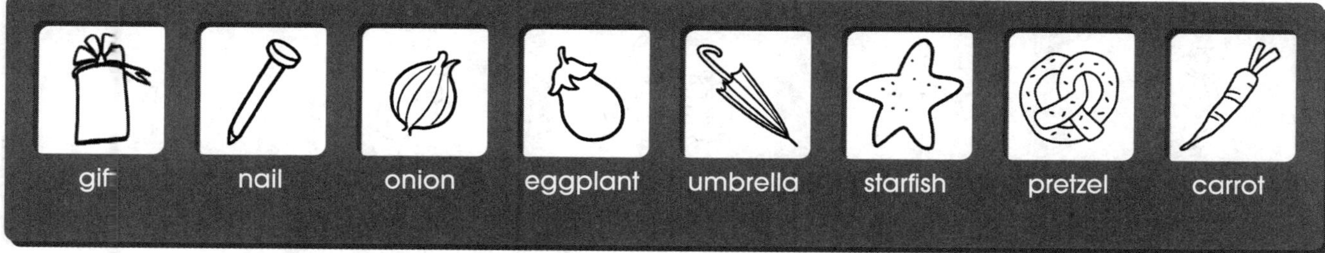

©School Zone Publishing Company

BARNYARD PARTY

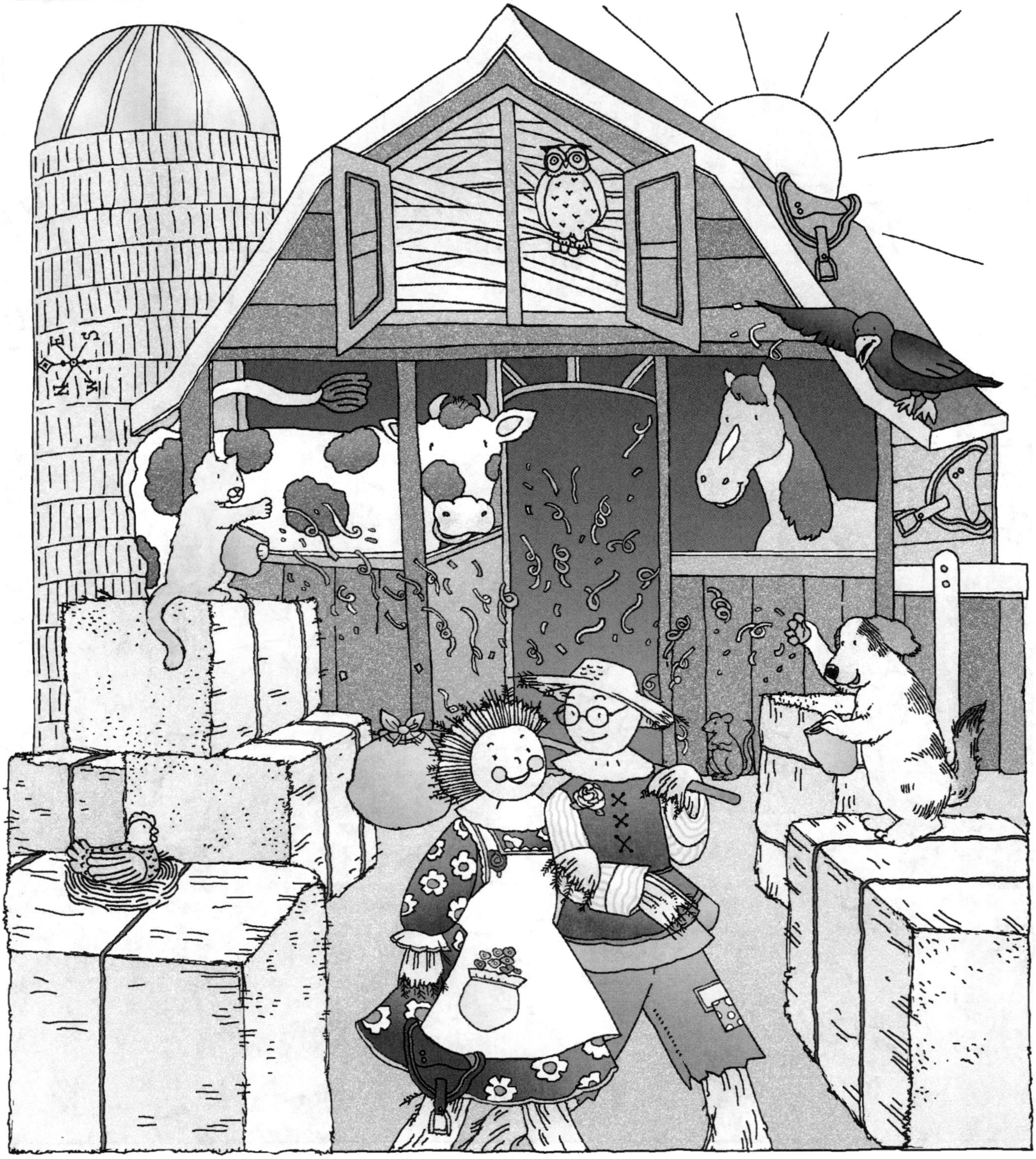

Find and circle the hidden pictures.

Find 1
owl

Find 1
weather vane

Find 1
hen

Find 1
mouse

Find 3
saddles

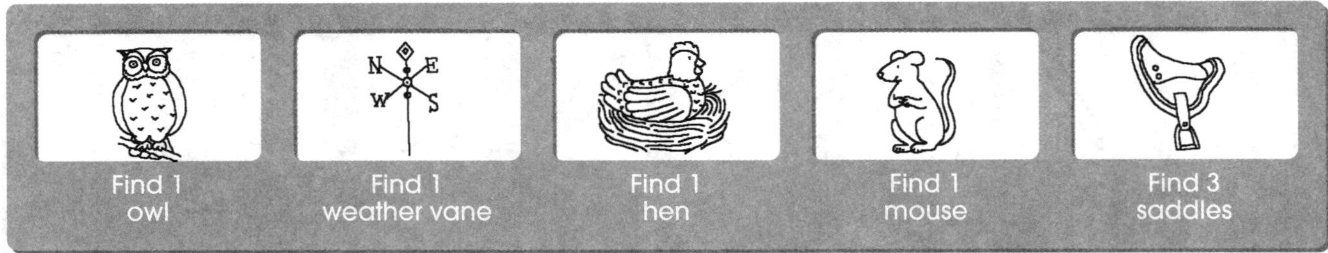

©School Zone Publishing Company

PIONEER TOWN

Find and circle the hidden pictures.

Find 1
railroad sign

Find 1
yield sign

Find 1
crossing sign

Find 1
one way sign

Find 1
hospital sign

Find 2
stop signs

SINGING IN THE SWAMP

Find and circle the hidden pictures.

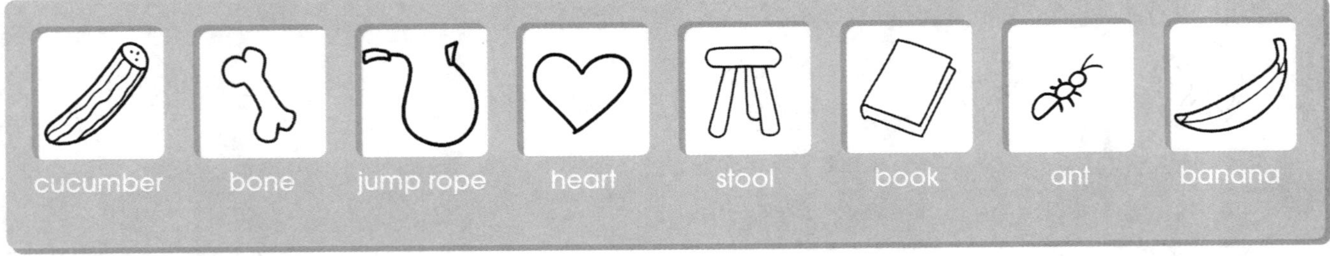

©School Zone Publishing Company

INSIDE THE BARN

Find and circle the hidden pictures.

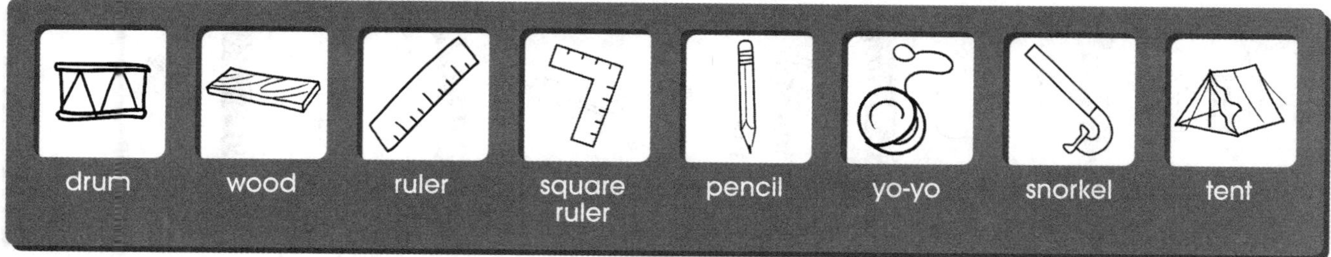

©School Zone Publishing Company

INTO THE SKY

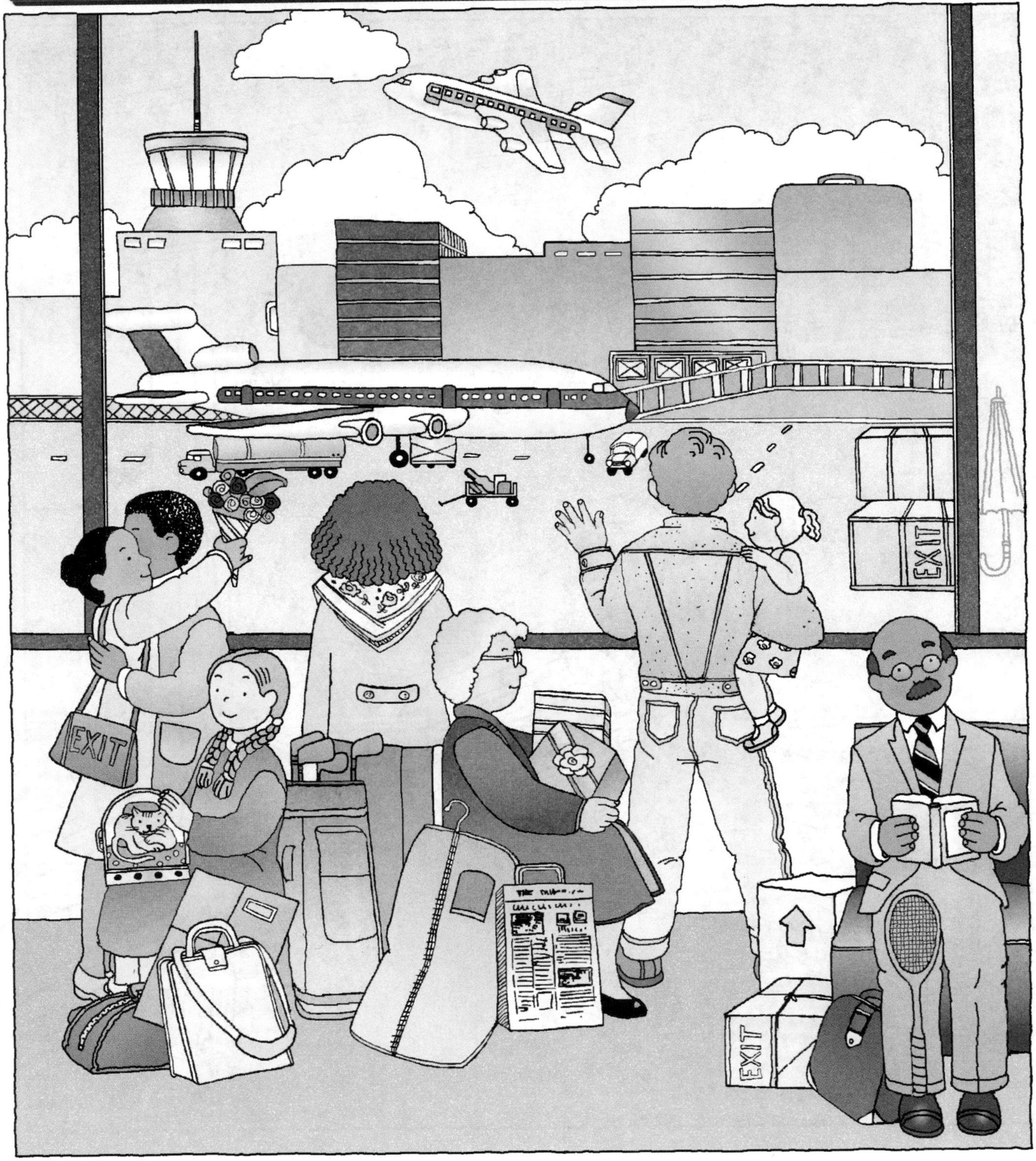

Find and circle the hidden pictures.

Find 3 exit signs

Find 2 suitcases

Find 1 newspaper

Find 1 umbrella

Find 1 set of golf clubs

Find 1 racket

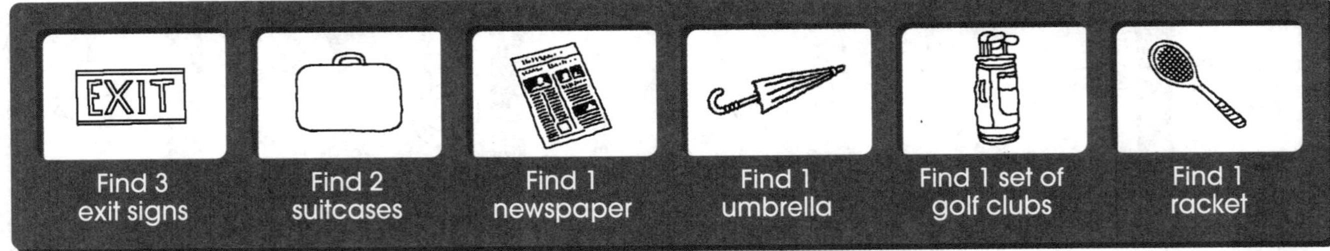

 ©School Zone Publishing Company

AT THE ZOO

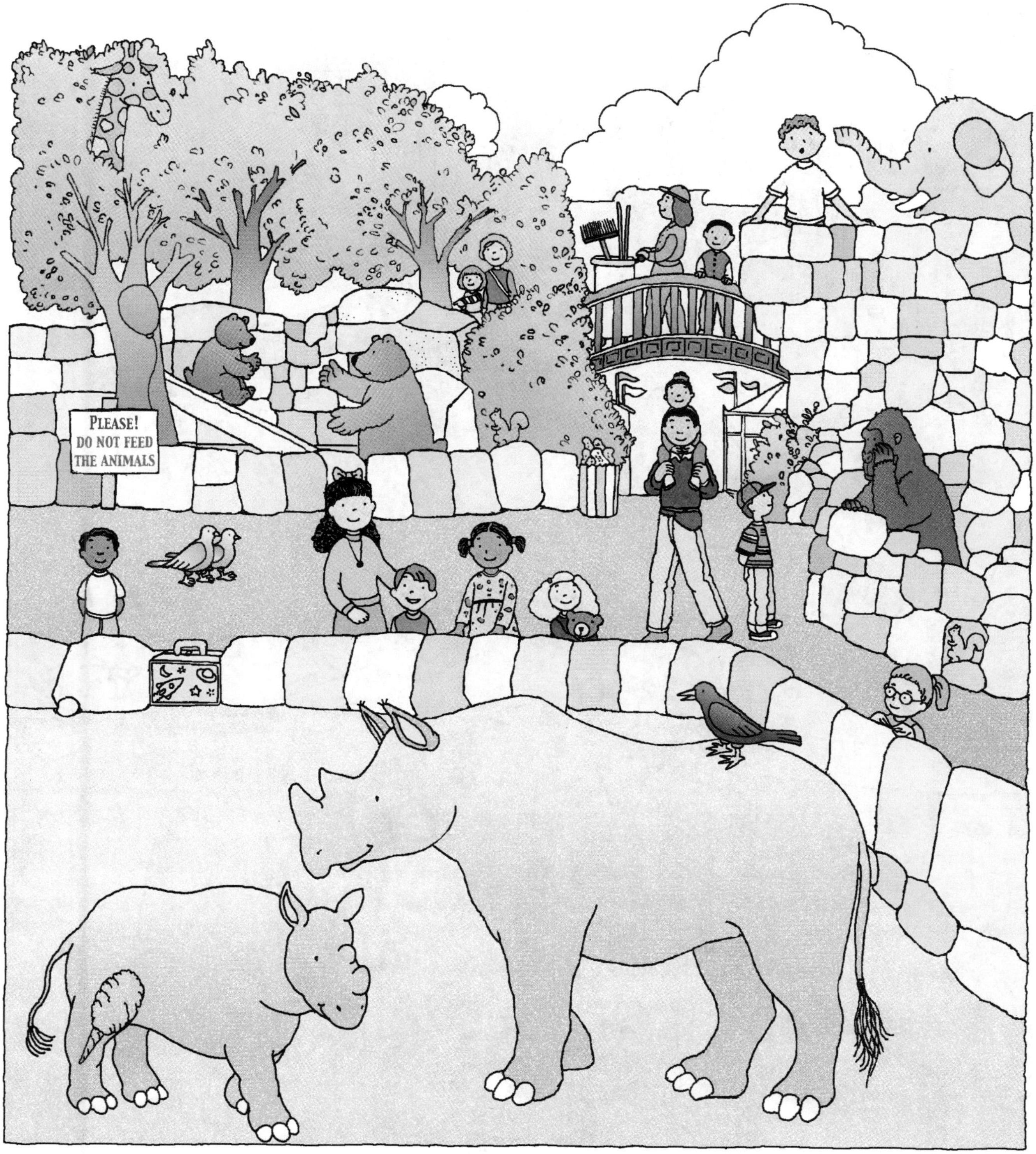

Find and circle the hidden pictures.

Find 1
lunch box

Find 1
giraffe

Find 1
cotton candy

Find 2
balloons

Find 1
bag of peanuts

Find 2
squirrels

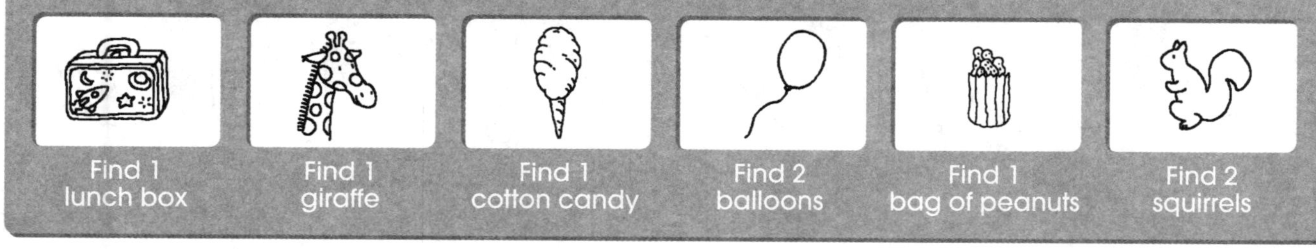

GARBAGE DAY

Find and circle the hidden pictures.

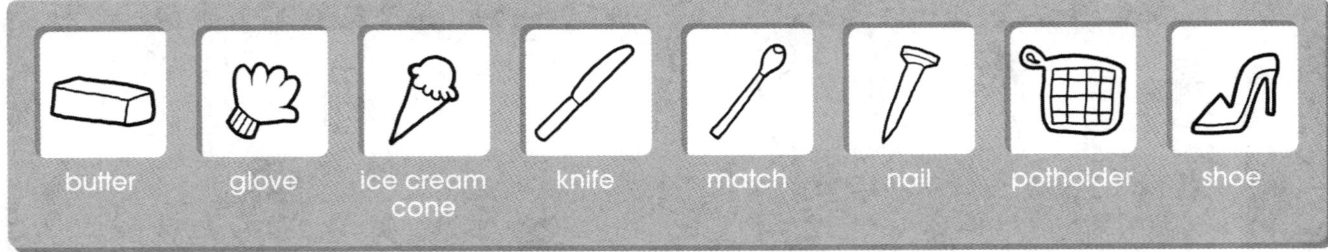

©School Zone Publishing Company

STARGAZERS

Find and circle the hidden pictures.

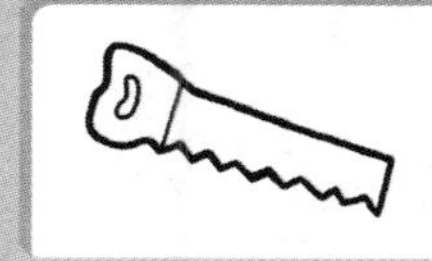

Find 1 saw

Find 2 arrows

Find 3 bats

Find 4 envelopes

Find 5 lightbulbs

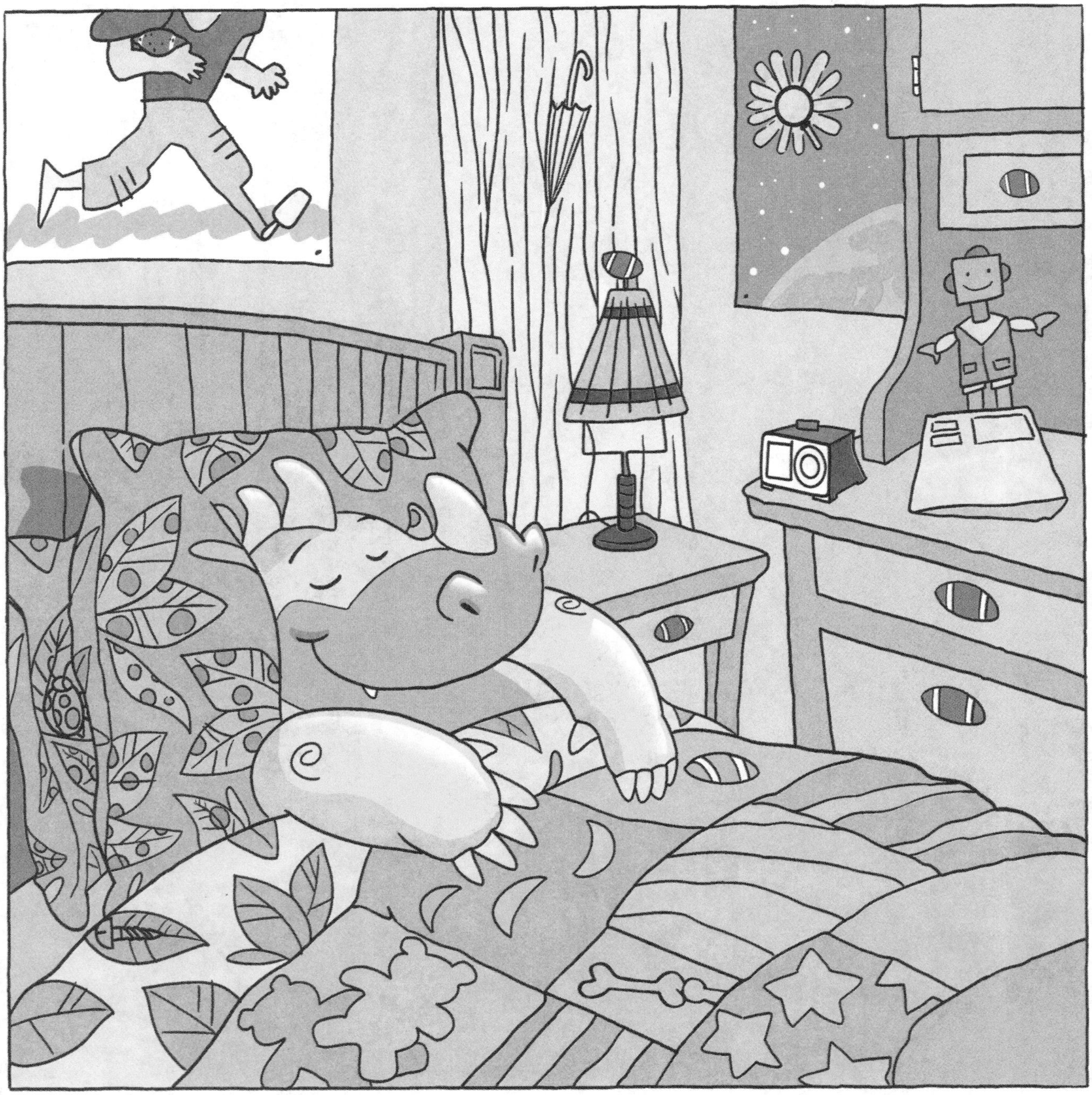

SWEET DREAMS

Find and circle the hidden pictures.

©School Zone Publishing Company

CATTLE GOTHIC

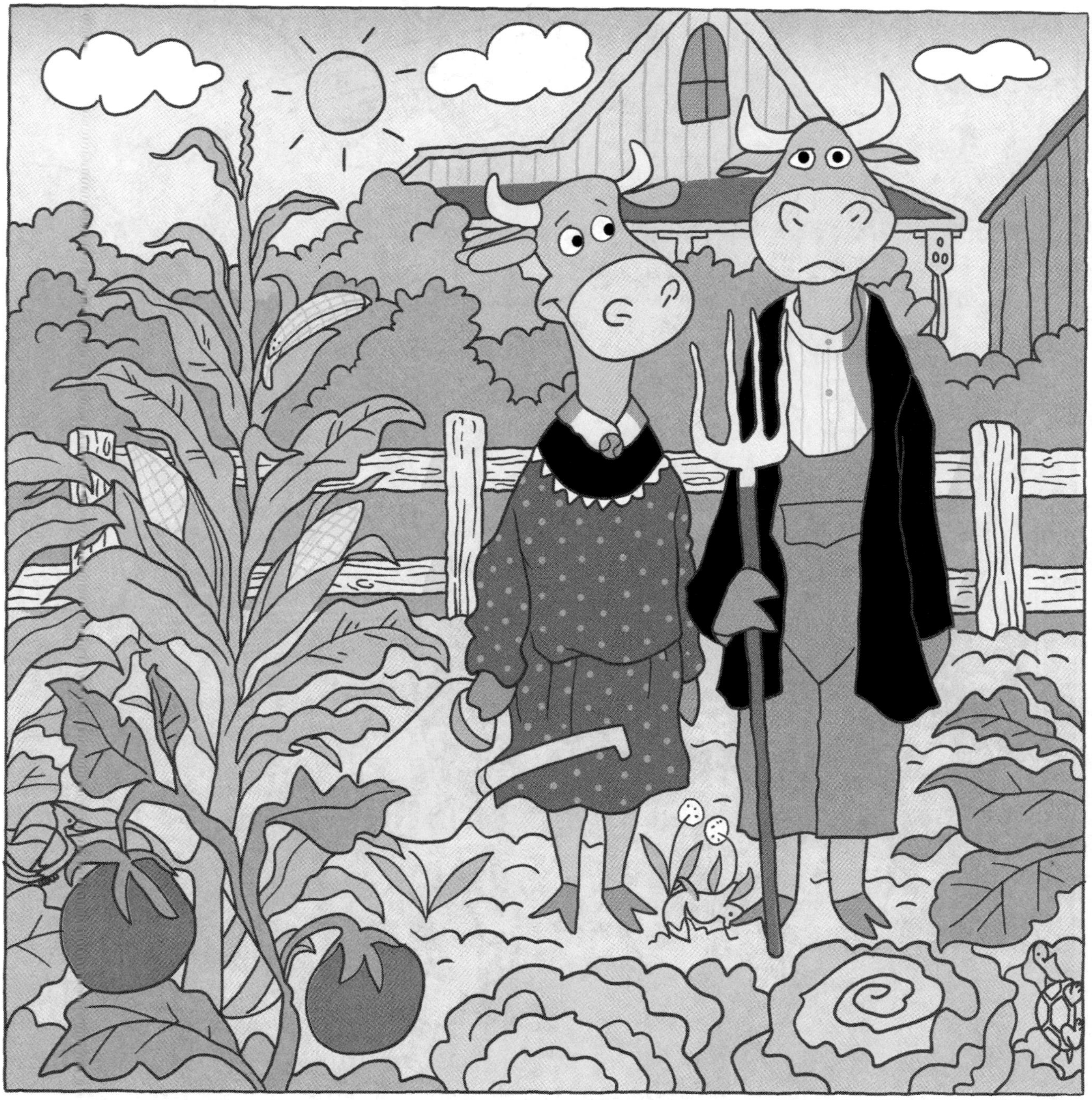

Find and circle the hidden pictures.

hot dog party hat squirrel spatula turtle woodpecker banana baseball

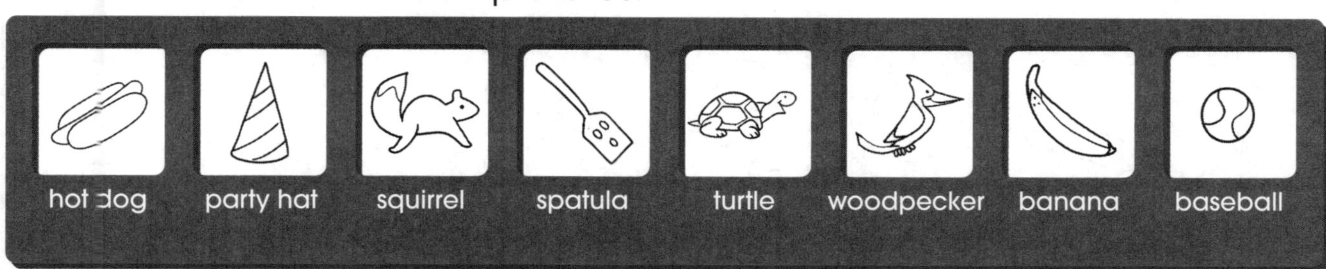

FRIENDLY FARMER

Find and circle the hidden pictures.

boomerang

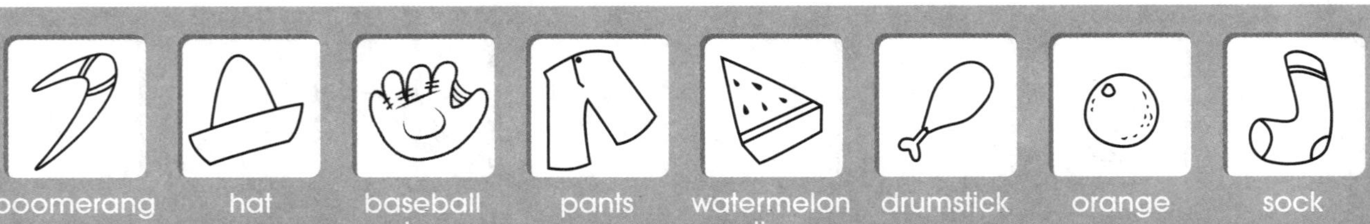

hat

baseball glove

pants

watermelon slice

drumstick

orange

sock

©School Zone Publishing Company

ANTICIPATION

Find and circle the hidden pictures.

bone

cat treat

cheese

dog bowl

kitten

pet bed

rope toy

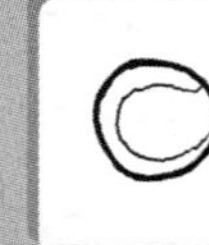

tennis ball

©School Zone Publishing Company

COMMUNITY GARDEN

Find and circle the hidden pictures.

Find 1
pail

Find 2
cacti

Find 3
frogs

Find 4
butterflies

Find 5
snails

 ©School Zone Publishing Company

THE WAVE

Follow the maze from start to finish.

SLITHERING SWIMMER

Color the picture below.

1 = blue green 2 = **brown** 3 = yellow 4 = **blue**

5 = orange 6 = **black** 7 = green

2 / 5	2 / 2	2 / 2	2 / 2	2 / 7	7 / 7	7 / 3	3 / 3	3 / 3	3 / 2	2 / 2	2 / 2	2 / 5	5 / 2	2 / 2
2 / 2	2 / 2	2 / 2	2 / 3	7 / 7	7 / 2	2 / 2	2 / 2	2 / 2	2 / 2	2 / 2	5 / 2	2 / 2	2 / 2	2 / 5
2 / 2	2 / 2	2 / 2	3 / 3	7 / 7	7 / 7	3 / 3	3 / 3	3 / 3	2 / 2	2 / 2	2 / 2	2 / 2	5 / 2	5 / 5
5 / 2	5 / 2	2 / 2	2 / 2	2 / 2	2 / 2	7 / 7	7 / 7	7 / 7	7 / 7	7 / 7	7 / 7	2 / 2	2 / 2	2 / 2
2 / 2	2 / 2	5 / 5	5 / 2	2 / 2	2 / 2	2 / 2	2 / 2	2 / 2	7 / 3	3 / 3	3 / 3	7 / 7	2 / 2	2 / 5
2 / 2	2 / 5	2 / 2	2 / 2	2 / 2	2 / 2	2 / 2	2 / 2	2 / 2	2 / 2	2 / 3	3 / 7	7 / 7	2 / 2	2 / 2
5 / 5	5 / 2	2 / 2	2 / 7	7 / 7	3 / 3	3 / 3	3 / 7	7 / 7	7 / 7	7 / 7	7 / 7	7 / 2	2 / 2	2 / 2
2 / 2	2 / 3	7 / 7	7 / 7	7 / 7	7 / 7	7 / 7	7 / 3	3 / 3	3 / 3	7 / 7	7 / 2	2 / 2	2 / 2	2 / 2
2 / 2	3 / 3	3 / 3	7 / 7	7 / 2	2 / 2	2 / 2	2 / 2	2 / 2	2 / 2	2 / 2	2 / 2	2 / 2	2 /	/
2 / 2	3 / 3	3 / 3	7 / 7	7 / 3	2 / 2	2 /	/	/ 4	/	/ 4	/	2 /	/ 4	4 / 1
2 / 2	2 / 2	3 / 7	7 / 7	7 / 3	3 / 3	4 / 4	4 / 4	4 / 4	4 / 4	4 / 4	4 / 4	4 / 4	4 / 1	1 / 1
2 / 2	2 / 2	2 /	7 / 7	7 / 7	3 / 3	3 / 3	3 / 7	4 / 7	7 / 7	4 / 4	4 / 4	4 / 4	1 / 4	4 / 4
2 / 2	/	/ 4	4 / 4	4 / 4	7 / 7	7 / 7	7 / 7	7 / 7	7 / 7	7 / 7	7 / 7	4 / 4	4 / 4	4 / 4
/ 4	4 / 4	4 / 4	4 / 4	4 / 4	4 / 4	7 / 7	7 / 7	3 / 3	7 / 7	7 / 7	7 / 7	7 / 7	4 / 4	4 / 1
4 / 4	4 / 4	4 / 1	1 / 4	4 / 4	4 / 4	4 / 4	7 / 7	7 / 7	7 / 7	7 / 7	6 / 7	7 / 4	4 / 4	1 / 4
4 / 1	1 / 4	4 / 4	1 / 1	1 / 1	4 / 4	4 / 4	4 / 4	4 / 4	4 / 4	4 / 4	4 / 4	4 / 4	4 / 4	1 / 4
4 / 4	4 / 4	4 / 4	4 / 4	4 / 4	1 / 1	1 / 1	1 / 1	4 / 4	4 / 4	4 / 4	4 / 4	4 / 1	1 / 4	4 / 4

 ©School Zone Publishing Company

PIPELINE PANDEMONIUM

Follow the maze from start to finish.

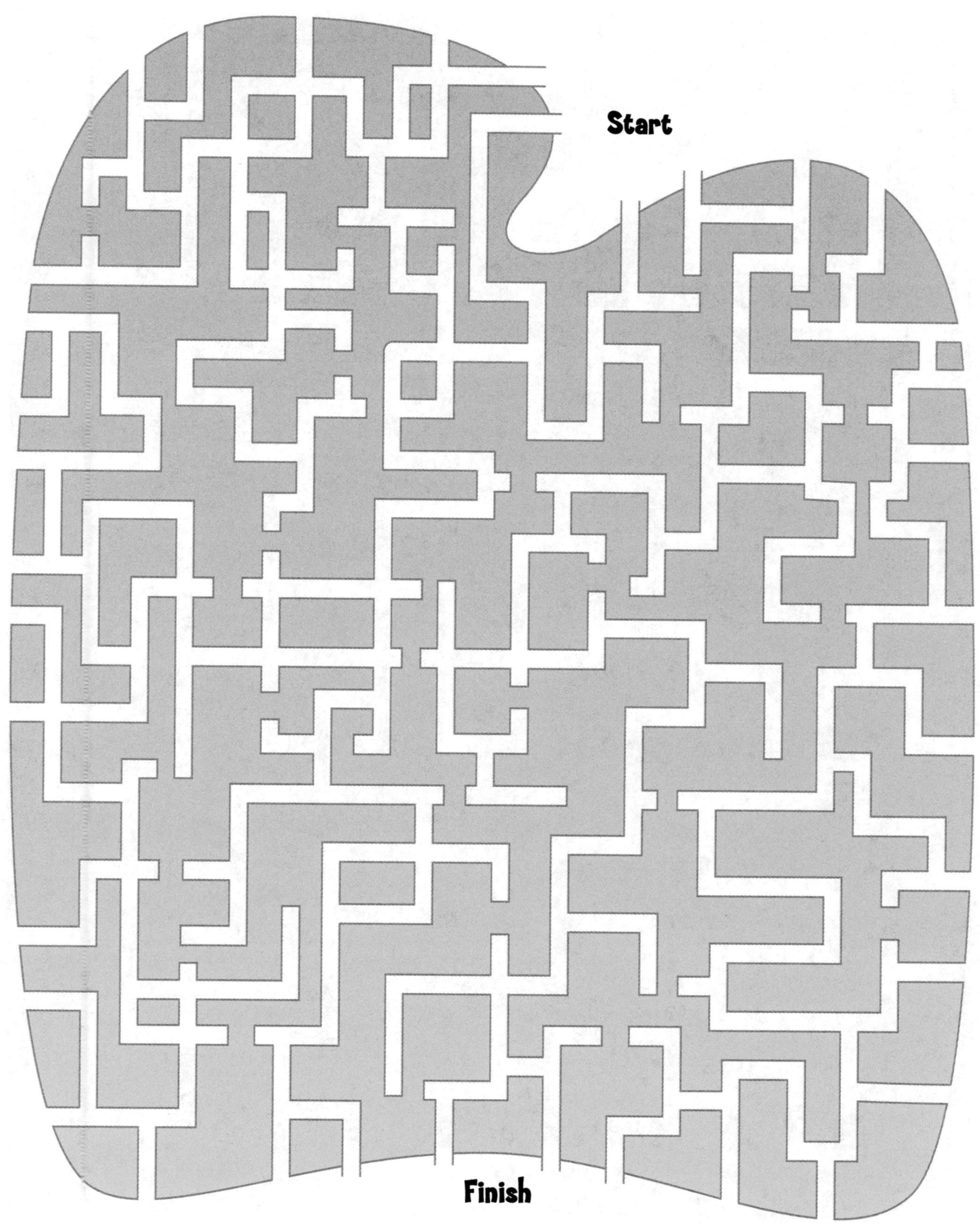

THE LABYRINTH

Follow the maze from start to finish.

 ©School Zone Publishing Company

BOXED IN

The object is to complete the most squares. Each player takes a turn drawing a vertical or horizontal line between two dots. When you complete a square, write your first initial in it. You then can take another turn. Your turn can include forming several boxes. A single line may form more than one box. Your turn is over when you draw a line that does not form a box.

The game ends when all of the possible boxes have been formed and filled. The winner is the player with the most initialed boxes.

L	P	L	P	P
L	P	L	P	P
P	L	L	P	L

Challenge!

You can also play this game by joining lines to form the fewest number of boxes. The players take turns drawing lines without forming boxes. The winner has the fewest number of boxes.

BOXED IN

Extra Playing Page: Directions can be found on page 253.

©School Zone Publishing Company

BOXED IN

Extra Playing Page: Directions can be found on page 253.

BOXED IN

Extra Playing Page: Directions can be found on page 253.

 ©School Zone Publishing Company

OUTER SPACE EXPLORATION

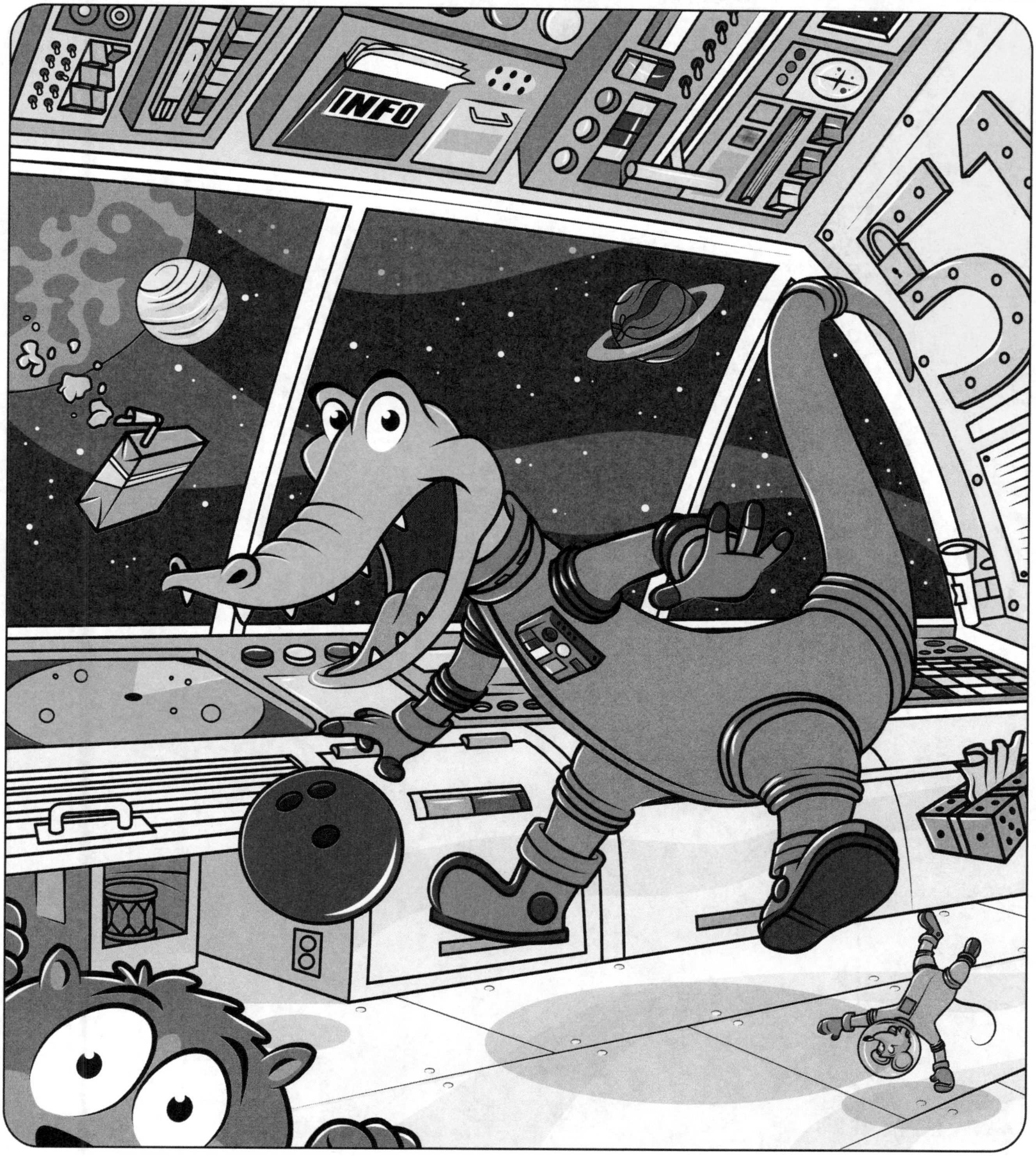

Find and circle the hidden pictures.

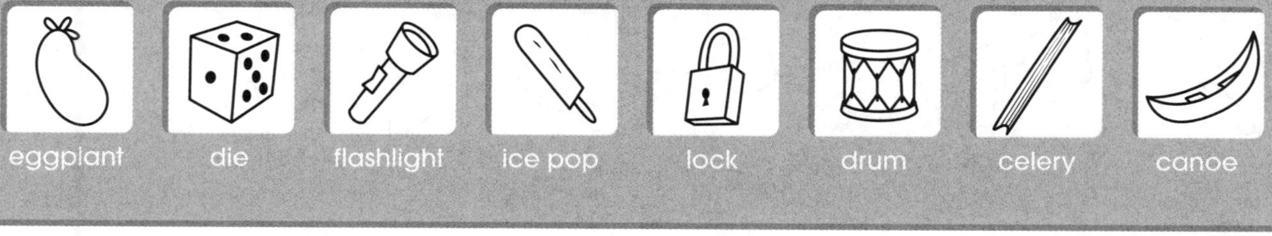

eggplant

die

flashlight

ice pop

lock

drum

celery

canoe

TOURIST TIME

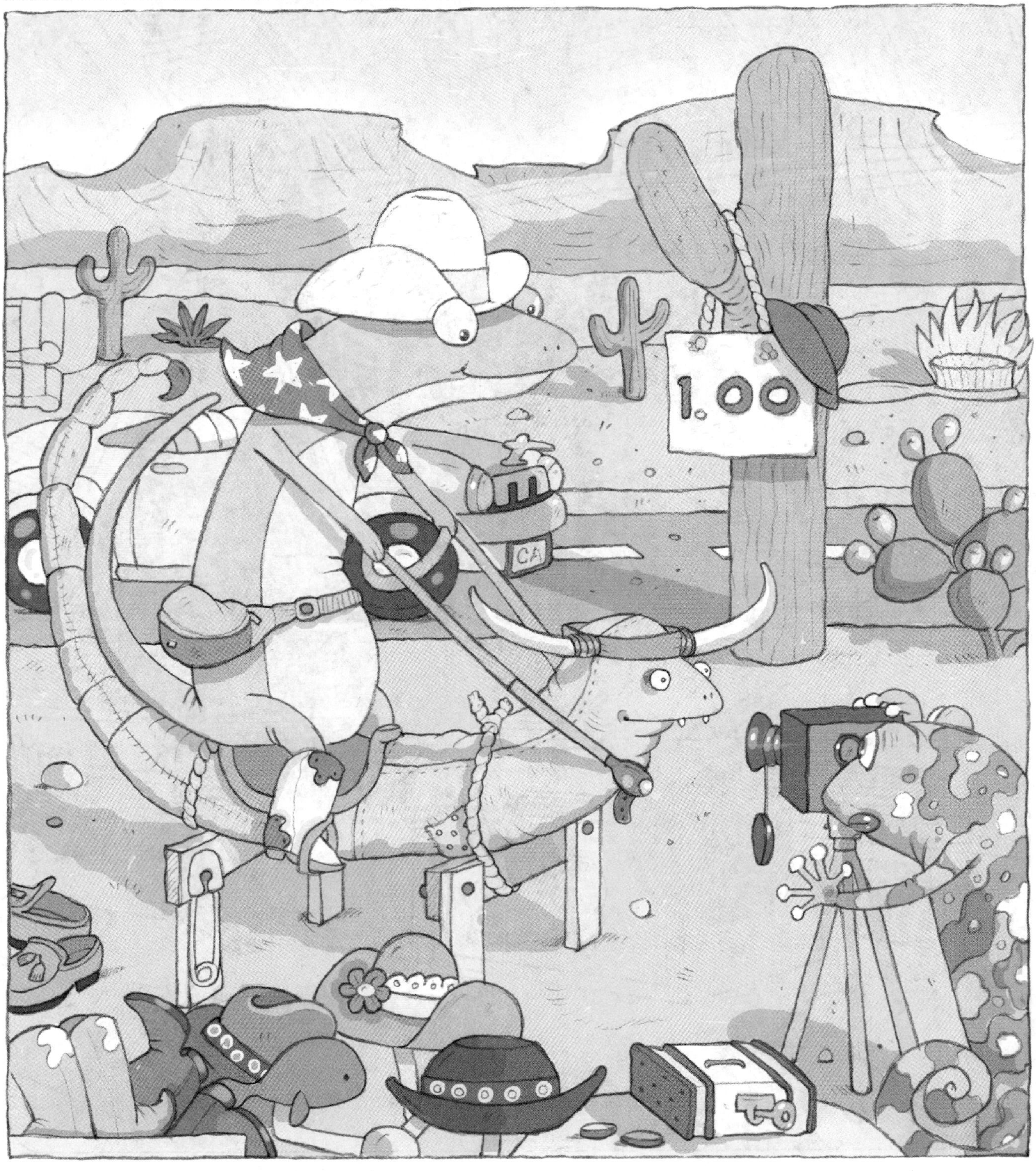

Find and circle the hidden pictures.

brush | chair | E | fish | ice cream sandwich | match | pickle | pin

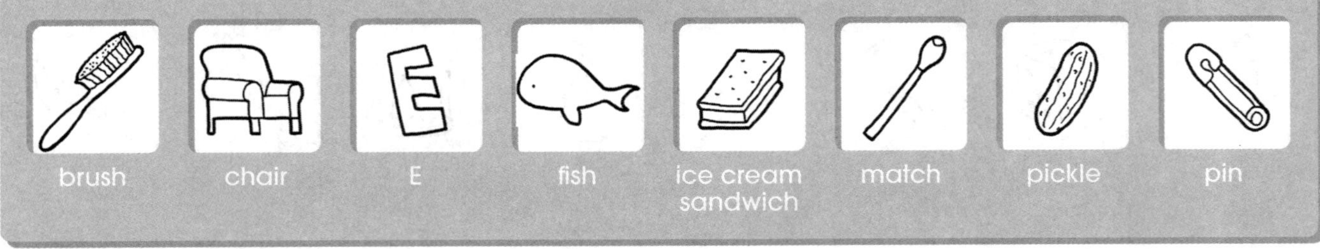

©School Zone Publishing Company

GARAGE SALE

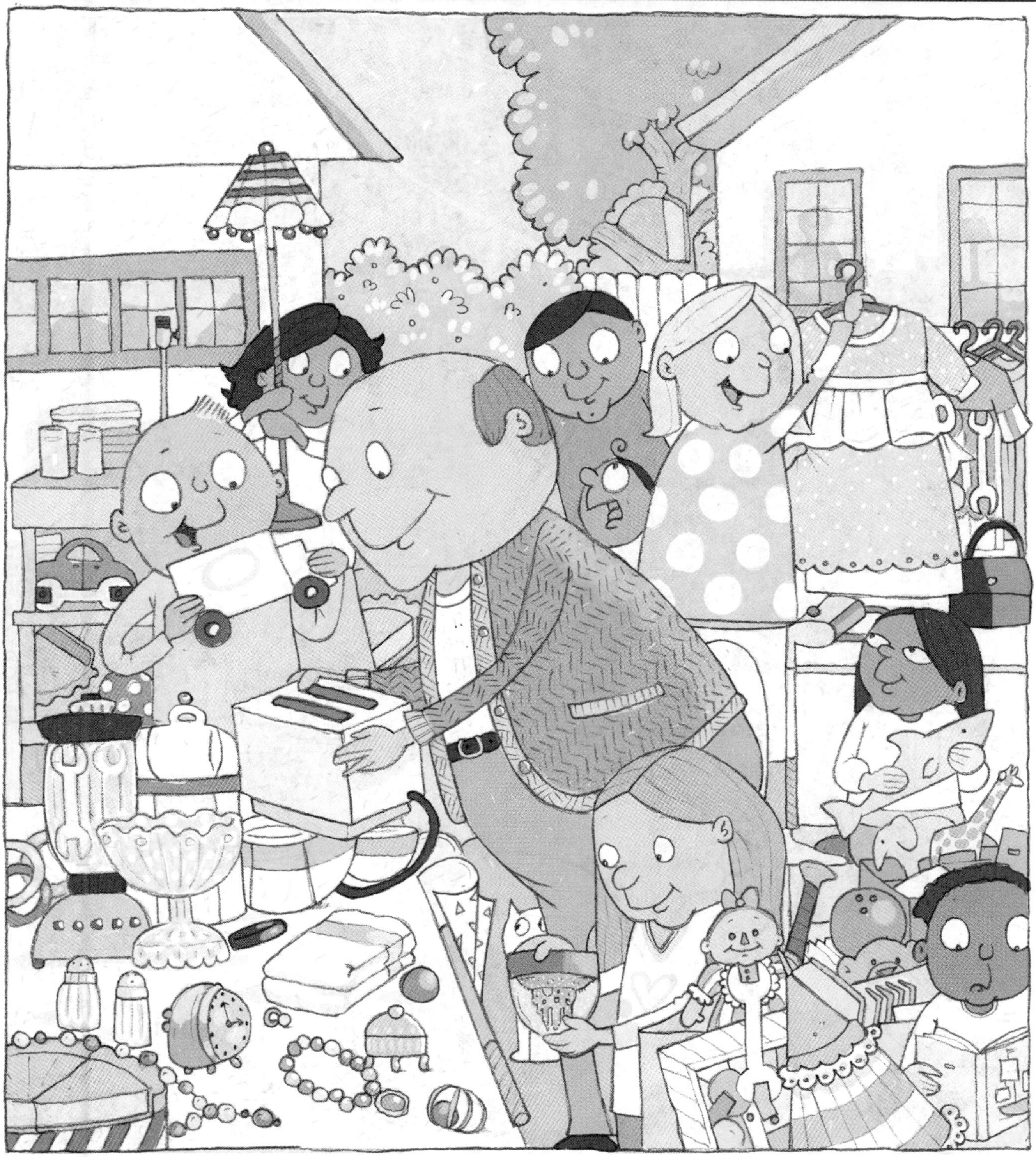

Find and circle the hidden pictures.

Find 1
hat

Find 2
cups

Find 3
golf clubs

Find 4
wrenches

Find 5
pie slices

©School Zone Publishing Company

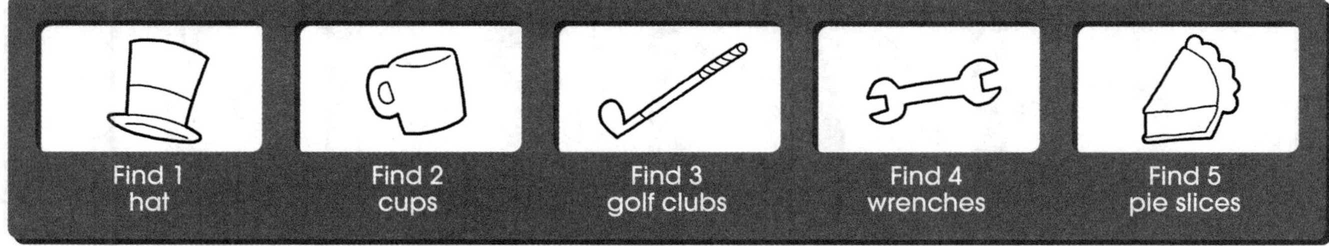

UNDER THE BIG TOP

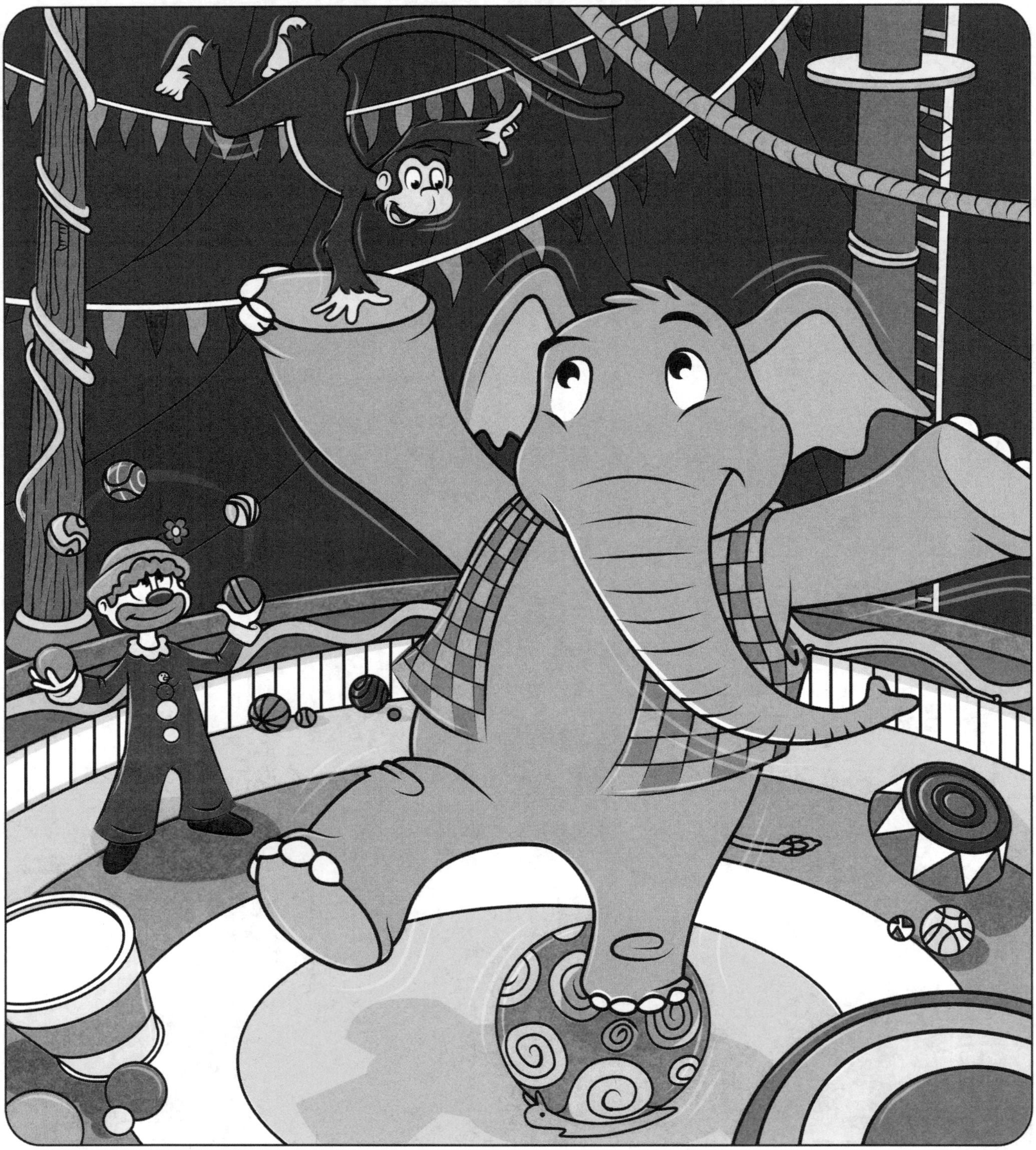

Find and circle the hidden pictures.

toothbrush | snail | asparagus | bow | milk carton | baseball | pot | snowman

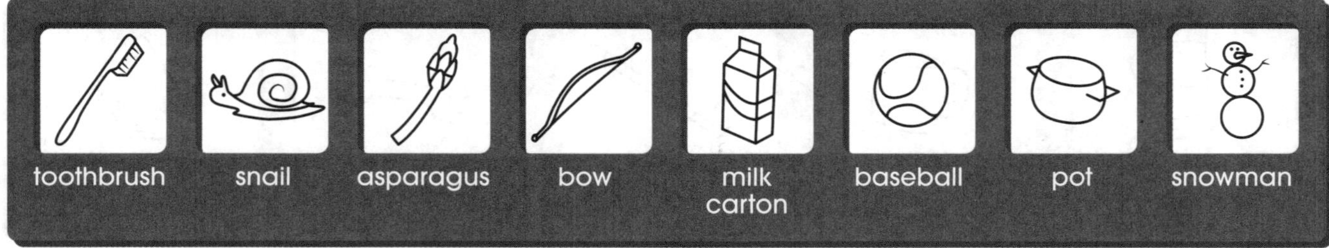

 ©School Zone Publishing Company

ARE WE THERE YET?

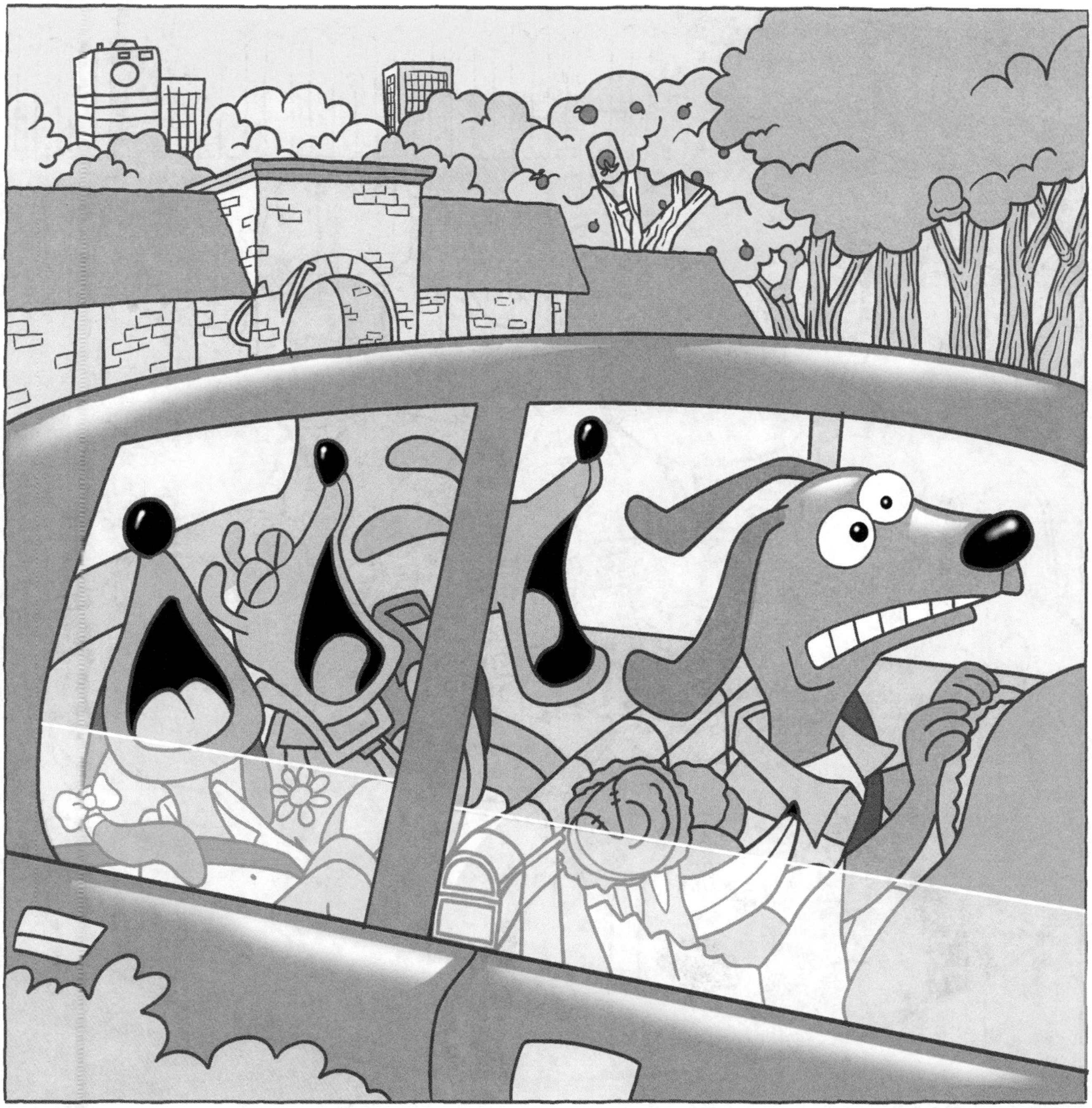

Find and circle the hidden pictures.

ketchup bottle

ice cream cone

flower

catcher's mitt

camera

watering can

bone

chest

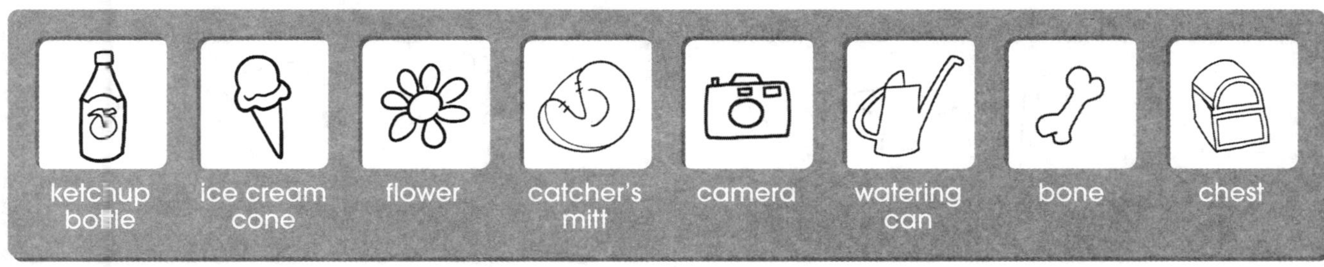

POOL PARTY

Find and circle the hidden pictures.

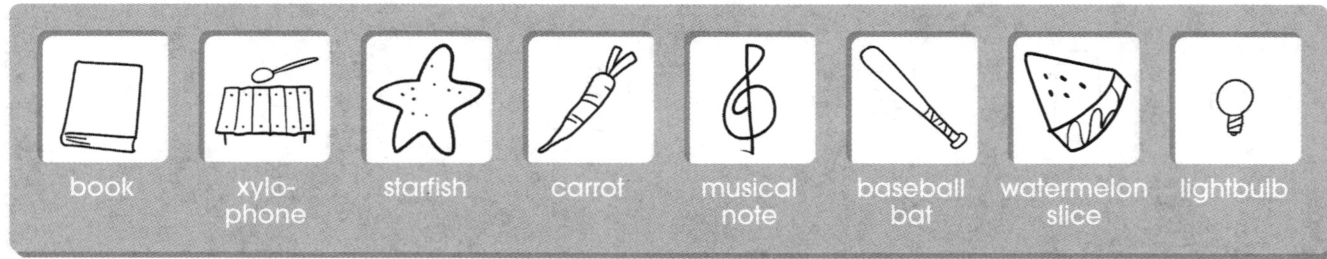

©School Zone Publishing Company

SANTA'S WORKSHOP

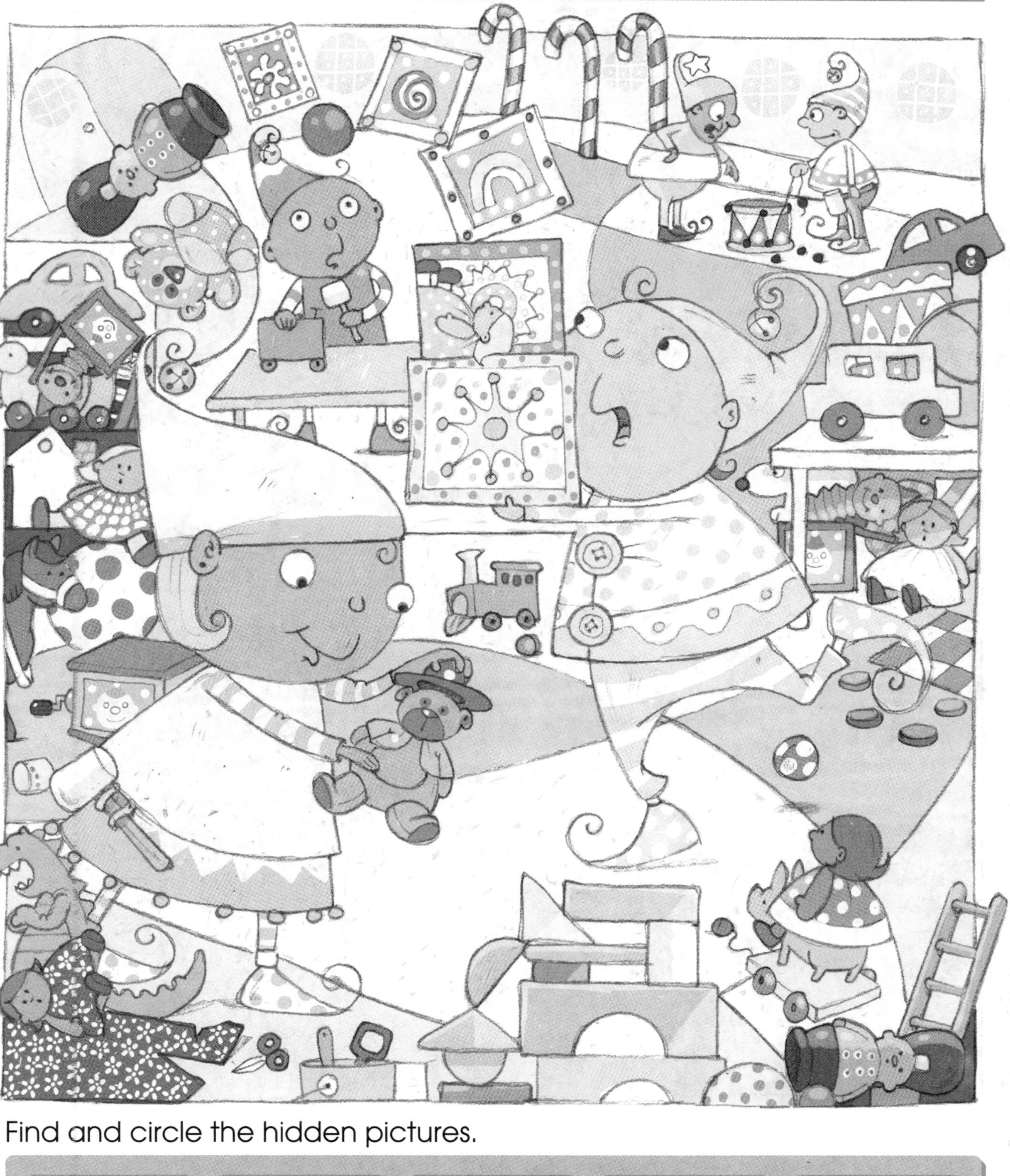

Find and circle the hidden pictures.

Find 1
star

Find 2
toy soldiers

Find 3
jack-in-the-boxes

Find 4
mallets

Find 5
dolls

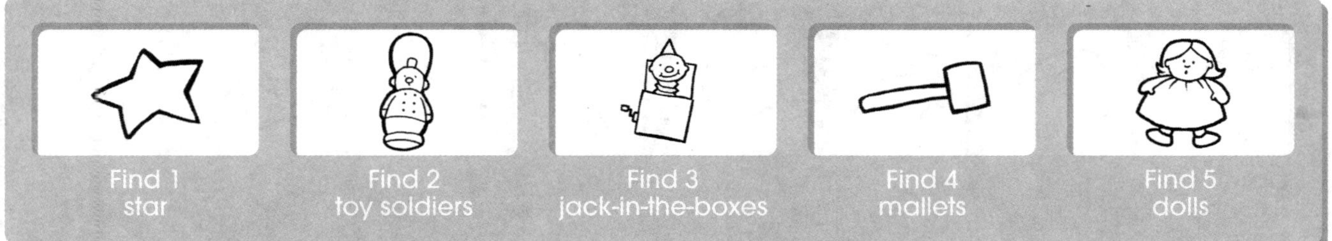

JUNGLE FUN

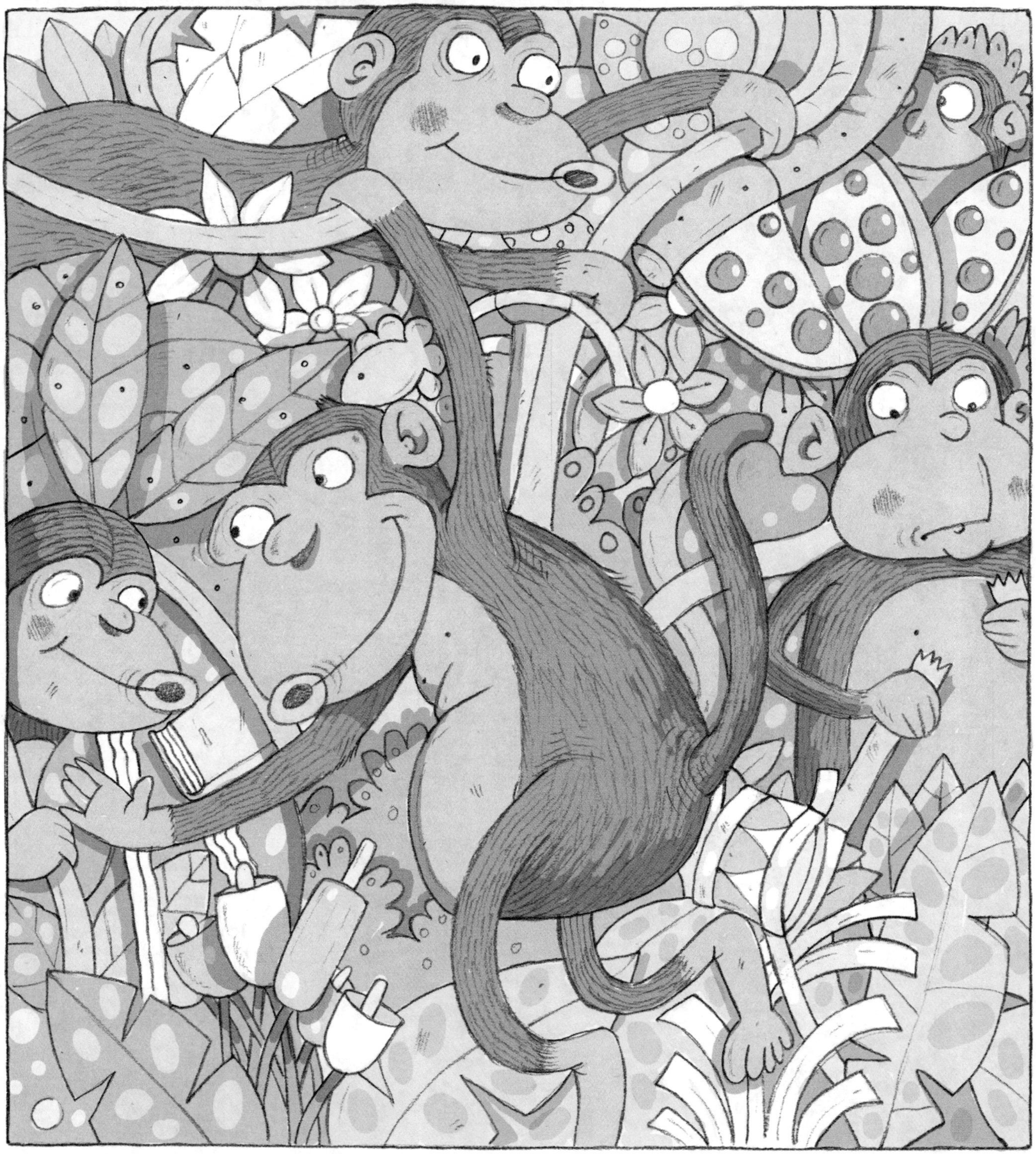

Find and circle the hidden pictures.

book drum fish heart ice pop nail pizza slice pine tree

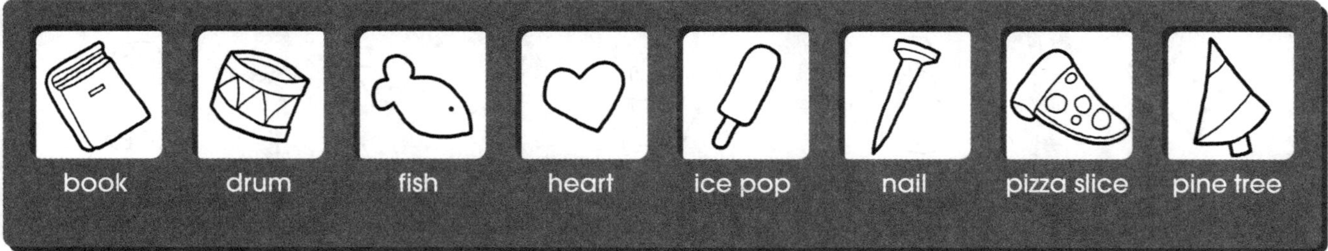

©School Zone Publishing Company

CAMPFIRE STORIES

Find cnd circle the hidden pictures.

©School Zone Publishing Company

NICE DINOSAUR...

Look at the picture and find:

1 hedgehog	**4** cats
2 mice	**5** birds
3 reptiles	**6** spiders

©School Zone Publishing Company

HODGEPODGE 3

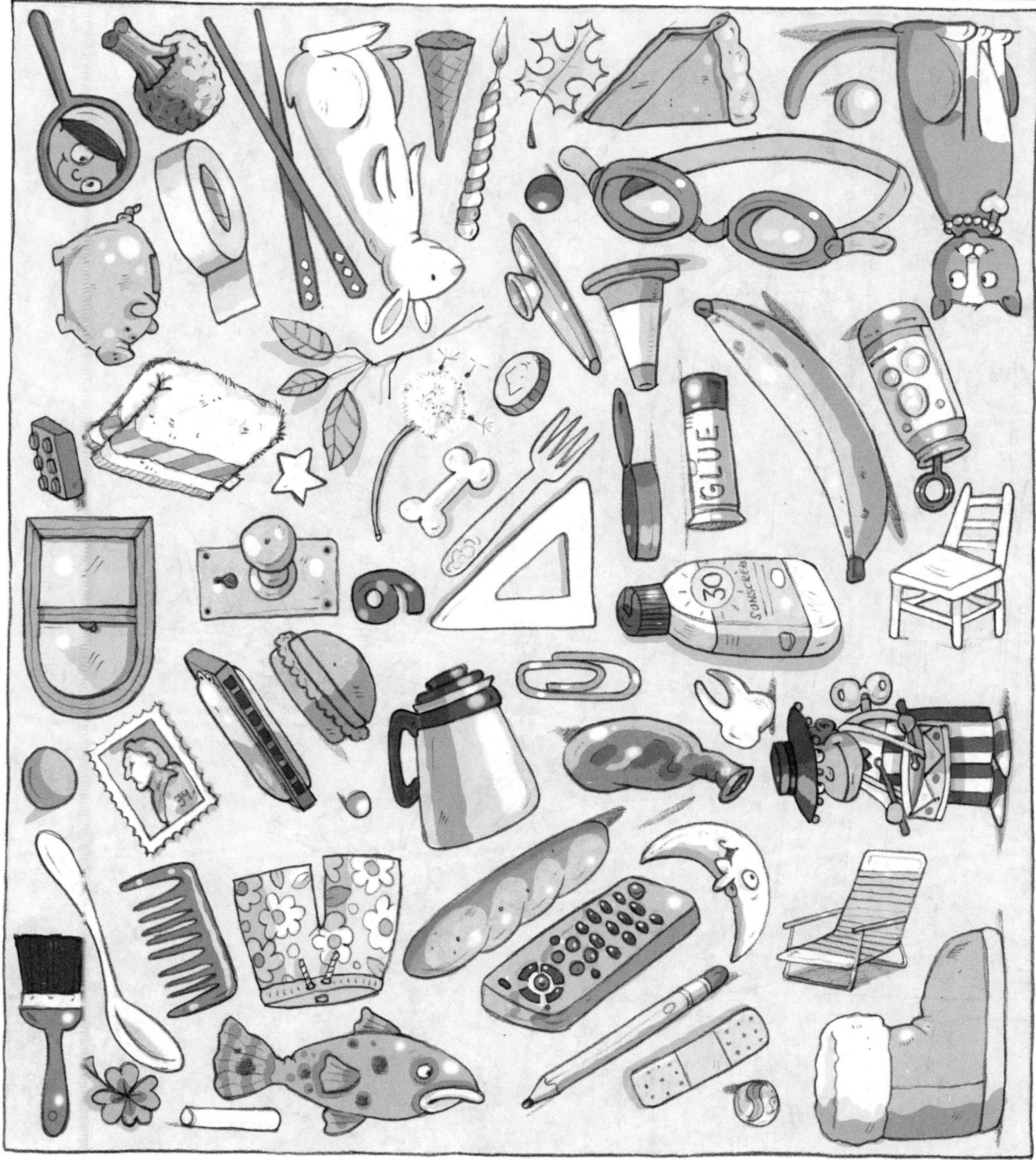

Look at the picture and find:

1 thing to peel

2 things to turn

3 things to eat with

4 things that stick

5 things for the pool

6 things to blow

©School Zone Publishing Company

MOUNTAIN CLIMBING ADVENTURE

Find and circle the hidden pictures.

candy cane

tie

wrench

clothespin

nail

watch

envelope

match

 ©School Zone Publishing Company

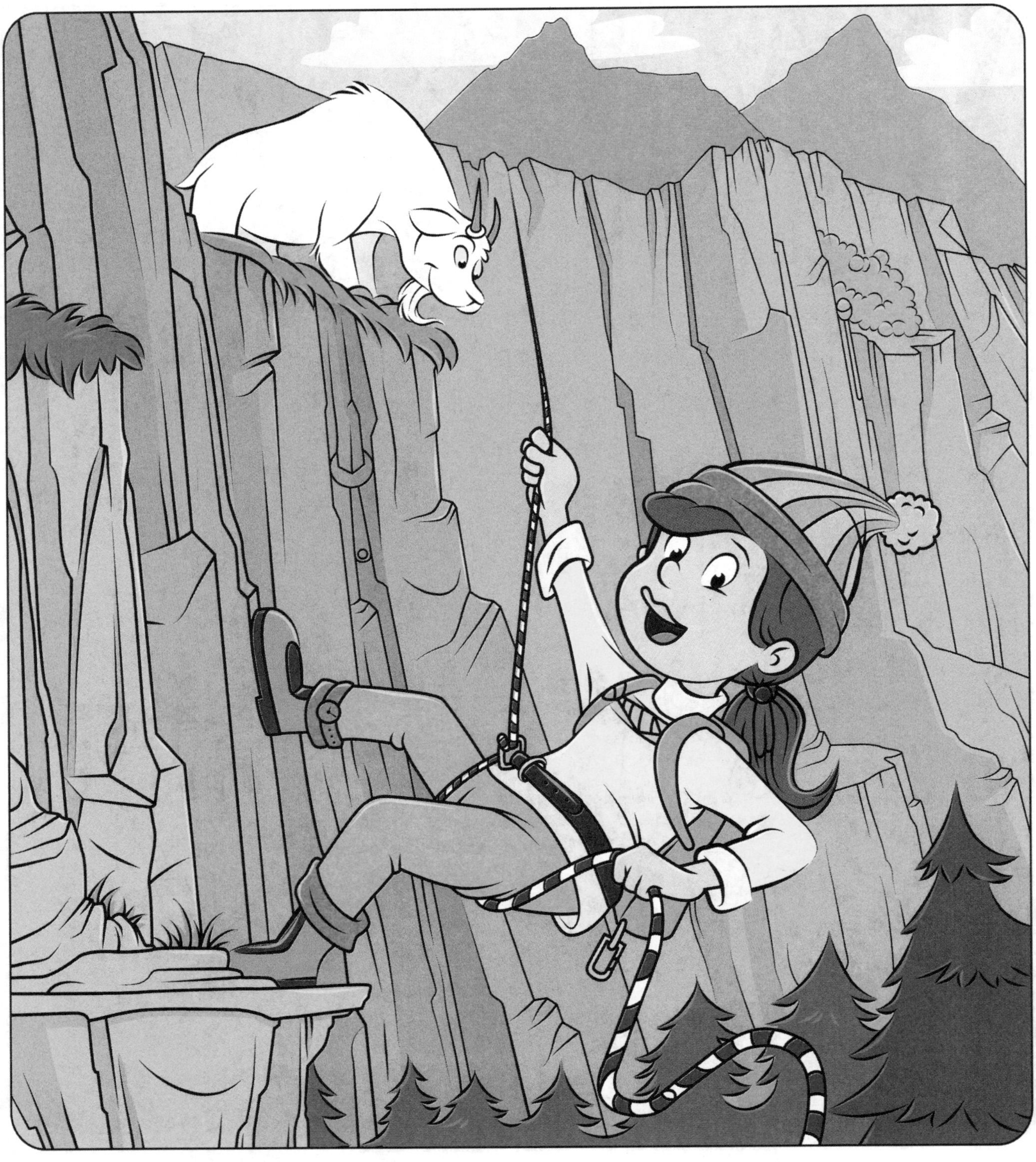

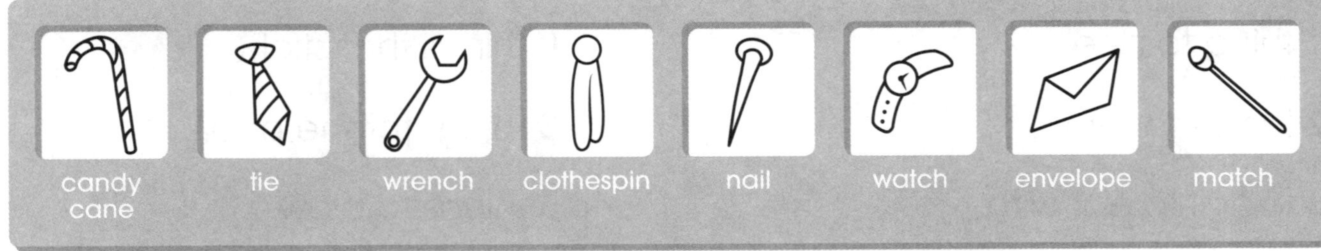

DOG SHOW

Find and circle the hidden pictures.

Find 1 trophy

Find 2 collars

Find 3 medals

Find 4 crowns

Find 5 pencils

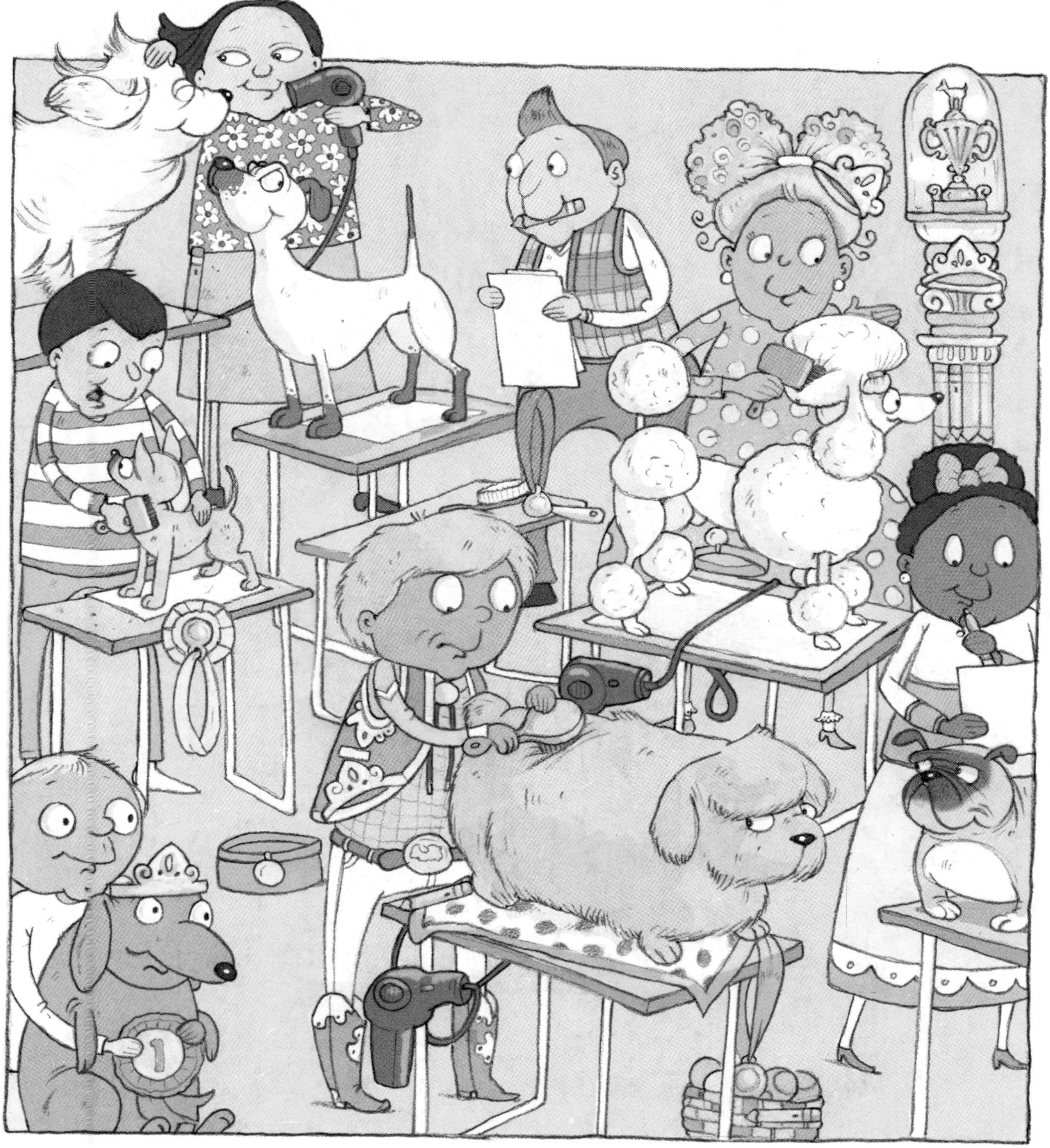

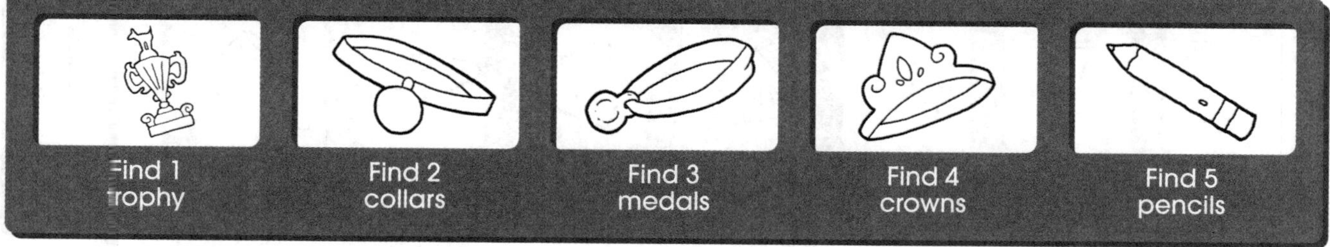

MAGIC SHOW

Find and circle the hidden pictures.

©School Zone Publishing Company

WHAT'S IN THE ATTIC?

Find and circle the hidden pictures.

ENJOYING NATURE

Find and circle the hidden pictures.

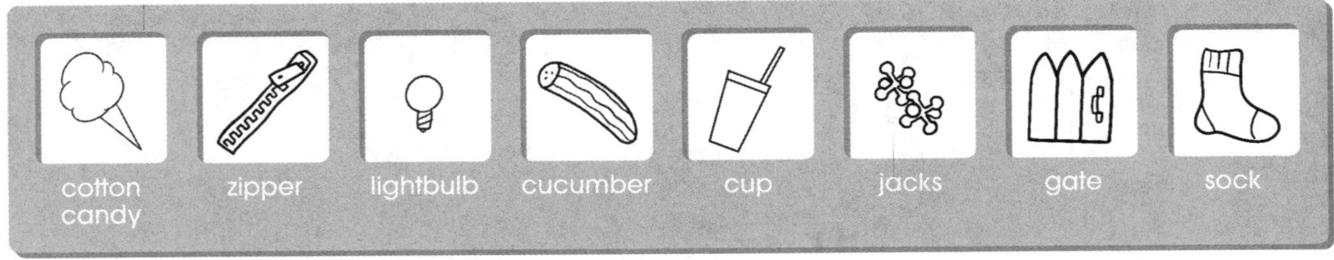

©School Zone Publishing Company

COFFEE BREAK

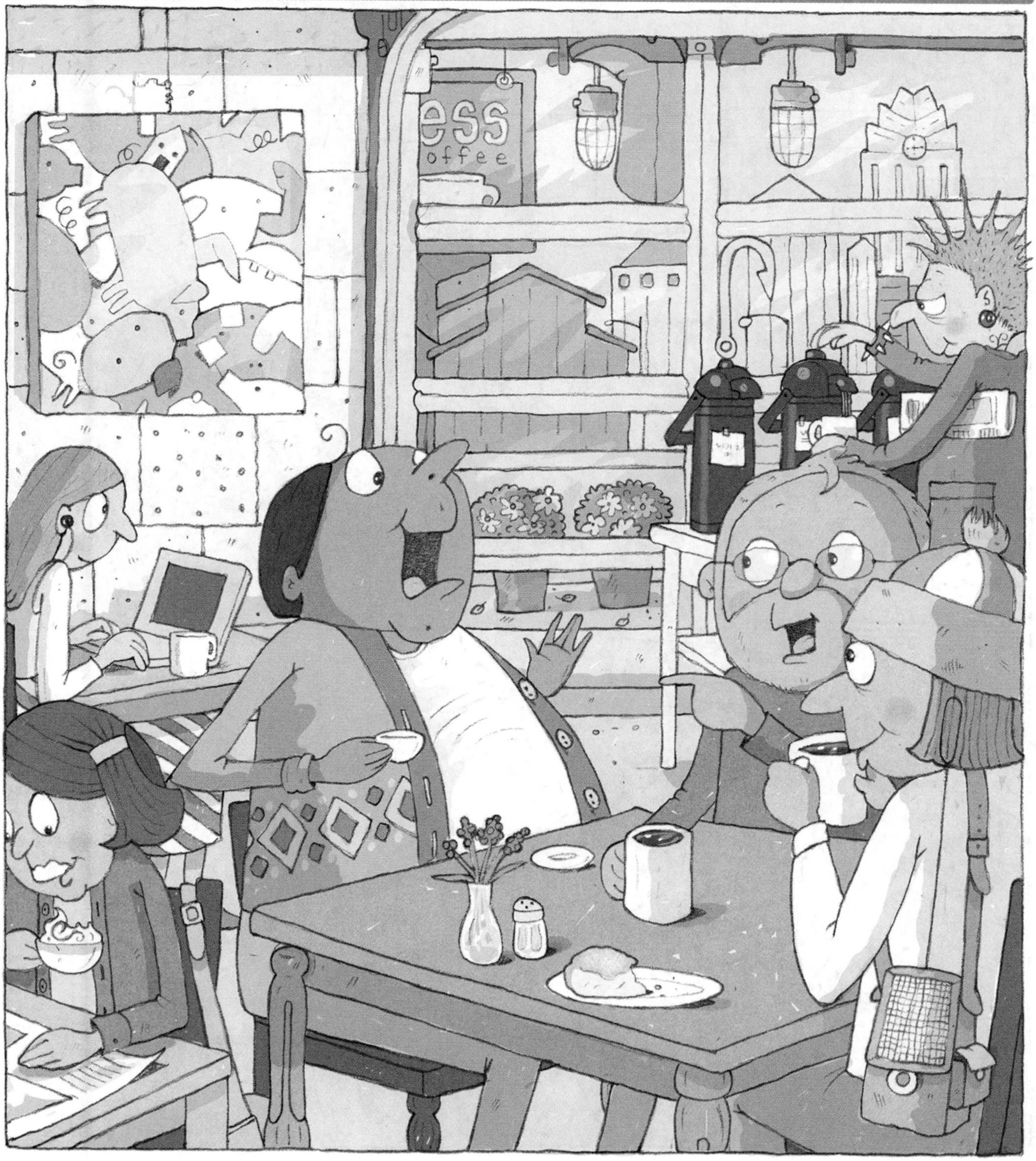

Find and circle the hidden pictures.

party hat

boot

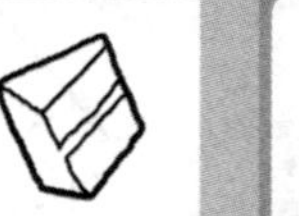
cake slice

clothespin

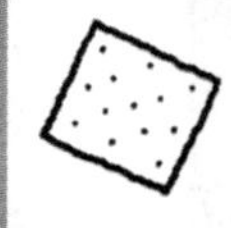
cracker

flyswatter

hook

pig

UNDER CONSTRUCTION

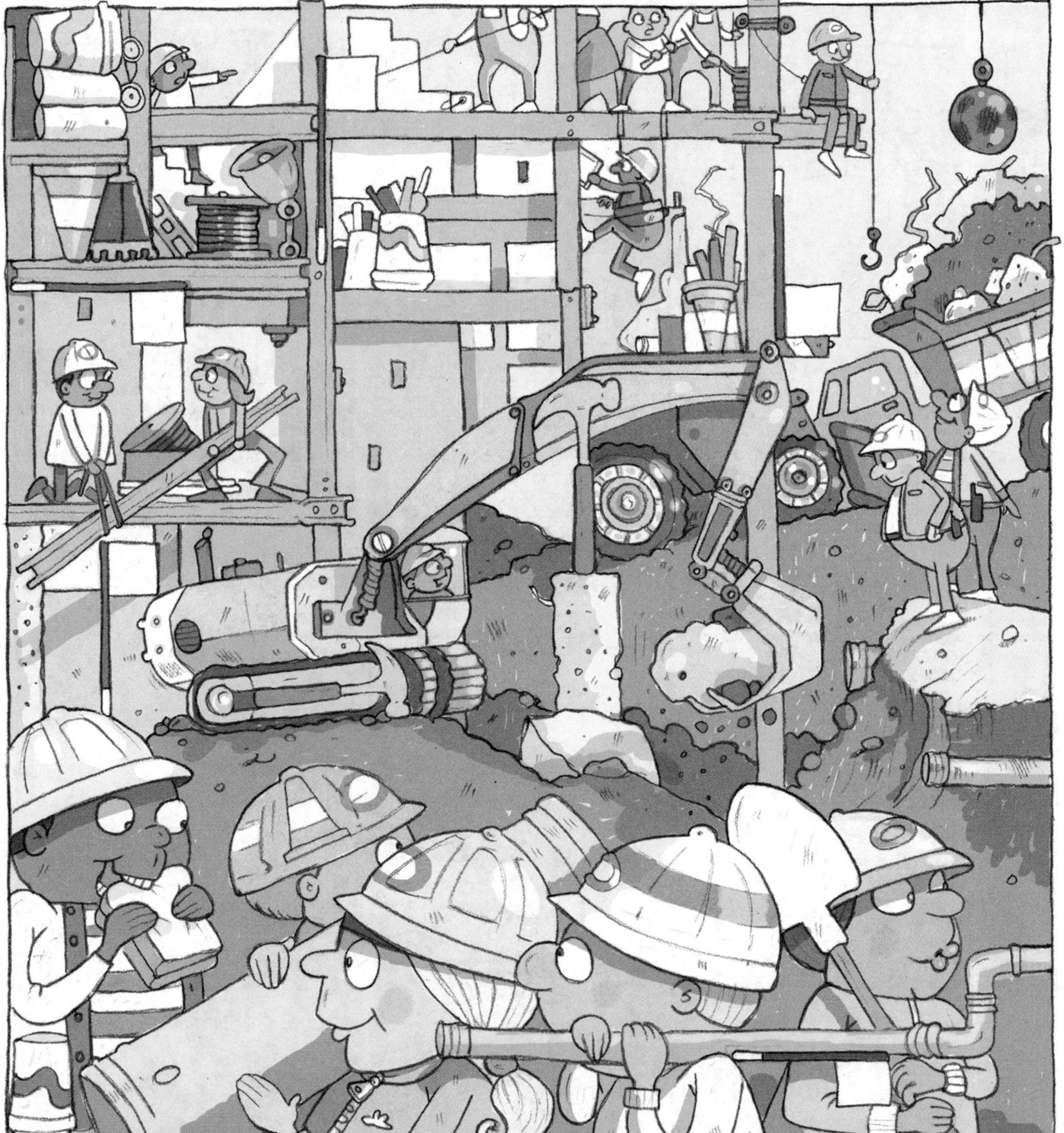

Find and circle the hidden pictures.

Find 1
bell

Find 2
hammers

Find 3
coffee cups

Find 4
emergency cones

Find 5
flags

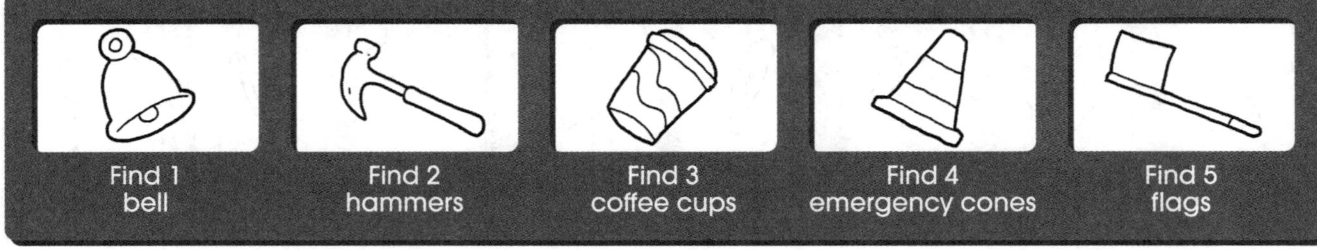

©School Zone Publishing Company

TROTTING THROUGH THE FOREST

Find and circle the hidden pictures.

©School Zone Publishing Company

MAKE A WISH!

Find and circle the hidden pictures.

 ©School Zone Publishing Company

UNDERSEA CASTLE

Find and circle the hidden pictures.

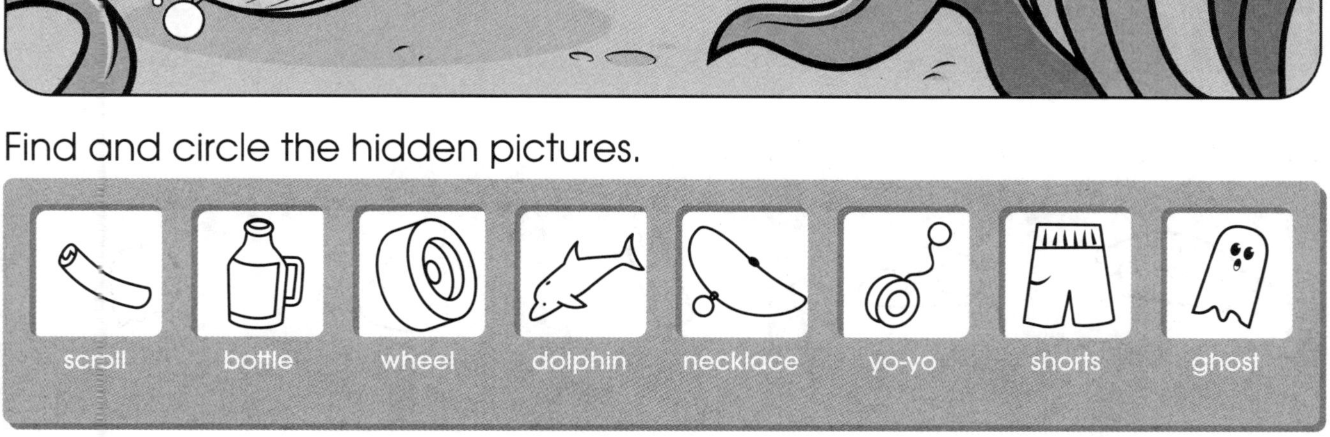

scroll

bottle

wheel

dolphin

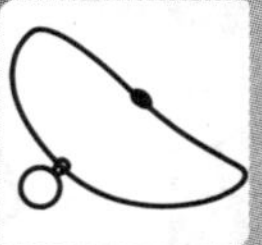

necklace

yo-yo

shorts

ghost

SANTA'S SLEIGH

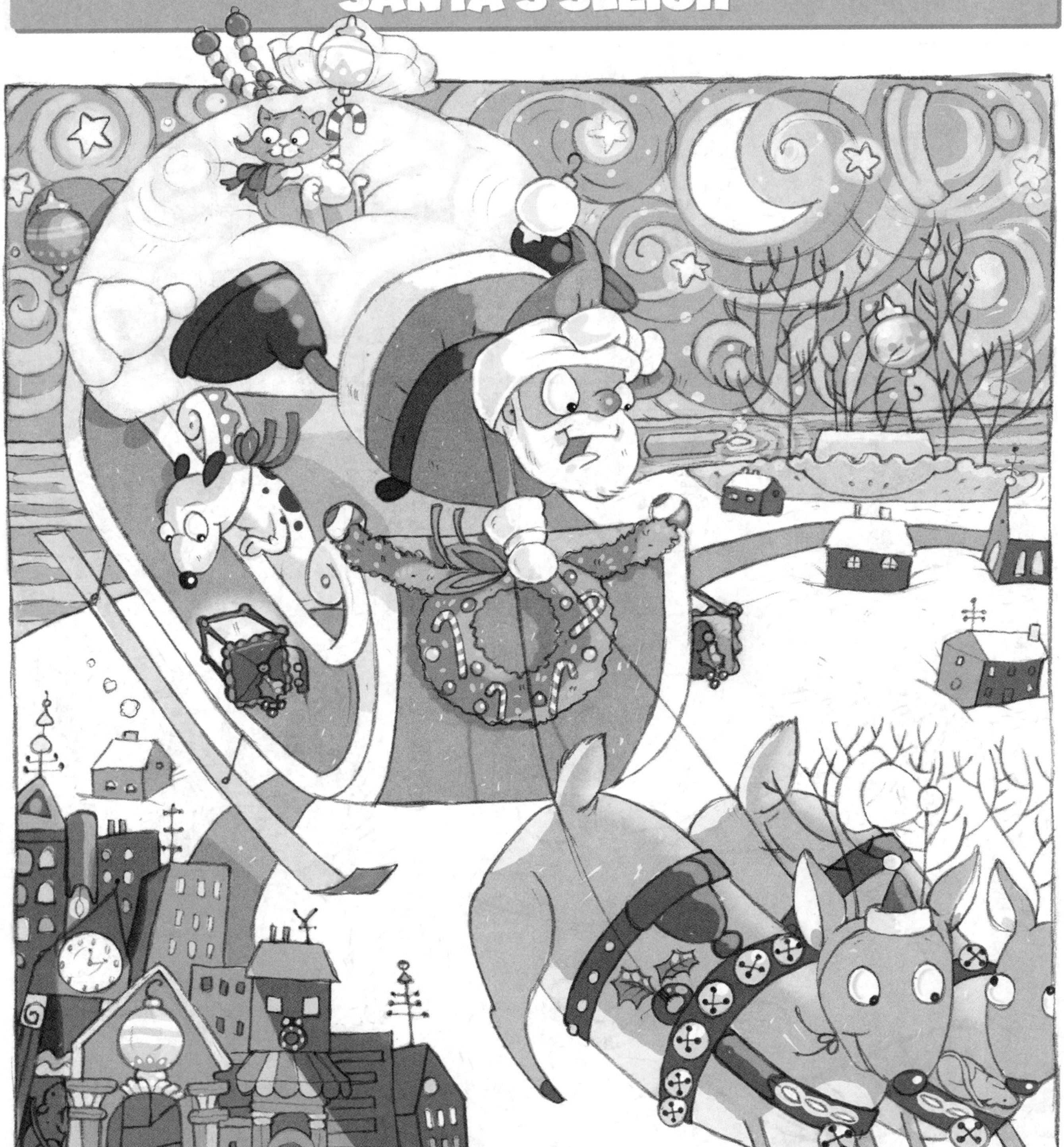

Find and circle the hidden pictures.

Find 1 pie	Find 2 mice	Find 3 candles	Find 4 hats	Find 5 ornaments

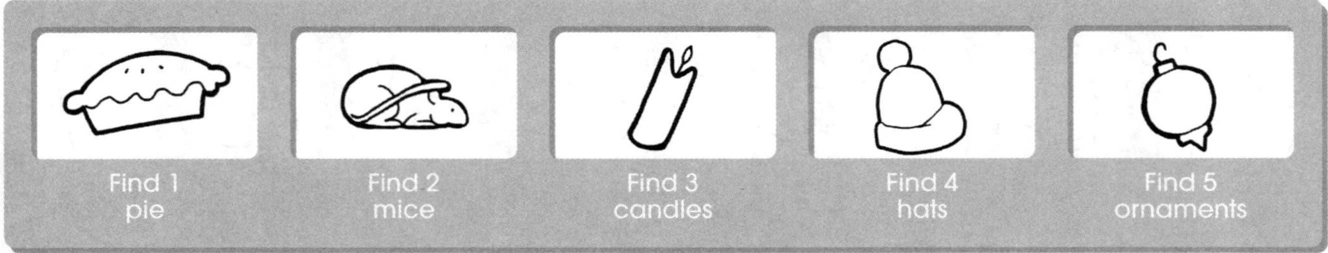

 ©School Zone Publishing Company

PARTY TIME

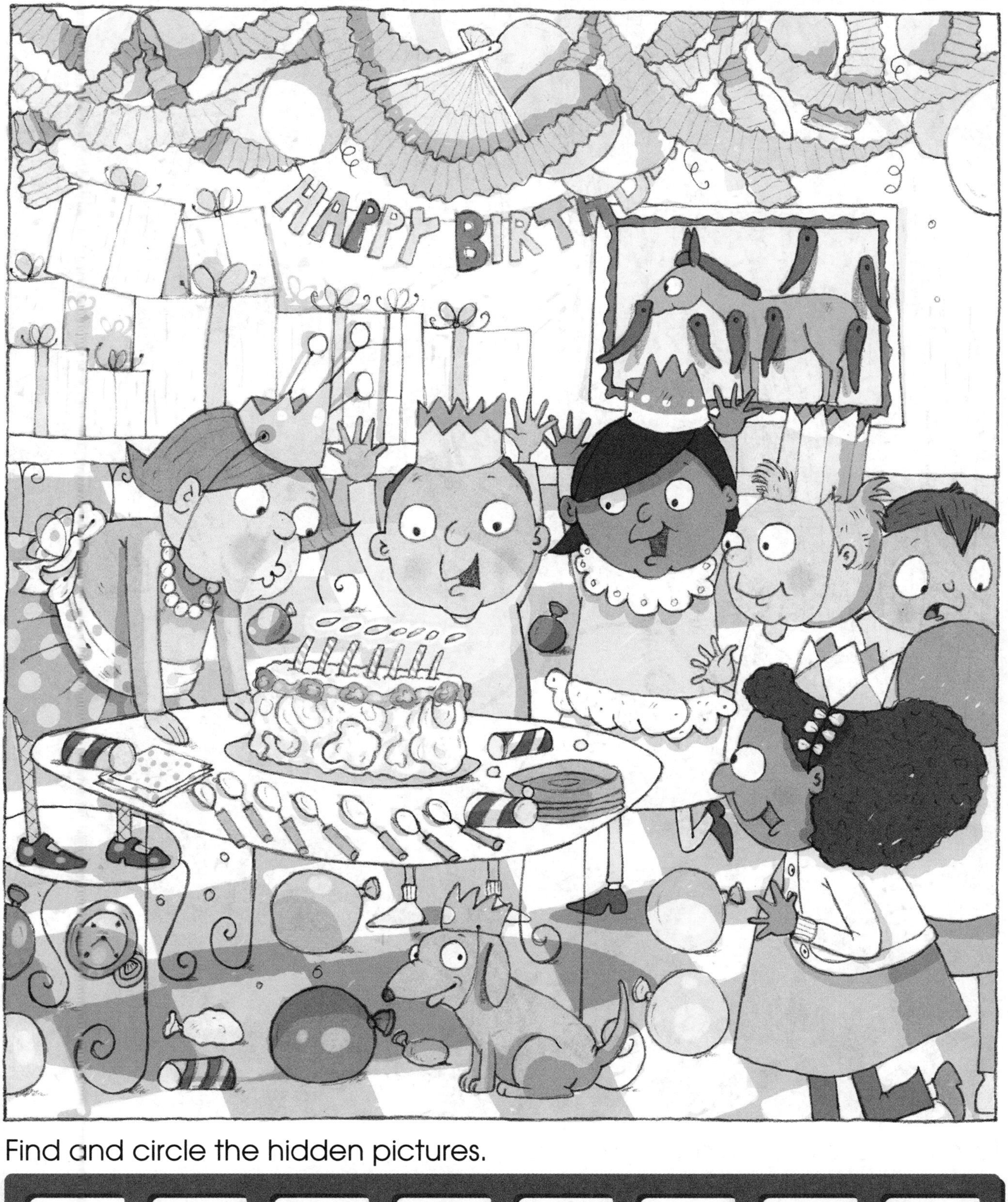

Find and circle the hidden pictures.

bread

butterfly

collar

fan

kite

musical note

tooth

pocket watch

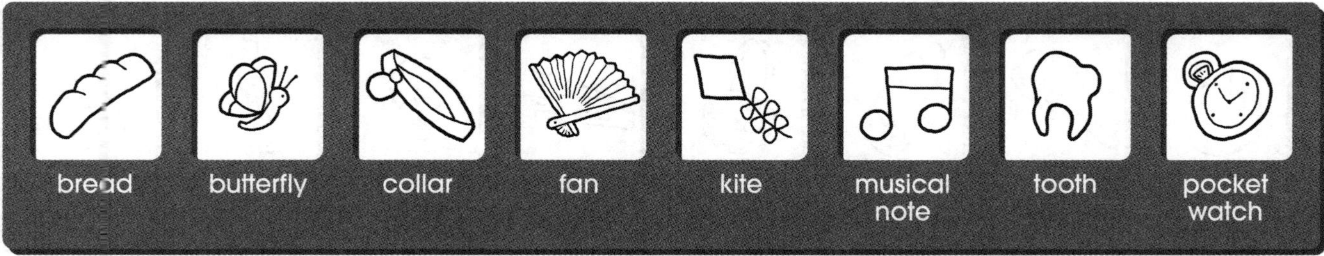

BASEBALL FOR MONKEYS

Find and circle the hidden pictures.

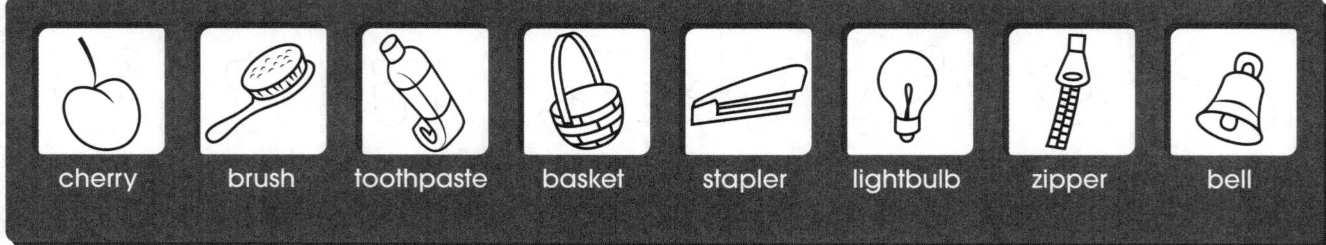

 ©School Zone Publishing Company

BY THE SHORE

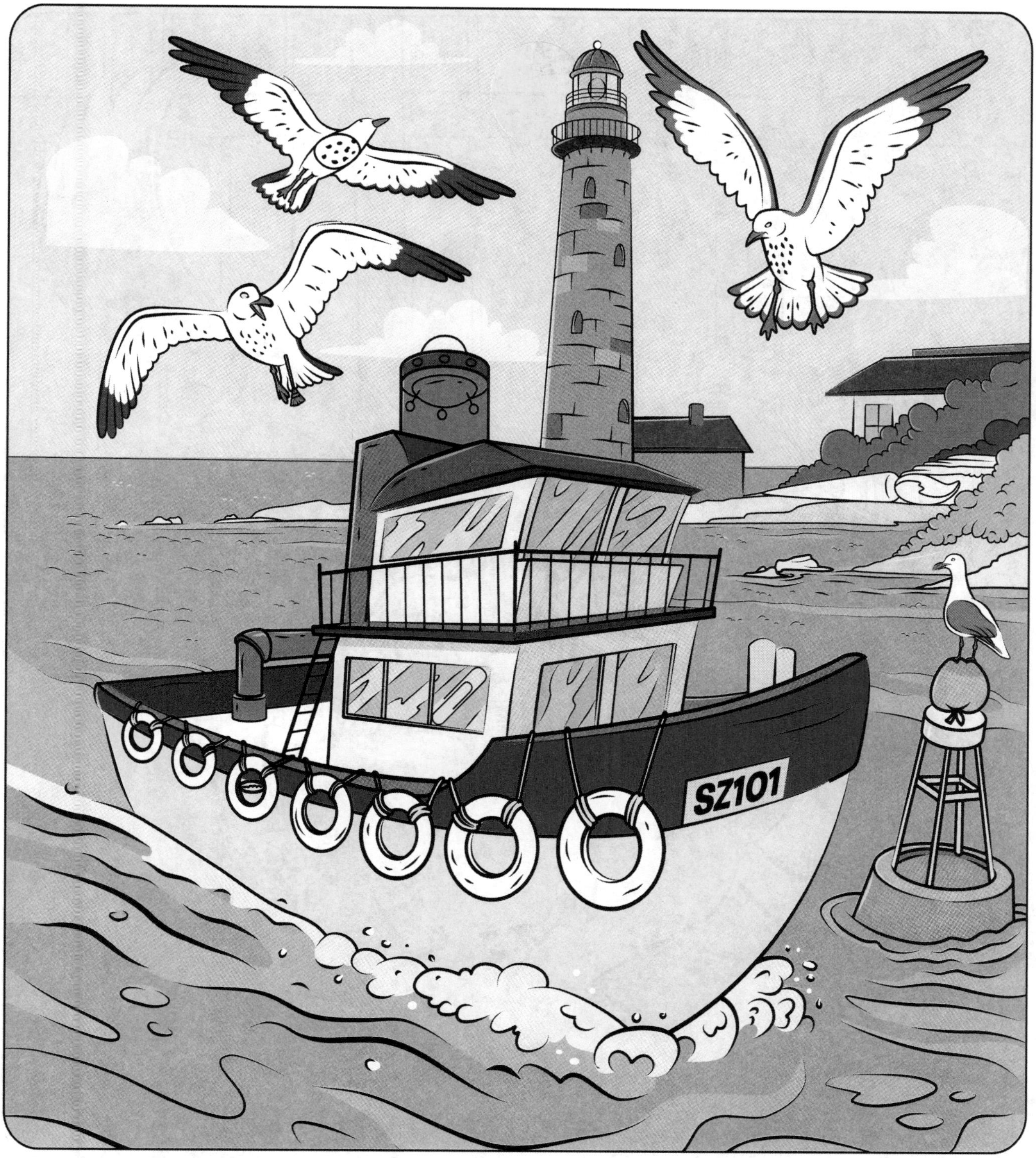

Find and circle the hidden pictures.

hat

apple

paintbrush

cookie

broom

bowl

paper clip

spaceship

©School Zone Publishing Company

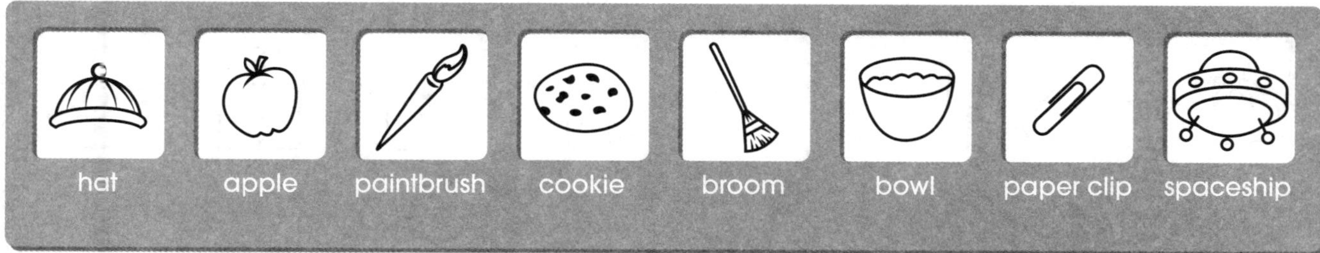

FURRY FRIENDS

Find and circle the hidden pictures.

©School Zone Publishing Company

UP IN THE ATTIC

Find and circle the hidden **a**, **b**, **c**, **d**, **e**, **f**, **g**, **h**, and **i** pictures.

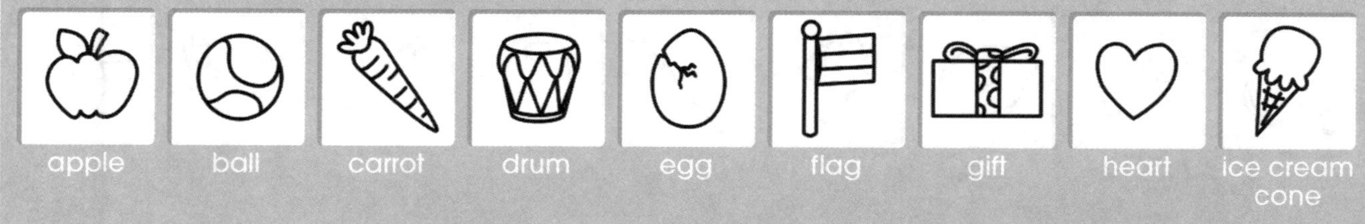

MORE STORAGE

Find and circle the hidden **j**, **k**, **l**, **m**, **n**, **o**, **p**, **q**, and **r** pictures.

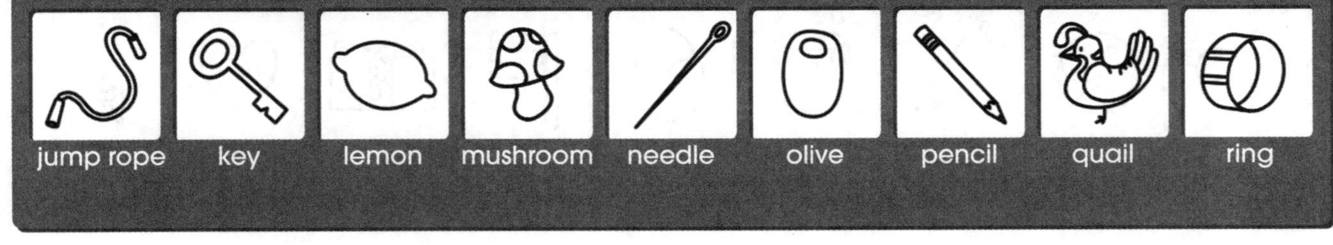

©School Zone Publishing Company

FRESH PRODUCE

Find and circle the hidden **s**, **t**, **u**, **v**, **w**, **x**, **y**, and **z** pictures.

CHEERS!

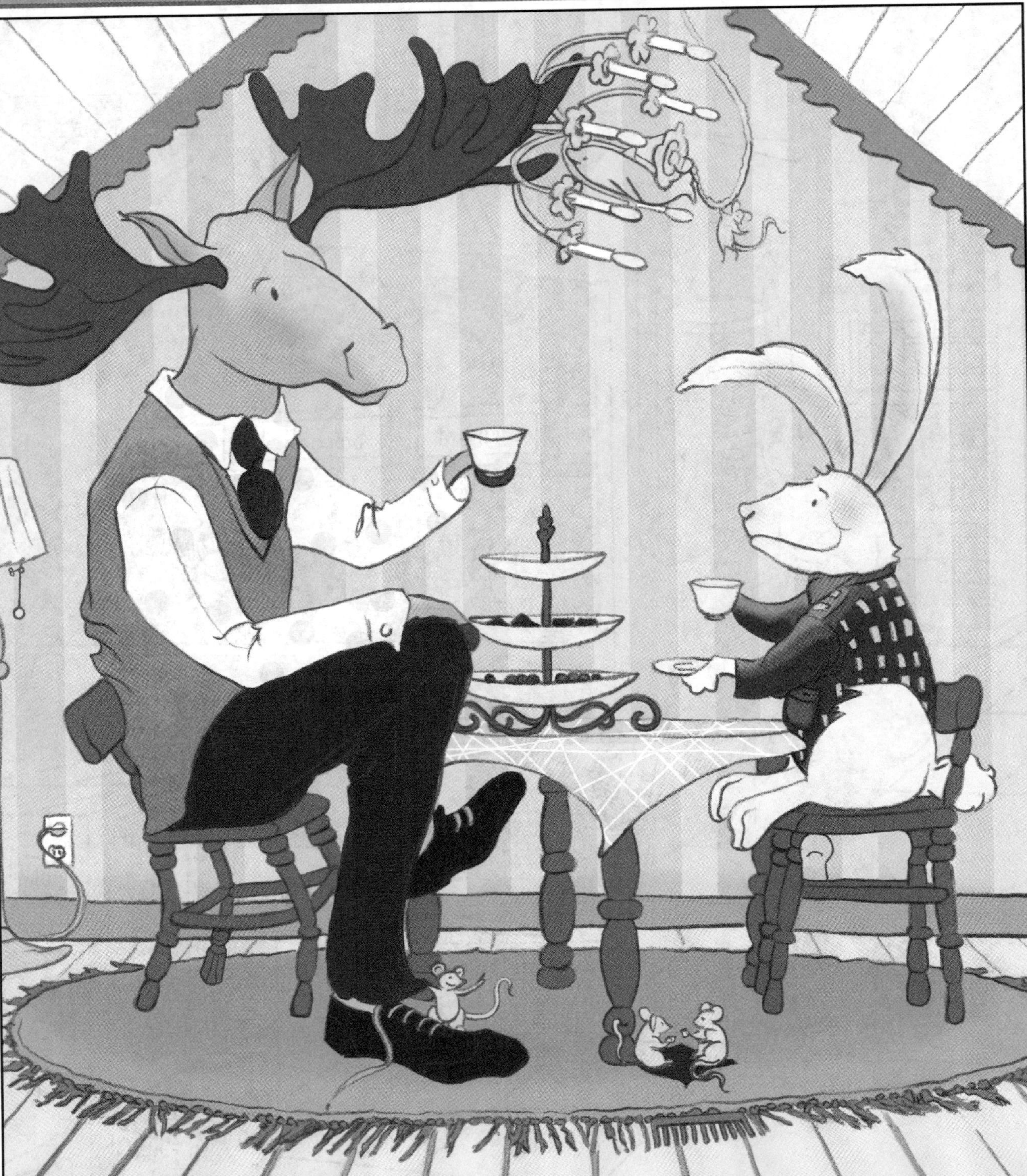

Find and circle the hidden pictures.

asparagus

bread

comb

dolphin

earring

pinecone

saltshaker

tea bag

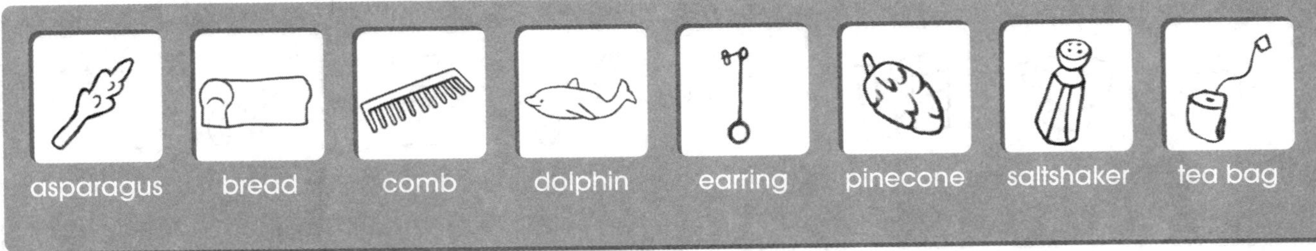

 ©School Zone Publishing Company

ALL THAT JAZZ

Find and circle the hidden pictures.

bandage

broccoli

marble

paper clip

pizza slice

ship

spoon

tooth

©School Zone Publishing Company

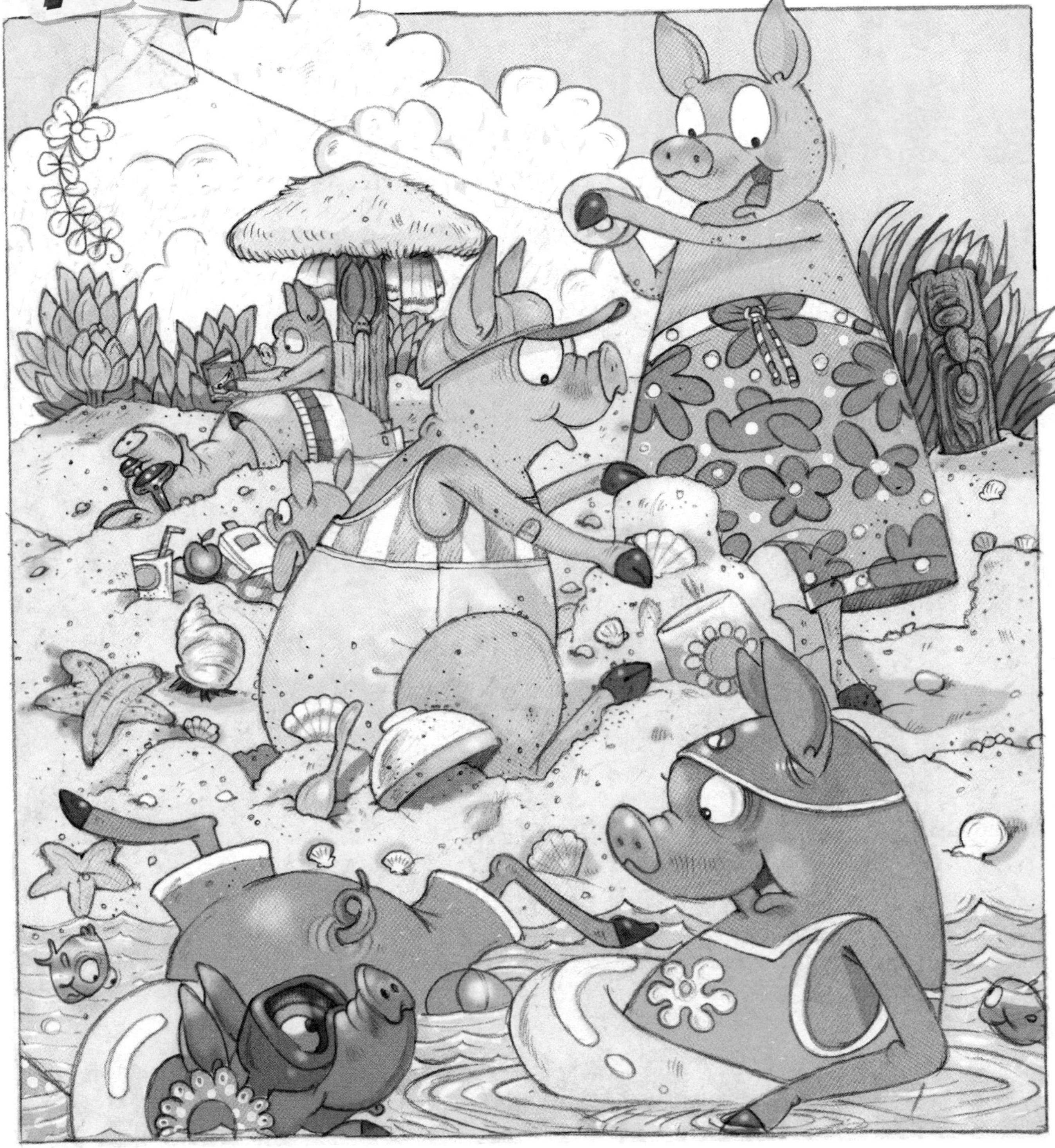

A B LETTER FUN

Find and circle the hidden pictures.

 ©School Zone Publishing Company

LETTER FUN CD

Find and circle the hidden pictures.

clothespin | comb | crab | cup | dart | dish | doughnut | duck

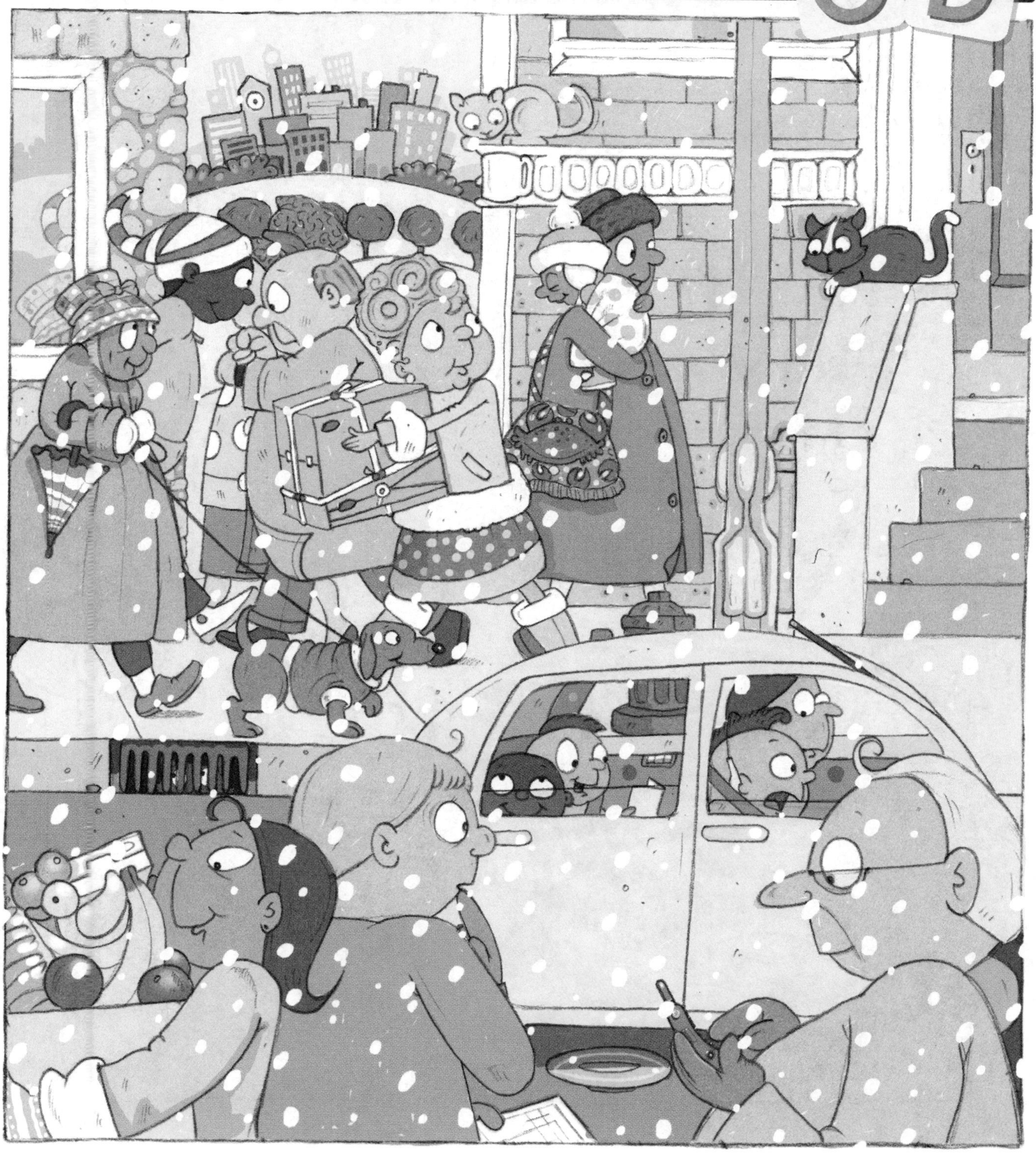

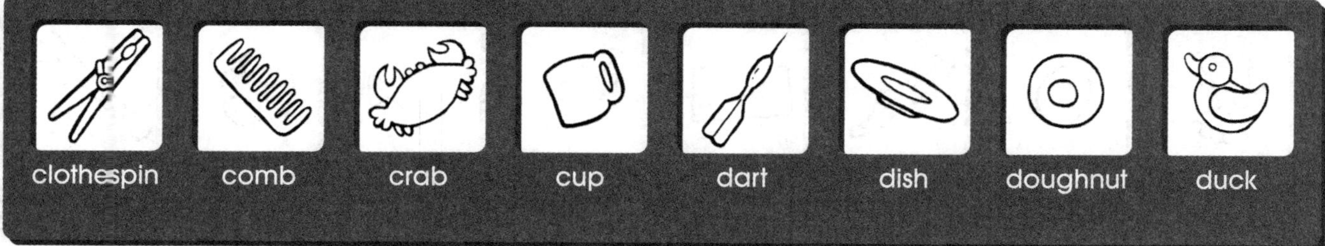

E F LETTER FUN

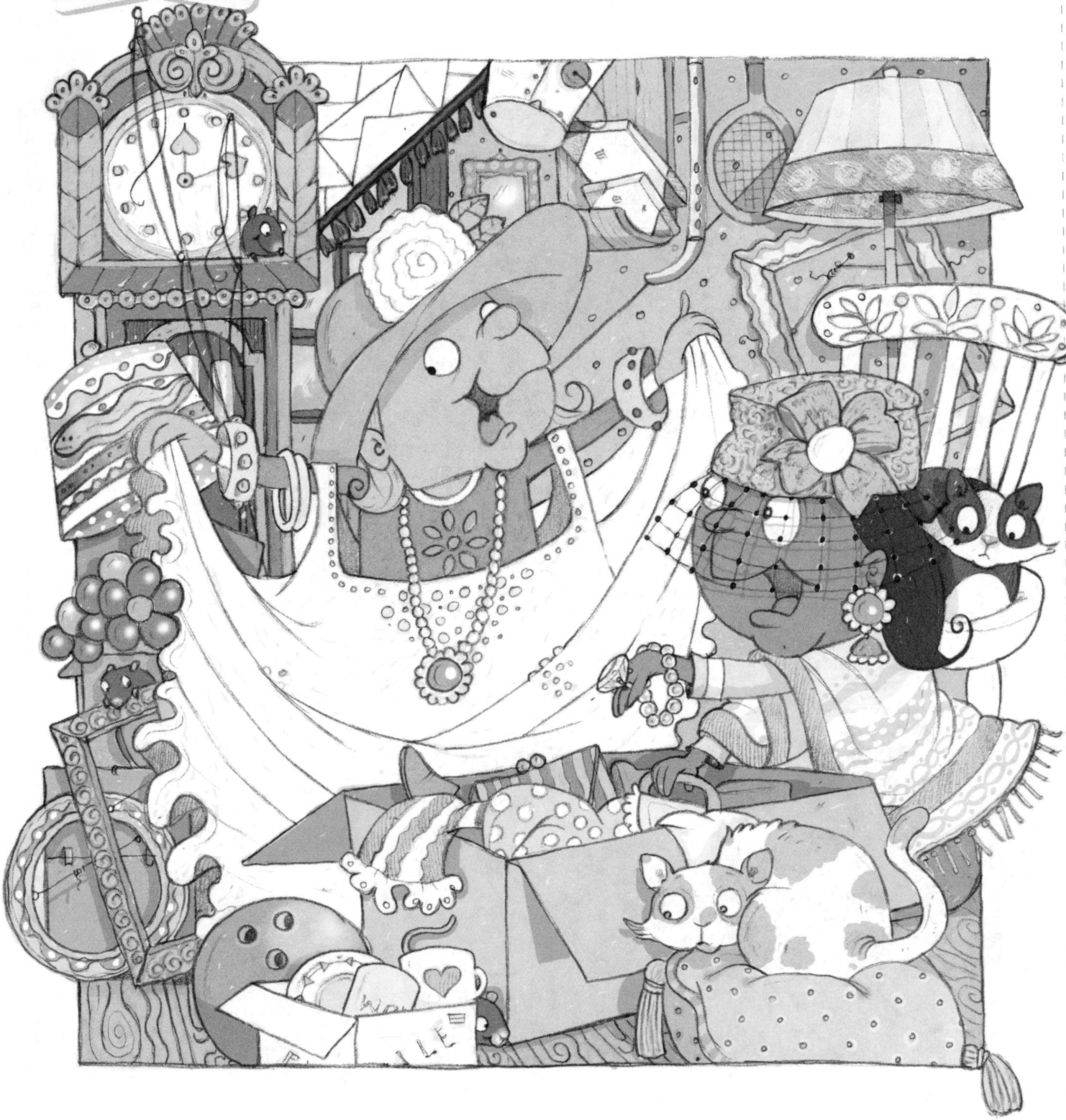

Find and circle the hidden pictures.

Find and circle the hidden pictures.

gate

gecko

ghost

gift

hammer

hanger

hare

heart

I J LETTER FUN

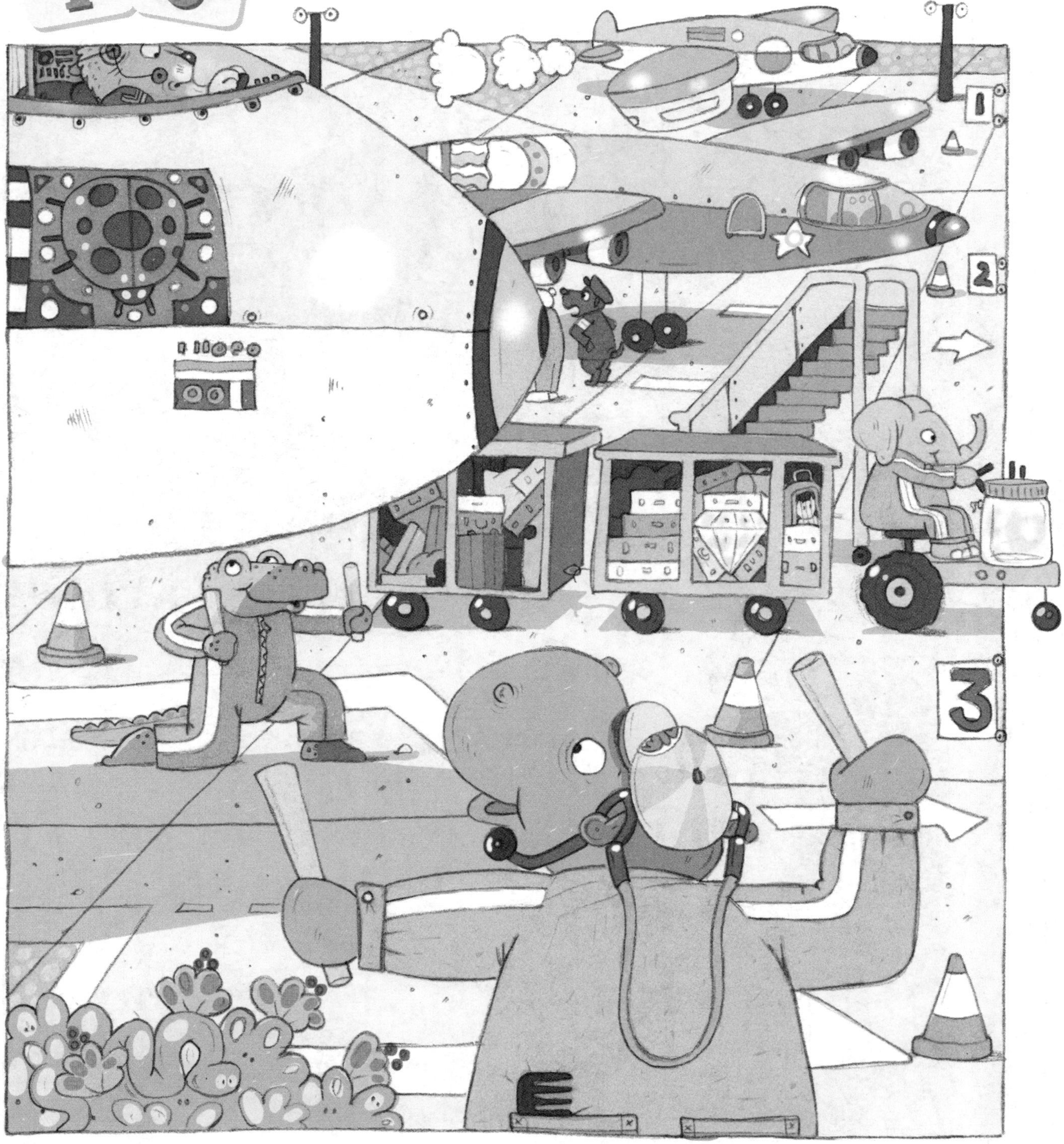

Find and circle the hidden pictures.

ice cream cone

inchworm

insect

iron

jar

jellyfish

jewel

jump rope

 ©School Zone Publishing Company

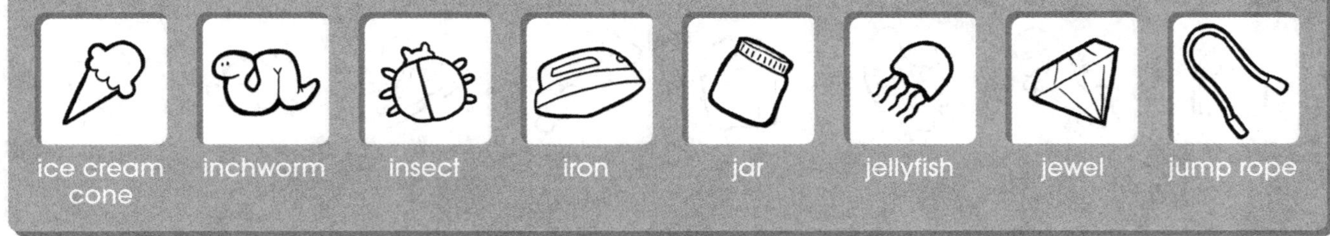

Find and circle the hidden pictures.

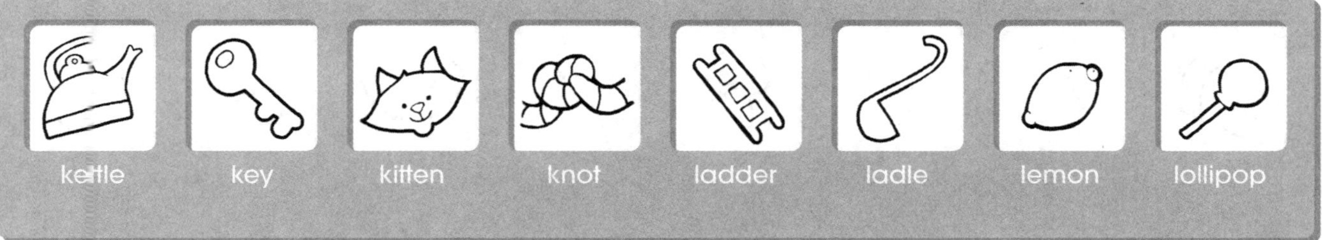

©School Zone Publishing Company

MN LETTER FUN

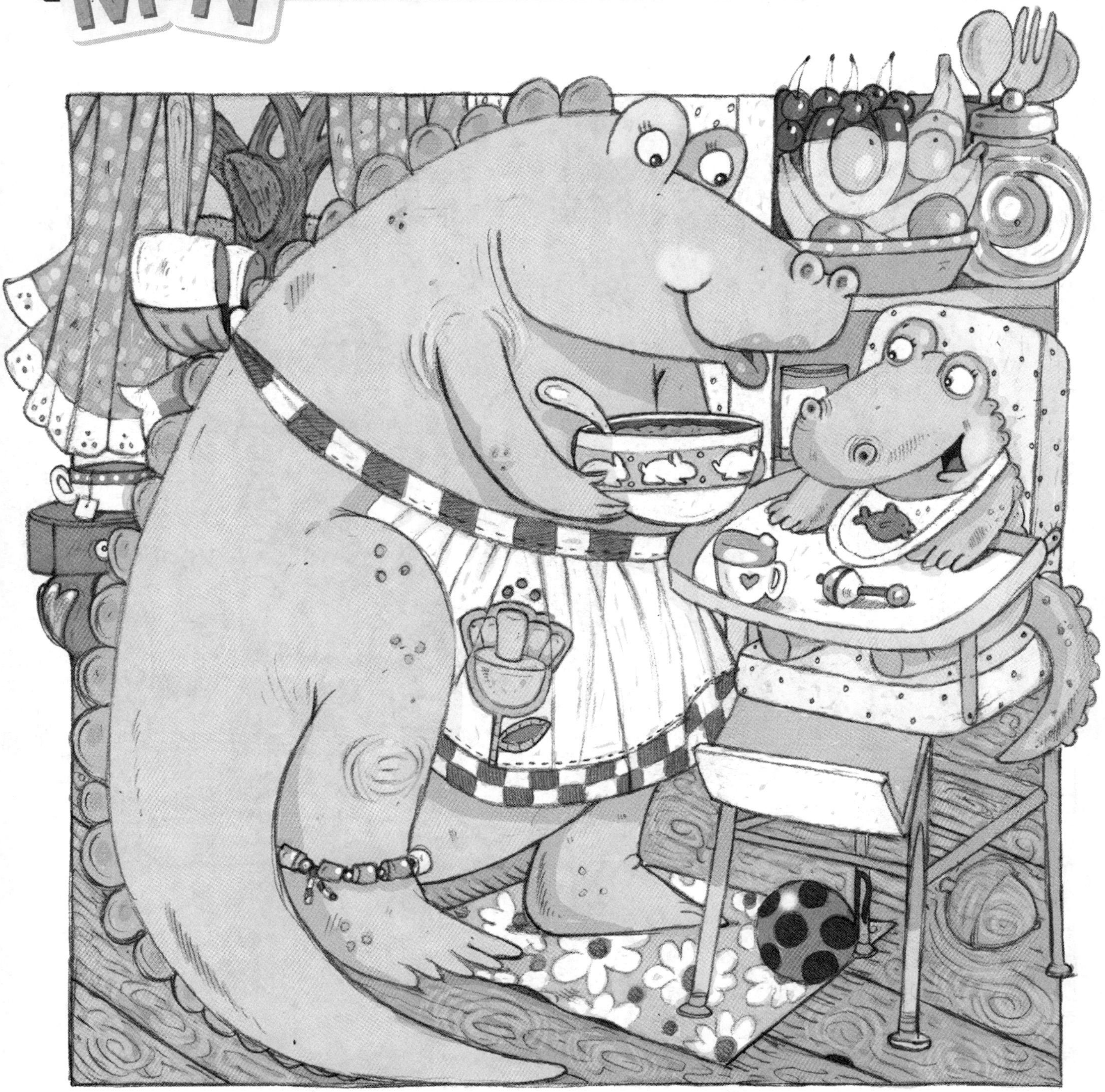

Find and circle the hidden pictures.

magnet mallet moon mushroom nail nest note nut

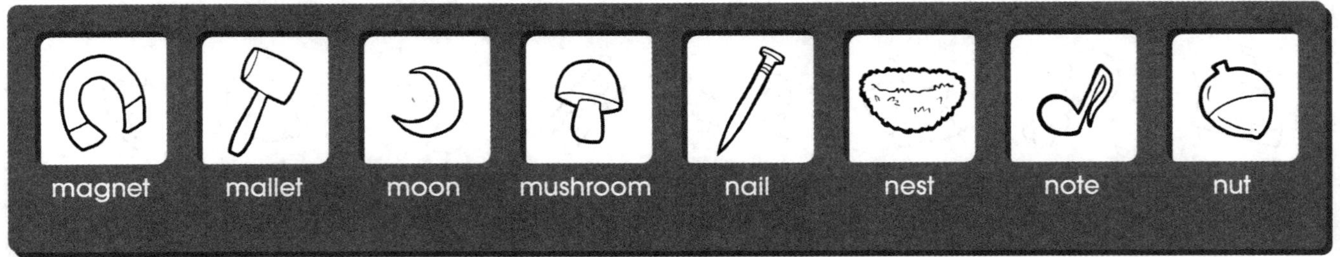

 ©School Zone Publishing Company

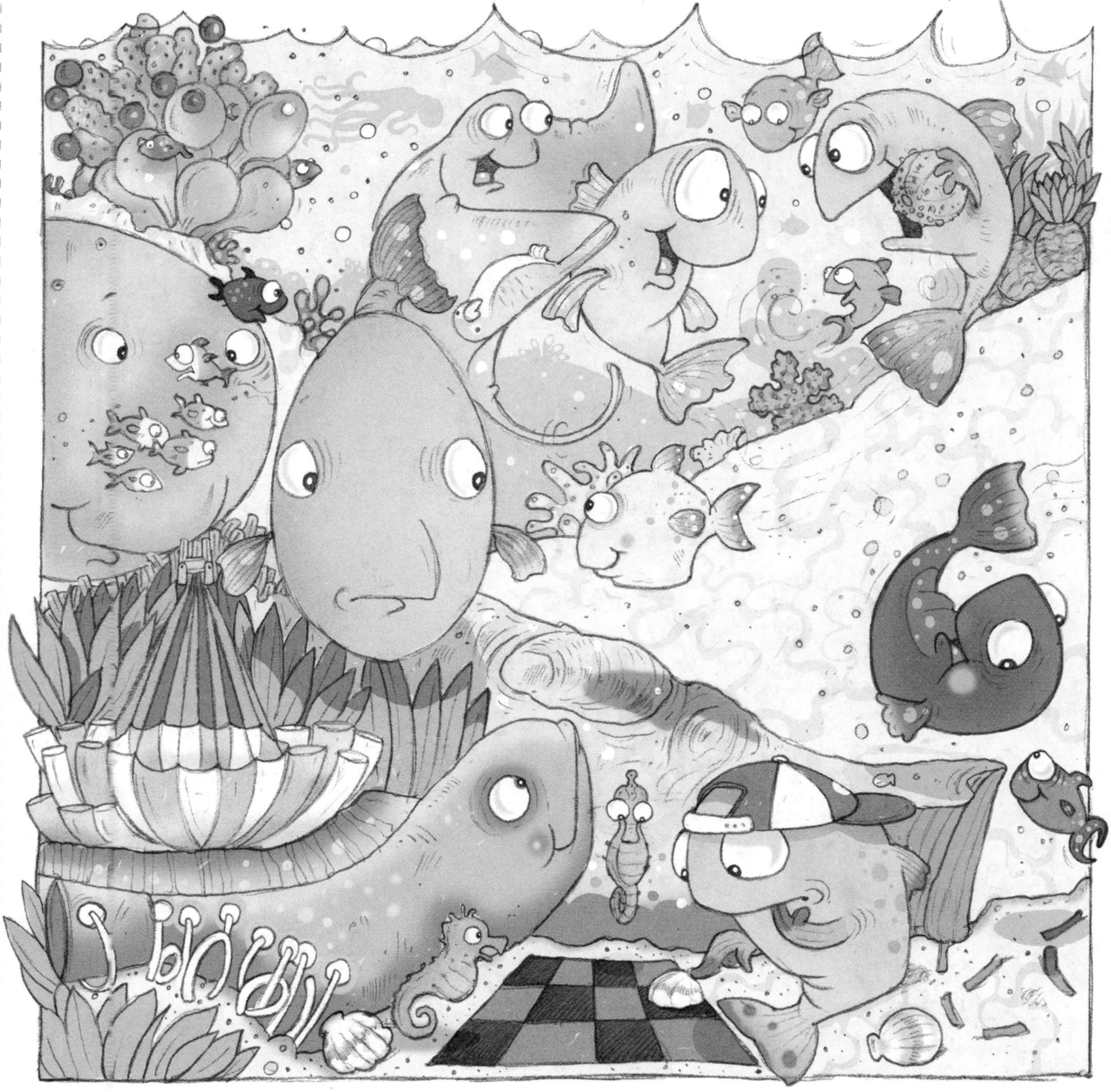

LETTER FUN O P

Find and circle the hidden pictures.

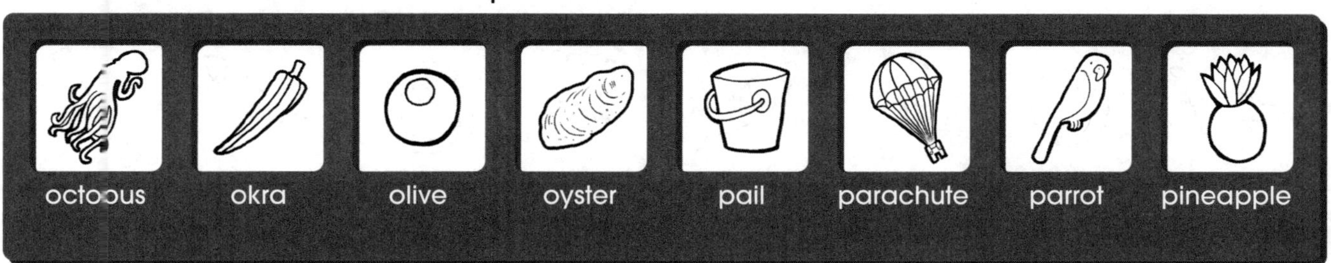

Q R LETTER FUN

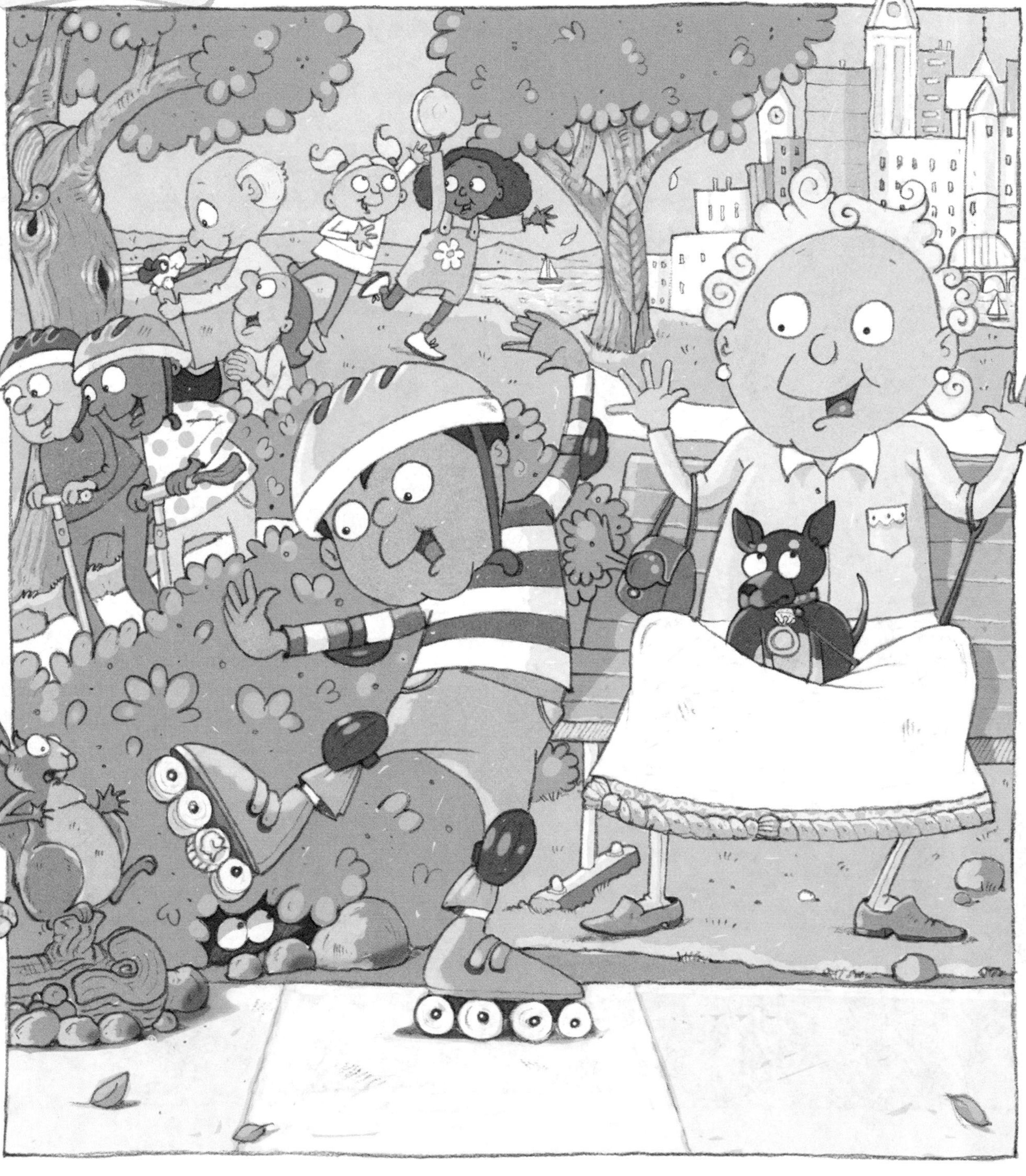

Find and circle the hidden pictures.

quail

quarter

question mark

quill

radish

ring

rocket

rope

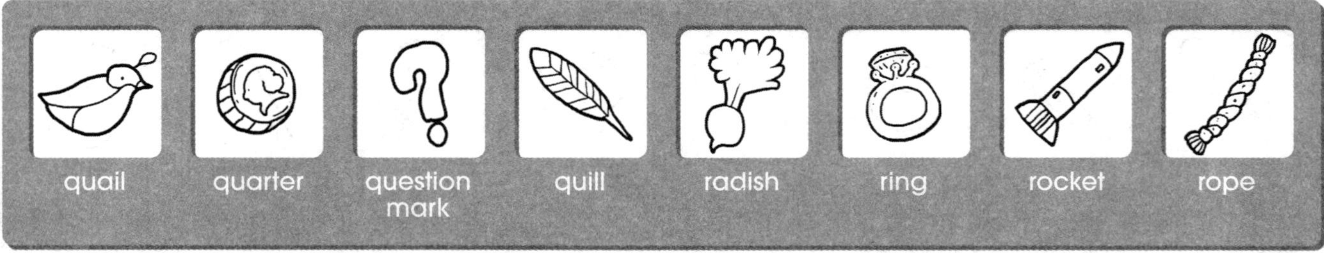

 ©School Zone Publishing Company

LETTER FUN

S T

Find and circle the hidden pictures.

U V

LETTER FUN

Find and circle the hidden pictures.

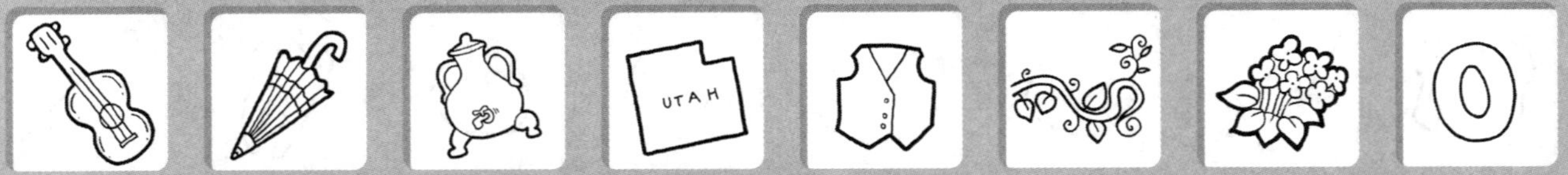

ukulele

umbrella

urn

Utah

vest

vine

violet

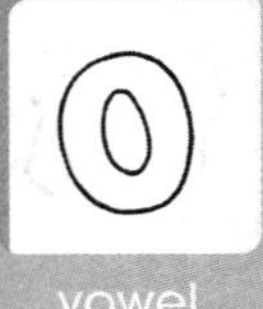

vowel

©School Zone Publishing Company

W X

LETTER FUN

Y Z

Find and circle the hidden pictures.

©School Zone Publishing Company

ANSWER KEY

Note: Only one solution is shown for each maze, but other paths are possible.

Page 1

Page 2

Page 3

Pages 4–5

Page 6

Page 7

Page 8

Page 9

Page 10

Page 11

Page 12

Page 13

Pages 14–15

©School Zone Publishing Company

ANSWER KEY

Page 16

Page 17

Page 18

Page 19

Page 20

Page 21

Page 22

Page 23

Pages 24–25

Page 26

Page 27

Pages 28–29

ANSWER KEY

Page 30

Page 31

Page 32

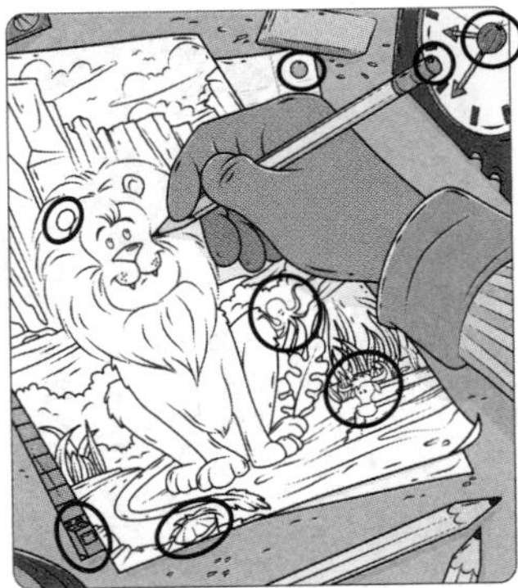

Page 33

Pages 34–35

Page 36

Page 37

Page 38

Page 39

Page 40

Page 41

Pages 42–43

 ©School Zone Publishing Company

ANSWER KEY

Page 44

Page 45

Page 46

Page 47

Page 48

Page 49

Page 50

Page 51

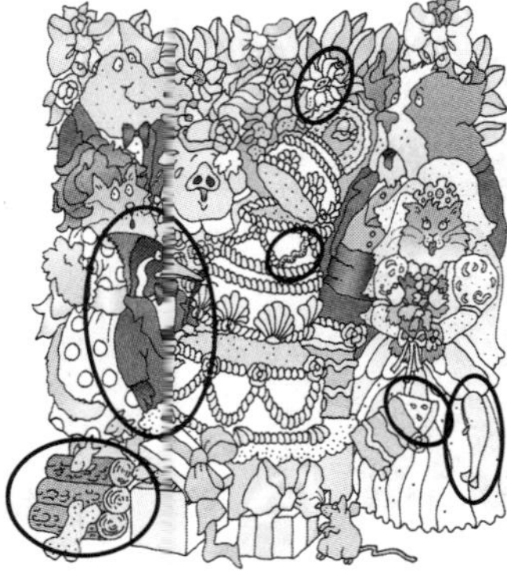

Pages 52–53

Page 54

Page 55

Page 56

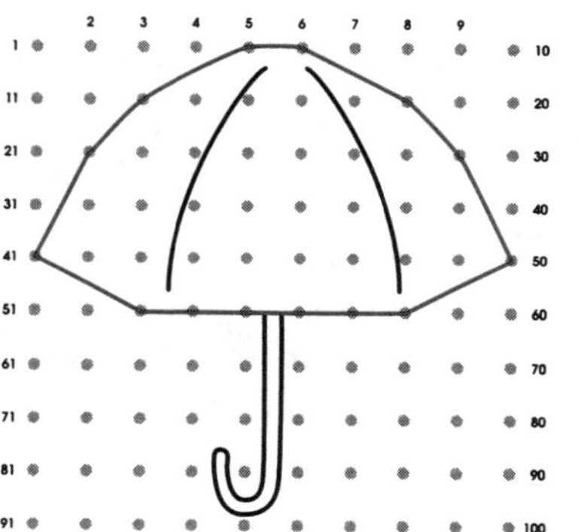

Line 1

1. 50
2. 29
3. 18
4. 6
5. 5
6. 13
7. 22
8. 41
9. 53
10. 54
11. 55
12. 56
13. 57
14. 58
15. 50

Page 57

ANSWER KEY

Page 58

Line 1
1. 18
2. 17
3. 16
4. 15
5. 14
6. 13
7. 12
8. 22
9. 32
10. 42
11. 52
12. 62
13. 74
14. 86
15. 98
16. 99
17. 89
18. 79
19. 69
20. 59
21. 28
22. 18

Line 2
1. 12
2. 23
3. 34
4. 46
5. 57
6. 69

Page 59

Page 60

Line 1
1. 7
2. 6
3. 5
4. 4
5. 13
6. 22
7. 32
8. 42
9. 53
10. 64
11. 75
12. 76
13. 67
14. 58
15. 49
16. 39
17. 29
18. 18
19. 7

Line 2
1. 86
2. 85
3. 95
4. 96
5. 86

Page 61

Page 62

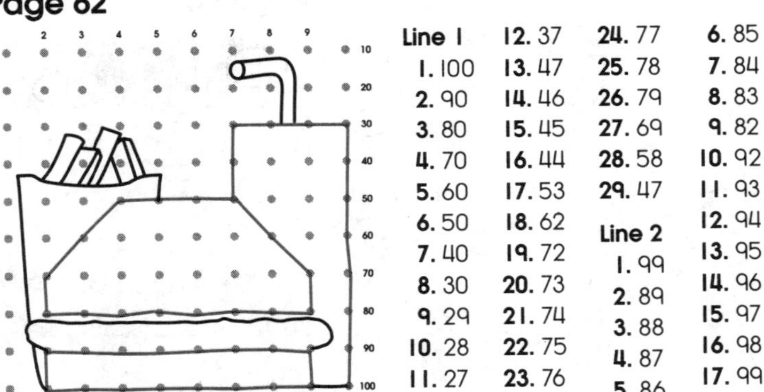

Line 1
1. 100
2. 90
3. 80
4. 70
5. 60
6. 50
7. 40
8. 30
9. 29
10. 28
11. 27
12. 37
13. 47
14. 46
15. 45
16. 44
17. 53
18. 62
19. 72
20. 73
21. 74
22. 75
23. 76
24. 77
25. 78
26. 79
27. 69
28. 58
29. 47

Line 2
1. 99
2. 89
3. 88
4. 87
5. 86
6. 85
7. 84
8. 83
9. 82
10. 92
11. 93
12. 94
13. 95
14. 96
15. 97
16. 98
17. 99

Page 63

Page 64

Page 65

Page 66

Page 67

©School Zone Publishing Company

ANSWER KEY

Page 68

Page 69

Page 70

Page 71

Page 72

Page 73

Page 74

Page 75

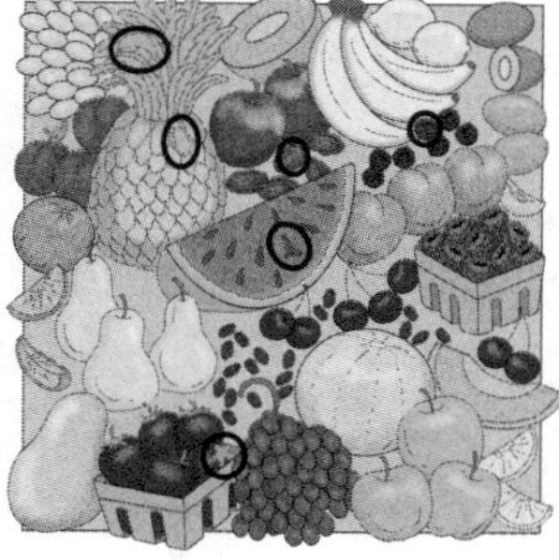

Page 76

Page 77

Page 78

Page 79

Page 80

Page 81

Page 82

Page 83

©School Zone Publishing Company

ANSWER KEY

Page 84

Page 85

Page 86

Page 87

Page 88

Page 89

Page 90

Page 91

Page 92

Page 93

Page 94

Page 95

Page 96

Page 97

Page 98

©School Zone Publishing Company

ANSWER KEY

Page 99

Page 100

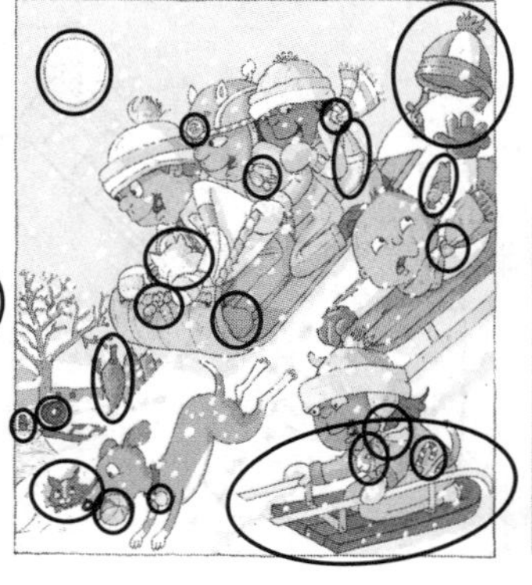

Page 101

Page 102

Page 103

Page 104

Page 105

Page 106

Page 107

Page 108

Page 109

Page 110

Page 111

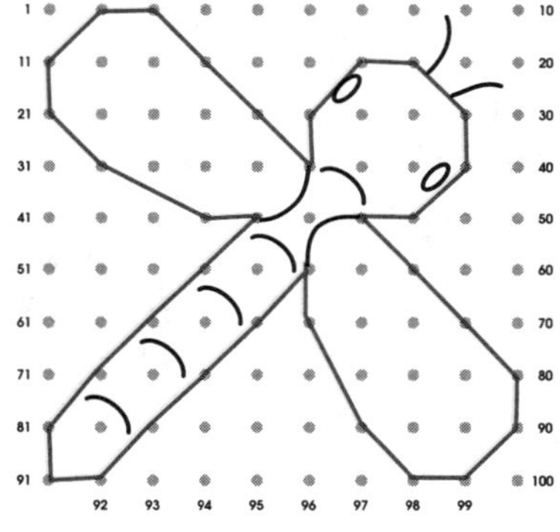

Line 1

1. 47	**11.** 3	**21.** 81	**31.** 99
2. 48	**12.** 2	**22.** 91	**32.** 90
3. 39	**13.** 11	**23.** 92	**33.** 80
4. 29	**14.** 21	**24.** 83	**34.** 69
5. 18	**15.** 32	**25.** 74	**35.** 58
6. 17	**16.** 44	**26.** 65	**36.** 47
7. 26	**17.** 45	**27.** 56	
8. 36	**18.** 54	**28.** 66	
9. 25	**19.** 63	**29.** 87	
10. 14	**20.** 72	**30.** 98	

ANSWER KEY

Page 112

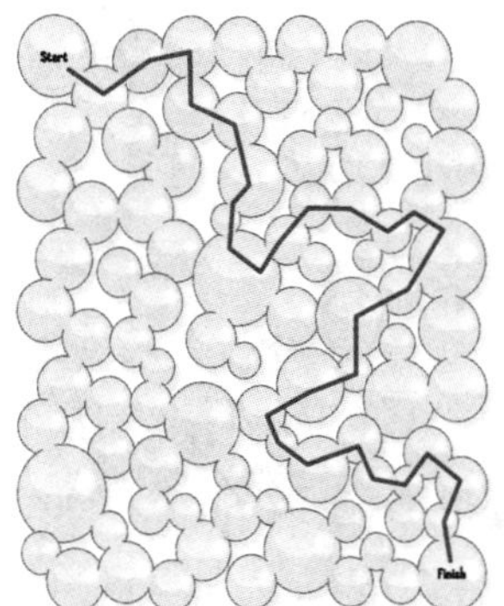

Page 113

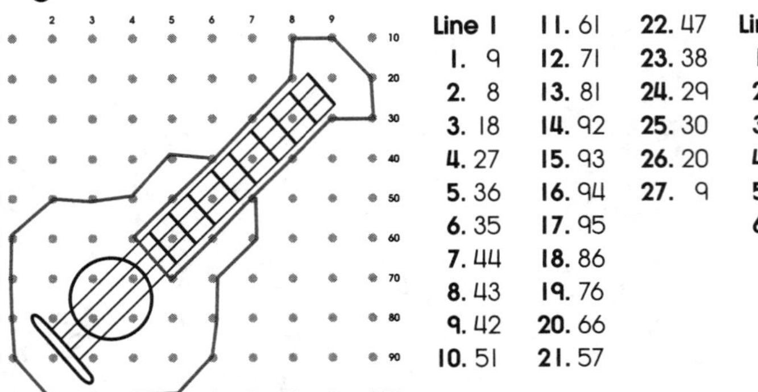

Line 1			Line 2
1. 9	11. 61	22. 47	1. 36
2. 8	12. 71	23. 38	2. 45
3. 18	13. 81	24. 29	3. 54
4. 27	14. 92	25. 30	4. 65
5. 36	16. 94	26. 20	5. 56
6. 35	17. 95	27. 9	6. 47
7. 44	18. 86		
8. 43	19. 76		
9. 42	20. 66		
10. 51	21. 57		

Page 114

Page 115

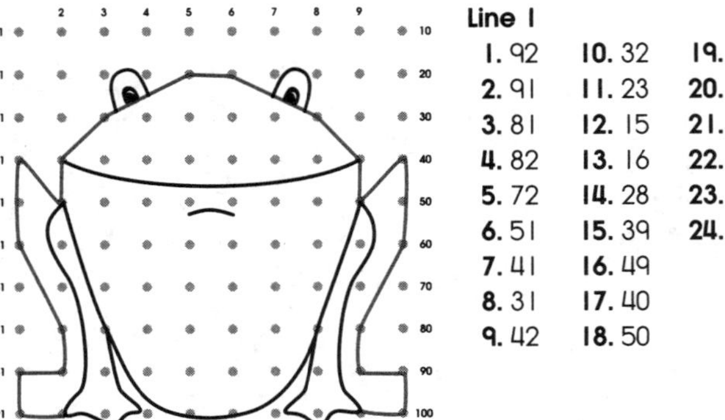

Line 1		
1. 92	10. 32	19. 60
2. 91	11. 23	20. 79
3. 81	12. 15	21. 89
4. 82	13. 16	22. 90
5. 72	14. 28	23. 100
6. 51	15. 39	24. 99
7. 41	16. 49	
8. 31	17. 40	
9. 42	18. 50	

Page 116

Page 117

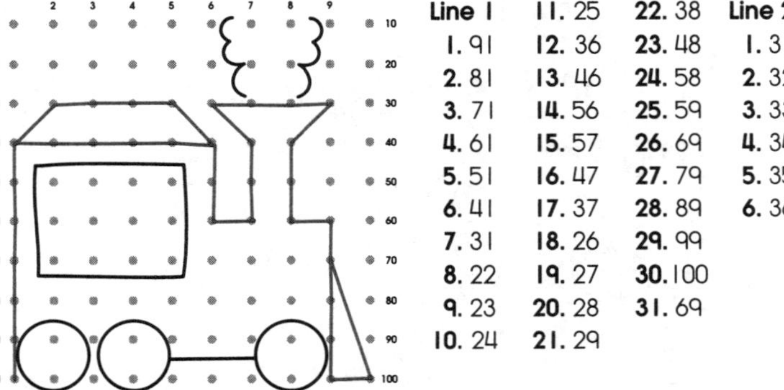

Line 1			Line 2
1. 91	11. 25	22. 38	1. 31
2. 81	12. 36	23. 48	2. 32
3. 71	13. 46	24. 58	3. 33
4. 61	14. 56	25. 59	4. 34
5. 51	15. 57	26. 69	5. 35
6. 41	16. 47	27. 79	6. 36
7. 31	17. 37	28. 89	
8. 22	18. 26	29. 99	
9. 23	19. 27	30. 100	
10. 24	20. 28	31. 69	
	21. 29		

Page 118

Page 119

Page 120

Page 121

©School Zone Publishing Company

ANSWER KEY

Page 122

Page 123

Page 124

Page 125

Page 126

Page 127

Page 128

Page 129

Page 130

Page 131

Page 132

Page 133

Page 134

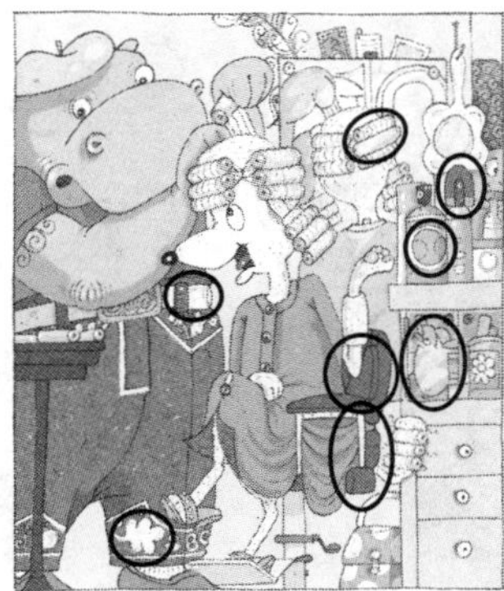

Page 135

ANSWER KEY

Page 136

Page 137

Line 1
1. 30
2. 29
3. 19
4. 8
5. 7
6. 6
7. 15
8. 25
9. 35
10. 34
11. 43
12. 52
13. 41
14. 51
15. 61
16. 72
17. 83
18. 84
19. 85
20. 86
21. 87
22. 88
23. 79
24. 69
25. 59
26. 48
27. 38
28. 39
29. 40

Line 2
1. 46
2. 45
3. 44
4. 53
5. 62
6. 73
7. 74
8. 75
9. 76
10. 67
11. 57

Page 138

Page 139

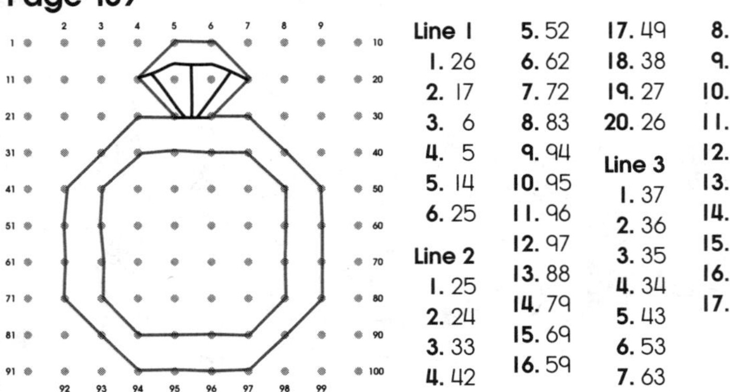

Line 1
1. 26
2. 17
3. 6
4. 5
5. 14
6. 25

Line 2
1. 25
2. 24
3. 33
4. 42
5. 52
6. 62
7. 72
8. 83
9. 94
10. 95
11. 96
12. 97
13. 88
14. 79
15. 69
16. 59
17. 49
18. 38
19. 27
20. 26

Line 3
1. 37
2. 36
3. 35
4. 34
5. 43
6. 53
7. 63
8. 73
9. 84
10. 85
11. 86
12. 87
13. 78
14. 68
15. 58
16. 48
17. 37

Page 140

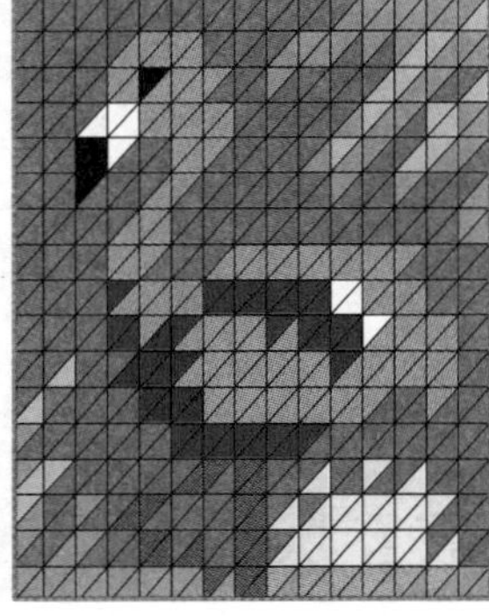

Page 141

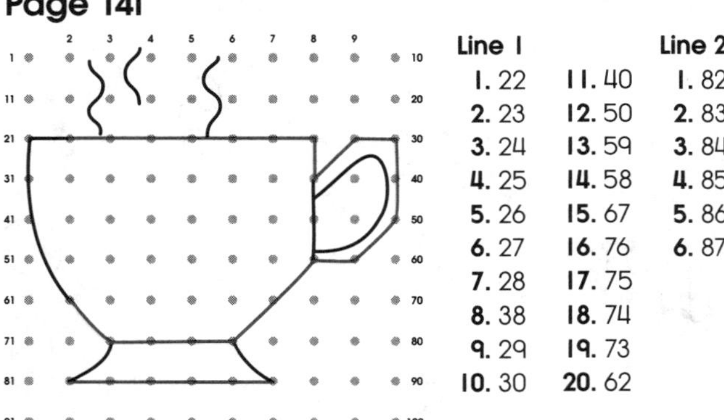

Line 1
1. 22
2. 23
3. 24
4. 25
5. 26
6. 27
7. 28
8. 38
9. 29
10. 30
11. 40
12. 50
13. 59
14. 58
15. 67
16. 76
17. 75
18. 74
19. 73
20. 62

Line 2
1. 82
2. 83
3. 84
4. 85
5. 86
6. 87

Page 142

Page 143

Pages 144–145

©School Zone Publishing Company

ANSWER KEY

Page 146

Page 147

Page 148

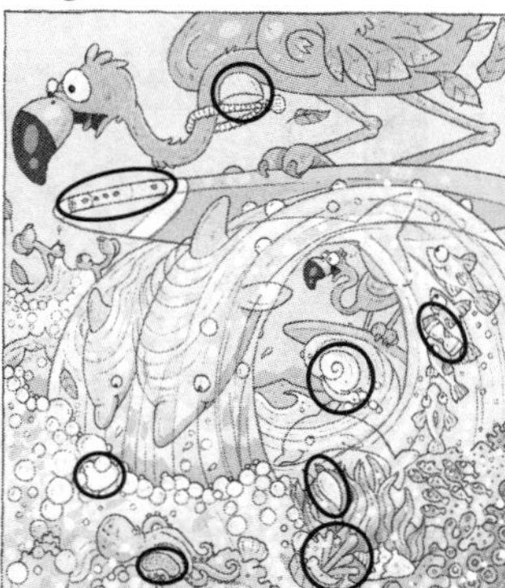

Page 149

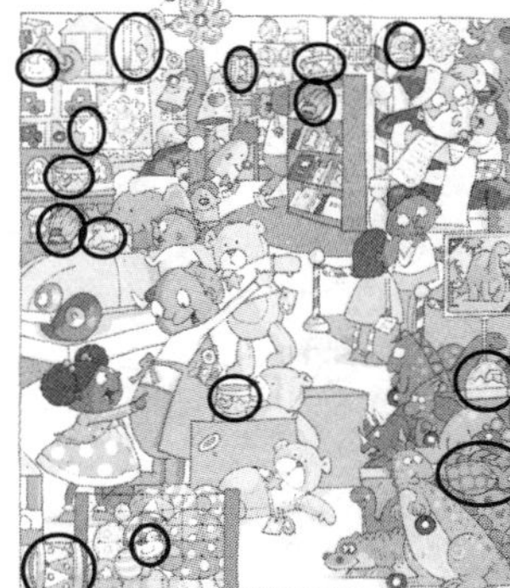

Page 150

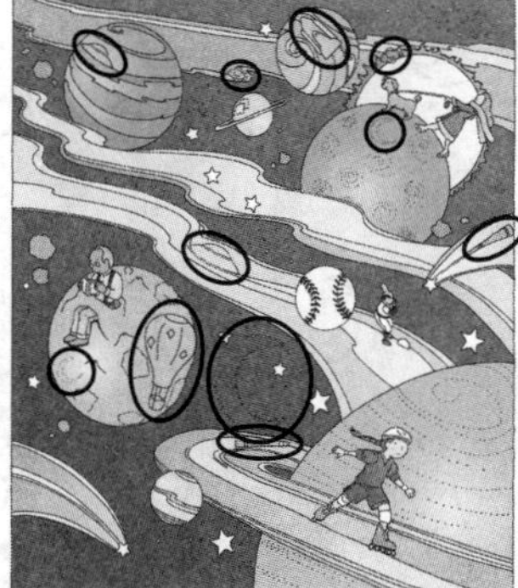

Page 151

Page 152

Page 153

Page 154

Page 155

Page 156

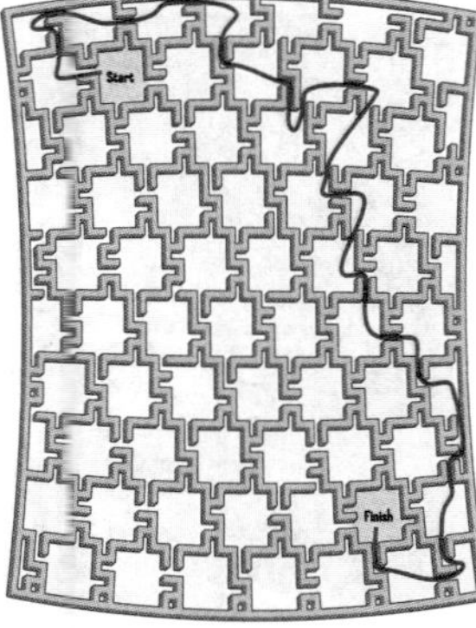

Page 157

Page 158

Page 159

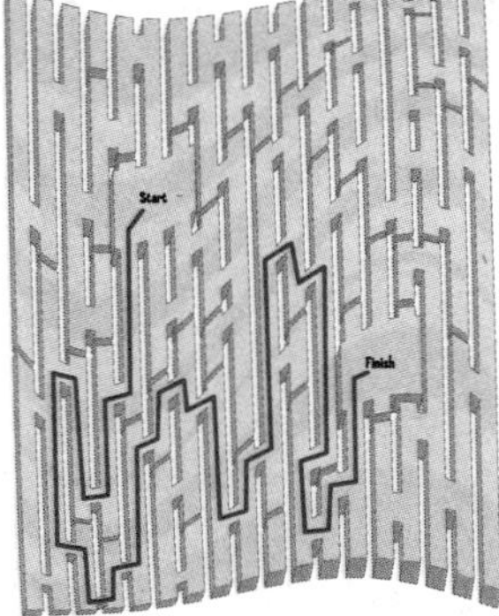

ANSWER KEY

Page 160

Page 161

Page 162

Page 163

Page 164

Page 165

Page 166

Page 167

Page 168

Page 169

Page 170

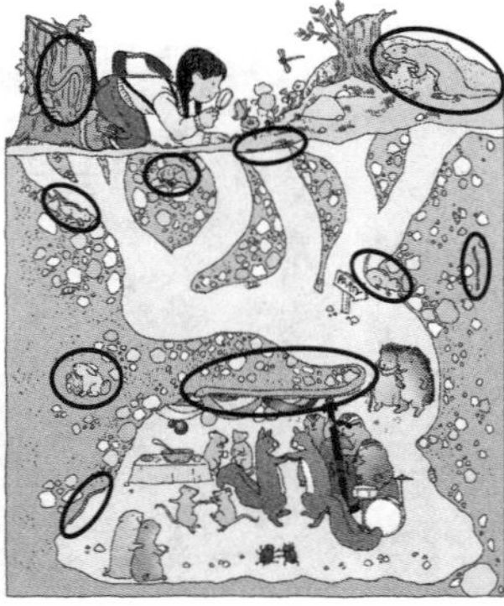

Page 171

Page 172

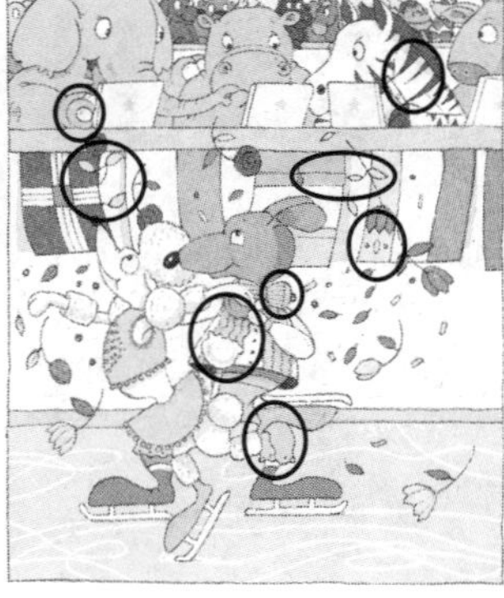

Page 173

Page 174

 ©School Zone Publishing Company

ANSWER KEY

Page 175

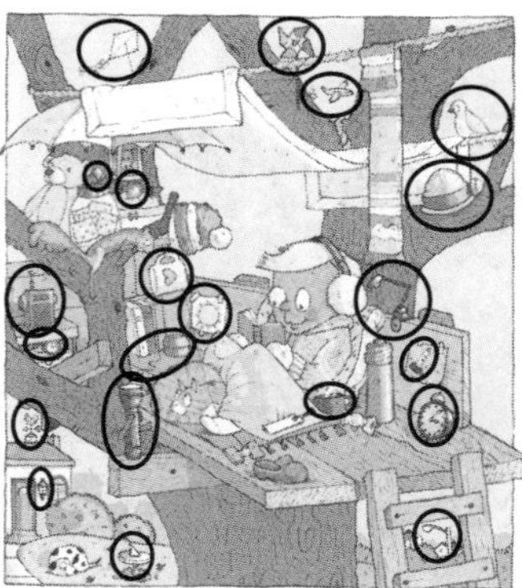

Page 176

Page 177

Page 178

Page 179

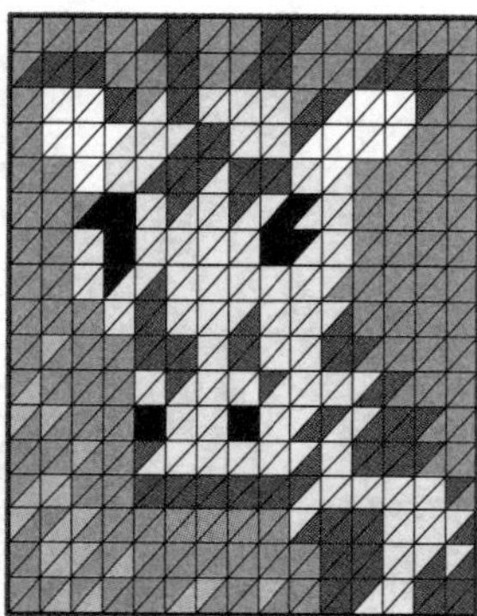

Page 180

Page 181

Page 182

Page 183

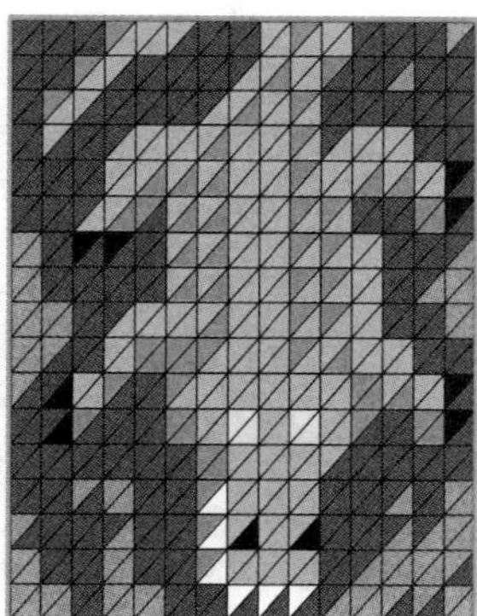

Page 184

Page 185

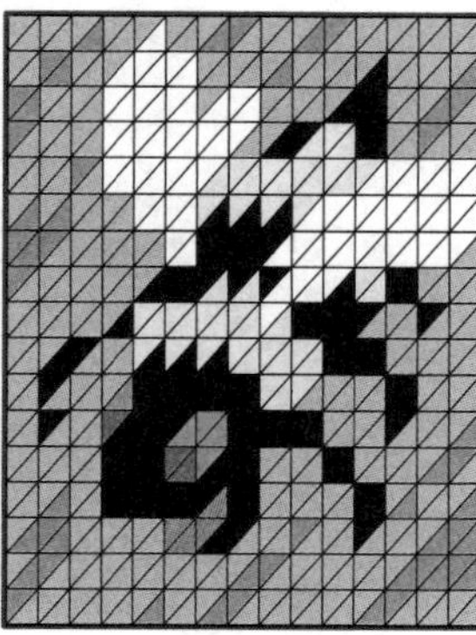

Page 186

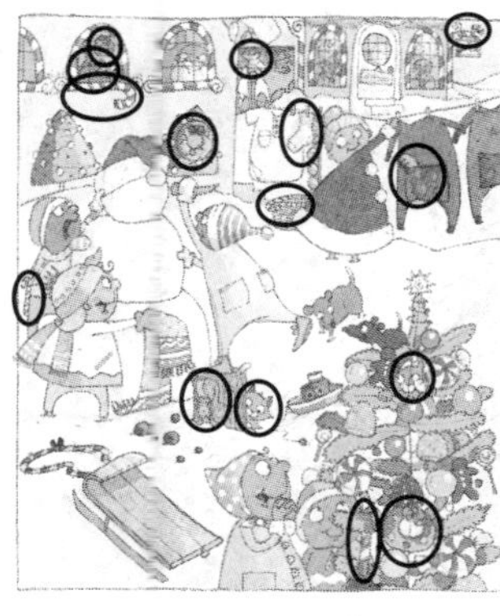

Page 187

Page 188

Page 189

ANSWER KEY

Page 190

Page 191

Page 192

Page 193

Page 194

Page 195

Page 196

Page 197

Page 198

Page 199

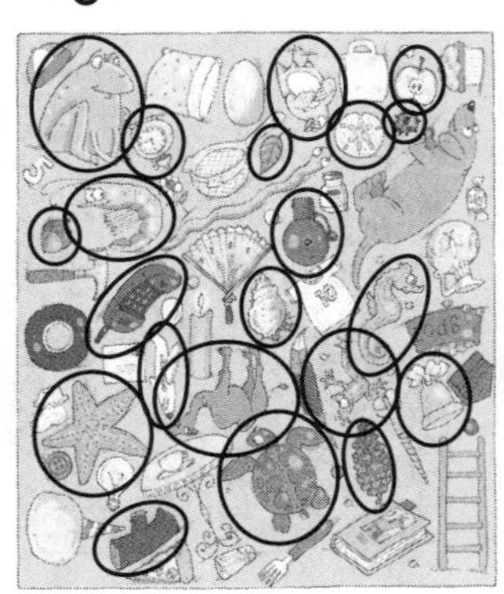

Page 200

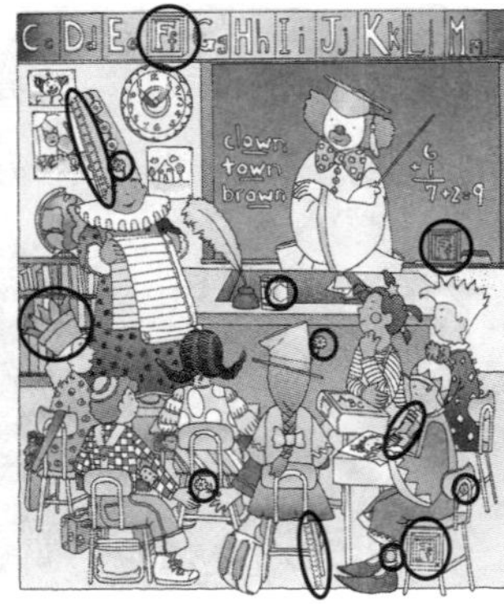

Page 201

Page 202

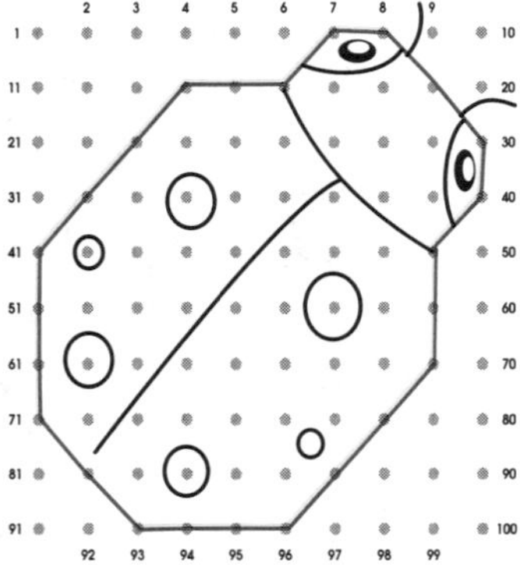

Line 1

1. 8	10. 61	19. 69
2. 7	11. 71	20. 59
3. 16	12. 82	21. 49
4. 15	13. 93	22. 40
5. 14	14. 94	23. 30
6. 23	15. 95	24. 19
7. 32	16. 96	25. 8
8. 41	17. 87	
9. 51	18. 78	

Page 203

Page 204

Page 205

Pages 206–209

Solutions will vary.

Page 210

Page 211

Page 212

Page 213

Page 214

Page 215

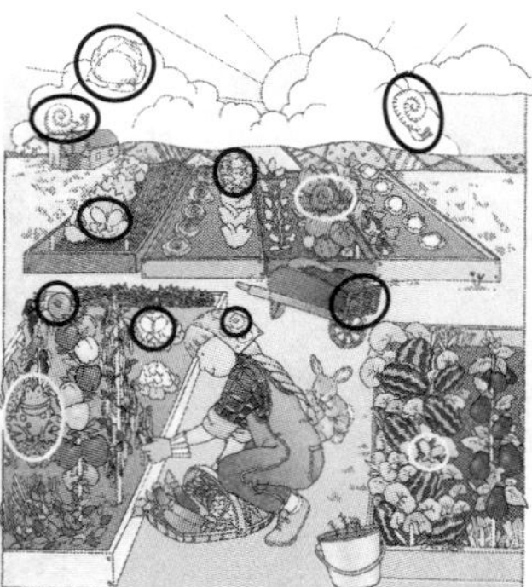

Page 216

Page 217

Page 218

Page 219

Page 220

Page 221

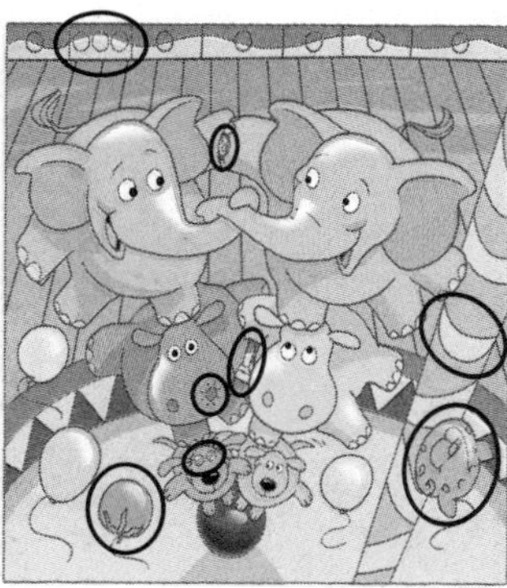

ANSWER KEY

Page 222

Page 223

Page 224

tassel: castle
man: can, fan
camp: lamp, ramp, stamp
far: car, guitar, jar, star
cool: jewel, pool, spool, stovol, tool
low: bow, crow, doe, hoe, snow, toe

Page 225

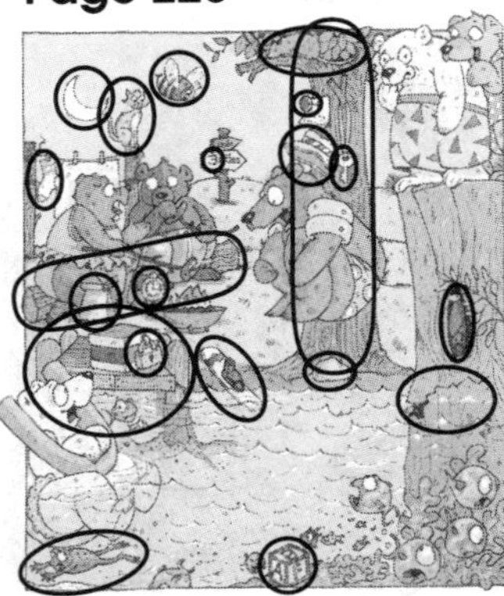

spoon: moon
dog: frog, log
black: crack, sack, tack
sat: bat, cat, hat, rat
see: bee, key, ski, three, tree
smock: block, clock, dock, lock, rock, sock

Page 226

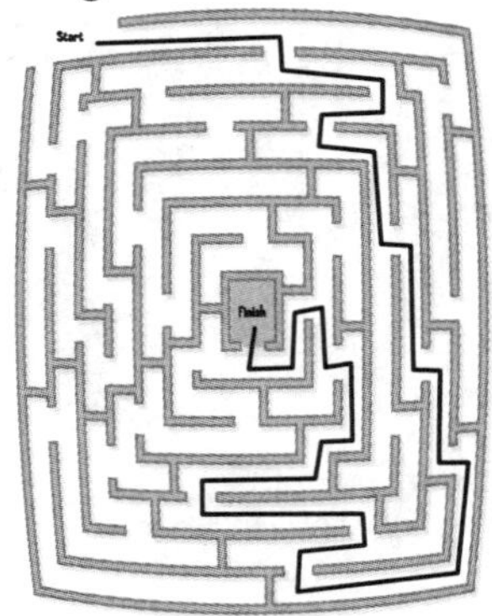

Page 227

Page 228

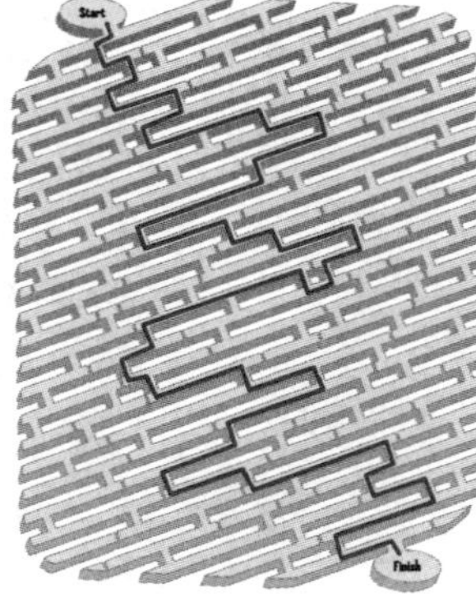

Page 229

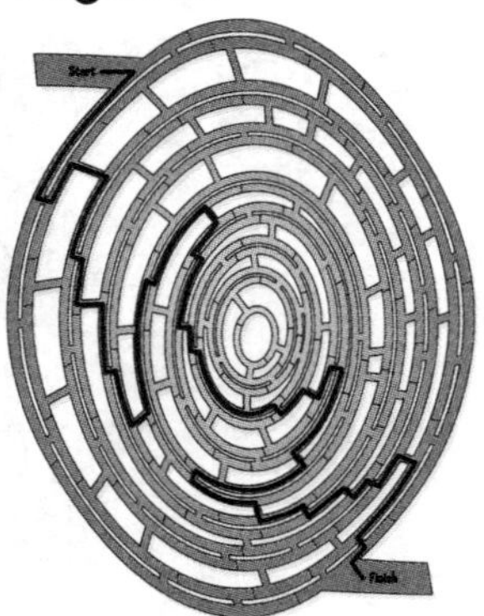

Pages 230–233

Answers will vary.

Page 234

Page 235

Page 236

Page 237

©School Zone Publishing Company

ANSWER KEY

Page 238

Page 239

Page 240

Page 241

Page 242

Page 243

Page 244

Page 245

Page 246

Page 247

Page 248

Page 249

Page 250

Page 251

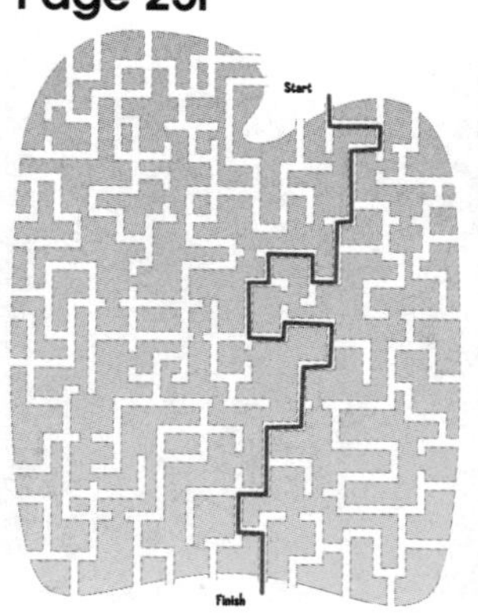

Page 252

ANSWER KEY

Pages 253–256

Solutions will vary.

Page 257

Page 258

Page 259

Page 260

Page 261

Page 262

Page 263

Page 264

Page 265

Page 266

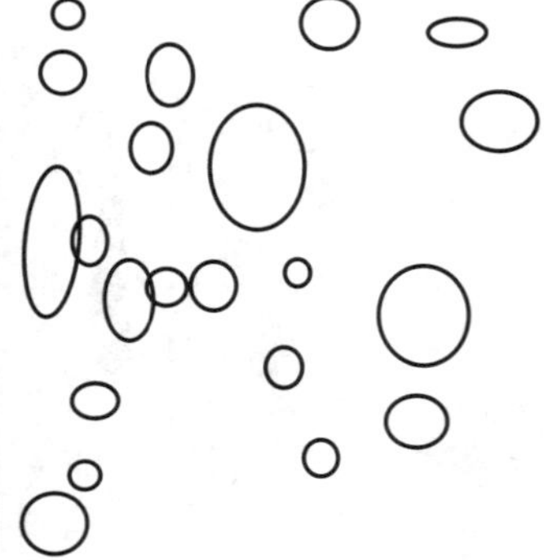

Page 267

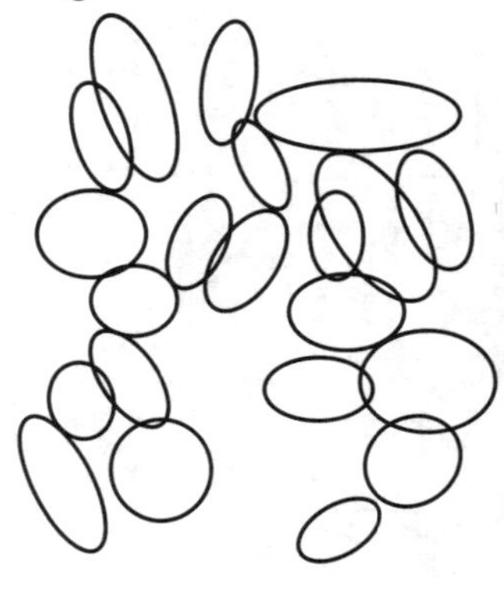

Page 268

Page 269

Page 270

 ©School Zone Publishing Company

ANSWER KEY

Page 271

Page 272

Page 273

Page 274

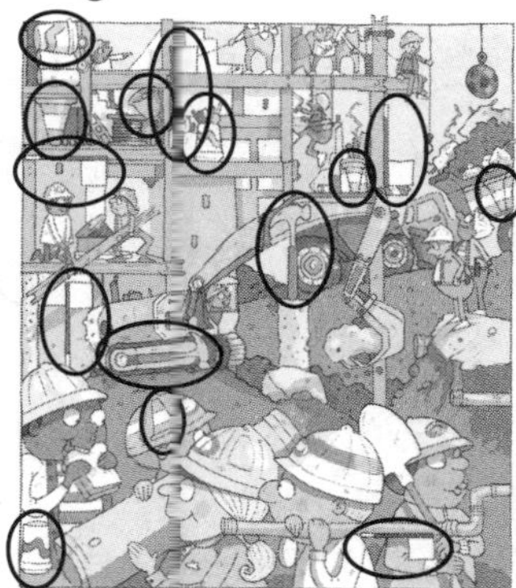

Page 275

Page 276

Page 277

Page 278

Page 279

Page 280

Page 281

Page 282

Page 283

Page 284

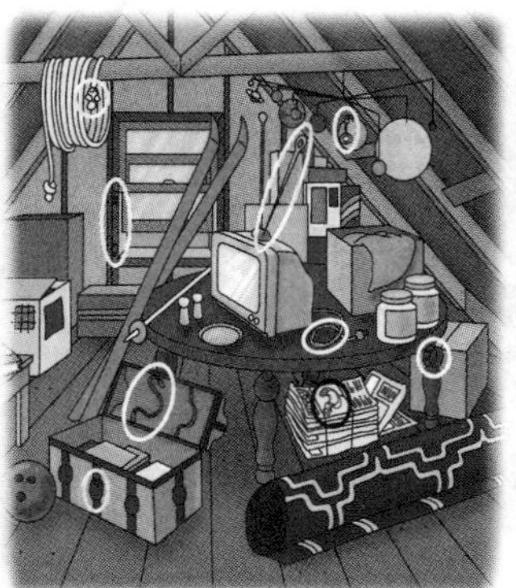

Page 285

ANSWER KEY

Page 286

Page 287

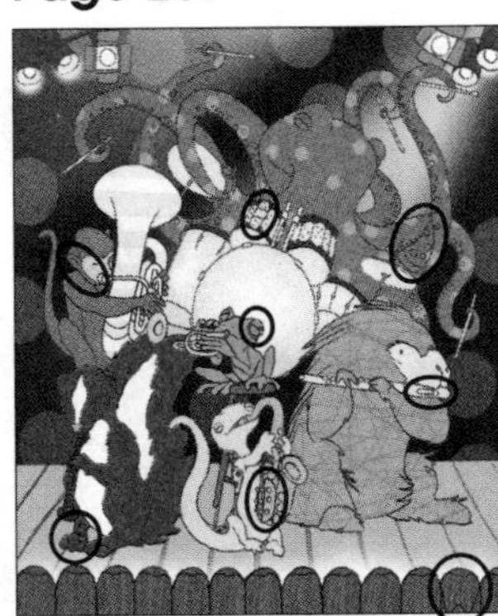

Page 288

Page 289

Page 290

Page 291

Page 292

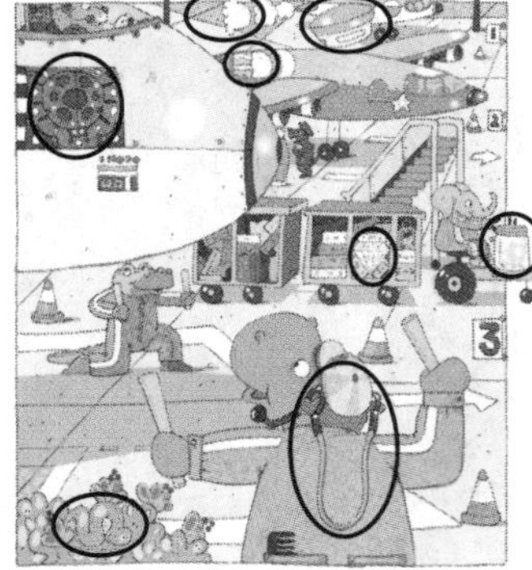

Page 293

Page 294

Page 295

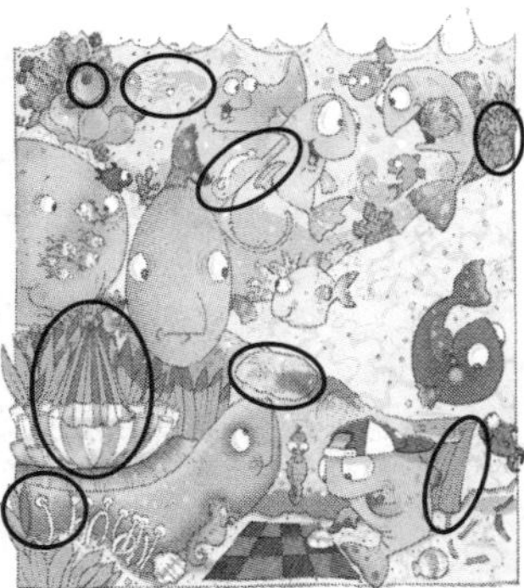

Page 296

Page 297

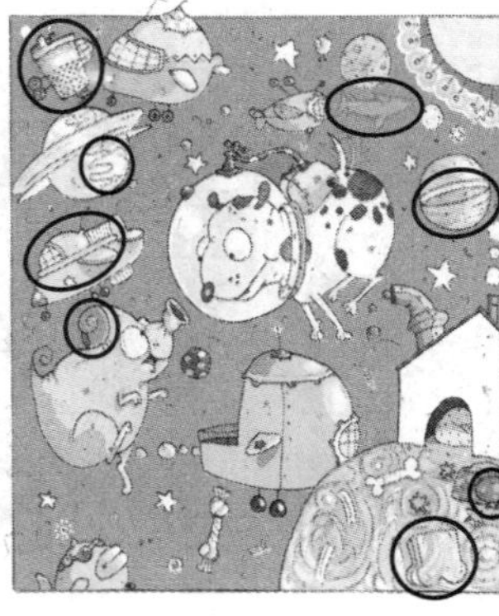

Page 298

Page 299

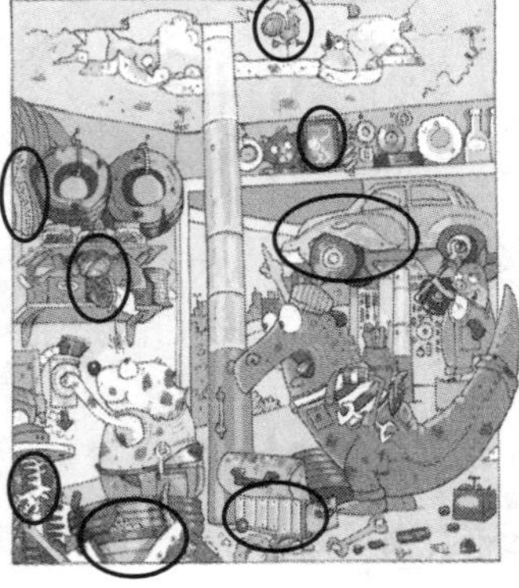